THE SIXTH WISCONSIN

and the

Long Civil War

CIVIL WAR AMERICA

Caroline E. Janney and Aaron Sheehan-Dean, editors

This landmark series interprets broadly the history and culture of the Civil War era through the long nineteenth century and beyond. Drawing on diverse approaches and methods, the series publishes historical works that explore all aspects of the war, biographies of leading commanders, and tactical and campaign studies, along with select editions of primary sources. Together, these books shed new light on an era that remains central to our understanding of American and world history.

A complete list of books published in Civil War America is available at https://uncpress.org/series/civil-war-america.

THE SIXTH WISCONSIN
and the
Long Civil War

The Biography of a Regiment

JAMES MARTEN

THE UNIVERSITY OF NORTH CAROLINA PRESS

Chapel Hill

This book was published with the assistance of the William R. Kenan Jr. Fund of the University of North Carolina Press.

© 2025 The University of North Carolina Press

Designed by Jamison Cockerham
Set in Arno, Cutright, and Scala Sans
by codeMantra

Cover art: 1st Lt. Mair Pointon of Co. A, 6th Wisconsin; and detail of Thure de Thulstrup, *Battle of Antietam*, ca. 1887. Courtesy of Library of Congress Prints and Photographs Division, Washington, DC.

Manufactured in the United States of America

LIBRARY OF CONGRESS CATALOGING-IN-PUBLICATION DATA
Names: Marten, James Alan, author.
Title: The Sixth Wisconsin and the long Civil War : the
biography of a regiment / James Marten.
Other titles: Civil War America (Series)
Description: Chapel Hill : The University of North Carolina Press, [2025] |
Series: Civil War America | Includes bibliographical references.
Identifiers: LCCN 2024047464 | ISBN 9781469684239 (cloth ; alk. paper) |
ISBN 9781469684246 (epub) | ISBN 9781469684253 (pdf)
Subjects: LCSH: United States. Army. Wisconsin Infantry Regiment, 6th
(1861–1865) | Soldiers—United States—Social conditions—19th century. |
Wisconsin—History—Civil War, 1861-1865—Regimental histories. | United
States—History—Civil War, 1861–1865—Social aspects. | United States—
History—Civil War, 1861-1865—Influence. | United States—History—
Civil War, 1861–1865—Regimental histories. | BISAC: HISTORY / United
States / Civil War Period (1850–1877) | HISTORY / Military / General
Classification: LCC E537.5 6th | DDC 973.7/475—dc23/eng/20241218
LC record available at https://lccn.loc.gov/2024047464

TO MY FRIENDS AND COLLEAGUES

in the history department at

MARQUETTE UNIVERSITY

and in the

SOCIETY OF CIVIL WAR HISTORIANS

CONTENTS

ILLUSTRATIONS

ACKNOWLEDGMENTS

Just as the men of the Sixth Wisconsin took comfort from the communities they formed during and after the war, my own community of historians, archivists, and students were instrumental in completing this book. I owe a great deal to a great many people.

First, I want to thank Lance Herdegen and William J. K. Beaudot, whose publications and the archive they created at the Kenosha Civil War Museum provided extraordinary starting points for my particular take on a unit they knew intimately.

More traditional thanks for material aid and encouragement go to:

Marquette University, which awarded me a Regular Research Grant in 2020 and a Way Klingler Fellowship in 2021–22, and the American Philosophical Society, which awarded me a Franklin Grant in 2021.

The following archivists: Amanda Fuller, Dawes Arboretum; Gina Radandt, Kenosha Civil War Museum; Russell P. Horton, Wisconsin Veterans Museum; Lee Grady, Wisconsin Historical Society; Kevin Abing, formerly of the Milwaukee Historical Society; Katherine Vollen, National Archives and Records Administration; Ranger Matthew Atkinson and Tom Greaney, Gettysburg National Military Park Library; and Carol Krogan, Vernon County Museum and History Center. I also want to thank Tara Baillargeon, dean of libraries, and all the staff at Marquette's Raynor Memorial Library, my home away from home at the university.

Kathryn Shively and Caroline E. Janney for allowing me to try out some of my ideas in "'The Battle for Which We Had So Long Been Yearning': The 6th Wisconsin at Brawner Farm," in *The Second Manassas Campaign* (Chapel Hill: University of North Carolina Press, 2025); Steve Rogstad for inviting me to give a talk at the annual meeting of the Sheboygan County Historical Research Center that was published as *Bearing Their Part Equally:*

Sheboygan County and the Iron Brigade (Sheboygan, WI: Sheboygan County Historical Research Center, 2022); and Terry Johnston, who published a much-extended version of a section of chapter 8 as "A Disappointment to His Friends: The Unknown Story of the 'Brooks Expedition,'" *Civil War Monitor* 13, no. 4 (Winter 2023): 40–45.

Numerous student researchers, especially Christian Krueger, who created the original database from which all other databases grew, and Maddie Anderson and Bridget Neugent, whose incredible instinct for history and patience with Ancestry.com was vital to the project. But a number of other graduate and undergraduate research assistants helped with the databases and newspaper research, including Zach Bukowski, Cory Haala, Megan Holland, Shane Kruse, Fr. Patrick Lapacz, Melanie Lorenz, Laurence Matthews, Kenny Pangbourne, and Drew Wilson.

I profitably shared my ideas about the Sixth Wisconsin with a number of friends and colleagues, especially Caroline E. Janney; our walk over the battlefield and past the Sixth Wisconsin monument near the now-finished railroad cut nine years ago inspired me to write the book. She also commented on an earlier, much longer version of the entire manuscript, as did William A. Blair, Alison Clark Efford, and CJ Hribal. Frances Clarke and George Rable offered advice and encouragement on the final manuscript. I hope they all find evidence of their wise and helpful comments; any remaining shortcomings remain, of course, my responsibility.

Other colleagues who answered queries, sent documents, and talked about the project over its long gestation, including Stephen Berry, Keith Bohannon, Thomas J. Brown, Matt Gallman, Scott Hartwig, Earl Hess, Brian Luskey, John Sacher, and Michael Waricher.

At the University of North Carolina Press, the book was improved through the enthusiasm and thorough and insightful comments of Mark Simpson-Vos and the copyediting of Iza Wojciechowska. Thomas Bedenbaugh, Alyssa Brown, Mary Carley Caviness, and the rest of the staff at the press eased the progress of the project from manuscript to book.

I've dedicated this book to my colleagues in the Department of History at Marquette University and in the Society of Civil War Historians. I retired from Marquette University at about the time the research was winding down and the writing was ramping up. I treasured my years in the history department at Marquette, which it was my profound privilege to chair for sixteen years. Each of the dozens of colleagues I had during my thirty-six years on the faculty shaped my career and life in his or her own way. I also had the great pleasure of being involved with the Society of Civil War Historians almost since its founding; I served as president and in other capacities and cherish the memories of the "three Amigos"—Steve, Bill, and me—working together during the society's formative period.

Finally, Linda Gist Marten probably heard more about "my guys" in the Sixth Wisconsin than about any other book I've written over the last forty years. For that she will have my eternal gratitude and, as always, my love.

THE SIXTH WISCONSIN and the Long Civil War

Introduction

This book tells a story of how men made war and what the war made of those men through the lens of a single regiment, the Sixth Wisconsin. The Sixth fought with four other regiments from Wisconsin, Indiana, and Michigan in one of the most famous units on either side of the war: the Iron Brigade. Serving with the Army of the Potomac in every campaign and most of its battles between August 1862 and April 1865, the Iron Brigade suffered more casualties than any other brigade in the Union army.

Wisconsin, a state for only thirteen years when the Civil War began, followed a complicated political path to war. Although a small minority of abolitionists promoted emancipation and racial equality, most residents favored preventing the expansion of the institution into new territories while at the same time adamantly opposing suffrage for African Americans. Wisconsin's opposition to the Fugitive Slave Act of 1850 cast it superficially into the states' rights side of the debate over federal power. By 1860, the Republican Party—promoting moderate views on race but supporting the Union wholeheartedly—easily won in every race, capturing the governor's chair, the state's congressional delegation, and large majorities in both the state senate

1

and assembly. The party's candidate for president, Abraham Lincoln, won the state by a majority of 20,000.[1]

Reflecting its state's ambiguous attitudes about race but strong attachment to the Union, the Sixth Wisconsin went to war not to free the slaves but to oppose Southern secession. The fall of Fort Sumter in Charleston was the catalyst in Wisconsin, as in much of the North, for an outpouring of warlike patriotism. Madison's *Wisconsin State Journal* declared that "the recent news from the South has aroused our people." Two of the city's most prominent private militia companies paraded through the streets and to the state capitol, followed by a "large concourse" of people. They offered their services to Governor Alexander Randall, whose speech the newspaper paraphrased. "The time had come," he said, "when parties and platforms must be forgotten, and all good citizens and patriots unite together in putting down rebels and traitors." Fort Sumter must be retaken, "though it cost fifty thousand lives and a hundred millions of dollars—what was money—what was life—in the presence of such a crisis?" His listeners may have thought Randall's valuation of the battered fort was laughably high, although some may have feared it was heart-stoppingly low. But thousands of Wisconsin men offered to join the 75,000 soldiers Lincoln called to put down the rebellion.[2]

Among them were the men of the Sixth Wisconsin, which rose from cities, hamlets, and farms throughout the state. By the end of the war, over 400 different communities would send their sons, fathers, and husbands to the regiment. Although more than half were farmers, farm laborers, or farmers' sons, they were also lumbermen from the north woods, Irish and German mechanics and laborers from Milwaukee, and rising lawyers, merchants, and clerks from towns large and small. Only a tiny fraction had seen any military service, although some Milwaukee recruits came out of prewar private militia companies. In these ways they resembled countless other regiments forming in the great rush to arms in the spring and summer of 1861.

The green recruits spent a few weeks in training a mile west of Madison at the old state fairground—named Camp Randall, after the governor. Madison was home to over 6,500 people and the brand-new University of Wisconsin, yet it still displayed elements of a frontier town; recruits complained about the dust and wind and their assignment to repurposed cattle pens for barracks. Seventy thousand Wisconsin soldiers would pass through Camp Randall over the next four years, along with a few hundred Confederate prisoners of war, before it reverted once again to a fairground. A half century later a "Memorial Arch" honoring the veterans of the Civil War was erected near the university's football field—still called Camp Randall.[3]

Soon after the Union defeat at Bull Run in July 1861, the Sixth traveled east, where it occupied several different positions in the Washington, DC, defenses. It eventually formed a brigade with the Second and Seventh Wisconsin and Nineteenth Indiana under the command of Brig. Gen. Rufus King, a West Pointer and former Milwaukee newspaperman whose undistinguished Civil War career is remembered mostly in the name of the sports teams at Milwaukee's Rufus King High School: the Generals. The Sixth wintered on Arlington Heights across the Potomac from Washington—in the middle of the current national cemetery—and spent the spring and summer training, marching, guarding, and pining for their first taste of battle.

When King was promoted to divisional command in March 1862, he was replaced by a regular army artilleryman, Brig. Gen. John Gibbon, who hammered the brigade into shape with incessant drilling and hard discipline. He also dressed them in their distinctive uniform: tall black Hardee hat, frock coat, and white gloves and leggings. When Gibbon led the men into their first battle in late August 1862, they responded with an enthusiasm forged by a year of waiting and months of hard drill and strict discipline, honed by a bitter disregard for most generals but faith in their own officers, and buttressed by their nearly arrogant confidence in themselves. Within a month, the Sixth and their comrades had earned one of the most famous nicknames of the war.

This is not a regimental history. Such works have filled countless volumes in the vast literature on the Civil War, typically chronicling in meticulous detail a unit's military exploits in major campaigns and particular battles. In the case of the Iron Brigade, Lance Herdegen and Alan Nolan have provided such narratives.

Instead, I intend to offer a regimental biography. I have spent the better part of eight years studying the lives of the nearly 2,000 men who served at some point in the Sixth Wisconsin. They cannot properly be considered a "random" sample, but they comprise a large and meaningfully diverse one.[4] I have documented the communities from which the soldiers came, the ones they formed during the war, and the ones to which they returned afterward. I have considered their lives and experiences as a kind of laboratory to study the gathering of the Union army and its years of fighting, dying, surviving, and remembering the war. Like any biography, this one traces the birth, education, maturation, aging, and decline of its subject. The book is shaped by the notion that the regiment, throughout its long "life," was in a sense a living organism.[5]

Framing the life of the Sixth as a biography allows us to explore its entire history, to provide an inclusive approach to the lived experience of its men and their families. Many historians have examined soldiers' experiences, the effects of the war on communities, the many versions of memory, and the lives of veterans. But none have followed a single regiment through the entire gamut of experiences, from peace to war and back again. At its most ambitious, then, this story of a single regiment from one of the Union army's most famous brigades provides a capsule history of the war and its aftermaths.

We know these men because they were *soldiers* who participated in a war that was by any measure exceptionally well documented, both in official records and in the words and recollections of individuals. Because this is a biography of men at war, several chapters necessarily feature extended narratives of combat. They establish the regiment's reputation, allow us to record its inevitable losses, and, accordingly, help us understand everything that came afterward. Yet at its heart this is a social history of the men of the Sixth, and the narrative rests on several key foundations and goals.

First, important as the military history shared by these men is, the survivors' much longer lives as veterans are equally important. As a result, I have sought to integrate my subjects' wartime experiences with their long-term effects. One example is a grueling week in early August 1862, when the regiment suffered dozens of casualties due to sunstroke and other ailments caused by a particularly difficult forced march. In that and other cases, I show how a particular moment could influence men's lives for decades. This work proceeds, then, from a framework that some historians call the "long Civil War" or the "enduring" war. Though such terms have gone out of fashion in certain scholarly circles, the framework has steadily—and productively, I would argue—disrupted the idea that the Civil War should be understood according to a political and military chronology of battles and surrenders. Instead, as the editors of a recent anthology write, a long view of the war "probe[s] widely, deeply, and expansively, identifying progressions of subjects, themes, topics, and tropes that emerged decades before the secession crisis . . . and lingered long after the last federal troops left the less-than-reconstructed South."[6] Unlike traditional regimental histories, then, this book offers the long view of the Sixth Wisconsin. For this regiment, the conflict began when 1,000 Wisconsinites responded to what they believed to be a fundamental threat to the United States. Another 1,000 men would join the Sixth—at different times, in different circumstances, and, in many cases, for different reasons. The war—or, to put it more precisely, the effects of the war—ended decades later when the last survivor, William Riley, died in 1939. In between were hundreds of experiences and moments shaped by the war, directly and indirectly.

Second, this study intends to enrich and complicate the way we think about common soldiers' experiences. Thinking about the Civil War soldiers' lived reality began with the countless memoirs published in the decades after the war and the still lively genre of published letters and diaries from the war years. The work continues with the periodic reboot of studies of the daily lives of soldiers. My approach is less like Bell I. Wiley's famous examinations of the lives of "Johnny Reb" and "Billy Yank" and more along the lines of work by Gerald Lindermann, Earl Hess, and Peter Carmichael. But even their works are more inspirations than models, as I narrow their broad scope to a single regiment, lengthen their chronologies by several decades, and worry less about *how* soldiers survived and more about *what* they survived.[7]

Brian Matthew Jordan has eloquently argued that Union soldiers returned home "afflicted with guilt, sorrow, and purposelessness." Their lives had broadened but had also become more brutal. "The rules governing their daily lives" as soldiers, writes Lindermann, changed again, almost overnight: "Killing once again became homicide; foraging was again theft, and incendiarism arson. Even language was a problem: Camp talk had to be cleaned up."[8]

Yet, however compelling and even logical those concerns are—*of course* every war has a tragic side and every combat veteran has to readjust to peace—the postwar lives of the men of the Sixth Wisconsin were too complicated to fit into either a cheerful "swords into ploughshares" narrative or a gloomy, even tragic tale of despair and decline. Part of the problem—perhaps the main problem—facing historians seeking to impose order on the disparate lives of millions of survivors of the war is that the vicissitudes of life in the Reconstruction era and the Gilded Age followed hard on the war itself. The war had thundered into soldiers' lives at critical times, just when they were starting out or had just settled into family life or economic independence, and it is unimaginable that it would not have some large or small impact on the lives of virtually every soldier and his family. Moreover, veterans' lives did not unfold in a linear fashion. Men veered in and out of good fortune and bad. Even the life arcs of contented men living their best lives sometimes featured tragedy and hardship. Thus has it always been, and we must take care before we give ourselves over to a single approach to the war's aftermaths.

Third, I want to consider how the Civil War generation invented the very idea of war. The men who went to war in 1861—and their families, friends, and communities—had virtually no idea what they were getting into. This is hardly an original thought, but it bears repeating and remembering as one follows the men of the Sixth to Camp Randall, to Virginia, and beyond. They were, in effect, inventing war—or at least inventing a vocabulary, a series of acceptable responses, a way of explaining it to others and to themselves.

As soldiers, they experienced *two* kinds of war. In one, they could identify their individual and unit contributions, assign reasons for victory or defeat, and distinguish their own unique outcomes from those of the army as a whole. In the second, they came to recognize that they were simply cogs in a brutal machine—a meat grinder, to use a metaphor applied at the time and ever since—and that they were the flesh being ground.

Once engaged in the grim business of killing and dying, they experienced massive casualties and deadly diseases, leading to a second "invention": new ways of managing and thinking about medical care. One of the fantastic—to define the word as nineteenth-century men and women would, as something surprising, frightful, or out of some kind of fantasy—elements of Civil War casualties was, of course, their scale. Adding the even larger number of men requiring treatment for the myriad, often debilitating diseases that plagued soldiers throughout the war, the most common experience for most Civil War soldiers was spending time in a field, regimental, divisional, or general hospital.

After the fighting ended, the survivors of the Sixth Wisconsin and other members of the Civil War generation also "invented" commemoration. Americans had always been keen on remembering their history—or at least versions of it—and there were monuments here and there to Revolutionary War battles and heroes and to founding fathers, especially. But, as in everything else, the magnitude of the Civil War inspired large-scale commemoration that democratized public memory even as, in some cases, it narrowed what was being remembered.

Last, I wish to highlight the Civil War regiment as a particular kind of constructed community. As an institution, the Sixth Wisconsin existed for almost exactly four years. In many ways, however, the Sixth was disembodied from the nearly 2,000 men who belonged to it. A few survivors would write about the Sixth and its men as though it had been a coherent group; a few more would later gather from time to time and talk about their experiences as though they had been shared by all. But the Sixth Wisconsin was an invented organization fabricated out of necessity and at some level for ease of bookkeeping. In fact, there were multiple "Sixth Wisconsins," as illness, wounds, desertion, and transfers guaranteed constant change. The endless turnover of officers and men and the replacement of veterans by enlistees, draftees, and substitutes eventually created an instability that needs to be comprehended to fully understand the history of the Sixth Wisconsin and any other regiment.

Adding to the regiment's blurred identity was the significant minority of original members—nearly 150—who served in other regiments, mainly from Wisconsin, usually after being discharged from the Sixth for wounds or illness. Thirty-nine enlisted men became officers in their new regiments; two accepted commissions in the US Colored Troops. An additional six dozen men of the Sixth, too sick or injured to go back to duty in the field, joined the Veteran Reserve Corps, which was organized in the spring of 1863 as the Invalid Corps. They often worked with provost marshals to track down and arrest deserters and served in support roles in hospitals.[9]

Each soldier no doubt created his own versions of the regiment and its history. Half of all the men who served in the Sixth entered the war at much later dates and in different circumstances than the original cohort, giving them their own sets of experiences and memories. Moreover, a majority clearly did not participate in veterans' activities, and virtually none formalized their reflections in prose. All of this means that referring to the "Sixth Wisconsin" as though it were a single entity is simply a matter of tidying up a complicated history—a process that began almost as soon as the war ended—rather than conveying a historic fact.

Reid Mitchell wrote years ago that military companies became extensions of the communities from which they came, and that holds true for the Sixth Wisconsin. Such histories, of course, also track the splintering of communities, or the more gradual drawing apart that occurs as they grow or respond to outside forces. For the Sixth Wisconsin and probably most Civil War regiments, the moment when soldiers and families and friends finished their lingering handshakes and Godspeed hugs was the moment when the experiences of soldiers and civilians diverged. There were cracks before that, of course; at public meetings, the enthusiastic young men signing pledges to serve their country heard speeches about patriotism and sacrifice differently than those who had no intention of shouldering a musket. Those cracks no doubt widened during the days before the companies finally left for camp. Time went too slowly for the men and boys who wanted to get this adventure started or get their service over with; it sped by all too quickly for mothers and wives and others who feared the future.[10]

Despite all the similarities and connections between Civil War soldiers and the people who waved them off to war, the recruits had deployed an imagination unavailable to the old, the young, and the female. Unlike the others, they exposed themselves to challenges and dangers and indignities that they could only vaguely have anticipated. Later enlistees and draftees would have access to more information about war fighting—whatever friends or acquaintances in the army were willing to share—and after making grim financial or moral calculations they went to war with different mindsets than the men who had gone before them.

Civilians invented their own wars, and where appropriate this book will highlight the ways in which the experiences and thoughts of soldiers and civilians diverged or intersected. When the war ended, the soldiers rejoined their families and communities, even as they formed new communities of commemoration and celebration and of the damaged and disabled. Many realized that their wars were logically and irrevocably separate; many in both groups no doubt believed they might meld back into comfortable prewar relationships. As we will see, that was not necessarily the case.

——— ——— ——— ——— ——— ———

The famed historian Bruce Catton deeply admired the Iron Brigade. In *Glory Road* he quotes an officer who described "that famed body of troops" marching, "full of life and spirit, with steady step, filling the entire roadway, their big black hats and feathers conspicuous." He watched them with "the pride of looking upon a model American volunteer." Catton argued that soldiers' admiration for officers' personal bravery meant more when it came from the Iron Brigade, "where they tended to be connoisseurs of courage."[11]

But Catton gets us only so far in understanding the Sixth Wisconsin. Look at the young men in 1861 daguerreotypes: stiff in their scratchy uniforms; embarrassed, perhaps, in their first sitting before a camera; eyes wide with the strain to remain still—or perhaps eager or anxious to confront the mysteries of war and human endurance that would soon be revealed to them. Then look into the eyes of the aging gray survivors in photographs taken decades later, sometimes with wives or fellow men from the Grand Army of the Republic. Bewhiskered and calm, they have seen things and learned things and know, unlike those boys in the earlier pictures, that courage was both a blessing and a burden.

1

Willing Hearts and Strong Hands

Gathering

Edward Bragg had been preparing for war since the summer of 1860. A thirty-four-year-old lawyer from Fond du Lac, a town roughly halfway between Milwaukee and Green Bay, Bragg had represented Wisconsin at the 1860 Democratic National Convention in Charleston, South Carolina. That was the convention at which the party of Thomas Jefferson and Andrew Jackson had finally splintered under the weight of internal conflicts about the present and future status of slavery. According to a friend, Bragg returned to Fond du Lac and predicted that the collapse of the convention due to the demands of Southern fire-eaters "meant war between the North and the South." The ambitious future soldier was, of course, right. In less than a year seven states would secede from the Union to form the Confederate States of America, and Bragg would play a critical role in the war he had predicted.[1]

Wisconsin responded like most Northern states when the secession crisis came to a head in April with the attack on Fort Sumter in Charleston Harbor. Wisconsin was led into the war by the Republicans elected to virtually all of the important state and national offices. Communities throughout Wisconsin held enthusiastic rallies after the surrender of Fort Sumter and President Lincoln's call for troops. Men, women, and children flocked to these meetings to encourage young men to join the fight and other citizens to dig deep into their purses.[2]

Alexander Randall, Wisconsin's two-term Republican governor, provided a thundering articulation of the moral and patriotic motivations that would drive men to volunteer in the first months of the conflict. A "spirit . . . is abroad among the liberty-loving people of the land," he said in a speech to the state legislature, animated by a conviction that the government must "be preserved, by the willing hearts and strong hands of those to whom it belongs." In his fiery finale, Randall declared that "the Supreme Ruler can but smile upon the efforts of the law loving, government loving, liberty loving people of this land, in resisting the disruption of this Union. These gathering armies are the instruments of His vengeance, to execute His just judgments; they are His flails wherewith on God's great Southern threshing floor. He will pound rebellion for its sins." Randall had 5,000 copies of the speech printed and distributed throughout the state.[3]

Randall provided practical as well as rhetorical leadership. On April 22 he requested "loyal citizens" to organize companies of seventy-seven men and then elect officers, who would then apply for commissions. "Usually some one man, who hoped to be captain, undertook the work," wrote an early historian of the state's mobilization. "After the first few weeks of enthusiasm and spontaneous offering, the latter would generally get out a handbill" promoting his company and detailing the pay, bounty, and (eventually discarded) possibility of a land grant. "After getting a congenial group of village boys, he would drive out into the country and get the farmer lads to pledge themselves. Meantime the people of the town . . . would pledge themselves to look after the families of those who went." The expenses for raising such a company were small, usually paid by the prospective captain or a group of enthusiastic friends.[4]

Although only charged by the War Department with providing one regiment, Randall insisted on raising six regiments of what were temporarily called the Wisconsin Active Militia. The First and Second Wisconsin were thrown together as three-month regiments and sent east in June. The Second fought at the First Battle of Bull Run, where their gray uniforms attracted

A prewar map of Wisconsin featuring county lines, major towns, and railway lines. Wisconsin Historical Society, Madison.

friendly fire. Upon returning home, both regiments were reorganized into three-year units and went on to distinguished service, the First in the West and the Second in the Army of the Potomac—where it would be brigaded with the Sixth.[5]

The kernels of the Sixth Wisconsin began sprouting in earnest in April and May. Disparate in region, character, politics, and ethnicity, the ten companies of the Sixth Wisconsin each had their own name and origin story, similar one to another but with particular details that became part of regimental and community folklore. The largely German Citizen Corps of Milwaukee was raised by a tall, 300-pound Prussian; the Beloit Rifles recruited more than three dozen men from out of state, especially from just across the border in northern Illinois and ten men from Berrien County, Michigan; a Swiss graduate of a military school who had fought in Italy with Giuseppe Garibaldi led the creation of the Buffalo County Rifles along the Mississippi River in the far northwestern part of the state; the Prescott Guards, in another Mississippi River town, had to scrounge for recruits across the state line in Minnesota, but the first few dozen men began to drill and study tactics every day and adopted makeshift uniforms of black pants, red shirts, and gray caps.[6]

Willing Hearts and Strong Hands

The Sauk County Riflemen came out of west central Wisconsin just northwest of Madison and would become Company A. Their recruiting arc shows just how fast some companies were raised—and how aggressive recruiting throughout a county or region could help organizers fill a company. The company originated in Baraboo, the Sauk County seat, at the town's first war meeting on Friday, April 19. F. K. Jenkins chaired, Elon Wyman was appointed secretary, and D. K. Noyes gave a speech. Jenkins and Noyes would both serve as officers in the Sixth. On the following Tuesday, April 23, another meeting featured enthusiastic speeches and a wave of volunteer recruitment. On Wednesday this first group of Riflemen and a local brass band rode four wagons into Reedsburg, about sixteen miles west; one participant remembered that "this trip resulted in a good time for the boys and ten recruits." After several more volunteered on Thursday, on Friday the company traveled to Merrimack, about twelve miles southeast on the shores of Lake Wisconsin, and gathered a few more recruits. That evening the company assembled at the county courthouse and formally resolved to tender their service to the governor "with the assurance that our highest aim is to support the Government and the Constitution and aid in the enforcement of the law." By Saturday there were seventy-seven men and a full slate of officers.

On May 4 they assembled for their first drill, joined by more volunteers from Reedsburg and nearby Delton. Community members thronged around the newly enlisted troops; a woman of the community presented each recruit with a red, white, and blue rosette. The volunteers drilled again a week later, and county residents feted the men with more speeches and a dinner in the grove. Men from out of town lodged with families in Baraboo. Another entertainment for the company was held at Delton on May 18, and by May 28 the officers were notified of their assignment as Company A of the Sixth Wisconsin. Eight more men joined when the company visited Prairie du Chien and Sauk City, roughly halfway between Baraboo and the capital of Madison, where the festivities and food created fond memories for the recruits. One recalled, "Many a time afterwards when rations were scarce and water scarcer, on hot, fierce marches under a burning sun, some of the boys would yell out, 'Say, boys, do you remember the doings' on those two golden days, and shout 'let's go down there again!'" By the time they returned to Baraboo they had 108 men. The company had its daguerreotype taken on June 19, two months to the day after Baraboo's first war meeting; it was "a very good picture" and was hung in the courthouse. About this time Lt. Col. Julius Atwood—who served with the regiment for only a few months—mustered the company for a flag presentation and said, "If there were any that were faint hearted or for any other cause did not wish to go for the three years they could retire." Although many men had believed they were signing up for a much shorter time—the federal government had only recently began demanding three-year terms of enlistment—no one did.[7]

The Sixth's Company D formed rather differently. It drew from the community of Irish immigrants or their sons who formed the core of Milwaukee's Montgomery Guards, a private militia company formed late in the 1850s. By mid-June the Guards had more than 100 men and seemed poised to be called to Madison. But as one of the state's few extant militia companies, it was called into local service earlier than expected. By June, Milwaukee's banks, many of which were backed by bonds from Southern states, were facing great difficulty as they struggled to respond to the uncertainty of the secession crisis. Faith in banking was already low in a state that had been rocked by panics in the previous decade, but suddenly the public faced the reality that their banknotes were worthless. In late June, violence erupted; a mob armed with bricks, clubs, knives, and pistols broke windows, damaged furnishings, and destroyed records in several banks. The mayor, several other city officials, and some bank executives were injured in the riot. In response, the Montgomery Guards formed up and advanced down Michigan Street with bayonets at the ready. The outnumbered militiamen were immediately assaulted by stones thrown from all sides, striking several in the head or body. Although a far cry from the Cornfield at Antietam or Railroad Cut at Gettysburg, the afternoon of violence during the "Bank War" gave the company a taste of blood.[8]

Bragg's Rifles, which would become Company E, used the reputation of their first captain (and a future commander of the Sixth), Edward Bragg, the rising lawyer and politician who had predicted war a year earlier; he left a murder trial to help lead a war meeting in spring 1861, where he gave a very short speech that one old veteran remembered years later. He could not afford to contribute money to the cause, "but I bequeath my loved ones to your protection and will go myself." He concluded, "This is no time for vain vaporing. All who are ready to fight sign this muster roll with me." With that he slammed the paper down on the table before him. A company soon formed and chose him as captain.[9]

The men who joined Bragg often did so on impulse. For instance, in Shawano, on the frontier north of Fond du Lac, "the war excitement rage[d] . . . with unabated interest" with each new report from the East encouraging new recruits. Throughout the last week in June, men left in groups of as many as ten to join Bragg's company. In the same week, an emissary from Bragg enlisted six men, who all agreed to leave immediately. A day or two later, at four in the morning, "the cannon commenced firing" to alert the town to the departure of this small band of volunteers. Four more men joined them, including a man who borrowed a neighbor's coat so he would not have to return home for his own coat where, he feared, his family would beg him to change his mind. Another volunteer recalled working in the field when he "dropped his hoe and sent word to his family that he was going to the war and would come back as soon as he got 'one fair *pop* at Jeff. Davis.'" A crowd followed the men down to the ferry on Lake Winnebago and gave "three lusty cheers and a tiger—a lusty growling noise"—when they passed the American flag flying from the liberty pole.[10]

Bragg's company would fill up when a rival group in Appleton—located on the opposite, northern shore of Lake Winnebago from Fond du Lac—had to disband. A recruiter from Chicago snapped up thirty of them, but about forty others joined Bragg's Rifles. In return, their leader, J. H. Marston, was voted first lieutenant in the combined unit.[11]

A detailed look at the formation of one more company is in order, if only to focus on the emergence of one of the regiment's most prominent soldiers. Rufus Dawes would fight with the Sixth Wisconsin through late summer of 1864 without suffering a single wound. He led the regiment in its two most famous and catastrophic battles and later wrote the best-known and most useful memoir by any member of the regiment. But in 1860 he was a rather disgruntled recent college graduate, living temporarily with his father in remote Juneau County in western Wisconsin. He had attended both Marietta College in Ohio and the University of Wisconsin. His parents were divorced and his mother still lived in Marietta, where virtually all of Rufus's friends and family lived and where he would eventually return. During school breaks, however, he worked with his father, farming and lumbering on the Wisconsin frontier.

Dawes's diary from 1860 betrays some contempt for the locals, making fun of their habit of pronouncing chairman "cheerman" and dropping g's from words like "getting" and "meeting." But he seemed to have warmed to the community when he became one of the organizers and orators for a July Fourth celebration. "After discussion the people called out speakers," Dawes recalled. First to the front came John Kellogg, a local attorney who would join Dawes as one of the longest-serving members of the Sixth. But as Dawes reported, Kellogg "did bunkum," leading the assembled to call for Dawes's best. It was, by chance, Dawes's twenty-second birthday. He regaled the crowd with a reading of the Declaration of Independence, followed by taking the lead in a processional that attracted "three hundred in my army—the largest regiment I have marshalled." In a telling revelation of personal ambition, Dawes wrote that "the people of this settlement need badly some one to lead."[12]

Dawes found the attention flattering. As the presidential campaign of 1860 heated up, he became one of the more popular local speakers on behalf of Lincoln and the antislavery movement. In an undated note in his diary, Dawes listed the locations of a dozen stump speeches he had given around the county, with brief notations like "Large crowd and good time," "Large and enthusiastic," and "Very good Discussion."

Dawes's politicking made it natural that he would be among the leaders at the public meeting of the Freemen of Juneau County to organize a "VOLUNTEER MILITARY COMPANY" less than a year after his triumphant appearance on July Fourth. "Brave hearts are needed to protect the rights and liberties guaranteed us in our time-honored Constitution," proclaimed the *Mauston Star*. "Come then one and all. Old men to give counsel. Young men to give strength." Dawes's father served as president of the meeting, which passed resolutions and observed over forty young men pledge their lives to the Union by signing a pledge of service. Within a few days the Lemonweir Minutemen—named after a lovely little stream that meanders through the county—had unanimously chosen Rufus Dawes as captain.[13]

Dawes was overjoyed. In a series of letters to his family during the summer, he marveled at his men and expressed supreme confidence in himself and the outcome of the war: "I am Captain of as good and true a bunch of patriots as ever rallied under the Star Spangled Banner," he wrote his sister. "My men are terribly in earnest and they will stand by me to death." The company had "no rowdies, no drunkards, no off scourings of society but the very flower of Juneau, Adams & Bad Axe Counties. I shall esteem it an honor worth a better life than mine to be permit[t]ed to lead them in this glorious struggle."[14]

In mid-June Dawes predicted to his brother Ephraim that his company would "be called into quarters soon." He was getting impatient "but will be ready in ample time to go with the grand expedition down the Mississippi to hold a Merry Christmas in New Orleans." Dawes would never see New Orleans, however, and of the twenty-two men who signed the pledge on that dramatic night in Mauston and served in the Sixth Wisconsin, six would die of wounds or disease, one would go missing in action, and five would be disabled by illness.[15]

The men gathering in these widespread sections of the state represented a true cross-section of Wisconsin men and communities. Later in the summer, the *Wisconsin State Journal* provided brief introductions when each company arrived at Camp Randall. They were proud descriptions of skills, excellent fighting qualities, and high character—qualities that civilian journalists unfamiliar with war in any real sense imagined would make these green recruits into effective soldiers. The Sauk County Riflemen "give renewed evidence of the muscular resources of Wisconsin. No company raised in the State can surpass these Sauk county boys in brawn." It would be hard to find "a better looking or a more healthy set of men" than the Prescott Guards, while the Buffalo County Rifles were "a remarkably hardy set of fellows—many of them lumbermen, who are inured to camp life, and will make the best of soldiers," and "nearly every member of" the Lemonweir Minutemen "is a temperance man in the strictest sense of the term."[16]

Although the *State Journal* imagined most of these distinctions, there were actually a number of more substantial differences worth noting. Sauk County's Company A and Vernon County's Company I, more than any other units, were companies of farmers; about two-thirds of the members of the former for whom we know occupations were either farm owners or laborers, and an even greater proportion—fifty out of fifty-seven—of the latter reported themselves as farmers of some sort. Company E, by contrast, dominated by the thriving small cities of Appleton and Fond du Lac, had only a dozen farmers (but sixteen skilled workers, fourteen laborers, and nine clerks, lawyers, and white-collar workers), along with three college students and two tavern owners. Milwaukee's Company F included twenty skilled craftsmen (although we have 1860 occupations for only about half the company). Not surprisingly, the companies that came out of the lumber districts of the west and northwest, particularly Companies B and K, had significant numbers of "lumbermen"—eighteen and eleven, respectively. Milwaukee's Company D, coming from a major Lake Michigan port, boasted ten sailors.

By the end of the war, over a third of the men in the Sixth were married before enlisting or being drafted, but only about 28 percent of the enlistees of 1861 were married. There were interesting differences among the companies, however. While over 30 percent of the men from the more established farming region of Vernon County (Company I) and the town-based men of Company E were already married, less than 10 percent of Pierce County's Company B, recruited in far-flung communities and lumber camps, were married. Relatively few of the men in Company F were married—only 14.4 percent—perhaps because they tended to be more recent arrivals from Europe, still finding their footing in the new world.

Every company had a complement of immigrants—there were a total of 216 immigrants in the 1861 class of enlistees, or 21.2 percent of the total—but Company F had by far the most immigrants with at least fifty-two (more than half its total), mostly from German-speaking countries. On the other hand, fewer than ten known immigrants enlisted in either Company C from Prairie du Chien or Company I from Vernon County. Although well over a third of the immigrants spoke German, clusters of other nationalities appeared in a few companies, with fifteen Swiss recruits in Buffalo County's Company H and ten Canadians in Juneau County's Company K. Interestingly, the so-called Irish Company D had only sixteen known Irishmen, although it is likely that many more were of Irish descent; less is known about the origins of the men in Company D than almost any other unit. As the war ground on, the percentage of immigrants—driven largely by late-war draftees—would rise to nearly 28 percent, and the percentage of those men born in German-speaking countries would rise from 38.6 percent to about half.[17]

What does this examination of the makeup of the original members of the Sixth Wisconsin tell us about the nature of this little segment of the Union army? In many ways, by mid-nineteenth-century standards, the Sixth Wisconsin was fairly diverse, with recruits from many national and ethnic backgrounds; a wide range of economic circumstances and occupations; settled men with families and single men with few prospects; and residents of cities, towns, and isolated farms. Yet they must have shared at least two beliefs: that the Union was worth fighting for and that this regiment was worth fighting with. Their government may have seemed for most an abstract if noble idea. But their membership in the community—communities—that embraced the concept of "Union" gave them a concrete, practical identity that in 1861 required defending. Although they could not yet imagine just how "long" their Civil War would be, the many different paths that brought them to the Sixth Wisconsin would merge into a single road leading to blood and glory, to a place where their differences meant nothing and their commitment to the regiment meant everything.

Many a Stern Face

The day of departure would come. The men were not yet soldiers, really; they would not actually be mustered into federal service until they reached Camp Randall. They didn't have guns, or even uniforms, although some had tried to find clothes or hats to distinguish themselves from civilians. Some had been drilling assiduously; others were no doubt more casual about their preparation. The final moments of speeches, fetes, presentations, prayers, and songs provided superficial connections between them and the folks they were leaving behind, but it is hard not to imagine that, in fact, the thoughts of the not-quite soldiers were already far away, imagining great deeds, unknown challenges, and possible heartbreaks. Their departures followed a script duplicated with minor differences in countless Northern communities.

Like most of the companies in the Sixth, the Prescott Guards, destined to become Company B, received orders in late June to travel from their homes along the Mississippi River to Camp Randall with just two days' notice. Their departure "called together the largest crowd of people we ever saw in Prescott," reported the local paper. "The parting was a touching scene; how could it be otherwise, when sons and brothers say good bye to those who love them as parents, sisters or lovers, to brave the hardships of the camp and perils of the battle field." But as they embarked on the riverboat taking them part of the way to Madison, "the boys . . . cheerily," if ironically, sang "In Dixie land I take my stand, To live and die in Dixie." Before they embarked, Capt. John Marsh thanked the crowd for its support and well-wishes, and Sgt. Michael Fitch declared that the volunteers "went to the war with the motto that the Spartan mothers always put upon the shield when they presented it to their sons,—'bring it home, or be brought home on it.'" After an artillery salute, "cheer after cheer rang from the volunteers and the people on shore, and with the best wishes, the sincere hopes for their safe return in due time, and the prayers of the people of the county."[18]

The Appleton contingent of Company E left on the southbound train to Madison at about the same time. They and a large number of citizens gathered in a local park, where the volunteers received numerous gifts, some more practical than others: a copy of the New Testament, towels, socks, and sewing supplies, as well as "a large and very tastefully arranged bouquet of flowers, from the hands of the patriotic ladies of Appleton." As a brass band led them to the depot, they made slow progress through the throng of well-wishers, who often interrupted their march "by words of cheer and a fervent wish for their prosperity, a 'God speed,' or the silent pressure of the hand by some who were too deeply affected to give utterance to their feelings."[19]

The "largest gathering of people . . . that had ever been seen in Baraboo" sent off the Sauk County Riflemen. Wearing only gray caps trimmed with green for uniforms—in contrast to their escorts, the fully uniformed Baraboo Fire Company—they were serenaded by a choir performing an original song by a local minister. All of the men accepted pocket Testaments and Capt.

A. G. Malloy received a richly bound Bible. Fifty-two wagons filled with over 260 volunteers and supporters snaked out of town, stopping later in the day for more speeches and a meal.[20]

Most of the Anderson Guards were from the eastern part of Bad Axe (Vernon) County. They came into Viroqua on June 30, when they were sworn into state service and then underwent perfunctory—too much so, it would appear later—medical examinations. "Some were too old, some too young, or could not get consent of parents, some were unsound," but ninety-four departed by wagon the next day, heading for De Soto on the Mississippi River, where they picked up another ten recruits and boarded a steamer to Prairie du Chien and from there a train to Madison. "The boys will have few harder battles to fight than the one they fought on parting, to keep their tears and sighs within their fountains," opined a local editor. "Many a stern face was wet with tears and the hot floods dimmed the eyes and bathed the cheeks of hundreds of ladies who had relatives, friends or neighbors in the ranks." As they departed, the men sang "Hurrah for the Union," a song written by Sgt. Henry Didiot and set to the tune of "Wait for the Wagon." "Come, brothers, all unite with us, join us, one and all," it began.

> United we must conquer, but divided we shall fall;
> Our Flag is for the Union, and we have a gallant crew,
> Who have raised it, and who love it—'tis the Red, White and Blue.

The recent violence in Milwaukee muted the departure of the Citizens' Corps and Montgomery Guards. Only a few family members and friends saw them off at the station of the Milwaukee & Prairie du Chien Railroad for the seventy-mile journey to Madison.[21]

Since spring the *Wisconsin State Journal* had covered the assembling host as it began to arrive in Madison, noting the recruiting efforts, the local selection of officers and granting of officers' commissions by the governor, and the transmission of orders for companies to go to camp. Indeed, in its columns one gains a palpable sense of the Sixth Wisconsin slowly coming together all over the state. Although brief mentions of the Sixth's individual companies had begun appearing in mid-April, the first mention of the regiment itself came late in May, when a list of senior officers for the first six Wisconsin regiments were named. In mid-June, the new requirement that men agree to three years of service rather than three months or a year threw some companies into disarray. In fact, a few companies originally assigned to the Fifth and Sixth Regiments "failed to muster full for three years" and had to be replaced, including the Union Guards of Fond du Lac, National Guards of Janesville,

Scott Guards of Racine, and Lodi Guards. Other companies who had not yet been ordered to Madison suddenly had to reassemble. This included Rufus Dawes's Lemonweir Minutemen, who had temporarily disbanded assuming they would be called later in the summer or fall. One of Dawes's recruits, Cyrus Spooner, hurried to marry his sweetheart, Pearl, the day before they departed for Madison.[22]

Despite these disruptions, the unit's formation quickened in mid-June, when the *Wisconsin State Journal* recorded the mustering into federal service of several of the Sixth's companies and began tracking their dates of departure from home and arrival at Camp Randall. The Prairie du Chien Volunteers reached Madison first. All the other companies had arrived by July 6, when Dawes and the out-of-practice Lemonweir contingent finally stumbled into camp to become Company K.[23]

A number of soldiers sent letters to hometown newspapers over the next few weeks. A typical missive from Company I's William E. Minshall described the trip to Madison from Vernon County. Although they had gotten lost in the fog on the Mississippi, they eventually reached Prairie du Chien, where they "paraded through the streets" before boarding a train for Madison. Later in the day they met their colonel, Lysander Cutler, gave him three cheers, ate "a good Soldier's dinner," and then, after resting in the barracks, watched the Fifth Wisconsin drill. The next day they were part of a Fourth of July parade that "kicked up such a dust that we could not see our hand in front of us," but basically the regiment enjoyed the festivities. "Our company are all in good spirits, and I think they all would fight. All the officers of our regiment are good men, our captain is a regular man."[24]

Minshall's letter had described Colonel Cutler as "a man that is a man." A relatively recent arrival to Wisconsin from New England, Cutler had experienced many highs and lows in his fifty-plus years. As a young man he had been a district schoolteacher in Massachusetts until moving to Dexter, Maine, where he became a prosperous woolen mill owner, a one-term state legislator, and a member of several boards of directors of educational institutions and a railroad company. Ruined in the Panic of 1857, he came to Wisconsin, where an old friend offered him a job as a prospector and surveyor for a mining company exploring the country along Lake Superior. He came south to Milwaukee in 1859 to become a grain merchant. He was the founder of a private militia company a quarter century earlier and a lieutenant colonel and post commander in the 1839 Aroostook War, a conflict over the boundary between Maine and New Brunswick, Canada (in which no shots were fired).

Throughout the ups and downs of his life, Cutler had always emerged as an effective leader of men, which would be key to the development of the Sixth.[25]

A few days after the regiment had filled up, the *State Journal* bragged with typical puffery that "the 5th and 6th regiments are in our midst—soon expecting to leave for the wars; and, if it were possible that more robust, active and determined men could be found than those who have gone before them—we should claim that the men of the 5th and 6th regiments were more than equals." Later the same week, after the regiment was sworn into federal service, the *State Journal* summarized the sorts of things civilians wanted to believe about the new Union army: "A remarkable state of feeling exists here in both regiments. Everyone seems satisfied with his neighbor, and the men with their officers, and the officers with their men. A spirit of good-natured competition, void of jealousy, pervades the whole camp." More important, the paper opined, "the improvement in drill is astonishing; and it is the opinion of all military men, that these two regiments are composed of material good enough to become first class."[26]

Only four men from the Sixth did not take the oath on July 17, the day they entered federal service and actually became soldiers for the Union. One simply refused and went home, but the others were honorably discharged, apparently for reasons that satisfied their comrades and protected their honor. Less honorable were the departures of two men from the Prescott Guards, who deserted within a week of taking the oath. Publishing their names, the *Prescott Transcript* declared, "They are too mean for men to despise, but little boys can hoot at them."[27]

Despite the optimistic outlook of the *State Journal*, the new leaders of the Sixth had little to no military experience and scrambled to learn how to become infantry officers or, at the very least, to figure out what they still did not know. At least early on, the federal government gave no instructions on how regiments should be trained; each new colonel needed to decide how he would prepare his men for service, and junior officers scrambled to obtain and to study military manuals. As Governor Randall had declared, "This legislature must determine for Wisconsin . . . the way of arming, equipping and uniforming its own citizens for military purposes. . . . The men sent to war should be soldiers when they go, or there will be few of them living soldiers when it is time for them to return."[28]

To that end, the state ordered the printing of an edition of *Chandler's Tactics, Compiled from Scott and Hardee, for the Use of Wisconsin Volunteers*; each regiment received 300 copies. A plagiarized version of the manual currently in use by the US Army, it did not make learning new concepts easy. One imagines the confusion of an eager young captain when in the first few pages he discovered that regiments would be called "battalions"; that the companies posted on a regiment's flanks would be called "grenadiers" or "light infantry" (usages discarded once the war started in earnest); that the companies would be posted, from right to left, in the order of first, fifth, fourth, seventh, and so on but once in line would be designated from right to left as first company, second company, and so forth; and that regiments would further be divided into a right wing and a left wing, companies paired up into divisions (also numbered right to left), and companies divided into first and second platoons. Each soldier would belong to five different, identifiable segments of the regiment—all with its own numerical designation.[29]

No wonder that, in one of Capt. Edward Bragg's first letters to his wife Cornelia, the daily schedule he provided was weighted so heavily toward drill: "Rise at a little before five and drill till breakfast—Attend officer Drill an hour from nine o'clock—Attend Company drill from ½ one till ½ two Attend Battalion Drill from 3 till 5 PM-Dress parade ½ 6 till 7. And Company Drill again from 7 till Eight. Superintend the general wants of the Company & study till ten then sleep in my clothes on a cot." Bragg revealed the mix of confidence and trepidation that many officers and most men no doubt felt when they considered the experiences that were to come. He was confident that his regiment would become a "superior" unit if it was only given time to learn "the science & practice of military evolutions." On a personal note, he wrote, "Camp life agrees with me—and I am hardening up to the work."

He ended his letter with concerns and advice that was almost universal among the men who left families behind. He urged Cornelia to tell the children that "they must be good and learn to mind you in everything—I should be very sorry to come home and find them wild & ungovernable." He ended with heartfelt sentiment and more than a hint of the ambition that drove young men like Bragg, Dawes, and others in the Sixth: "Remember that when this trouble shall cease, we shall be together again, and your husband will be a patriot soldier, as well as a lawyer. Never fear but there is still a bright, long, happy future in line for us yet."[30]

But for the most part the men focused on mundane matters or concerns closer to their own priorities. A recruit from a different regiment complained that Madison itself was "miserably dull . . . offering scarcely any amusement. But worse than all this and more to be deplored . . . there is scarcely a pretty woman here." Others were less concerned with local women. Two members of Company A made fast trips home to get married.[31]

Even as they took the first ragged steps toward becoming soldiers, the men of the Sixth no doubt kept an eye on newspapers reporting from the "seat of war," as the First and Second Wisconsin headed east and, in the case of the latter, into battle. Their experiences would no doubt color the Sixth's responses to training and to the prospect of facing a real enemy. In Cleveland, a member of the First was accidentally stabbed through the mouth with a bayonet; in Maryland, the men complained about the heat and army food. They were called to arms one night, but rather than fighting Rebels, they were sent to arrest a few drunken US Regulars. A more sobering hint of the dangerous business of soldiering was the news of a man from a different regiment losing a leg after an accidental shooting.[32]

The only Wisconsin regiment to see combat at Bull Run on July 20 was the Second, serving in Gen. William T. Sherman's brigade and suffering nineteen killed and 114 wounded. News of the Union's defeat hastened the timetable for the Sixth's departure. Reuben Huntley wrote—on patriotic stationery with a picture of the partially finished US Capitol dome and the labels "Our Country" and "Camp Randall"—that "the disastrous result of the battle at Bulls run has entirely altered our arrangements here. We are now under marching orders & shall leave this week." He closed hurriedly with "God bless you and believe me the only thing that could distract me from my duties is the recollection of my family at home. Good bye." The Fifth would depart for the front almost immediately, while the Sixth would follow a few days later.[33]

Although not engaged at Bull Run, the First Wisconsin did experience small skirmishes, and a letter from a local boy describing "Shooting a Rebel—First Experiences" was no doubt read with interest by members of the Sixth. "I cannot describe my feelings at all. There was more curiosity than anything else." Like all new soldiers, he had been eager to get a look at the Rebels. As the regiment advanced—perhaps as a line of skirmishers—"I got down in a corner of the fence, and saw a fellow in the act of firing at our men. I deliberately took aim at him, and had the pleasure of seeing him roll over, and two men carry him off the field; so I concluded I have done my country some service already."[34]

The men of the Sixth would find out soon enough how they would measure their own duty to the country.

About 2,000 men would eventually serve in the Sixth Wisconsin. The regiment does not represent the origins and makeup of every unit in the Union army, but it is very likely that it reflects the experiences of those raised in the summer of 1861, particularly in the "northwest," as it was called then, or even in other rural areas of the North.

The Sixth shared many characteristics with other Union troops, although their differences—some slight, some rather large—stand out. Their median age of twenty-three matched the median age of the army as a whole, although they were somewhat more likely to be married at the time of enlistment (35 percent, compared to 30 percent). At least 555 members of the Sixth were immigrants (27.9 percent), a fifth again more than the estimated 23 percent who served in the army as a whole. Men from Germany or German-speaking countries made up almost exactly half that number—well above the army-wide average of about 36 percent—while 10.8 percent of the Sixth were Irish-born, 9.5 percent English-born, and 5.8 percent Canadian-born, compared to the overall estimates of 28.8, 9, and 10 percent, respectively, for all Union troops. An additional 6.5 percent were born in Switzerland and were mostly from a small pocket of Swiss immigrants living southwest of Milwaukee.[35]

Most companies grew from a small core—as few as a dozen, as many as a few dozen—of men who came from specific towns or, more likely, counties. At least two-thirds and as many as 80 percent of the men in each company came from its "home" county; most of the rest came from contiguous counties. Yet by the end of the war, every county in the state and 439 cities, towns, and villages would send men to the regiment. This geographical diversity is underscored by the fact that just under 8 percent of the first 1,000 recruits came from other states, mainly Michigan and Minnesota but also Iowa, Illinois, New York, and even Virginia. There is some evidence that a few recruits went shopping for regiments—Henry Matrau, who would serve throughout the war with the Sixth, was one of the contingent of perhaps a dozen men from Berrien County, Michigan, who joined the company from Beloit—but mostly the out-of-staters simply traveled to nearby border towns like Beloit in the south or Prairie du Chien in the west to enlist. Others may have had family connections in Wisconsin or were in the state for work when the war broke out.[36]

As a result, although there were clear attachments to one or two communities among the original enlistees, the Sixth does not fit the stereotype of Civil War regiments reflecting fairly small and tight-knit communities. And that diffusion of geographic origins becomes much more obvious when the men are divided into cohorts by enlistment dates. Although it varied somewhat by company, in general each company was made up of three separate cohorts. Cohort 1, logically, consists of the roughly 1,000 men who enlisted during the initial enthusiasm for the war in spring and summer 1861. A few men drifted into the regiment during the next year or so, but cohort 2 enlisted during the fall of 1863 and early 1864. Just over 200 belong to this cohort, but the number of men entering individual companies during that time varied greatly, ranging from seven in Company E to over fifty in Company I. All but one company received a major infusion of men from the fall 1864 draft; these more than 450 draftees make up cohort 3. Company H received only twenty-five draftees, but Companies B, D, and E each gained over sixty men. Company G received only three draftees, but it was the main beneficiary of the disbandment of the old Second Wisconsin, whose survivors were integrated into Companies G and H of the Sixth. A few other enlistees and several dozen substitutes also joined the regiment during this time, although they are not included in the cohorts.[37]

A particular segment of cohort 1 deserves mention: the 122 men who would serve as officers in the Sixth Wisconsin. All but eight came out of the 1861 enlistees, and at least four of those eight had been officers in the Second Wisconsin before transferring to the Sixth. Nearly 60 percent began the war as enlisted men. The prewar backgrounds of the men who served as officers in the Sixth were rather different than the sample provided in a recent analysis of Union soldiers, however; the percentage of officers in the Sixth who were farmers in 1860 was 35.1, compared to 19 percent in the army as a whole, while fewer were skilled artisans (14.9 percent to 36 percent), and slightly more were merchants or white-collar workers (19.1 to 16 percent). They did share one characteristic with their fellow officers: casualties among them were appalling, especially among the thirty-eight who served as captains or brevet captains; eight were killed and thirteen wounded for a combat casualty rate of 55 percent.[38]

A more complicated question than geography requires a bit of imagination to unpack. Historians have explored the motivations of Civil War soldiers for a century or more, yet the reasons that men joined the Union cause are difficult to pin down. There is every reason to believe that the men of the Sixth Wisconsin shared the same bundle of motivations as other Union soldiers, from patriotism and an idealistic sense of Republican democracy, to a desire for adventure and peer pressure, and on to a hatred of slavery and of the so-called slave power. And at least some would have agreed with the young Irishman who declared just after the war that he had "enlisted (not for my country being nothing but a boy did not know what that meant; did not know what my duty to country was), but for the sake of seeing the sunny south that I had heard so much about and to be considered brave."[39]

Few, if any, recruits in 1861 admitted that financial considerations played a role in their decision to enlist. Of course, the opportunity for large bounties would come later, but military service as a financial transaction rather than a political or patriotic statement would come to dominate the rhetoric of volunteering as early as fall 1862. Thus it is fairly easy to assume that for at least some of them—first-wave recruits, later enlistees, and substitutes alike—economics played a role. Perhaps the men from Milwaukee shared the impulses displayed in Dubuque, Iowa, where Russell Johnson has shown that the economic crisis inaugurated by the Panic of 1857 led many to perceive a social disintegration that might be solved by military service for young men cast adrift in an unstable economy. The panic caused business instability, shattered confidence in Dubuque's long-term economic development, and led to more people demanding public relief. Johnson argues that military service became a "strategy" for some sons in uncertain times.[40]

A century-old but still useful study of Wisconsin's economy in the Civil War era suggests that during the fall of 1860, the likely election of Lincoln drove down the value of the bonds and stocks from Southern and border states that supported much of the currency issued by Wisconsin banks. The Panic of 1857 had already rocked Wisconsin; it caused grain exports to plummet, along with their prices. Wheat fell from ninety-four cents a bushel in August to sixty-five cents in December and remained at about that level through the spring. Although the panic, even in the West, had largely subsided by summer 1860, the sectional crisis—which reached a fever pitch in late 1859 with John Brown's raid and intensified with the 1860 presidential campaign—and especially the secession of most of the slave states, plunged the North into a two-year recession that corresponded with the outpouring of volunteers in the summer of 1861 and 1862. While Wisconsin escaped most of the labor unrest that occurred during the late 1850s, it suffered its own peculiar economic ramifications of secession with the Bank War, which provided an odd prologue to the state's mobilization for war. The statewide depression continued into 1862. It is difficult to track the effects of several years of economic distress on individual Wisconsinites, but it is hardly a stretch to suggest that economic conditions played a role in the decisions of small farmers, recent immigrants, younger sons, and other young men—even boys—who had yet to establish their economic independence or stability.[41]

The Western Brigade

Before the Sixth Wisconsin and the other regiments in their brigade earned the nickname they would wear proudly into history, they were usually called the "Western Brigade" by newspapers and even commanding officers. They were a novelty as the only brigade in the Army of the Potomac to come from the "West"—although they were still from east of the Mississippi and many of its soldiers were actually born in Ohio, Pennsylvania, and New York. The men themselves took some pride in being unique among the units fighting in Virginia and sometimes complained about eastern regiments receiving undeserved "newspaper puffs," or publicity.[42]

But it is less clear what exactly distinguished them from eastern soldiers. The biggest demographic difference is that, at least in the 1861 cohort of recruits, far more were farmers than the average in the Army of the Potomac (46.8 percent of those for whom we know occupations, compared to 30 percent in the army as a whole), and far fewer were laborers (9 percent compared to 42 percent).[43]

These occupational differences—if they were even aware of them—do not seem to have been the key factor in soldiers identifying as "westerners." At a certain level, the terms "western" and "eastern" were simply practical labels; they hailed from a part of the country that in 1860 was the "West," after all. On the other hand, the men of the Sixth loved to scoff at the poor performance of some of the eastern regiments at Second Bull Run, South Mountain, and Antietam. As we will see, New Yorkers came in for severe criticism from the Wisconsin men, and they took not-so-grim satisfaction out of putting down a short mutiny among two-year regiments from the Empire State just before Gettysburg. Sometimes being a westerner simply meant possessing a certain skill set; before an amphibious attack across the Rappahannock, their commander referred to their "western breeding" and "skill as oarsmen"—which would only have applied to those few men who had been rivermen in the western part of the state.

But their western identity also seems to have become something of a shorthand for a set of values and assumptions articulated by Iron Brigade historian Lance Herdegen, who wrote in his magisterial history of the brigade that its origin in "the frontier West was significant." He associated the brigade with the development of the Northwest Territory as a Free Soil enclave "with a distinctive sectional interest and identification," a place developed by "folk of ambition and vigor, men and women interested in making a future." Frontier communities judged people "less by their family connection and money than for their skill with axe and plow and the strength needed to take a wilderness." The open, diverse (for their time) societies, where men could make something of themselves and education and industry were respected, created "a new kind" of Americans, who would become soldiers "with a certain dash and sense of themselves never before seen in the United States."[44]

Yet it is hard to translate this regional identity into a set of military values. Perhaps the most telling indication of the limits of the brigade's western identity is their disdain for one of the most "western" commanders they ever had, Kentucky-born and Illinois-raised Gen. John Pope, who had come from the West to Virginia in summer 1862. His style never resonated with the Wisconsin men, and his poor leadership during the Second Bull Run campaign cemented their contempt for this most western of generals. Being western would come to mean less; by May 1864 there would be at least two dozen regiments in the Army of the Potomac from western states, mostly from Michigan, but also including the Fifth Wisconsin. Perhaps it is enough to say simply that identifying themselves as "western," however vaguely that applied to their roles as soldiers and officers, gave them an emotional and psychological edge to survive the long and bloody war to which they had committed their souls. As one member of the brigade recalled years later, in remembering the pressure they put themselves under entering their first battle, as "the only Western soldiers in the entire army ... we would have died rather than dishonor the West."[45]

We Will Have Some Hard and Bloody Fighting

The Sixth Wisconsin saw the Fifth Wisconsin off to Washington, DC, on July 24. As the cars slowly rolled away, the men of the Sixth waved their caps and "gave their late comrades nine rousing cheers." The Sixth got its marching orders two days later. They spent July 26 packing, getting paid, and being inspected. The *State Journal* published the final list of field officers and staff, as well as the captains and lieutenants of each company. "The officers and men are in the best possible spirits, and will leave their noble State with light hearts and strong hopes." The Sixth's Julius Murray wrote home that "all are anxious to leave," for doing the same "thing over and over from day to day is getting to be rather monotonous and tiresome." Although everyone was excited to go, Murray feared that "this war will not be brought to a close as soon as a great many imagine. I think we will have some hard and bloody fighting and a great many companies will lose some of their number from the muster roll before they return." With unusual prescience, he predicted that "we will have to suffer privation and hardship in every way and in my opinion sickness will thin off our ranks faster than the enemy." Yet, he assured his family, "my chance is as good as any one's to come back but it is not likely that we will all return."[46]

The Sixth left "at the appointed hour yesterday morning," announced the *State Journal* on the twenty-ninth. "There was no confusion or hesitation in their movements. Each company knew where it was to go, and got on board without any noise or delay." Colonel Cutler's first general order announced that the regiment would break camp at 5:00 a.m. and "take up the line of March for Washington" precisely at 9:00. He also gave the itinerary for their train trip east and the order in which they would enter the cars (Company A first and so forth through Company K). For those with rifles (perhaps one company actually had arms by this time), bayonets would be unfixed when entering the cars but fixed whenever they left them; officers and men would be seated in the cars in roughly the same order as in formation, with sentries posted at each exit; roll calls would be taken every morning; soldiers leaving cars without permission or leaving stations would be treated as deserters; no cheering would be allowed unless ordered by an officer; and "perfect decorum will be preserved by all officers and men during the march."[47]

Lieutenant Kellogg of Company K assured his hometown newspaper just before the regiment entrained that "the boys are all well." They "went off" with half a dozen pails of lemonade, wheels of cheese, and barrels of crackers to snack on during their long journey. "They are in the best of spirits, and only anxious to meet the traitors."[48]

2

Coming Events Are Crowding Thickly upon Us

Waiting

On a hot night in Baltimore, Sgt. Earl M. Rogers of Company I let rumors of war and his own imagination get away from him. It was the Sixth's first night of actual military duty. They had encamped within the old breastworks in Patterson Park, where during the War of 1812 the Americans had successfully turned back the British in the battle that inspired "The Star-Spangled Banner." It had become a public park a few decades before the Civil War, and its view of the harbor made it a popular promenade. But now the military had again taken it over, and the park was full of green recruits.[1]

Perhaps the park's history got to Rogers, or the stressful march from the depot when the regiment had arrived in the city a night or two before. Although the state remained in the Union, many Marylanders supported both slavery and secession. A pro-Confederate mob had attacked the Sixth

Massachusetts as it marched between railway depots back in April; a dozen civilians were killed and three dozen soldiers injured, and the violence had helped spur enlistments in Wisconsin. The Sixth Wisconsin had experienced its own, much smaller attack. Rufus Dawes wrote his brother just afterward that the largely unarmed regiment had supplied itself with "paving stones and brick bats" and was accompanied by 200 armed policemen. "The streets were jammed with people ... and the excitement was intense." The "rebel plug uglies" launched an attack on Company E, but the Baltimore police escort fought them off.[2]

Whatever the cause, feeling the weight of responsibility and fearing the possibility for violence, Rogers saw "enemies of the country walking, plug uglies crawling towards me, ghosts, specters, skeletons, all after me—my hair sings, my very flesh quivers, my limbs tremble." Perhaps Rogers was on duty the night that a few dozen shots had been fired at the Union guards and a "secesher" had been shot in the leg by return fire.[3]

This real or imagined encounter would soon enough seem trivial to the Sixth Wisconsin in general and to Earl Rogers in particular—indeed, three years later, at Spotsylvania, a bullet would splash a general's brains and blood all over him. But the excitement during those dark hours in Baltimore was, for all intents and purposes, the regiment's first introduction to a conflict zone.

Leave Soldiering to Those That Like It

The journey east was long, and one captain would complain that the weather was "excessively hot," the cars crowded, and "the men boisterous & unruly." Yet the heat, boredom, and boorish behavior were interrupted from time to time by enthusiastic receptions and food, flags and flowers, cheers and kisses, and heartfelt expressions of gratitude and concern. Sixteen-year-old Henry Matrau, who had added two years to his age when he talked his way into the Beloit Rifles, filled his letters to his parents with descriptions of the journey to war: "At every place we stopped the people came out in great numbers, cheered, and shook hands with us and at most places they filled our canteens with water and some with hot coffee." Henry became a bit of a tourist when he recalled a schoolbook, *Old Mitchell's Geography*, that "told the truth when it said that Pittsburg was remarkable for its smoke. . . . You can smell smoke, feel smoke, & I will go so far as to say you can taste it."[4]

The regiment would never be as large or as healthy as it was when it left Camp Randall. The losses began before they left, when George Moser of Company B stepped in a hole while drilling at Camp Randall, rupturing his "heel cord," or Achilles tendon. He traveled east with the regiment but could do only light duty around camp. Moser was discharged in November; witnesses claimed a decade later that his leg had since shriveled up, rendering Moser unable to make a living.[5]

Two more men died on consecutive days from disease. Nathaniel Dilameter was forty-two years old and had four daughters. He injured his leg while changing trains in Chicago, perhaps the first of hundreds of veterans of the Sixth disabled in the line of duty. The wound became infected, and the regiment left him behind in Harrisburg, Pennsylvania. Dilameter died days later, and he was buried there, far from home and from the front lines alike. A few days later Benjamin Campbell died in Baltimore. He was apparently a heavy drinker, or had been, according to the decree granting his wife Ursula a divorce a few months before his enlistment. Yet his commanding officer believed Campbell died of exhaustion brought on by a recent case of measles and the long, hot train ride. Campbell was first sergeant of Company D, and in his testimony on behalf of the widow, Capt. Thomas Kerr would later swear that Campbell had overexerted himself "looking after the men." Yet a newspaper report blamed the deaths of both Campbell and Dilameter on "dissipation."[6]

Despite these reminders of the serious business at hand, some men remained confident. Pvt. Braeton B. Morris wrote smugly from Camp Kalorama, one of the forts defending Washington, DC, that "everything goes on like clockwork in our camp," as each man went about the business of preparing for their first sight of enemy troops. The food was "coarse" but wholesome and plentiful; the regiment's health was good. Morris ended with a bit of bluster: "I now prefer gunpowder to butter on my bread, and can sleep perfectly comfortable upon the sharp edge of a rail." Yet like young men in any war facing camp discipline and the great unknowing of events outside their control, some complained. "A soldier is not supposed to know anything outside of his own camp," young Matrau told his parents. "When we are ordered to sling knapsacks & prepare for march we don't know what it is for or where we are going." He told his parents to warn his brothers that "if they want to be free & not be obliged to come & go at the beck of an officer to stay at home & leave sogering to those that like it."[7]

Perhaps united in ignorance, communities soon began to form within the regiment. Surgeon Chandler B. Chapman had brought along his seventeen-year-old son Chandler P. to work as a hospital steward. "With all the men (sick and well)," the surgeon wrote his wife, "it makes a large family to care for, and they are possessed of such variety of qualities as give both pleasure and pain at the same time." He had "established a rule that profane words shall at once forfeit a place in the hospital." A few days later the elder Chandler again compared the regiment to a family: "The most gratifying good will seems to prevail almost every where in our midst."[8]

Later in the fall, a member of Company C penned a rosy report to the *Milwaukee Sentinel* and reported that Col. Lysander Cutler also had a fatherly way with his "Wisconsin boys," describing daily proofs of his almost parental anxiety for the welfare and improvement of his men, and solicitude in providing for our comfort." The "standard of morality in our army is high," the man from Company C continued. "The amount of crime is less, considering the number of men and the scope for all manner of misconduct, than in any previous war of which I have ever read." He described an unlikely tranquility among the men. "Our soldiers are exceedingly domestic in their habits, and each tent resembles a little family, every member of which tries to do all in his power to advance the good and promote the enjoyment of the rest." They spent their evenings around a fire, reading "*Harper[*'s Weekly*]*, or if taste of fancy lead . . . to ruminate over *Jane Eyre, Don Juan,* or a daily news paper." Perhaps at least some of the men needed to believe this about themselves and their comrades; certainly, many wanted the folks back home to believe it.[9]

The officers were also getting more comfortable with one another. Rufus Dawes complained mildly about Capt. Edward Bragg's seniority over him. A few days earlier, Dawes had had to help Bragg call out commands during drill. Yet, he admitted with admiration, Bragg was "the smartest man among our officers. He is keen as a whip. He was a delegate to the democratic national conventions at Charleston and Baltimore. And it is enough to make a dog laugh to hear his experiences." He also admired Colonel Cutler, who was "stern, and unflinching in the performance of his duty, and I believe he will prove of determined courage."[10]

What they all wanted was action—if not a battle, at least some movement that would remind them that they were in a war. A month after the brigade's arrival, a Wisconsin newspaper declared that "there is only one thing the boys really need, and grumble because they cannot get. That is a fight. They are spoiling to put their drill into practice." This was hardly an unusual feeling for green Union troops in the late summer of 1861. Except for those who had fought at Manassas in July, most regiments in the Army of the Potomac had to wait many months to test their mettle in a real battle.[11]

They thought they might get their chance in late September, when the Sixth, with a number of other regiments, marched from Maryland into

Virginia. A letter from a Green Bay man serving on Gen. Rufus King's staff filled two full newspaper columns with news of the dramatic, if anticlimactic, evening. Suddenly ordered to pack their knapsacks, the men were issued forty rounds of ammunition. They marched to the Potomac River on a clear but moonless night, dust rising from the dry road. "There was no noise but the dull and heavy tramp of four thousand men, and the occasional clatter of the wheels of the provision wagons and ambulances upon the loose stones along the road." They passed quietly through Georgetown and halted at the Chain Bridge, which the Fifth Wisconsin was ordered to cross. The four-hour march had worn out the men. As if to underscore how new the officers and men were to war, General King had brought along his fifteen-year-old son Charlie (who would later have a close relationship to veterans of the Sixth) and decked him out in a colorful Zouave uniform and a toy pellet gun of some kind; the boy marched along as if he were an actual soldier. As it turned out, the operation was a previously planned movement to occupy strategic locations along the river, but it was all very exciting to men longing for action.[12]

In mid-October the Sixth broke camp and crossed over into Virginia for good. Late afternoon "found us on the 'sacred soil' of the Old Dominion—the State which will be entirely in the hands of the Union forces before the snows of another winter shall whiten the bosom of mother earth." The letter writer made a little more than he should have of this minor change of location, but his enthusiasm reflected the frustration that was already emerging among the men.[13]

Even when they chafed at not getting into the action, however, the new soldiers were impressed by the sheer scale of the war effort and of the army they had joined. The late summer rise of Maj. Gen. George B. McClellan to command the force now called the Army of the Potomac raised the bar for military professionalism. For the men and boys from Wisconsin who had come from the scattered farmsteads and lumber camps of the north woods, the market villages in more settled parts of the state, and the rough towns along the Mississippi, the size of the army being built on the bluffs and flatlands near Washington was extraordinary. At least 70,000 men participated in the grand review held for the benefit of General McClellan and President Abraham Lincoln on November 20. That was more than half again as many men as there were people living in Milwaukee (about 45,000); the next largest city in Wisconsin was Fond du Lac, home of many men from Company E, with just under 13,000 people. Most others lived in or near towns of a few hundred people. Reuben Huntley wrote to his wife that the review was "by far the grandest thing I efer saw such a vast assemblage of people, but you can form no idea of the scene as you were not an eye witness. I would have been glad for you to have seen it."[14]

"There was a sea of heads, horses and bayonets the like of which was never seen in America before," Lieutenant Colonel Bragg wrote to his wife. "The display commenced at the firing of signal guns and sound of the bugle." McClellan and the president "rode at a dashing gait along the entire lines in front of each battalion—cheer after cheer filled the air as he passed, caps were flung in the air and such shouting you have never heard except at an old fashioned town meeting." The westerners, unlike their eastern counterparts, remained silent rather than breaking into cheers, "their heads and eyes steady to the front." Bragg bragged that "we have been taught and teach our men that perfect silence in the ranks is evidence of the true and well disciplined soldier." The general and the president acknowledged the compliment by removing their hats as they passed.[15]

Less than a month later, the Sixth conducted an actual—if routine—military operation when it went out on picket duty to keep an eye on Confederate forces in Fairfax County. The experience was worth another long letter from Bragg, who told of spending two nights in brush shanties and eating cold meals in the "land where Washington spent his boyhood and did his first surveying." The countryside was beautiful, if ruined: "There is a death like stillness about—that speaks of war and devastation. You can scarcely hear any thing—except the faint sound of a drum or discharge of volleys of blank Cartridges within our lines, or in the distance toward Fairfax & Centreville."

This may have been one of the first times the men encountered African Americans outside of camp. Most of the white people had gone south; those remaining were "old decrepit & stupid." The slaves left behind, wrote Bragg, were found "lounging" about "& happy as ever around the old homestead." There was a little excitement when one of the sentries thought he saw "a scout of the enemy & fired—which put our camp in alarm—but upon inspection we found nothing & went to sleep again." When they spotted a party of Rebel scouts across the river, Bragg galloped up the hill to get a better look. "We were anxious to have a small discussion with them, but they evidently had come out for a different purpose" and "rapidly disappeared."[16]

Hardy Men and Patriotic Ladies

It is likely that at least some of the men had access to newspapers from back home, where they could have read about the ways in which their communities had responded to the first year of the war. The men of Company E may already have enjoyed the martial stylings of Henry Pomeroy, a professor from Lawrence University in Appleton, who in July advertised for "Hardy Men of Good Character" to join his proposed regiment. They must be at least eighteen years old; five feet, four inches tall; and have a sound constitution, "good habits," and "good principles." He wanted "mechanics in wood, metal and leather; good shots; good axemen; and skilled woodsmen." Pomeroy assured potential recruits that "from the outset, pains will be taken to bring each member up to a high condition of both physical and moral health, tone, and vigor."[17]

Captain Pomeroy was still sharing "Facts and Thoughts for Volunteers" in September, after the Sixth had been in Virginia for about a month and the men were already getting a sense of what it meant to be in the military. The army, Pomeroy wrote, "is a noble field for men of spirit, industry, courage and character," offering many chances for advancement. He offered three "Foundation Virtues" for ambitious young soldiers: obedience, courage, and "cheerful" patience. Without them, a man "is no soldier but is a pest to himself and his comrades and an abhorrence to his officers." Pomeroy offered more wisdom about martial character in a later issue; although he never managed to form his own regiment, he did serve as a cavalry officer through much of the war.[18]

Readers from the Sixth may have noticed advertisements in local newspapers that blatantly connected the home front to the battlefront, as advertisers sought to market books, flags, and other war items and deployed military jargon and breaking news to attract attention and boost sales for virtually any product. In May a Grant County blacksmith had headed his new ad with an eye-catching "War At Home!" while a couple of weeks later a Lancaster farm equipment store announced the "Latest from the War!" in its ad for Bulls Ohio Reaper, which "has arrived . . . after its many victories."[19]

Actual news and commentary on the war could be obtained from panoramas—giant paintings that scrolled across a stage accompanied by music, narration, and sometimes special effects—that toured the country. Almost before the Sixth settled into its Virginia encampment, Madison's Baptist church hosted a "Panorama of the War!!" that depicted "Views of all the Principal Camps, Battle Fields, Forts, &c." and also a "Comical After-Piece relating to the war." The music was "excellent" and the narrator "has a vein of dry humor which spices his descriptions and embellishes his stories." The *Appleton Crescent* promoted "Willis's Panorama of the War," urging locals to "go and see the battles fought by our brave men, in defence of the Union and

Constitution." That there was a market for these entertainments speaks to the desire of men, women, and children on the home front to make a connection with the men fighting the war.[20]

The summer and fall of 1861 saw the first attempts to provide aid to soldiers and their families, with the women of Wisconsin taking the lead in establishing this most direct link between the home front and battlefront. Their efforts would continue throughout the war and, while not equivalent to picking up a gun and standing a post, would provide civilians with a sense of patriotic sacrifice. Communities raised funds and collected supplies, eventually merging into national and regional groups administered from Washington or Chicago. At the same time, towns and counties set up small funds to help families survive the absence of husbands, fathers, and sons, and the state government established a payment of five dollars per month to needy families of soldiers. Although the campaigns to help soldiers were rarely controversial, the efforts on behalf of soldiers' families were fairly quickly equated with charity by some observers—and not in positive ways.

One of the first mentions of war work for Wisconsin women appeared during the first week of May in the *Wisconsin State Journal*, which reported on the "patriotism of the ladies" who had begun making flannel shirts for the volunteers. The women "are as patriotic as the men, and are now proving that they are made up with the same spirit that was evinced by the women of the revolution." However, the number of women helping fell precipitously, with many dropping by for only an hour or two after supper. "It is too bad to make a few do all this work, when by a general effort it might be accomplished at once."[21]

By fall, more permanent organizations had begun to spring up. In November, Appleton women organized a Florence Nightingale Union Society, whose purpose was "to enlist all of Woman's tender sensibilities and sympathies." Chartered in June 1861, the US Sanitary Commission would become the umbrella organization for gathering supplies and accepting donations for Union soldiers. Its first call for aid had appeared in Wisconsin in fall 1861; by late May 1862, women had gathered five boxes of vital supplies, earning thanks from the head of the Wisconsin chapter of the US Sanitary Commission, Henrietta Colt, who declared, "Never since the world began has there been a war where the nation and government have been one, like a large family of loving brothers and sisters."[22]

No surviving letter or diary by a member of the Sixth actually commented on home-front efforts to help their families or, for that matter, on formal contributions from the Sanitary Commission. Yet, whenever they unpacked boxes full of jams and socks and other delicacies and useful items, whenever they managed to read a weeks-old newspaper from home, whenever a wife or mother wrote them with relief that a government program or individual kindness had eased their hardships for a month or even a few days, they would have realized that they were part of a national war effort.

The Right Must, and Surely Will, Triumph

That war effort would eventually address the issue of slavery. The men of the Sixth had encountered enslaved people since shortly after their arrival in Virginia, although most did not think deeply about the institution, which may have indicated an indifference to the issue of race. Not surprisingly, Rufus Dawes reflected on slavery and emancipation more than most. In April 1862, he wrote in a letter home that "our camps are now flooded with negroes, with packs on their backs, and bound for freedom. No system of abolition could have swept the system away more effectually than does the advance of our army.... The right must, and surely will, triumph in the end." In his memoir he added, "Our military authorities refused to have anything to do with the negroes. But with the sympathy and active assistance of the soldiers, the poor slaves were breaking their fetters in spite of their masters."[23]

Dawes and surgeon John Hall whiled away one muggy evening with a debate over whether "the negro has any love of liberty," with Dawes strongly believing they did and Hall apparently less sure. They tested the issue by asking the six "Africans accessible"—suggesting the ubiquity of African Americans in and around their camp—the following question: "Which would you prefer—to be a slave with a good master, not much to do, plenty of hog and hominy, and a coon dog, or be a free man and have to scratch for your living?" A modern observer would note the biased wording, but in any event, one of them "took my side," but the others "followed the coon dog." Their spokesman, Mink, "argued that if he could pick his master, he had rather be a slave than a Brigadier General. There was no better position": an easy life with no responsibility. It was far better than being a free Black man. "He said a free nigger was 'spized' everywhere he had ever been" and that being free was no better than having a "bad master."[24]

Despite his liberal sensitivities, Dawes found the accents and behavior of the fugitives who came into the regiment humorous and occasionally lapsed into the racist language of the day. In his memoir he repeated the oft-told story of Colonel Cutler's servant fleeing camp when a Rebel shell knocked a nearby coffeepot twenty feet into the air. "The darky ... left the field at the speed of a race horse." A similar incident occurred late in the year, when the regiment was again opposite Fredericksburg in the days following the disastrous battle. Cannon fire from Confederate batteries sailed over the regiment, but the shelling caused a panic among the "colored servants, who were following the regiment . . . loaded down with coffee pots, frying pans and officers' rations." The fugitives "fled hastily over the river bank, tumbling from top to bottom, and scattering our officers' provisions." Later, another servant, an older man named Matt who had grown up on a nearby plantation, pleaded with members of Company C not to cut down a certain stand of trees that were precious to his old master. "The darky could not contain himself," crying, "Boys, what you doin' dar! You brake dat old man's heart if you cut down dat tree! His grandfather planted dat tree!"[25]

When Dawes briefly commanded a small outpost near a plantation on the south bank of the Rappahannock in August 1863, he described in a letter to his fiancée Mary "an exodus from this neighborhood of children of Ham (and they took all the hams with them) last night, to the number of about forty. 'Dey's g'wine ter git out dis yer place 'fore de southern gemman come.'" With some satisfaction, he predicted that "this morning, for the first time in her life . . . the old rebel lady of this house cooked a very poor breakfast for herself."[26]

Like many Union officers, Dawes enjoyed the services of an African American servant named William for much of the war. He came to refer to him as "our chief steward," rather than simply as a "darky," and admitted that the officers with whom he messed "should be badly off if it were not for William."[27]

Another close relationship developed between a teenaged African American named Richard Epps and a young private in Company E, Jake Diener. Epps served as a cook and jack-of-all-trades for the rest of the regiment and soon befriended young Diener, who started to teach him to read. Epps narrowly escaped being killed by Rebel sharpshooters, and when Diener himself was wounded, Epps carried him to safety. Despite the young fugitive's round-the-clock nursing, Diener died a few days later. Epps buried his young friend in a wooden box used to haul muskets.[28]

Dawes was rare in his unusually nuanced, if at times problematic, attitudes about African Americans. But most men of the Sixth saw the African Americans they encountered—if they mentioned them at all—as background scenery, sources of humor, and cheap labor. George Fairfield recorded a nighttime encounter with enslaved people who had followed the regiment away from their plantation. After the soldiers had built fires, "the darkies which followed us back sung and danced for our amusement till nearly morning & fiddle was obtained and the music, the uncouth dancing of negroes and the liveliness in our camp was exciting to one as unused to them as my self." The men of Company A encountered "an old darky slave" who took "a great interest" in the rebuilding of a bridge during the brutal marches in August 1862. "It took we uns four years to build dat dar bridge, and de Yankee soldiers done gone and build dat dar bridge in three days," he remarked. "We all laughed at the darky's catching on to the soldier of it."[29]

Years after the war, James Sullivan offered a sympathetic but casually racist account of "How We Lost Our Cook," which revolved around the appearance in June 1862 of a fugitive with "curly hair and prominent lips, who had concluded to 'lay down de shubble and de hoe,' and seek independence and affluence." The matter of what to do with escaped slaves, at least according to Sullivan's memory, was still unsettled. Dawes became the butt of the story, as the captain gathered the company around "and explained, in glowing terms, the advantages" to both parties that would accrue "from an alliance . . . between company K and the person Ben Butler disrespectfully classes as contraband of war." With Dawes paying half his wages and the men the other half, the arrangement went well. In the evenings, the man "would relate to an attentive audience stories of his former slave life in de cotton and de cane and terbacker fiel's of de souf." When the regiment came under fire, however, the servant fled, followed by the cheers and catcalls of the men. This incident provided "an infinite fund of amusement to the regiment," with men frequently teasing the captain by asking if he had "heard anything from his nigger."[30]

The formerly enslaved men, women, and children that the Sixth encountered provided help around camp and a distraction from the hard realities of war. But sometimes the enslaved were seen as actual human beings with feelings. When the regiment went into King George and Westmoreland Counties in May 1863—an area previously undisturbed by federal troops— enslaved people "flocked to us in droves," according to Sullivan. "Such a medley of sights and sounds as our brigade presented on that march was probably seldom witnessed during the war. Ox carts with one ox and a cow for the motive power, family carriages, mules, donkeys, darkies of all ages, sizes, and complexions, 'toting' on their heads feather beds, bed clothes, stoves, wash tubs, iron kettles, household goods of all kinds, clothing, crockery and anything else their fancy and avarice prompted." Sullivan and others used such scenes as local color, but behind it seemed to be a general satisfaction that the "slaveocracy" was finally being punished for their role in starting the war and a bemused appreciation for the enslaved people's enthusiastic embrace of freedom. "The news of our coming had spread . . . and at each plantation and cross roads we would meet crowds of contrabands shouting 'We's gwine wid you all,' and filling the air with such a joyful chorus as was never heard in all of the Northern Neck before."[31]

Only a handful of men in the Sixth Wisconsin actually expressed an opinion about the institution of slavery. Yet whether they were abolitionists or proslavery Democrats or something in between, most agreed that slavery was the cause of the war. Moreover, like many other Northern soldiers, they tended to be open to changing their minds about African Americans and, by extension, slavery when they came into contact with the institution and with the enslaved.[32]

Of course, it was impossible to separate ideas about slavery and race from politics, although the *State Journal* had tried to do exactly that in late 1861. "Let us not stop to wrangle over such questions [as slavery].—Let the war go on, and let slavery take its chances. The first great duty is to put down the rebellion. Leave to the march of events the question of slavery."[33]

Civilians in Wisconsin could take a rather abstract view of slavery, at least at the beginning of the war. But another issue soon embroiled soldiers in state politics: whether soldiers living outside the state should be allowed to vote. Democrats opposed the idea, declaring that it violated the state constitution and would lead to the manipulation of soldiers into blindly supporting the government's policies. The Republican *State Journal*, on the other hand, asked, "Who is better entitled to vote—the brave and loyal man who hastens to the support of his country's flag in the hour of danger, or the wretched and cowardly sneak who instead of responding to her call attempts to escape into Canada to avoid a draft?" It could not be "good policy to disfranchise the patriotic soldier while the sneak is permitted to vote for his representative."[34]

The very fact that this was being debated at all must have been disheartening to soldiers on the front lines. Although the legislature passed along party lines the bill allowing soldiers in the army to vote—Republicans in favor, Democrats against—the fact that anyone would challenge that right could not have been received well by men in the field. Not surprisingly, in the state election of 1863, the first chance soldiers had to express their displeasure at the polls, Wisconsin soldiers voted 8,373–2,046 for James T. Lewis, the Republican candidate for governor.[35]

There is no record of how the Sixth Wisconsin voted, although the *Crescent* finally admitted that the elections "have gone nearly unanimously Abolition." It blamed shenanigans by Republicans and indifference and disorganization among Democrats for the loss. At least one Republican paper took no small amount of glee from the outcome of the election and the outrage of the Democrats: "The Democrats charge that the officers of the Wisconsin regiments compelled their men to vote just as they desired. Judging from the unanimity of the election returns, we say that they have got their men in a high state of discipline."[36]

No Place for a Man without a Sound Constitution

While they impatiently waited to confront the Rebels face to face, the soldiers of the Sixth encountered significant challenges in adapting to their new environment and the threat of disease. James Conklin deserted after his wife, who had apparently accompanied him to camp, died of typhoid fever. He may have returned home to care for their two children.[37]

Poor sanitation and close proximity to each other in camp left members of the Sixth, like other soldiers in the newly formed army, as likely to miss service for illness as other causes. Reports from Sanitary Commission agents who visited the regiment in August 1861 described a narrow pond of "sludgy, green" water that "will breed mischief between the camps of the Fifth and Sixth Wisconsin." An inspector also complained that some men did not bother to go to the "regulation pits" to "void" themselves and that officers had little interest in sanitation, saying "that there was too much bother about the sick."

A fairly urgent health issue facing the regiment in the first weeks of their sojourn in Virginia was the availability of watermelon and cantaloupe; the men loved the exotic fruits, but they wreaked havoc on their digestive systems. Surgeon Chapman told the inspector that he had "never before seen diarrhea follow so surely and rapidly on eating" melons; he also noted a "great difficulty with the seeds of Blackberries in some of his patients."[38]

One inspector blamed the regiment's poor health on its camp's location on unshaded, slightly elevated land with a "bad reputation" for malarial fevers. The camp was far from complete, with drainage ditches still under construction, tents crowded, bathing spots unavailable, and a certain "odor of decay" hanging over the area. Many medical provisions were in short supply, especially painkillers, and no ambulance system had been set up. On the other hand, rations were good and very little liquor was available—although on average a man was sent to the guardhouse for alcohol-related issues about once every day or two. The "prevailing diseases" were "measles, malarial fever, and diarrhea"—which matches the commentary of soldiers from the same period.[39]

Surgeon Chapman's report for September 1861 indicated the inevitable results of the poor campsite. Seventy-six men had already been reported sick during the previous thirty days, with thirty-one suffering from various fevers, twenty-five with measles, thirteen with diarrhea or dysentery, and a sprinkling of other maladies (and one broken limb). Twenty others had taken sick in August and remained off duty more than a month later. All told, nearly 10 percent of the entire regiment had become ill enough to be removed from the duty list.[40]

By November, the Sixth had moved to its more permanent camp near Arlington House, but an inspector reported little improvement. Most of the trees in the area had been cut away over the summer. The men kept their camp "moderately clean" but still wore their original gray uniforms and had only cheap overcoats that were already "somewhat worse for wear." In answer to the question about whether the men "bathe frequently," the inspector answered, "Not very"; later, he reported that the men were "somewhat" infested with vermin. Surgeons were in the process of vaccinating the men for smallpox. Medical supplies and preparations seemed adequate, although the health of the men remained problematic. The "prevailing diseases" were remittent fever, bronchitis, and rheumatism. There were twenty-two patients each in the regimental and general hospitals and eighty "sick in quarters" (defined as "slight cases in their own tents"). Over the previous two weeks, the average number of men being treated in the regimental and general hospitals and in their tents was twenty-five, twenty, and seventy-five, respectively. Still, the agent reported that the general health of the men was "improving."[41]

By February, although the regiment was still plagued by cold-weather complaints such as catarrh (a catchall term for a respiratory infection) and rheumatism, the number of men being treated in hospitals or in camp had declined. Officers still sent, on average, about one man to the guardhouse each day, "chiefly from intoxication," although discipline in the regiment was "rather better" than average. Interestingly, the "length of time the men are on drill daily" was "hardly any now."[42]

The diseases that plagued the regiment emerge as the most severe enemy the men faced during its first months in Virginia. Benjamin Smith of Company E had managed a short furlough while at Camp Randall to get married. His wife Christiana was a widow by Christmas and in May 1862 became one of the earliest applicants for a widow's pension. Measles had rippled through the Sixth even as they traveled east. Lorenzo Pratt claimed in his pension affidavit that he suffered from the disease from the time they were in Harrisburg until well into the fall. It rendered him "unable to speak above a whisper," and ever afterward "he was continually coughing," although he remained with the company. Smallpox also struck at least a few men, who were quarantined in an abandoned old house and cared for by men who had already recovered from the illness and other "immunes." A number of men would later claim that their initial exposure to camp life would lead to lifelong—if vague—health problems, particularly rheumatism. Adolph Sulzer joined the Sixth in the summer of 1861; at one of the first encampments in Virginia, which a surgeon recalled as being swampy and uncomfortable, and where a number of men came down with fever, Sulzer claimed he had an attack of rheumatism. It hit the little fingers of both hands hardest, to the extent that they curled inward and made it hard to handle his gun. He was eventually discharged early in 1862, but the rheumatism never went away.[43]

The scale of disease led to a certain callousness about the victims. When a member of Company E died, Jerome Watrous seemed to brush it off: "He was a young man of exceedingly delicate health, and like many others should not have enlisted. The Army is no place for a man without a sound constitution." Late in the fall, Edward Bragg admitted that "there is considerable sickness in camp" that had caused eight deaths in the regiment (records suggest it was more like a dozen by November 1861). Yet, he claimed, that was "not a very great mortality list for a thousand men, in six months, under all the attendant circumstances, of changes of climate, & habits of living."[44]

But the growing number of absences by death or discharge were not so easily dismissed by others. A number noted the first men to die in their companies. Eighteen-year-old Edgar Ames of Company A died in January 1862; his comrades all chipped in to send his body home. As it turned out, "he was the only comrade sent home," one wrote. "They came too fast later when the fighting was on" and the soldier's wage of "thirteen dollars a month did not go far," especially when the government required that bodies sent north had to be embalmed—which cost fifty dollars for officers and twenty-five dollars for enlisted men.[45]

The death of one of his men profoundly affected Capt. Edwin Brown, who seemed to admit that his inexperience as an officer might have played a role in the man's death. In a letter to his wife Ruth, Brown wrote that she might remember a certain member of his company: "I think he called at our house when I was trying to fill up our Company." He was middle-aged and stocky and had, as it happened, married a Madison widow while they were at Camp Randall. "He was ambitious & desirous of promotion and did not get as high a position as he would have liked, and became sick & tired of the Army." He tried and failed to get a discharge based on an old injury, "where-upon he began to grow sick. Most every one supposed he was shamming illness, until I saw that he lost flesh & appetite." The surgeon continued to insist that the man was simply "discouraged and homesick," and although he had rallied briefly when he thought he might get a discharge after all, he "gave right up again" when the surgeon again refused to sign off on his request. Although "no fault attaches to me," Brown regretted that he "did not have charity enough for his feelings" to advocate more strongly on his sergeant's behalf.[46]

Sickness, death, and disillusionment filled a diary kept by a soldier in Company H. Isaac Tucker was a forty-two-year-old private who had enlisted in summer 1861 and seems to have been unwell throughout his fifteen months in the Sixth. Never particularly happy with the medical care extended to soldiers, whenever he was ill he would simply leave camp and stay in a private home. Months later he was finally sick enough to go into the hospital at Fairfax Seminary. He recovered somewhat, but while he was still too ill to return to the regiment, he helped out at the hospital, apparently recommend-ing patent medicines and ordering men around. On at least one occasion he pulled the tooth of an old African American woman. By May he had decided that the main policy of the medical corps was to keep men in the hospital as long as there was a chance they could return to duty. "Nine cases out of ten," he declared, "if they were discharged" from the army it "would prolong their lives and if not to say the least of it they would be with their friends to die and not among strangers." His anger grew after every funeral of a "victim of misplaced confidence," until he suspected that politicians and profiteers were somehow benefiting by keeping the war machine running. "Men are used more like dogs than human beings." After surviving a bout of mumps, he returned to the regiment in August but was discharged for disability two months later.[47]

The Sanitary Commission inspectors offered hints of why so many men might have been discharged: they were in poor health before they entered the army. A questionnaire they submitted as part of their reports asked if the men had received a "medical inspection" at the time of their enlistment. "None worthy the name," one sniffed; surgeon Chapman had been far from thorough in the original examinations, and none had been conducted since. The upshot, an inspector asserted in February, was that at least seventy-five men would have been rejected if they had received a vigorous examination before their swearing in.[48]

A scorecard of the losses and other changes in Company B appeared in the *Prescott Journal*. "Promotions, deaths, and desertions account for the large percentage of the company's original men who are now gone," Benjamin Meeds reported (he would later be wounded and discharged himself). "Company B is a dwarf in comparison with what it was the day we left Prescott. Since that day, one has died, one has been discharged, two more have surgeons' certificates of disability, one has been transferred to Company H, four have been promoted to positions in other companies, two do duty in the martial band, four have been transferred to the artillery, four are in the hospital, and FIVE HAVE DESERTED, making a total of 24." The sheer scale of change caused him to "involuntarily" compare it to "rats leaving a fated vessel." Meeds went on to say that "if the war lasts three years there will be but a very few of the men who were in the company when we left Prescott with us on our return."[49]

On top of all the other changes in the regiment, in late October the Sixth experienced what Rufus Dawes would later call "a violent wrench," when a raft of captains and lieutenants were dismissed and replaced with junior and noncommissioned officers, often from other companies. Dawes admitted that some of the men had been poor leaders, but "several very promising officers were arbitrarily driven out of the regiment" by Colonel Cutler "under thin disguise of failure to pass examination before a certain commission of officers." Many years later Dawes admitted Cutler's "courage of his conviction, and his justification must be found in the fact that good results ultimately followed." It was an unusual beginning to the Sixth's war. Wisconsin's adjutant general, in his 1861 report summarizing the creation and staffing of the state's regiments, remarked that there had been "more change" among the officer corps of the Sixth "than all other regiments combined . . . for some reason not known to this department."[50]

As the Sixth settled into what would become their winter quarters on Arlington Heights, they drilled, took target practice, cut wood, and performed all the regular duties of soldiers, but in this season of relative safety and innocence, they also wrestled and boxed, drank, sang, and read books. A correspondent from the Sixth described the camp as a veritable "New England Village." And though they waited to make history on the field of battle, in November they helped make history of a different kind—or so some came to believe—when the poet Julia Ward Howe visited the army with a small group of Unitarian dignitaries. They came to witness a review of Gen. Irwin McDowell's division, including the western brigade. Reports of a small skirmish between picket lines a few miles away interrupted the review, and Howe and her party headed back to Washington. The fighting petered out, but the Unitarians found themselves riding among two Wisconsin regiments, whose watch fires sparkled among the trees and hills ahead. As it did on occasion, singing rumbled up from the ranks, and one of the songs was the popular "John Brown's Body." Howe's group returned to the Willard hotel, and by morning she had written a nearly finished draft of the "Battle Hymn of the Republic."

Rufus Dawes wanted to believe that his regiment had inspired the composer of that famous fighting hymn. He suggested that when one of the regiment's best singers, Sgt. John Ticknor, launched into the verse beginning "We'll hang Jeff Davis on a sour apple tree," the whole regiment joined in. Dawes claimed that Howe "has said that the singing of the John Brown song by the soldiers on that march, and the scenes of that day and evening inspired her." Although Howe never confirmed that she found her muse among the Sixth's singers, Dawes cheerfully accepted credit on behalf of his comrades.[51]

An Elastic Tread and Jaunty Air

The Sixth spent the winter and much of the early spring in camp on Arlington Heights. They satisfied their martial ardor with picket duty and a few raids, along with the formal reviews they came to hate, even as they took pride in their professional appearance. In March, brigade commander Gen. Rufus King announced to the regiment after a dress parade near Arlington House, "Boys, I will find you warm work within ten days."[52]

Yet they were limited to make-believe battles that the *Washington Chronicle* called "sham" fighting. "Every morning" King's brigade was "out in the grounds in the rear of the camps going through the motions of a real battle, company pitted against company, and wing against wing. Blank cartridges are used, and powder is burnt freely." Although "troops are vanquished and victories won, and prisoners taken, and colors raised," it was hardly the real thing; it was simply "excellent sport for the boys and accustoms them to the smell of powder."[53]

The Sixth and its brigade had already earned reputations as well-drilled outfits, but late in spring 1862 they would come under the command of the man who would turn them into the Iron Brigade. John Gibbon was an old army officer and had commanded Battery B in the US artillery; he received his brigadier's star and took over the brigade when King was reassigned in May. He was not a stranger to the men; for some time Battery B had been attached to the brigade, and a number of Wisconsinites had been detached to the battery. Years later, Gibbon noted the men's "quick intelligence" and potential to make excellent soldiers. Gibbon admitted that he was in over his head, at least during his first few weeks in command. Although the men were disappointed not to have joined the march on Richmond that spring, Gibbon saw it as a kind of reprieve that he improved by familiarizing himself with the brigade and with his responsibilities as an infantry commander. Like most officers from the antebellum army, he "had never before seen so large a body of men" drill all at once. The moment that seemed to push him over the edge was overhearing one of his subordinates saying that "Gibbon was only an artillery officer and did not know anything about infantry drill." He soon found a copy of an old drill manual, and although it "was slow work at first," boring both soldiers and officers, progress was eventually made, and the men "eventually took a greater interest and even pride in the work."[54]

Gibbon standardized the brigade's uniforms to match US Regulars' outfits, including the tall, 1858 model dress hat that gave the westerners one of their early nicknames, the "Blackhats." He got the regiments to tidy up their campsites, stepped up the drill regimen, and held officers and noncommissioned officers accountable for the discipline and cleanliness of their men. Frank Haskell, who had begun the war as a lieutenant in the Sixth, became Gibbon's adjutant and hatchet man; the officers and men hated both for trying to impose "regular army" standards on volunteers. "We have one of the meanest Brigadier Generals that ever lived," one member of the brigade declared. He predicted that "if we ever get in a fight, he will be the first to fall." They would actually grow to appreciate the training they received under Gibbon. The six months he spent as their commander would, as most veterans would come to understand, make them into one of the best units in the army.[55]

Even as the Sixth grudgingly accepted Gibbon's regime, they continued to chafe at the lack of action. When most of the army mounted the massive Peninsula Campaign in spring 1862, the Sixth stayed behind to shield Washington. They were called out occasionally, and undertook a few marches, but were never sent to the front. A private in Company B put a humorous face on it in a letter to his brother: "The six regt dont have any fighting to do the rebels run away every time." But Edwin Brown was not amused. When division commander McDowell appeared again in July 1862 after an absence of two months, Brown complained, "Of course we have a review." He despised McDowell: "His presence among us is very unwelcome [with] disgust & contempt appearing on every countenance. . . . there is no way to get out of this 'Hell on Earth' except by death or promotion." Even so, Brown took pride in his regiment. "I will say one thing however that no regiment yet to be raised in our State can be made to equal the Sixth Wis., in nicety of drill, cleanliness of appearance, completeness of dress & equipment and that elastic tread & jaunty air that marks the 'Espirit du Corps.'"[56]

Rufus Dawes was less likely to betray his own strong feelings than Brown—at least in this stage of the war—but even he could not resist writing a sister in mid-July that "I am not near Richmond nor like[ly] to be soon the way the matter looks now." He blamed McDowell, "a thick headed pompous popinjay—tyrannical to inferiors and in the same measure cringing and sycophantic to superiors."[57]

Despite this optimistic assessment and never having raised their hand against the enemy, the regiment continued to dwindle. A correspondent with a hometown newspaper—probably Sgt. Howard Huntington—wrote in the summer of 1862 that Company A's "appearance has changed much within a year." The company had shrunk to sixty-five men. Nineteen were on detached duty; seventeen had been discharged, and four had died. "Thus are our companies, regiments, and armies reduced." Huntington believed that "had we been placed in more active service, where our movements were of a character to animate a soldier, and inspire him with confidence in their propriety and the earnestness of leaders, I am quite certain that the health of the whole army would have been much better." The enlisted men of his company, the "Baraboo Generals," he called them, "are becoming dissatisfied. . . . They see not the fruits of their labor, and wonder why we have been 'playing soldier' so much."[58]

Instead the war continued to claim victims in unexpected ways. Two more men from Company C died of disease in July. And nineteen-year-old Homer Lillie, "while bathing in the Rappahannock, was seized with a 'cramp,' when a current of the ocean tide hurried him beneath the swift rolling waters. We heard a shriek," wrote a soldier in Company C to his local newspaper, "and by the time the words 'Boys, O boys,' struck our ears, Homer was beyond help." After his body was found a few days later, the company held a formal military funeral, complete with a tribute of six volleys—one of the last held for a private soldier from the Sixth. "Disease visits every camp and frowns upon every soldier," the man from Company C admitted. "Sickness or death threatens us all, and really, life is stript of nearly all its beauties and charms. But the *love of country* and the prospect of *victory* prompts us to endure all."[59]

That patriotism and confidence helped the men through the mundane forms of death that seemed to be sapping the regiment's strength. Yet few lost sight of the larger purpose. "Coming events are crowding thickly upon us," a sergeant wrote his father in mid-February 1862. "Those who cannot or will not take a part in this struggle must stand aside and let those in who will. For in God's name I believe the time has come for this rebellion to be crushed, slavery abrogated and peace, liberty and prosperity restored to our now distracted country." By early summer 1862 those thickening events would set in motion the Sixth's rendezvous with history.[60]

3

Tall Fighting

Fall 1862

In a letter to his hometown newspaper in mid-August 1862, Jerome Watrous reported that the "Wisconsin men" serving in Gen. John Gibbon's brigade "have got a good name, and if we get together when in battle, we can do a huge amount of tall fighting." But the opportunity to prove it came haltingly, even as Gen. George B. McClellan finally stirred his massive Army of the Potomac into action in the spring of 1862, moving it to the Virginia penin- sula for a direct attack on Richmond. "I read from Samuel," Earl M. Rogers recalled, tongue in cheek, that "it came to pass . . . at the time when Kings go forth to battle, that Abraham sent little Mac and his servants, and all the army to destroy the children of the South and besiege Richmond." Gen. Irwin McDowell's I Corps and the men of the Sixth Wisconsin were still waiting to board transports when they were recalled by President Abraham Lincoln and Secretary of War Edwin Stanton, who feared that not enough troops had been assigned to defend Washington. The Sixth's campaign was over before it had begun. Instead, they grew sick from marching in the sleet and rain and, on one dreary night, Rogers recalled, all the officers "but Capt. Dawes" became a "little worse for whiskey."[1]

The Sixth Wisconsin finally "went forth" at dusk on a hot Virginia evening in late August 1862, when they and the rest of the brigade fought a much larger force under Maj. Gen. Thomas "Stonewall" Jackson at a battle they would forever call Gainesville (although historians now call it Brawner's Farm). They fought three more battles over the next few weeks. By the end of September, the surgeon's "Report of Sick and Wounded" would note only one condition on the form's checklist of dozens of major and minor diseases: *vulnus sclopeticum*—Latin for "gunshot wound." There had been 212 cases and forty deaths.[2]

The hard fighting during those six autumn weeks completed the Sixth's transition from recruits to combatants. The narratives of combat they put on paper immediately after the battle or, later, in reminiscences were full of exciting details, dramatic images, and brave words. They mourned their dead and maimed comrades and acknowledged the naïveté that had wished them into battle, but they betrayed no sense of despair. Although sometimes angered by poor leadership at the higher levels, they could fit the killing and maiming into a narrative of pride and accomplishment, even in defeat.[3]

Aching for a Fight: Gainesville

George Fairfield had kept a diary since he went into the army in 1861. At first he wrote only sporadically, but over the summer, sensing that he would finally have something interesting to report, he "took much pains with it." His entries increased in July as he and his comrades struggled through some of the hardest days they had thus far experienced, reflecting a gradually increasing sense of purpose and danger.

The men first had to battle the heat. Fairfield and his fellows endured seemingly endless hot, dusty marches that pushed them to the edge of their endurance. "I was several times so near gone that I would think I could not go much further," he wrote, until "a breeze would spring up, we would start down a hill, or the order would be given to rest." The Sixth's commanders increased the duration and intensity of drills, anticipating the time was drawing near for real fighting. "Some said they could hear cannon in the direction of Richmond," Fairfield recorded.[4]

On August 4, the test stiffened, when at 2:00 a.m., the men of the Sixth, accompanied by a small cavalry unit and a section of artillery, left their camp near Fredericksburg to begin a raid on the Virginia Central Railroad. With Col. Lysander Cutler in overall command, Lt. Col. Edward Bragg took over the regiment. By late morning, through blistering heat and over a "very serpentine road," they had marched nineteen miles. They covered another eight miles to Mount Pleasant late in the afternoon. After a brief and troubled night of rest, they began another long march early the following day, including an unnecessary ten miles added when their guide got lost. With his men's physical strength sagging, Cutler left the 150 most affected by the heat to guard the bridge over the North Anna River, then proceeded to Frederick's Hall Station. There, according to Cutler, the troops destroyed two miles of track, burned a small bridge and several railroad buildings, and destroyed a warehouse containing Confederate whiskey and 1,000 bushels of corn. After recrossing the North Anna and burning that bridge, they stopped, having marched thirty-two miles in a single day over difficult terrain. By the time they returned to Fredericksburg, they had marched ninety miles in three and a half days under a broiling sun. Cutler was full of compliments for his officers and men: "They all suffered severely from heat and fatigue, but were all ready at any time to execute any order given. The only murmurs I heard were those of disappointment at not meeting an enemy."[5]

Fairfield's diary told a different story. "The boys fell by the way in great numbers," he wrote, and Bragg had to threaten some with the bayonet to get them back on the road after a short rest. By the end of the day, only a "skeleton" of the regiment remained in the ranks. Fairfield admitted that the infantry was "too tired to make much headway" with the mission's purpose and that the cavalry carried out most of the destruction. As the Sixth staggered into camp at the end of the expedition, the officers "lost command of the men and if an order was given it was not heeded"; the officers "were about as tired as the men and took no notice of their disobedience." The regiment had almost literally melted away, and stragglers drifted into camp a few at a time.[6]

The brutal August marches became legendary among the men of the Sixth, and records suggest that they did significant damage to the regiment. During August, September, and October of 1862, twelve men deserted the regiment, hinting at the possibility that the early August raids had been a last straw for men already fed up with army life. During the same time, twenty-five men were discharged for disability, suggesting they may have fallen victim to sunstroke or exhaustion.[7]

For years after the war, men would trace their poor health to August 1862. In one case, assistant surgeon A. D. Andrews noted in his affidavit for Peter Hansen that his was just one of the "very numerous instances that came under my observation & treatment of overheating or sunstroke incurred while making a long & rapid march under a burning sun." Hansen suffered convulsions that left him blind in one eye and deaf in one ear; he was discharged later in the year. Although he eventually recovered his sight, twenty-seven years later he was harvesting grain on "a very hot day" and suffered another attack, during which "my brain was affected and matter run from my right ear and my right eye turned red." A few days later he had "apoplexy" and lost the sight in his right eye and much of his hearing.[8]

Over the years, Stephen Long blamed a multitude of health problems on that early August expedition, from nausea and an inability to withstand high temperatures to heart trouble and vertigo, from chronic meningitis and constipation to "nervous dyspepsia" and an eye affliction, and from headaches and "confusion of the brain" to "general prostration" and sleeplessness. By 1884 he was complaining that his "mind at times is easily excited, followed by great mental depression." He told an examining surgeon that he was unable "to follow his occupation of teaching as it would set him crazy. His memory is very poor [and he] cannot make mathematical calculations." He was "troubled with depressed feelings and is afraid he will go crazy." Yet by the turn of the century he was working as a clerk in the Washington, DC, Pension Bureau.[9]

Another narrative from surgeon Andrews recorded that Lt. Samuel Birdsall became "disabled by sickness" during the march on August 4–7, 1862, "producing an attack of inflammation of the kidneys and acute dysentery, with extreme prostration and debility." He had partially recovered by the end of August but relapsed later in the month. Several weeks later he was ordered to the hospital "as the only means of saving his life." He apparently stayed in the hospital for well over a year. Pension and medical records suggest he never truly recovered, chiefly suffering from chronic dysentery, bladder disease, and, by the 1880s, paralysis on one side.[10]

The August marches contributed to the alarmingly steady deterioration of the regiment during its peaceful first year of service. By mid-August, a total of at least 236 men had left the regiment. Twenty-one had died of disease and one had drowned; sixteen had been transferred; fourteen had resigned; and twenty-eight had deserted (although that number, according to postwar officials, was highly suspect—authorities may have lost track of many of those men while in hospital, while some may have returned unnoticed from an approved leave). All the rest—156—had been discharged due to "disability." Later accounts would estimate the regiment's combat strength at 500–600 men, suggesting that even more men were temporarily—and unofficially—indisposed and out of action due to the early August marches.[11]

But the nearly constant marching continued for the rest of the month, as the brigade fruitlessly searched the Virginia countryside for Stonewall Jackson. Poor leadership and indecisiveness from Maj. Gen. John Pope, commanding the newly created Army of Virginia to which the Sixth was attached, down through corps commander McDowell and division commander Gen. Rufus King forced the Sixth and its fellow regiments into a series of pointless, draining journeys. Yet the Wisconsin men began to get a better idea of what it meant to be on the sharp end of war. Reuben Huntley warned his wife, "Do not be scared if you here that gibins brigade has had a fite for that is where we are now." Their general certainly seemed ready for a "fite." One morning as Gibbon and his staff were eating breakfast, a message came that they were about to be attacked by Confederate cavalry. Some of the staff members mounted up and galloped away. But "the Gen'l . . . arose, lighted his pipe, drew his revolver and stood by the side of a tree and said, "d——n 'em, let 'em come."[12]

Come they would, although it took a few more days. Soon after the Sixth's infamous raid on August 4–5, Confederate troops began moving north after successfully defending Richmond and seeking to seize the initiative. Robert E. Lee split his Army of Northern Virginia in two, with one wing under Stonewall Jackson and the other under Lt. Gen. James Longstreet. Jackson's forces drove northwest toward Cedar Mountain, while Longstreet moved more directly north toward Manassas and Washington.

Once more the Sixth Wisconsin was called to march with Pope's forces, but this time with even greater urgency. After covering forty-five miles and making a night-time crossing of the Rappahannock River, the brigade reached Cedar Mountain late on August 9, having just missed a fierce fight between Jackson and Maj. Gen. Nathaniel Banks. Rufus Dawes, who had been promoted from captain of Company K to major earlier in the summer, reported that "we were obliged to bury many of the rebel dead whose corpses, left half buried upon the field, were intolerable. This was our first contact with one of the real horrors of war." A Sauk County veteran recalled his disgust at seeing the tops of the shallow graves "moving like gentle waves with living corruption"—the larvae squirming around the decaying bodies.

They stayed on the broiling, stinking battlefield for a week, while Pope, initially believing Jackson was in retreat, pondered his next move.[13] But Pope lost track of the opposing force and ordered his men to fall back, retreating over the Rappahannock on August 20. The Sixth spotted Confederate cavalry across the river that afternoon, and the next day the Sixth came under artillery fire for the first time. Hoping to draw out the enemy, Cutler threw Capt.

Edwin Brown's Company E and part of Company B out as skirmishers, and they became the first members of the regiment to fire on Confederate troops, killing and wounding a few and capturing an officer and two men. Thus, wrote Dawes, Brown and his men "won the first glory for the Sixth Wisconsin on the field of actual battle." A day or two later a few men from the Sixth—as part of the brigade's Headquarters Guard—helped repulse a Confederate raid on a wagon train. Distant dust clouds revealed that the Rebels were also on the move and convinced the regiment that these small tastes of combat would soon be followed by a much bigger portion.[14]

As part of Pope's efforts to concentrate his forces, Gibbon's brigade, along with the rest of King's division, was ordered to Manassas via the Warrenton Turnpike. August 28 saw even more signs of war: the growling of distant artillery, Union skirmishers trudging along the flanks, and sightings and alleged sightings of Confederate cavalry and even infantry. Confederate and Union foragers stumbled across one another in an abandoned farmhouse; the men marched by three dead bodies lying under bloodstained blankets and stared as a group of Confederate prisoners trudged past.[15]

By the time King's division wearily passed a hardscrabble farm rented by one John Brawner, Gibbon's brigade stretched along the Warrenton Turnpike from near Groveton to a point a few miles east of Gainesville, roughly ten miles northwest of Manassas. The rest of the division had also become rather stretched out, with Brig. Gen. John P. Hatch's brigade ahead of Gibbon's and those of Brig. Gens. Abner Doubleday and Marsena Patrick behind. In the battle to come, only two of Doubleday's regiments and none of Patrick's would join the fight.

The turnpike paralleled an unfinished railroad bed, concealed by a tree line running along a low ridge about a half mile north of the road; the field lying before it was interrupted by a slight depression about halfway up. Much of this was open ground, although there was an old orchard near the farm and a small wood—less than a quarter mile wide—starting just east of the farm and extending down to the turnpike. Skirmishers from Hatch's brigade had reconnoitered the area around the farm, and a battery had lobbed shells toward the woods a little earlier in the day, but the few mounted Confederates in sight had quickly retired, and no one could blame the men and officers of the Sixth for thinking they were in no danger.

In fact, they were in extraordinary peril. Jackson's entire wing was concealed behind the embankment or not far from it, and Jackson now had a chance to destroy a significant piece of Pope's army. As the Confederates prepared to attack, Gibbon's isolated brigade of under 3,000 men faced a first line of over 5,000 Confederates, with close support from another 6,300 and less immediate support from an additional six brigades. The Confederate line also included guns from several different batteries, with more on the way. "We were completely surprised," Gibbon would later write. He had received no intelligence about Confederates in the area and was unaware that "no precautions [had] apparently been taken to protect that flank."[16]

As Gibbon's frustrated complaint indicates, no one in the regiment or brigade had any notion that their year of training and frustration was about to take a very bloody turn. The regiment marched, recalled one veteran, "with arms at will, with no thought of battle." There was no singing, drumming, or bugles, although one soldier recalled the men "were . . . chatting, joking and laughing in their usual manner." The sounds of tramping feet and quiet conversation, the clanking and thudding of arms and other equipment, and the occasional mounted officer or messenger trotting along the line must have obscured the sounds of thousands of Confederates stepping out of the tree line and deploying in the open fields around and north of the farm. Foliage and topography gave them cover.[17]

At about the same time that Gus Kline of the Sixth—who would receive a battlefield promotion a few hours later—exclaimed, "I tell you this d——n war will be over and we will never get into a battle!" a shot from a Confederate battery screamed over their heads. That oft-repeated story is almost too perfect, but another private's tale rings true: "Every head was down in an instant, till the missile struck the ground, when the heads were all up again and laughing at each other."[18]

While the Sixth scrambled for cover in the ditch running along the turnpike, another battery opened fire at the other end of the brigade's line of march. Gibbon, believing these to be unsupported artillery units, ordered Battery B to suppress the first battery and the Second Wisconsin to assault the second. As the infantry maneuvered to the left of the woods and advanced on the Confederate guns, Confederate skirmishers appeared on their right flank. The Second wheeled and drove them back, but more Confederates emerged on their left, near the farm buildings. Gibbon pushed the Nineteenth Indiana forward to meet the new threat.

By now Gibbon had begun to understand that he was outnumbered and outflanked. He issued a flurry of instructions: hurrying the Seventh Wisconsin up to the right of the Second; requesting help from his divisional commander, King, and from the other brigade commanders; and ordering the Sixth Wisconsin to move forward along the right, or eastern, edge of the woods.

Artist Edwin Forbes's sketch of the opening phase of the Battle of
Gainesville. Although mislabeled as "Gen. Sigel's Division," other
notations clearly identify this as Gibbon's brigade. The infantry stepping
off in the left foreground is likely the Sixth Wisconsin, as the only
Union artillery unit in the battle, Battery B, deployed to the right of the
Sixth (*in right foreground*). Library of Congress, Washington, DC.

The fight the Sixth had been spoiling for was at hand, and the men of the
Sixth went into it with gusto. "'Forward, Guide centre' was the command,"
Dawes recalled, "and every man scrambled up that bank and over the fence ...
with just the same feeling of eagerness that one would hurry to save his dear-
est friend from great peril."[19] One private later admitted, "I don't know how
the others felt, but I am free to confess that I felt a queer choking sensation
about the throat." The regiment formed a line of battle, made a half wheel to
the left—"as accurately as if on the drill ground," according to Dawes—and
moved quickly forward. Their baptism of fire could not have occurred in a
more dramatic setting: Dawes described the "bloody red sun, sinking behind
the hills," and most of the battle was fought in thickening gloaming and then
darkness.[20]

A man from Company A remembered that "we heard a rip-rip, but did not
fully realize" Confederates were shooting at them "until the boys began to

fall." Another recalled that their forward movement took some time because of the failing light and having to clamber over a few fences. The Confederate line looked to one man "like a black mass or ridge of ground thrown up . . . not more than fifty yards distant." A sergeant in Company B later wrote to his hometown paper that the developing battle "was the grandest sight I ever saw," and that when the Sixth was ordered forward, "over the fence we sprang, and on a double quick *we went in.*" The dim light gave the Sixth a temporary advantage; apparently thinking that they were actually a Confederate regiment attacking the Federals' right flank, the Confederates opposite them hesitated until the Sixth opened fire. Even then, because they were on slightly elevated ground, the Rebels tended to aim high, saving the lives of many men of the Sixth.[21]

"We could see the enemy distinctly, as they could see us," one soldier recalled. Once the shooting started, the only orders he heard were "an occasional 'Give them hell! boys, give them hell!'" Gibbons was flanked on both ends, but aside from a few temporary—and bloody—advances by individual Confederate units, the two lines blasted away at each other for the duration of the battle with no more than seventy-five yards—well under a typical city block—and often as little as fifty yards separating them.[22]

Colonel Cutler soon took a bullet in the thigh, and Lieutenant Colonel Bragg led the regiment through the rest of the battle. In the gathering dusk, the rapid rifle fire and exploding artillery shells cast terrifying shadows in the smoke. Survivors from the Sixth were struck by the eerie illumination of the battle by flashes from thousands of muzzles. "During a few awful moments," wrote Dawes, "I could see by the lurid light of the powder flashes, the whole of both lines." He was struck by the image of a Confederate officer being shot off his horse. Both sides fired as fast as they could. One soldier wrote home after the battle that he had fired his gun forty-six times. Dawes remarked on being able to see officers of the Second and Seventh Wisconsin "working among and cheering up their men." Standing today on the ground held by the Sixth, where a thin stand of trees and a small creek traces much of the Union line, it is hard to imagine Dawes actually seeing the entire line, considering the darkness and billows of smoke and that the Sixth was on the far side of the small woods and slightly in front and below the other regiments. Perhaps being on horseback gave him just enough perspective; he could certainly have seen the Seventh in action.[23]

Eventually, Doubleday sent the Fifty-Sixth Pennsylvania and the Seventy-Sixth New York to fill the gap between the Sixth and the rest of the brigade, steadying the line. The firing continued until the Union regiments on the left began to give way slowly and darkness discouraged the Confederates from throwing more units into the line. Gibbon pulled his men back carefully, deploying skirmishers and collecting most of his wounded as he retired. Bragg ordered the Sixth to conduct a fighting retreat, walking backward, loading and firing as they went. When they reached the turnpike, he "called upon the regiment to give three cheers" in defiance of the more numerous Confederates. "No response of any kind was given by the enemy," which he and his men took as a kind of moral victory.[24]

The woods seemed to be filled with injured men, who had taken shelter during the fighting. "They were now scattered about under its dark shadows," wrote Dawes, "suffering and groaning and some were dying. In the pitchy darkness we stumbled upon them." A young private reported that the men "had not felt any horror" during the actual fighting, but now that "everything had become still," the groans of the wounded "were the most pitiful sounds I ever heard."[25]

One of those wounded, Matthew Kinsey, had to be left behind. As it turned out, his first battle would be his last, although his remaining quarter century on earth would, in fact, be one long fight against pain and debility. The Sixth's surgeon had hastily bandaged his wounded arm, but he was left untreated for three days, lying "upon the bare ground, without shelter or covering, and suffering more than could be told." A Confederate surgeon finally amputated his arm, but over several more days he "received no other medical attendance." He traded his hat to an African American servant for a piece of hardtack—his only "meal" for several days. On September 4 he was taken under a flag of truce into Union lines and transported to Columbian Hospital in Washington. By then "he had . . . entirely lost his appetite, and was sick and miserable, in consequence of having been allowed to eat too much, after his long fast, and the stump of his amputated arm was in a highly inflamed, dry and feverish condition, and so swollen that the stitches had torn out, leaving the incisions gaping open." He was barely able to travel when he was discharged on November 21 "and was reduced almost to a skeleton." The skin had sloughed away from his stump, leaving the bone exposed and rotting.

Kinsey returned to Wisconsin and boarded with a neighbor. Unable to do any hard work, the twenty-year-old attended school and when summer came he did "light work" around the farm. The next winter he collected taxes for the county. He married in 1865 and bought a piece of land but eventually sold that farm and started anew in Kansas. Despite his attempts to work, Kinsey was, according to his neighbor, "a broken down, sick weakly man after his return from the war." When he died in 1886, his widow Susan provided even more details. For instance, being left-handed he was able to do a fair amount of work for a few years; he could never eat "hog meat" or corn bread due to his weakened digestive system. Her narrative stressed respiratory problems; "he always suffered a great deal with his lungs & that was his principal trouble. He kept up his strength pretty well, but he appeared to gradually fail every year." They moved to Illinois and then to Missouri to escape the winters, but he continued to get colds that settled in his lungs, "and he always spit up matter & corruption." He died from consumption in 1886 at the age of forty-five.[26]

Men like Kinsey, left to the mercy of the Confederates, would face death or, if they were lucky, lengthy recoveries. The wounded who could walk or be moved were gathered up in the depressing darkness, and at midnight, tin cups and other equipment muffled, the brigade moved out for Manassas. Gibbon remembered it as "a sad, tedious march." A private wrote that "when we would halt for a few minutes one half would go to sleep, each man sitting or laying down upon the spot where he halted."[27]

A day or two after the battle, Reuben Huntley reached into his pack and pulled out another sheet of the patriotic stationery he had apparently bought from a sutler earlier in the summer; this time it featured a large three-color print of a battle scene. On it he scribbled that the "fite . . . was awful and it lasted tel dark, and then we fel back of the feld but we could here the s[hrie] ks of the wounded awl nite o sarah it is awful to think of." His thoughts turned to mundane, peaceful pursuits in the last words his family would read from him: "Dear so you must try and git hay to winter the cow for you now that the cow is a help to the family Do your best and you shall be rewarded." Huntley would be killed two weeks later.[28]

In his inimitable way, Bruce Catton described the brigade's first battle—"a baptism of total immersion"—as "a straightaway, slam-bang, stand-up fight with no subtleties and no maneuvering, no advancing and no retreating." All told, the brigade had lost about a third of its men: 133 killed, 539 wounded, and 79 missing. The Sixth came off with the lightest casualties, a total of seventy-two out of the 504 who had gone into the battle. With their comrades they had killed or wounded over 30 percent of the Confederates engaged.[29]

Although to most generals of the time and historians of the future those ninety minutes on a little farm west of Manassas would blend into the Second Battle of Bull Run, for the men of the Sixth it was a turning point. Proud of their role in standing muzzle to muzzle against a larger, more experienced Confederate force, they always recognized it as a separate engagement from the one that followed at Manassas. Although in the coming weeks they would fight equally hard and at far greater cost, the vivid images left by their first battle, fought in shadows and crimson smoke, would never leave the survivors. Having responded well after their year of longing for battle, they could build on that steadiness and reputation, which became a self-fulfilling aspiration in future battles.

The Army Is Discouraged: Second Manassas

After the grueling night withdrawal and without guidance from headquarters, King continued marching his division to the east, toward Manassas and Pope's gathering forces and away from Jackson. The next day, Pope determined that the Confederates were actually in the process of retreating to the west. But the opposite was true; Jackson was still dug in, and Longstreet and the rest of Lee's army were coming up fast. Nevertheless, Pope launched furious attacks against Jackson's position throughout the day and evening of August 29, unaware that Longstreet had arrived on Jackson's right flank. Gibbon's battered brigade stayed out of the inconclusive fighting on the twenty-ninth. Late in the afternoon of the thirtieth, however, it provided support for the other two brigades in their division, whom Pope sent in to attack the Confederates that he still believed were trying to withdraw. The day provided the Sixth with another chance to show off its pluck and discipline.[30]

Working through a thick wood along the Warrenton Turnpike a little over a mile from the previous day's battlefield, the Sixth Wisconsin and their comrades were out of sight of the forward battle lines. Confederate rifle and artillery fire decimated the New York regiments ahead of them; as one member of the Sixth scoffed, they "broke and skedaddled, crying out *our regiment is cut to hell, we are cut to pieces*." Gibbon angrily drew his revolver and ordered his men to shoot the stragglers if they refused to stop. Bragg shouted, "Kneel down! Captains, keep your men down! Let nobody tramp on them!" Some, a Wisconsin man wrote, "fell into our ranks and stood up like men," while others hesitated briefly and then continued fleeing when "our attention was drawn off by another squad of cowards."[31]

The collapse of the attack forced a general withdrawal of the Union men in the woods. The Sixth, however, had become separated from the rest of the brigade and had no idea that the other units were pulling back to the Union line. Gibbon remained with the Sixth as they hugged the ground under heavy fire from Confederate artillery and skirmishers. When Gibbon realized that the Sixth was the only regiment between the Confederate and Union lines, he ordered the men back to the edge of the woods, where they formed up and covered the remaining three-quarters of a mile over an open field at the double-quick. Impressed by his men's composure, and within sight of much of the Union army, Gibbon removed his hat to salute the Sixth's graceful withdrawal.[32]

Gibbon established his brigade behind a line of thirty-six cannon, where they crouched "on all fours looking under the guns." Gibbon allowed Longstreet's attacking Confederates to get so close that "we could see every detail of their outfit." As they witnessed the inexorable approach of Longstreet's advance—one of the largest single attacks of the war—the "nervous tension of the men lying" behind the line of guns "was awful." When he finally ordered the artillerymen to fire their double-canister loads, the men of the Sixth and other Iron Brigade regiments were stunned by the carnage. "The volley tore great bloody gaps in the Rebel lines and piled the dead and mangled in rows like hay raked in windrows in a hayfield." Despite the "awful slaughter," flanked again on both sides, the brigade soon retreated.[33]

By early evening the Union position had become untenable and Pope ordered his army to pull back. Gibbon's brigade covered the army's retreat. After the rest of the army had passed around or through their line, they built campfires to fool the Confederates into thinking they were still in position before beginning their own quiet departure. They made camp roughly four miles to the rear after working their way through the detritus of a defeated army. For the second time in three days, a nighttime withdrawal had followed a hard day of fighting.

The Sixth Wisconsin had played a relatively minor role at Second Manassas, taking light casualties. Yet the men could take pride in their steady performance in the face of heavy fire and in their own commanders' inspiring leadership. Gibbon's decisiveness and obvious pride in the performance of his brigade endeared him to the men, who previously had resented his strict discipline and old-fashioned ideas about uniforms. But the Sixth and the rest of the brigade were part of a tiny minority of Union soldiers who had been well led. The days—indeed, the months and years—following the battle saw recriminations and courts-martial and a drop in the morale of an army who thought they should have won the battle. The obvious failures of commanders at almost every level depressed and angered their men.[34]

Rufus Dawes complained years later that "the best blood of Wisconsin and Indiana was poured out like water, and it was spilled for naught ... against a dark background of blunders, imbecilities, jealousies and disasters." A couple of weeks after their baptism of fire, and just a few days before the Battle of South Mountain, where General McClellan would allegedly give the brigade its lasting nickname, Edward Bragg wrote his wife that "Pope is a braggart &

a villainous pervertor of facts & McDowell, too fussy & confused." In a hurriedly and nearly illegibly written letter to his wife, Edwin Brown excitedly declared that "three times has my life been in jeopardy. . . . You can say to your friends that your husband was no coward, when so many showed 'the white feather.'" So, too, the entire regiment had "maintained for themselves a good name." He saw more experienced and more famous regiments break and run "almost at the first fire, loosing [sic] more retreating than fighting." As a result, "the Army is discouraged, having no confidence in any one." He was not well and wished he could come home or at least get some rest. "I am weary & sick, if the enemy was off from our [territory] I should go to Hospital. Honor requires that every one who has any patriotism left should meet the insolent foe." Brown would go to Antietam sick and lame but determined to lead his company.[35]

A few men reflected on more immediate and personal experiences. Edward B. Hendrick of Company K wrote a letter to his mother that appeared in a local newspaper. He described the hot work on that afternoon at Second Manassas, when his friend Levi Gardner was shot through the head and killed right next to him. The sharpshooter who shot him turned to run; Hendrick reported with satisfaction that he shot him "through his back and he fell a corpse." He described the flight of the New Yorkers and the remarkable poise of the regiment when they withdrew under fire, but closed, "We have had a hard time lately. No one but a soldier knows what hard times are."[36]

It must have been hard for the men of the Sixth to remember that a few short days before, they had never been on an active battlefield, and it must have seemed to them that the entire experience of combat had been pressed into the hours they spent on those bloody Virginia hillsides. Dawes recalled a sergeant from Company F shot dead when he went out to help a wounded soldier, a retreating New Yorker killed almost immediately after Gibbon grabbed him and shoved him into the firing line, and the cries of a mortally wounded man to "give them hell!! . . . Poke it at 'em. Poke it at 'em, Boys." And he recalled the extraordinary weariness that came over the men during the retreat, when one exhausted guard accidentally shot his own brother-in-law.[37]

Some of the Wisconsinites reflected at the time or years later how their first battles had altered their perceptions of the war. After describing the various ways his comrades had been shot ("One poor fellow had his face stove up with a bullet, and two were shot through the left breast. Some in arms, and more in legs."), one man concluded, "I don't thirst for more fight, although if there is to be one I am in." No doubt some wondered how they could have been so naïve as to have sought battle. One of the older men in the regiment, Lucius Murray of Company E, wrote to his daughter soon after Second Manassas. He expressed sympathy for the recent loss of her eleven-month-old son, but he added that "death in all forms here have become so familiar to us that we hardly look on it with dread." Murray later wrote that while the fighting rages, "you do not much mind the shells bursting over your heads. The solid balls tearing up the ground and cutting the trees down around you, the incessant peal of musketry among the universal din sounds like pop guns. You become callous to those falling around you dead or wounded." Dawes later wrote with some irony that Gainesville had been "the battle we had yearned for." Like many men, Dawes admitted that the battle had changed him and his soldiers: That one night "had eradicated our yearning for a fight. In our future history we w[ould] always be found ready but never again anxious"; they would do their duty but not worry that they might be left out of the next battle.[38]

During the interlude following the fight at Manassas, Lieutenant Colonel Bragg had a chance to catch up with his wife Cornelia in a letter that was by turns reflective, caustic, and a bit prideful.

"It seems strange that one can escape, when every variety of death dealing missiles fill the air around," he wrote. Most escape uninjured, "but far more . . . escape, than are injured, and very many more run away from their colors, & carry back reports of losses & defeat—when they know nothing of the battle. A man who brings such news, is nine times out of ten a dastardly coward, who frames his story to excuse his shameful conduct." Yet, although "we lost the . . . battle on the 30th . . . we were not beaten—our men are of good cheer—and would have fought a good fight and held their ground until re-inforcements reached us." The ambitious lieutenant colonel had also heard that "the Wisconsin Brigade is the pride of the Corps" and agreed. "They never faltered—never yielded a point—but did what was assigned them—Every time."

Buoyed—perhaps relieved—by his regiment's performance, and his own, Bragg had discovered a confidence in his leadership and a pride in his cool-ness under fire. After only a few hours in combat, he had come to believe that he would not "suffer except it may be a slight wound." Yet the next line of his letter, as events would show, foreshadowed one of the weirdest examples of prescience by a member of the Sixth, or of any regiment: "No one can tell if it be my fate to fall," but if it were, "my body will be sent to you."

Yet Bragg was already looking forward to the war's end, yearning to be a veteran surrounded by his proud family. "Kiss the children many times for me, and when I come home again around the fire, I will talk the battles over again when it is not quite so noisy & uncomfortable as it was on the 28th of August." It would be a long time before Bragg would enjoy that dreamy night.[39]

Waiting for the Summons: South Mountain and Antietam

Over a week before Bragg sent his somewhat conflicted letter to Cornelia, Robert E. Lee had ordered his troops over the Potomac River into Maryland. McClellan was back in charge of Union forces, combining elements of Pope's Army of Virginia with the Army of the Potomac. The men were refitted and a number of command changes were made, including the replacement of division commander King with Brig. Gen. John P. Hatch. With the rest of the brigade and division, the Sixth trudged through Washington, resting for the night on the White House lawn, where Abraham Lincoln ladled late-night drinks of water from a bucket. The next few days saw the men moving north toward Frederick, Maryland. About this time Rufus Dawes wrote his mother. "My health is good and I am ready to take my chances," he assured her—although the letter was not, in general, very reassuring. He did "not feel that our task is easy or sure of successful accomplishment. The battle will be desperate and bloody, and upon very equal terms."[40]

Although none of the men in the regiment was aware of it, their job be-came somewhat easier when, in mid-September, McClellan was handed the famous "lost order" that laid out the details of Lee's campaign. One part of the plan was to recapture the Federal outpost at Harpers Ferry, which Jackson did on September 15. The other was to block the three roads leading through "gaps" in the Blue Ridge range at South Mountain to give Lee time to reassemble his army west of the mountains. McClellan's plan to catch Lee before he could concentrate his army required access to those passes, and Maj. Gen. Joseph Hooker's I Corps was given the task of clearing Fox's Gap, Turner's Gap, and Crampton's Gap, with Gibbon's brigade ordered to take the middle pass.

Gibbon moved his regiments up the old National Road that linked the Potomac River with the West (now US Highway 40). Although the road was solid macadam, it rose in a steep grade and was lined by patches of woods and orchards and flanked by rough and rocky ground, crossed occasionally by stone fences. It was, as brigade staff officer and former member of the Sixth Frank Haskell wrote, "an ugly looking place to attack." Gibbon arranged his regiments into two lines straddling the road. They were covered by a thin film of skirmishers, including Companies B and K of the Sixth, who traded shots with the Rebels from behind boulders, trees, and any other cover they could find. The Confederate skirmishers slowly fell back, but the brigade soon ran up against the main enemy force. When the Seventh Wisconsin was stymied by devastating fire from Confederates lodged behind a stone wall, Bragg redeployed the Sixth—which had been a few dozen yards behind the Seventh—to the right so that it could relieve their fellow Wisconsinites of the fire from that flank.[41]

Bragg's report described his complicated maneuver in the darkening woods, when he folded the regiment into two parallel "wings" (one under his direct command, one commanded by Dawes). Once he had the "left" wing into position behind Dawes's "right" wing, he called for Dawes to have his men lie down—"I am going over you." The wings alternately fired volleys and clambered up the hill, dropping to the ground as the other wing climbed through them. A forward line of Confederates was pushed back, although they still held the gap. Once again, the Sixth was within fifty or sixty yards of its enemy, and at times they could hear Confederate officers shouting orders.[42]

By this time, the regiment had nearly run out of ammunition. Bragg told his men to hold their fire "and trust to the bayonet." One can imagine the men, crouching in the dark, feeling in their nearly empty cartridge boxes, groping around them in hopes that a fallen comrade had a few last rounds. It is unclear whether Bragg actually ordered the men to fix bayonets, but the dramatic declaration by their colonel no doubt caused some to grip their rifles and clench their jaws more tightly. Soon, a single volley threw back a tentative attack by the Confederates. Then, "with three lusty cheers for Wisconsin, the men sat cheerfully down to await another attack; but the enemy was no more seen." They stayed on the field through the night until they were relieved by the Second New York. The New Yorkers "had been lying in the field, under cover of a stone wall," Bragg wrote with his characteristically arch sarcasm, "refreshing themselves with a good night's sleep, after a long and fatiguing march of some 10 miles." For the second time in a month the regiment had been left to fend for itself while its supposed support remained safely in the rear.[43]

Gibbon's two-paragraph description of South Mountain added luster to the reputation the brigade had begun to build two weeks earlier: "The conduct of the officers and men was . . . everything that could be desired, and they maintained their well-earned reputation for gallantry and discipline." General McClellan's report on South Mountain included a great compliment to Gibbon and his men: "General Gibbon, in this delicate movement, handled his brigade with as much precision and coolness as if upon parade, and the bravery of his troops could not be excelled." Those words—"precision," "coolness," and "bravery"—would come to embody the brigade and the Sixth, who would treasure them as long as they lived.[44]

They would relish another story even more. No one knows for sure when or how it occurred, but McClellan apparently always believed he had something to do with it. He witnessed the attack toward Turner's Gap, and when the brigade was identified he said something about their being "made of iron." Or perhaps he responded similarly to General Gibbon's question—or perhaps it was Maj. Gen. Joseph Hooker asking it—along the lines of "What do you think of my brigade now?" In any event, their new nickname—not the Western Brigade or the Black Hat Brigade but the Iron Brigade—first appeared in a Cincinnati newspaper just over a week after South Mountain. The reporter did not attribute the name to any one person but simply said that the brigade "has done some of the hardest and best fighting in the service. It has been justly termed the Iron Brigade of the West." An article that first appeared in a Chicago paper but was reprinted in the *Milwaukee Daily Sentinel* a little later, after Antietam, said that "the Western Brigade, under Gen. Gibbons [*sic*], has been badly cut up," with the survivors of the four regiments amounting to only a single regiment. "This 'Iron Brigade,' as Gen. McClellan dubbed them, has earned a glorious name by their indomitable courage and unparalleled power of endurance." Although a brigade of New York regiments had already been known as the "Iron Brigade of the East," the nickname stuck permanently with the westerners.[45]

Of course, no one in the regiment was aware of their new sobriquet, and the next day, when it was discovered that the Confederates had pulled back during the night, the brigade marched through the gap and over South Mountain. They continued along the National Road, passing by a stone tavern that still stands next to a trailhead for the modern Appalachian Trail. There they accepted the cheers of soldiers and a formal salute from II Corps commander Gen. Edwin Sumner and his staff, who had viewed their fight from the rear the day before. Trotting along with the weary and bloodied Sixth was a Newfoundland dog that had appeared in camp some time earlier and been adopted by gruff Capt. Werner von Bachelle of Company F.[46]

A contingent of about eighty just-arrived recruits destined for the brigade marched far back in the column; the roster suggests that about a dozen ended up in the Sixth, although they caught up to the regiment too late to fight in the coming battle. Yet one of them, George Fink, recalled half a century later the awesome and terrible sights that made them understand "the meaning of war more plainly than we ever had before." Passing through the aftermath of South Mountain, in the wake of the Army of the Potomac, "what we saw . . . was too terrible to tell. The dead, many of them had been left without burial. The bodies were decomposed. Dead horses, gun wheels, exploded shells and arms and accoutrements were on every hand." Unlike the original cohort of men who had enlisted in the summer of 1861, this small band, and the few score others who had drifted into the regiment in 1862 (almost all from February through April) did not have a year to prepare for combat, and this first glimpse of what lay ahead would have delivered a mighty shock. Two of these dozen recruits would be killed and nine would be wounded before the end of the war.[47]

After a pleasant, if brief, reception by the Union-loving residents of Boons-boro, the brigade then turned south and marched toward Keedysville, which would soon become the site of numerous makeshift hospitals that would care for many of the Sixth Wisconsin's wounded. After coming under fire from Confederate guns and stopping briefly for coffee and rest, the brigade, along with the rest of Doubleday's division, crossed the Upper Bridge over Antie-tam Creek and followed narrow country lanes toward the Hagerstown Pike north of Sharpsburg. It was hot and naturally dusty. Hemmed in by trees and tall rows of ripening corn—as some of these same lanes still are today—the men, marching four abreast, must have felt closed in, even claustrophobic. Eventually they looped to the north of the gathering army and came out onto open fields, settling on the army's far right flank near the road to Hagerstown. The regiment had reached its position on September 16 at about dusk and in a drizzling rain; as intermittent firing flared up in the distance, the soldiers lay along the turnpike with loaded muskets, still in marching formation.[48]

McClellan began the battle at first light on September 17. Those men of the Sixth who had managed to sleep awoke to a damp, foggy morning, artillery and scattered small-arms fire thudding and crackling somewhere to their front. The hungry men rose slowly, groggy after their uncomfort-able night—and then the generals started showing up. "General Doubleday came galloping along the line," Dawes remembered, ordering the brigade to move out of range of Confederate guns. "After much shaking and kicking and hurrying," the men got into formation and began to move east toward some farm buildings that would provide cover. This apparently got the attention of Confederate artillery batteries, which began firing on the haggard west-erners. They had gone just ten rods when a percussion shell exploded in the very center of Company A, killing two men outright and wounding eleven more. Capt. D. K. Noyes would lose most of a foot and nineteen-year-old

Arris Young parts of both arms. The sudden and deadly explosion in their midst became a staple of regimental memoirs and histories and perhaps inspired Thule de Thulstrup's 1887 chromolithograph *Battle of Antietam*. This unusually destructive shell proved to be a portent for the Sixth, which was advancing toward one of the most famous killing fields of the war: Miller's Cornfield.[49]

According to the brigade's commander, however, "the shock was momentary, and the column moved on leaving the mangled bodies of their comrades on the ground." Corps commander Joseph Hooker now appeared and ordered the brigade to advance along the Hagerstown Pike. The Sixth moved up the west side of the narrow road toward the Miller farm, where it encountered a heavy line of skirmishers and artillery fire. At this point Haskell, now on Gibbon's staff, rode up. He raised his cap in salute, presenting Gibbon's compliments, and passed along the general's order to "press the enemy as far as it is safe." Bragg raised his slouch hat and replied, "Col. Bragg's compliment to Genl Gibbon. It has been d——d unsafe here for fifteen minutes," before calling out, "Steady Six[th]—forward."[50]

At this point five companies of the Sixth slid over to the east side of the pike, as they worked their way through the Miller farm's orchards and gardens. Dawes, in command of that quintet of companies, had just sent John Kellogg's company forward as skirmishers. They "dashed across the field at a full run," driving Confederate skirmishers out of the orchard and outbuildings near the farmhouse. He then ordered Captain Brown of Company E—whom Dawes called "his best friend in the regiment"—to file through a gate and re-form in the garden; as Brown, sword raised, turned to shout the order to his men, "a bullet passes into his open mouth, and the voice is forever silent." A different account told of Brown screaming in agony after a shell fragment tore off part of his jaw. In any event, he died almost immediately. As Dawes struggled to get the company through the gate and into line—this would not be the last time he had to pull and shove his regiment through a picket fence—"the air above our heads filled with the screaming missiles of the contending batteries." Indeed, a few of Dawes's men were killed or wounded by friendly fire a little later as they crouched among the cornstalks.[51]

Once clear of the farm, Dawes's men pushed into a large cornfield (about to become "*the* Cornfield"). By then, Bragg had suffered what turned out to be a minor wound and Dawes had taken over the regiment. At this point Dawes's narrative becomes a frantic account of sound, furious action, and dramatic images—the Confederates fall back before them, beyond the corn, toward a little church they would later come to know as the Dunker Church. "The powder is bad, and the guns have become very dirty. It takes hard pounding to get the bullets down, and our firing is becoming slow. A long and steady line of rebel gray . . . comes sweeping down through the woods around the church [to the right and front of the Sixth]. They raise the yell and fire. It is like a scythe running through our line." Now the Sixth breaks and flees back into the corn; Dawes grabs the state flag and manages to stop the retreat in the corn. Years later, Dawes recalled sprinting "as fast as I could run . . . from the point where the regiment broke to the point where I reorganized" it; the entire operation from retreating to being ready to move forward again took, he estimated, five minutes.[52]

In the meantime, the companies on the regiments' right flank along the road were surprised by a sudden volley from hidden Confederates—the famous Louisiana "Tigers"—that riddled Captain von Bachelle's body with a dozen bullets. Many blamed Capt. Alexander Hooe for this ambush. His Company C had been sent out as skirmishers, but the captain's nerves had failed and he took cover behind a tree, leaving his men without orders and effectively useless. Alone among all the companies in the regiment, Company C suffered virtually no casualties that day. Hooe, a thirty-year-old widower, left the army in January 1863 and worked as a laborer and then as a federal employee in Washington, DC.

He never returned to Wisconsin.

Dawes led his regiment forward again, with the Second Wisconsin on his left (the other two regiments in the brigade fought most of the battle on the west side of the turnpike) and bolstered by a brigade of New Yorkers, who soon became mixed up with the men from Wisconsin. They slugged it out with Confederates at short range, pushing them back and advancing over the open ground just south of the cornfield. Then another wave of Rebel infantry—Gen. John B. Hood's Texans—slammed into them from their right and front, knocking down two out of every three men in the Sixth's front line, according to Dawes. The regiment hastily retreated back into the corn and beyond.[53]

Leaving the now-shredded cornfield behind—even in the middle of the bloodbath, the farmers in the regiment must have regretted the destruction of the nearly-ready-to-harvest crop—they withdrew into some woods, still under fire from Confederate infantry and artillery, with shot and shell and bullets rattling in the trees above them. There Dawes discovered that of the 280 men who went into the cornfield, 150 were already killed or wounded. The Second Wisconsin had it even worse; when its survivors reported to

Dawes, they were down to a captain and eighteen men. "This was the most dreadful slaughter to which our regiment was subjected in the war." While this was going on, Capt. John Kellogg, who was so sick he could barely walk, drew his revolver and pushed, shoved, and threatened hundreds of stragglers from other units into a makeshift regiment that took up position behind a stone wall near the regiment's starting point earlier that morning. The Sixth, "intermingled" with members of the Twentieth New York, retreated with the guns toward the North Woods, more or less where they had begun their day. There occurred one of the regiment's favorite stories about Gibbon. A few minutes earlier, with casualties among the artillerymen rising, he had dismounted and taken over a section of the battery. By the time the Sixth had regrouped, he rushed over, face "black with powder smoke," and told Dawes to come help. "He said 'By —— they shan't have these guns.'"[54]

The battle raged elsewhere for the rest of the day. As the musket and cannon fire thundered south and east of their position, the men cared for their wounded, rested, and greeted the small squad of reinforcements who had finally caught up with them. Bragg was back with the remnants of the regiment after having his slightly wounded arm treated at a field hospital. Using rough language that rather shocked at least one of the men, he refused to allow the regiment back into the fight. Most lay on the ground, exhausted, while some gathered around the newcomers, eager for news from home. Somehow Bragg had rustled up two barrels of molasses cookies, the only rations the regiment had eaten for two or three days.[55]

By day's end, the Army of the Potomac and the Army of Northern Virginia had fought each other to a standstill, and although the Union victory was far from complete, it ended Lee's raid into Maryland. Both armies spent September 18 burying their dead, and that evening the Confederates began to withdraw across the Potomac River, unmolested by their weary opponents.

Bragg recalled burying at least some of the men who had been killed near the Cornfield "under a locust tree" near Dunker Church—they may, like other burial parties, have chosen the spot near the tree to make it easier to find their comrades for more permanent reburial. Many were placed in a shallow trench scratched out with an artilleryman's hoe; Captain von Bachelle—found lying on his back, hat over his face, field glasses shattered—and his newly acquired dog were also buried near the tree. Earl Rogers's Company I, down to just "28 muskets," also buried its dead. Even after just a day, "the poor boys who had fallen were badly discolored and bodies swollen. They were placed in long lines with little covering of earth they were hidden from view."[56]

Given their close contact and the fact that a number of their comrades had been assigned to Battery B, many men in the Sixth would have heard with horror—mixed, perhaps, with bitter empathy—of the veteran cannoneer in Battery B who, in great pain, and knowing he had just hours to live, had drawn his revolver and shot himself in the head after saying, "Those few hours are not worth living."[57]

Soon, at least some of the men started to reflect on what they had experienced over the previous few days. Bragg wrote to Cornelia on September 21, the same day he wrote his official report of the battle. In the latter, he briskly provided highlights, described the death of the "genial" Captain Brown, and commended Dawes, "who discharged his duty . . . with signal courage and ability." The regiment "conducted itself during the fight so as to fully sustain its previous reputation"—a reputation that did not actually exist until less than a month earlier. He repeated some of the same information in his letter to Cornelia but also remarked, "I have not heard a cannon, in several hours, which is wonderful, in the times we are living." Although "my hand & arm pain me some this morning . . . I am in no danger, and wish all my brave fellows were so well off as I am."[58]

A First-Class Chance to be Killed

As the Sixth Wisconsin finally met Confederates on the field of battle, Wisconsinites at home were briefly distracted from the war in the East by a war in the West, as fears arose that a conflict in Minnesota between whites and Native Americans, which would become known as the Dakota War, would spill over into Wisconsin. Several newspapers reported panics in the less-settled parts of western and northern Wisconsin, where many peaceable Native Americans still lived. Even in Manitowoc, located nearly 200 miles from the border of Minnesota, reports of marauding bands of Indians threw residents into a brief frenzy. Although a few Wisconsin units would be sent west to fight in the Dakota War, the movement in Minnesota would be put down brutally and Wisconsin would remain safe from the perceived threat, which years later would be reduced to a humorous anecdote.[59]

No one was laughing about the war between the whites or about the very real need for more men to fight it. By May 1862, Wisconsin had mustered nineteen regiments of infantry and three of cavalry, along with eleven batteries of light artillery and part of a battery of heavy artillery.[60] For units like the Sixth that had been in Maryland and Virginia since 1861, the call for fresh manpower was nearly constant. Before he was reassigned as a lieutenant colonel in the Seventeenth Wisconsin, Capt. A. J. Malloy returned to Baraboo to recruit for the Sixth late in 1861. He had posted an ad in the *Wisconsin State Journal* asking for "young, able-bodied men—between the ages of 18 and 45" to "fill up the ranks." The regiment, he declared, already "has the reputation of being one of the best in the service." Men could choose to join any company in the regiment. An infusion of more than fifty recruits joined the Sixth between December 1861 and late March 1862.[61]

The recruitment issue became more urgent still in the summer of 1862. When Union victories in North Carolina and New Orleans and at Forts Henry and Donelson in the spring seemed to indicate an imminent end to the conflict, the War Department began to wind down its recruiting operation. But McClellan's defeat on the Peninsula and the sobering stubbornness of the Confederates made it clear by June that more troops would be needed. Lincoln issued a call for 300,000 additional three-year volunteers, and recruiting was bolstered by the Militia Act of July 1862, which empowered the president to set quotas of troops to be raised by each state and authorized governors to enforce the quota through a special militia draft if volunteering proved inadequate. The effort ultimately produced 421,000 new enlistees.

The men of the Sixth made direct appeals to those still in Wisconsin. "There is one very important fact we would urge upon the young men at home," one wrote to the *Appleton Crescent*. "The Union army needs reinforcing: we need the aid of all our old companions, school-mates, shop-mates and associates, to help us in this great work of reconstruction!" Neither comfort nor convenience should keep men from enlisting. The doom and gloom spread by discharged soldiers should be ignored: "Let no man make up his mind that he is unfit to serve his country! Hardships will stare you in the face at every road-crossing and on every side, but you will soon get used to that." In a passage foreshadowing Colonel Bragg's comment a few weeks later about longing to tell his children war stories before a comforting fire, the *Crescent* assured potential recruits that "it will make sport for you in old age, when your little grand children shall cluster around you, to listen to the stories of 'struggles fierce and wild.' Come, boys, turn out! Join us in the tented fields!"[62]

The situation became even more severe after Gainesville and Second Bull Run. "As you are aware," General Gibbon wrote to Wisconsin's governor Edward Salomon in a letter that was published in a number of state newspapers, "the Second, Sixth and Seventh Wisconsin Regiments in my Brigade were much reduced in strength during the recent engagements"—an old soldier's careful way of saying they had suffered hideous losses—"in which they earned a name for efficiency and gallantry which will not be soon forgotten in either the army or the country." Many other regiments had suffered major losses, and "I am exceedingly desirous of having these gallant regiments filled up to the maximum strength."[63]

Yet Federal policy was generally not to send replacements to existing regiments—at least, the effect of recruiting policies tended to result in regiments quickly dwindling, even as new regiments were being formed. In fact, the Sixth Wisconsin would not see a major influx of new recruits until late 1863 and early 1864. In the meantime, the conversation back home revolved around the very serious business of finding ways for individuals and communities to avoid state and Federal conscription.

Less than two weeks after Gainesville, the *Manitowoc Herald* only half-jokingly reported on the "Alarming Increase of Feeble Men," as Wisconsin prepared to conduct its first statewide draft. "Brain fever and spinal affection [*sic*] are alarmingly on the increase, kidneys are found to be weak, lungs are covered with tubercles, and the general anatomy suffers in common with everything else from the war." The *Baraboo Republic* reported that when word got around that persons without front teeth had been exempted from the draft because they could not bite off the ends of rifle cartridges, "a good many fellows, it is said, *have had their front teeth pulled*." The *Crescent* declared with contempt that "we should like to be able to publish a list of all the applicants for exemption from the Draft. It would be rich." A local doctor claimed to have turned down at least eight out of every ten applicants who had come in "a perfect rush. Many of them without a scratch or blemish. Shame on their manhood."[64]

The "momentous question" of "To Enlist or be Drafted" had become "the almost exclusive topic of conversation" among the young men of Wisconsin even before the bloody news from Virginia had arrived. In urging them to consider joining up, one editor reminded young men that volunteers would "receive ample bounty to leave your families well provided for, besides 160 acres of land [a common misperception at the time], your pay will be two dollars more per month, and you can choose your own company or reg't." On the other hand, "drafted men will receive but $11 per month and no bounty."[65]

But not everyone set the bar for proving their manhood that high, and the conversation about recruitment quickly became a discussion of what men owed their country and what the country would, in turn, owe those men who volunteered. Northerners faced nearly existential choices as they decided how to respond to the war, weighing the nation's needs against their own obligations. The government recognized the need to incentivize enlistments, not only by encouraging patriotic fervor but also by creating more concrete enticements.[66]

The notion that joining the army was more a matter of completing a transaction than fulfilling a patriotic obligation became more compelling as the war dragged on. As a historian of Madison wrote, "The easy gallantry and bravado of 1861 had given way to a much more calculating attitude." There were hints of such an approach soon after the war began and long before anyone suggested the need for conscription. When a new company formed in Viroqua late in 1861, the local newspaper added up the various bounties, wages, and benefits extended to soldiers and their families and concluded that the "the pay of the Union soldier" was "ample, whether he has a family or not."[67]

A few months later, hoping to encourage more men to enlist—and perhaps reflecting the hard times still affecting some parts of the state—the *Milwaukee Daily Sentinel* had promoted the benefits of bounties. In doing so, it stated blithely and irresponsibly that "we conceive it scarcely possible that the present war can last a year longer and the chances are that it will be terminated in six months." In short, even as the risk declined, the benefits of enlisting would rise. "Those who enlist now will have all the bounties provided by the State and Government, and in all probability will be back in their houses and businesses in six months." The state and federal bounties, along with the monthly pay of a private would, "in six months, put $228 in cash in the pocket of ever[y] man who enlists, besides his board and clothing. *Thirty-eight* dollars a month and found is good wages."[68]

The debate in communities across the state generally revolved around what kinds of financial incentives would be effective in encouraging enough enlistments so that towns and villages and counties could "escape" the draft. By August the *State Journal* and other newspapers began to fill up with stories about recruiting, quotas, and bounties. Towns and individuals alike offered bounties to volunteers. By late fall men were paying substitutes—men ineligible for the draft who would go in place of a draftee—as much as $300 in Appleton and up to $350 in Milwaukee.[69]

Although the draft was supposed to have been held in August, Governor Edward Salomon sought and received permission to delay Wisconsin's draft until after the fall elections, which gave most counties time to meet their quotas. Indeed, only Washington, Ozaukee, Sheboygan, Brown, Fond du Lac, and Milwaukee Counties—all in the eastern portion of the state, most along Lake Michigan, and many with high numbers of German immigrants, many of whom opposed the war and especially conscription—failed to meet their quotas. Salomon was himself a German immigrant, and although not politically aligned with his antiwar fellow countrymen, he was sympathetic to their objections to the draft. Yet he responded forcibly when resistance in those counties led to noisy processions, attacks on draft commissioners, and the assembling of armed mobs. Troops arrested the protesters in West Bend and in Port Washington, where a band of resisters had seized and destroyed militia rolls, assaulted the commissioner, and damaged his and a number of other homes.[70]

"Fear of the draft" had, in the words of an aide to Governor Salomon, a "truly wonderful" effect on recruiting. Yet, although well over 16,000 Wisconsin men volunteered that autumn, virtually all joined one of the fifteen new infantry regiments mustered into federal service from August through the end of December 1862. None of the 1,789 men mustered into service out of the 4,587 drafted ended up with the Sixth. Drafted men had ten days to provide substitutes or to volunteer in old regiments for three years with bounty or in old regiments for nine months without advance pay or bounty. Many of the draftees enlisted for nine months—without bounties—and were put into the Thirty-Fourth Wisconsin, which saw garrison duty at various posts before mustering out in fall 1863. Their wager to wait to be drafted rather than to volunteer for three years paid off. [71]

News of armed resistance and the failure of the draft to produce even a dozen recruits for the Sixth must have been discouraging. James Sullivan had, against his wishes, received a disability discharge in the fall of 1862 and returned home to Juneau County. He witnessed the lack of martial enthusiasm in person and, broke and disgusted with the state of affairs—high prices, complaining civilians, and too many "discharged invalids" bragging that they "had killed half the rebel army, and men . . . growling about the draft"—he reenlisted in the Sixth, "knowing that there would be a first-class chance to get killed."[72]

Sharp Times

Colonel Cutler, recuperating from his wound back in Milwaukee, missed the large and small tragedies and triumphs of the Sixth's recent battles. But his former lieutenant and current brigade staff officer, Frank Haskell, brought him up to date in a letter published in the *Milwaukee Daily Sentinel*. Haskell reported that the "Steady Sixth" had seen "some sharp times since last you led it." Only 200 men remained in the regiment "after the four hard battles they have fought," but, "Colonel, it would do you good to learn how splendidly the Sixth has done in all the battles." He described the calm retreat before the enemy at Second Bull Run and the way the regiment "covered itself with glory" at South Mountain. Antietam has been "the great battle of the war. The other battles were as nothing compared to this." He described the shell exploding among the men of Company A and the discovery of the battered bodies of Captain von Bachelle and his dog. "The dead are all buried now; those of the Sixth . . . all tenderly together under a locust tree, near where they fell; and their names are marked upon boards at the heads of their graves." Like a born officer, Haskell closed, "The boys are all cheerful, and ready again to meet the enemy. Many are the inquiries they make after you,—expressing their hopes and kindest wishes for your speedy recovery and return."[73]

The regiment would end 1862 secure in the triumphal narrative expressed by Haskell and others. Yet the idea of patriotic sacrifice, already ringing hollow on the home front, would become more abstract to the men in the ranks, where regimental identity would eventually be overshadowed by bitter confusion and a desperate desire to survive.

4

Where You Die, I Will Die

1863

"'The country demands' we advance, Richmond must fall, Lee's army must be 'bagged,' there must be a bloody battle, at least ten thousand of our brave soldiers must be killed and wounded," a fed-up Rufus Dawes wrote to his sister early in December 1862. "Nothing short of this will [appease] the blood thirsty appetite of our people." The army, he complained, "is cursed with second rate men from [Gen. Ambrose] Burnside" on down. "Our generals are not men who can hope for success upon any other stage," he declared with a certain conspiratorial flourish and, as a result, "many of them are accordingly not anxious for the war to end." Dawes ended dramatically: "This winter is the 'valley forge' of the war." He meant it from an emotional standpoint, it seems; no Union soldiers were leaving bloody footprints in the snow.[1]

Dawes penned these angry words shortly after the Army of the Potomac's defeat at the Battle of Fredericksburg. The Sixth had lost only a handful of men; the brigade's newest regiment, the Twenty-Fourth Michigan, bore the

79

brunt of the fighting against Stonewall Jackson's men on the Union left flank south of the town. Earlier in the fall the Sixth had seen much campaigning on the cold, muddy, and eventually snow-covered countryside of Maryland and Virginia. They would slog through the infamous "Mud March" in January 1863 before finally settling into their winter camp at Belle Plain along Potomac Creek, not far from Fredericksburg.[2]

Mourning their lost comrades—at South Mountain and Antietam alone the Sixth had lost thirty-four killed outright, with 194 wounded (a number of whom would later die)—the battered regiment welcomed the respite from combat, despite the difficult marching and short rations they experienced during those frustrating months. The greatest loss to the brigade was the promotion of John Gibbon to divisional command. "We are sorry to lose him," Rufus Dawes wrote, "for a brave and true man, tested as he has been, is a jewel here."[3]

When the spring killing season began in May, the Sixth would complete a stunning, if little-known and ultimately meaningless, cross-river attack to open the Chancellorsville campaign. Two months later, it would write another chapter in its unique history in a wild charge on the first day at Gettysburg.

Western Breeding

By late spring the regiment's strength had stabilized at roughly 250 men, although there continued to be a great deal of coming and going. Some of the wounded returned during the fall and winter, but many did not. Eighty-eight men received disability discharges due to wounds between the Battles of Antietam and Gettysburg; another seventy-seven were discharged for illness between October 1862 and June 1863. Only thirteen new recruits came to the regiment during that time. Earl Rogers attributed many discharges to men simply wearing down. "It takes 160 pounds of energy to make a soldier," he believed. A man weighing less "falls out, dies, a hospital case, or is sent home" so as not to become a "burden to the army."[4]

Despite the pause between campaigns, death remained a fact of life for the Wisconsinites. Rogers recalled the death from smallpox of "one of the Fox boys"—probably twenty-three-year-old William. "He was taken to a tent off by himself and not a funeral note was sounded and no one to this day knows where he lies. Such is the glory of dying for country with small pox." In Company B, George Cassidy was accidentally shot in camp and died a few days later.[5]

The regiment took part in a small but rewarding action in mid-February when it mounted a raid into Virginia's North Neck. The men marched rapidly inland, arresting a confessed smuggler and a Confederate official; confiscating mail, a few dozen horses and mules, five tons of bacon, and various other supplies; disrupting a meeting of local Confederate conscription officials; sinking several small boats that had been used to run the blockade; and liberating and transporting to freedom seventy "contrabands."[6]

By then Col. Lysander Cutler commanded a different brigade in the division. Edward Bragg was promoted to colonel and took charge of the regiment on March 25. "From your late commandant I receive you," Bragg declared solemnly at the commissioning ceremony. He continued with an odd metaphor paraphrasing a passage from the book of Ruth: "I hope that I wed not an unwilling bride. May your laurels never fade, but cluster thicker around your brow. You have been faithful to me in the past, I know that you will be in the future. Where thou goest there will I go, thy home shall be my home, where thou diest, there also will I be buried." The rhetoric might seem overwrought, even romantic, but Bragg, a tough and resourceful leader, had lived that sentiment through his two years' service with the Sixth and might have been drawn to the biblical Ruth's faithful service and sense of duty and shared sacrifice.[7]

The men did not so much look forward to the campaign that would inevitably begin once the roads were dry as they did to getting on with the job at hand. "All very anxious to move or get at some employment," George Fairfield wrote in mid-April. Ten days later he commented that "all is suspense. Dark clouds obscure the sky, & darker still seem the fortunes of war." That move was imminent. Joseph Hooker intended to cross the Rappahannock River with his army of 130,000 men to envelop Robert E. Lee's entrenched Confederates at Fredericksburg. The Sixth was part of the two corps that would cross the river south of Fredericksburg to threaten and hold Lee's right flank as the larger portion of the army tried to force Lee into the open west of the city.[8]

The Sixth—along with elements of the Twenty-Fourth Michigan and Second Wisconsin—started it with a grand and daring operation they would remember the rest of their lives. The I Corps had stalled at the river, as Confederate sharpshooters entrenched in rifle pits on the far side prevented pioneers from building the pontoon bridge. A bold plan came down to the brigade. As Adj. Edward Brooks later wrote to the *Appleton Crescent*, they were roused before midnight on April 28, with orders to cross the Rappahannock, "storm the rebel rifle pits," and clear the far riverbank. "Although we did

The Sixth Wisconsin launching its attack across the Rappahannock at Fitzhugh's Crossing. Rogers Collection, Vernon County Historical Society, Viroqua, WI.

not crave the job, the honor of being selected from among all the regiments of our corps was gratifying, and our hearts beat with a stern resolve to prove ourselves worthy of the trust." They spent a few hours on the bluff above the river, exchanging fire with the Rebels on the other side. The plan was to cross in pontoon boats, "flat-bottomed, square-bowed institutions, about twenty-five feet long, four wide and about three deep." The rifle pits across the river—about 300 yards away—"were swarming with 'confeds,' who could fire with safety at us" while the Wisconsin men fought the current in their little fleet of clumsy boats. The far bank rose forty feet from the river and was overgrown with vines and underbrush and very slippery from recent rains.[9]

"Col. Bragg made a short address," wrote another man, "telling us to show our western breeding and our skill as oarsmen." The regiment formed up, with Bragg at the front. He tugged his hat down and said, "'Come on, boys,' and that was all the orders we got." The men of the Sixth "felt the danger," wrote Brooks, but with the corps depending on them, "no one faltered and every man was in his place"; they actually *"kept step"* as they approached the river. The men cheered as they piled into the boats and pushed off, sent on their treacherous way by cheers from the men providing covering fire from the bluffs to their rear.[10]

Once in the boats, Brooks recalled, "*Jesu!* How the bullets did rattle against their sides. . . . Splinters from the gunwales of the boats flew in every direction." A man was struck in the temple, flopped over the side of his boat, and sank. Two other soldiers were killed and about a dozen wounded during the crossing. When the boats ground to a stop, the men clambered out and swept up the bank, shooting or capturing a couple of hundred Confederates, and securing the bridgehead. George Fairfield's laconic diary entry simply stated, "A charge was decided upon and several men picked up the boats and we made for the river double quick to mann [*sic*] them. We crossed and carried the heights. It rained in the evening."[11]

Far more excited was Colonel Bragg who, as was his custom, wrote his wife at about the same time he made his official report. "My regiment lead the 'forlorn hope' & forced the crossing below Fredericksburg, in open boats, in the face of a deadly fire, from a concealed foe," he boasted. "Such cheering & shouting you never heard—Everybody was crazy." His formal report was more restrained: "The conduct of every officer and man in my command was splendid."[12]

It was for naught. Hooker's grand plan collapsed and the Army of Northern Virginia once again prevailed at the Battle of Chancellorsville. The Sixth crossed back over the Rappahannock on May 6. As it was not involved in the embarrassing failure on the other end of the Union line, the Sixth could glory in its minor but stirring victory at the river. "It is called one of the daring exploits of the war—I am told," wrote Bragg with slightly false modesty shortly afterward. "The grandest fifteen minutes of our lives! *Worth one's life* to enjoy," agreed Philip Cheek and Mair Pointon half a century later.[13]

Casualties were very light in the Sixth at the start of the campaign, but one of the dead was Philip T. Shields, who lingered for months in a Philadelphia hospital before dying at the age of twenty in June 1864. His parents were able to bring his body home for a funeral, which provided a rare opportunity for public grieving at the death of a member of the regiment. "The death of this amiable young man," declared the *Daily Milwaukee News*, "is worthy of more than a passing notice," for he was "a kind, dutiful and devoted son and a gentle and affectionate brother" and "a youth of exemplary goodness of character and uncommon intelligence." When the war began, "the fire of patriotism glowed brightly in his bosom and actuated solely by a sense of duty he enlisted" early in the war. The knowledge that he was "fortified by the graces of those holy sacraments which the church provides for the children at the last hour" should "pour the balm of consolation into the hearts of his afflicted and sorrowing parents." Countless gallons of balm would be required before the summer was out.[14]

So Fine a Body of Soldiers

With the rest of the army, the Sixth waited in their camp near Fredericksburg for the rest of May, with most days featuring company and battalion drills, inspections, and sometimes a dress parade. One private complained that "it seems as if our colonel [takes] especial pains to drill us every hot day but I am of the opinion that I can stand it if he can." About the only excitement came when the Sixth and the Second Wisconsin put down a mutiny among a regiment of two-year men from New York. When the New Yorkers saw the Wisconsin regiments drawn up in line, bayonets fixed, reported one member of the Sixth with a certain grim delight, "they took their arms and went into the ranks, knowing that they would meet with no mercy at our hands, as we have the reputation of obeying orders."[15]

The post-Chancellorsville reorganization of the army had made the Iron Brigade the first brigade of the first division of the first corps of the army, a coincidence that they would always relish. Maj. Gen. John Reynolds commanded the corps, Brig. Gen. James Wadsworth the division, and Brig. Gen. Solomon Meredith, the former commander of the Nineteenth Indiana, the brigade. Late in June Colonel Bragg was kicked by a horse, and when he went to Washington to recover, Dawes became acting commander.

During the last three weeks of June, the Army of Northern Virginia left its lines near Fredericksburg, marched west, and proceeded down the Shenandoah Valley toward Pennsylvania. Hooker slowly pivoted to keep his army between the Confederates and Washington, but as Lee's intentions became clearer, the entire army lurched onto roads leading north. The Sixth, along with the rest of I Corps, left its camp on June 12.

On their first day on the march, the division witnessed the execution of a deserter from the Nineteenth Indiana by a firing squad drawn from the Sixth Wisconsin. As in numerous descriptions of similar scenes—executions were one of the set pieces of postwar memoirs—the focus was not only on the deserter but on the witnesses who were the target audience for this harsh bit of moral theater. Howard Huntington wrote in the *Baraboo Republic* that "soldiers who had been in many battles stood in breathless suspense. What a moment it must have been to the unfortunate victim who heard that awful click—the prelude to the last sound he was to hear on earth. He moved not a muscle. The signal—aim—was given, and then that final, fatal word—Fire!"

It was a depressing ending to Huntington's cheerful report from the front; how many readers wondered if they had ever written to their sons, brothers, or fathers words that might have inadvertently caused them to consider forsaking their comrades?[16]

The scene seems to have affected Dawes in exactly the opposite way it was supposed to. A few days later, the young acting commander of the regiment could write to his fiancée that "I had a chance to do a good thing this morning and it gave me pleasure." A "fat cheeked, sleepy boy" from Company I had been found asleep on guard duty—a court-martial offense. Rather than submitting him to the mercy of military justice, Dawes let him go with a "sharp lecture and a warning." The boy was killed eight days later at Gettysburg.[17]

Resuming the march, the men, of course, had no idea where they were going. Lyman Holford appreciated being able to buy fresh bread, milk, and butter from citizens along the way, which was "an agreeable change of diet," but fretted that "we can get no papers and are in ignorance of what is transpiring." A day later, after remarking picturesquely that when the army "wound slowly over the crooked mountain road" toward Frederick, Maryland, "it looked like a huge serpent," he again wondered what was going to happen next. "All kinds of rumors are afloat . . . but I do not know what to believe."[18]

Something big was clearly looming. On June 28, Maj. Gen. George G. Meade replaced Hooker. Dawes wrote his fiancée that Meade "lacked the martial bearing and presence" of his predecessor. "Few of our men knew him by sight," and the change seems to have been little remarked upon. Two days later, according to Sgt. John Johnson, the roads were filled with "an almost endless procession of wagon-trains; ammunition, subsistence, and quarter-masters', each drawn by six horses; also the cavalry, 10,000 strong; the batteries, with a large number of cannon and ammunition-wagons, some of them drawn by six; others by eight, horses; and last, but by no means least, infantry . . . each carrying his 60-pound pack." All were "marching and counter-marching, oftentimes at a double-quick; now along several parallel roads, now through the fields, through the unbroken country," beaten down by the sun and "enveloped" by "an immense dust-cloud." When they finally halted at the end of the day, the men collapsed on the open ground for a night's sleep, but the lieutenants and first sergeants in each company worked until daylight completing end-of-the-month paperwork. At breakfast on July 1, Johnson and his messmates Thomas Polleys and Lewis Eggleston drank coffee but had no appetite. "Something seemed to give warning of approaching disaster;

we knew not what, nor could we shake off the depression." Their foreboding would prove prescient; all three would be wounded within a few hours, and Eggleston would die of his wounds by the end of the month.[19]

The regiment started the day a few miles south of Gettysburg. They were not yet aware that part of the Confederate army was, even then, beginning a tentative advance on the thriving crossroads town, opposed only by a small division of Union cavalry. An observer from Battery B—which still contained a sprinkling of the fifteen men originally detached from the Sixth—was "riveted" by the Iron Brigade as it marched by. "No one now living will ever again see . . . the Iron Brigade . . . file by as they did that morning" just south of Gettysburg. The undulating road offered a memorable image of the brigade as it marched "down one slope and up the other," with "the effect of huge blue billows of men topped with a spray of shining steel, and the whole spectacle was calculated to give nerve to a man who had none before." Friendly banter between the foot soldiers and artillerymen may have been the last jokes heard by dozens of men, who would within an hour or two be locked in combat with the Confederates.[20]

Still unaware that they were marching into history, the Sixth literally sang their way onto the battlefield, starting with the Germans in Company F, who, James Sullivan remembered, performed "a soul stirring song in German." The rest of the regiment kept time with the song and gave "three rousing cheers" when they finished. Company K came next with a song, its tune apparently now lost to history, that began "On the distant prairie where the heifer wild, Stole into the cabbage in the midnight mild" and continued through endless verses connected by a chorus of "On the distant prairie, hoop de dooden doo." The drummers picked up the beat, and the singing "kept up from one end of the line to the other." That ditty finally over, the Irishmen of Company D launched into "Paddy's Wedding," a rollicking celebration of the drinking, dancing, drinking, feasting, drinking, toasting, and "bedding" at an Irish marriage ceremony. After a score of verses, it was "music enough for one day," recalled Sullivan. The regiment may never have sung again; indeed, one of Dawes's favorite singers would be dead by day's end, along with many of the Irish and Germans who had set the playlist of that morning's march.[21]

A certain poignance shrouds soldiers' descriptions of those first few hours of July 1. It was just another long, hard slog—until it became something else entirely—and the singing, the familiar swinging route step, the easy conversation in the ranks, the knowledge that others saw them as the *Iron Brigade*, even the dawning awareness of a battle, lent a rather elegiac tone to the memories of the men who survived the day.

As the regiment neared the Emmetsburg Road, about three miles south of town, Lieutenant Colonel Dawes decided to make a splash, almost as though he wanted to fashion a memory worth savoring. On that morning he commanded 340 officers and enlisted men—his own regiment plus the 100-man brigade guard comprising ten men from each company. All were in the highest spirits. He brought the drum corps to the front and had the colors unfurled. The drum major had begun "The Campbells Are Coming," and the regiment had closed its ranks and swung into step. "The people would infer," he thought, mostly in jest, "that the rebels are running, or would run very soon after" confronting "so fine a body of soldiers as the 6th Wisconsin."[22]

Then, the sound of cannon rolled in from the northwest, which, wrote Lyman Holford, "told us there was work ahead." The brigade in front of them—commanded by the Sixth's old colonel Lysander Cutler—veered west and north toward a rise they would come to know as Seminary Ridge. The Iron Brigade followed. Dawes stopped the music and started his men across the field over which Confederate general George Pickett would lead his doomed charge two days later.[23]

The brigade slanted toward the sound of the guns for several minutes. Cutler's brigade soon engaged the Confederates, while in their front corps commander Reynolds would within minutes be killed by a Rebel sharpshooter; the Sixth unknowingly saw his shrouded body carried to the rear. Maj. Gen. Abner Doubleday took command of the corps and, as the Confederate line continued to stretch south, he personally ordered the brigade into position in the woods west of the Lutheran seminary and its namesake ridge. "I deemed the extremity of the woods . . . to be the key of the position," he explained in his official report, "and urged that portion of Meredith's brigade, the Western men assigned to its defense, to hold it to the last extremity. Full of the memory of their past achievements, they replied cheerfully and proudly, 'If we can't hold it, where will you find men who can?'" Doubleday referred to them as the "Iron Brigade" throughout the rest of his report. The sweating soldiers from Wisconsin, Indiana, and Michigan rushed into McPherson's Woods, near a stream called Willoughby's Run. There they would capture most of a Confederate brigade while sustaining terrific casualties. Much of the Iron Brigade's historic reputation stemmed from its sacrifice on the first day at Gettysburg, where it would be virtually destroyed. The men of the Iron Brigade would never be the same emotionally, physically, or even organizationally.[24]

But the brigade would do it without the Sixth, who fought as an independent regiment throughout the morning and afternoon of the first day and would earn its own place in history at an unfinished railroad cut northwest of Gettysburg. Dawes's men jogged forward, loading their guns as they ran, expecting to go into line at the far left of the brigade. But a staff officer came with another order from Doubleday for the regiment to remain in reserve. The panting men stopped and lay down to await further orders—which soon came directly from the general himself. "The death of General Reynolds was followed by other disasters," Doubleday later wrote, one of which included the outflanking of Cutler's outmanned brigade north of the Chambersburg Pike, a road that led straight into town. If the Confederates overran Cutler, Doubleday realized, it might lead to "the defeat, perhaps the utter rout, of our forces. I immediately sent for . . . the Sixth Wisconsin . . . a gallant body of men, whom I knew could be relied upon." He directed them to attack immediately and Dawes ordered a charge, "which was gallantly executed." Doubleday saw the greater threat that the entire Union position was in jeopardy; Dawes and his men saw only the danger Cutler's defeat would represent to the other regiments of the Iron Brigade, whose right flank could be rolled up if Cutler fell back.[25]

The Sixth immediately got into line of battle and hurried forward at the "double-quick," this time toward the turnpike, just under 1,000 yards away. Dawes's horse was shot out from under him, and the regiment took numerous casualties. The men did not fire a shot until they paused at a rail fence along the road. By this time, many of the Confederates—the Second Mississippi and elements of two other regiments—had taken cover in an unfinished railroad cut and poured a deadly fire into the Sixth. Knowing that remaining in place was not an option, some of the men started shouting, "Charge! Charge!" Dawes ordered his men over the fence and then over a second fence along the north side of the pike. When he saw the Ninety-Fifth New York coming up on his left, Dawes ran over to the commander, Maj. Edward Pye, and shouted above the battle racket, "'We must charge!' The gallant major replied, 'Charge it is,' and they were with us to the end." Both regiments lurched forward in the face of a "fearfully destructive fire from the hidden enemy. Men who had been shot were leaving the ranks in crowds." The Sixth bent into a V, "with the colors at the advance point, moving firmly and hurriedly forward, while the whole field behind is streaming with men who had been shot, and who are struggling to the rear or sinking in death upon the ground." Some of the wounded left behind at the fence struggled to load and fire at least one more time.[26]

John Johnson recalled that in the few seconds before the charge, it occurred to him that they might die in another vain attack, "but we must raise

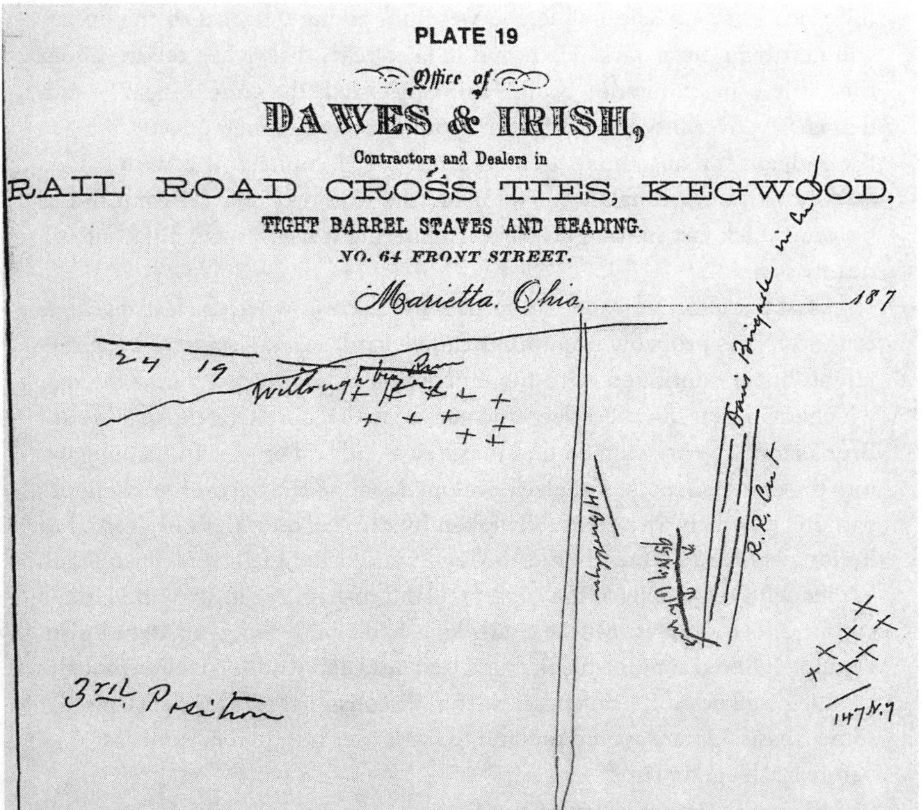

PLATE 19

Office of

DAWES & IRISH,

Contractors and Dealers in

RAIL ROAD CROSS TIES, KEGWOOD,

TIGHT BARREL STAVES AND HEADING.

NO. 64 FRONT STREET.

Marietta, Ohio, _____ 187

2 4   1 9

Willoughby Run

R. R. Cut

3rd Position

147 N.Y.

Gettysburg

643

Many years after the war, Rufus Dawes sketched the charge on the Railroad Cut on his business stationery. Beaudot Archival Collection, Kenosha Civil War Museum, Kenosha, WI.

the price as much as possible; we were not giving bargains to the enemy voluntarily in these days." He found in later years that, when talking about the battle, other comrades recalled thinking exactly the same thing. The sudden charge over fifty yards of open ground, he remembered, was costly to the Federals but absolutely "demoralized" the "Johnnies." The Sixth loaded as they ran; unfortunately for Johnson, the jostling caused his ramrod to become stuck fast in the gun barrel, rendering it useless as a rifle but still deadly as a club.[27]

A last Confederate volley from the railroad cut—when the leading angle of the "v" was probably no more than five yards away—staggered the regiment, but it continued onto the embankment to fire down into the cut, which was at least four feet deep and packed with Confederates. Adj. Edward Brooks took twenty men around to the east end and directed a flanking fire into the crowded ditch. A melee developed around the Second Mississippi's battle flag, which was eventually taken by the Yankees; the only medal of honor awarded to a member of the regiment during the war went to Frank Waller, who got credit for the capture. Hand-to-hand fighting swirled in the cut for a few minutes. Musket butts smashed skulls, blood spattered from wounds suffered at point-blank range, and dead and wounded fell among the scuffling Yankees and Confederates. The Wisconsinites would later claim that some Mississippians would pretend to surrender but then fire one last shot before finally giving up.[28]

When the commander of the Second Mississippi offered Dawes his sword, in the ancient ritual of surrendering, Dawes took it. "It would have been the handsome thing to say, 'Keep your sword, sir,' but I was new to such occasions, and, when six other officers came up and handed me their swords, I took them also, and held the awkward bundle" until he found someone to lug them into Gettysburg. They were later lost when the Confederates occupied the town and its hospitals.[29]

The charge of the Sixth Wisconsin blunted the Confederate attack along the Chambersburg Pike, which if not stopped would have had a major impact on the outcome of the battle. During the lull in the fighting that followed, Dawes moved his men forward, or west, from the Railroad Cut and spent the next half hour reorganizing his shattered companies. Two of his company commanders had been killed and five wounded, and Dawes—and no doubt everyone still standing with him—only then came to fully understand the tremendous cost of their bold attack. The Sixth had captured over 230 Rebels at the price of 29 killed, 111 wounded, and 20 missing—nearly half of the number that had left the Emmetsburg Road less than an hour earlier. By this time XI Corps, which had followed I Corps to the battlefield, was hard-pressed by Confederate forces coming down from the north and threatening the flanks of both corps. For a time the Sixth fought in support of Battery B. During this time the mortally wounded Frank King of Company E begged any comrade who passed by to put him out of his misery. None had the courage to shoot him.[30]

Dawes described the subsequent collapse of both I and XI Corps precisely, as he had one of the least obstructed views of what was happening of anyone on the field. The Union troops on both sides were falling back. Dawes thought at the time that his regiment had been forgotten, but it eventually received orders to withdraw back through town and onto the ridge to the south. The Confederates were advancing, it seemed to Dawes, in a giant U, with the Sixth caught in the open end. "If we had desired to attack [Gen. Richard] Ewell's twenty thousand men with our two hundred, we could not have moved more directly toward them." Dawes led the survivors of the charge on the run, through the Railroad Cut they had won earlier in the day, and then through a second cut closer to town. Confederate fire fell all around them, splattering them with dirt. At that point Dawes formed the men into a line of battle as they began jogging toward town. "It was an even race which could reach Gettysburg first, ourselves, or . . . Ewell's Corps." They were still alone, for all intents and purposes, and in mortal danger.[31]

The Sixth hurried through open fields and along a small creek. "The first cross street"—probably a railroad crossing just west of town—"was swept by the musketry fire of the enemy." Across the street a board fence enclosed a barnyard; a couple of missing planks created what the men called a "hog hole." Dawes grabbed the regimental flag and called for the men to follow him in single file across the street and through the narrow opening. "Taking position at the fence, when any man obstructed the passage-way through it, I jerked him away without ceremony or apology." Two men were shot in the crossing, but the regiment re-formed and proceeded into town. The three buildings of the Pennsylvania College—present-day Pennsylvania Hall and the President's House still stand as witnesses to the battle on the Gettysburg College campus—provided some cover from the Confederate troops driving from the north.

"The weather was very sultry," Dawes continued. "The sweat now streamed from the faces of the men. There was not a drop of water in the canteens, and there had been none for hours. The streets were jammed with crowds of retreating soldiers, and with ambulances, artillery, and wagons." The chaos was "depressing to my hot and thirsty men." They took fire as they neared the center of town, but the demoralized Yankees clogging the streets were a greater problem. Near the house in which Abraham Lincoln would stay when he came to Gettysburg to dedicate the national cemetery in November, they shoved their way through a swarm of Union stragglers, some of whom tried to surrender in their panic and haste. "I saw no men wearing badges of the First Army Corps in this disgraceful company," Dawes recalled with anger and relief.

After they exchanged volleys with Confederates firing from Baltimore Street, they re-formed yet again and continued down Washington Street, passing a number of buildings that still exist, including a Young Ladies Seminary and the home of Jack Hopkins, a prominent local African American who worked as a janitor at the college, and on into the countryside just south of town. They must have seen other Union troops drifting or running toward Cemetery Hill, where a rally point had been developed by the Union troops still arriving from the south and east. Indeed, that these reinforcements had time to establish the strong defensive position south of Gettysburg was a testament to the Sixth's action at the Railroad Cut and the desperate fighting by the rest of the brigade west of Seminary Ridge.

Perhaps the Sixth fell in with other members of the Iron Brigade who had finally been overwhelmed and were falling back. The Sixth left the road at about the same spot it had turned toward the firing earlier in the day, trotting east across farm fields and resting for a time near the gatehouse at Evergreen Cemetery—not far from where the president would deliver his famous address—and then worked their way to the relative safety of a position on Culp's Hill. It was a scene of great confusion, as officers tried to bring order to tangled regiments and companies without commanders. Acting division commander Gen. Thomas Rowley, possibly drunk, acted "positively insane," according to Dawes, as he incoherently tried to rally the men. Lt. Clayton Rogers—originally a Sixth Wisconsin man but now a staff officer—put Rowley under arrest and asked Dawes to assign men from the Sixth to escort him to the rear. The regiment had apparently gotten dispersed toward the end of its retreat; by nightfall only about 100 men were accounted for.[32]

It had been a long and tragic day. With the rest of the brigade, the Sixth threw up shallow breastworks—some of which can still be seen—and prepared to defend the Union right flank. For the most part their sector was quiet until late the next day. Although the Sixth saw action on both the second and third days of the battle, the regiment took few casualties. This gave a few men the chance to reflect and to write home.

Early on the second, Dawes started a letter—that he may not have sent—in which he stated simply, "I ordered a charge and we captured a regiment. . . . Lost 160 men." A member of Company A wrote a letter that would be published two weeks later in the *Baraboo Republic*. "In the field at Gettysburg, Pa., July 2d, 1863. The Iron Brigade lost 1140 men yesterday. It has 450 for duty this morning. We never did harder fighting." The letter described the charge to the Railroad Cut and the false surrenders of some of the Confederates. Nine of the fifteen men in the company who went into the battle were shot; two were killed. The newspaper added, "This company left Madison with about 111 men; now THEY CAN muster only six fit for duty."[33]

On July 4, Thomas Kerr of Company E wrote to his wife, who also shared his letter with the local newspaper. "I am all safe. We have had three days of the hardest fighting I ever saw. Our brigade is cut to pieces. . . . I had twenty-eight men with me when we entered the fight, and brought fourteen out again. The rest were all killed or wounded." He suffered a minor wound but did not leave the field.[34]

On the fourth, the regiment spent Rufus Dawes's twenty-fifth birthday burying bodies. For whatever reason, neither Dawes nor his men chose to describe the aftermath of the battle in such horrifying detail, but there is no reason to think they experienced their gruesome chore any differently than an officer conducting the same awful duty. His burial detail found corpses blackened and bloated—some bodies had actually burst—eyes bulging, arms stretched out at odd angles. The smell was overwhelming, and the odor that lay over the battlefield for many days was the most remarked upon feature of the battle's aftermath. One officer in charge of a burial detail reported that "in a short time we all sickened and were lying with our mouths close to the ground, most of us vomiting profusely."[35]

As the men wandered the battlefield, looking for dead comrades, they would have seen the same horrors that civilian observers reported. Near Culp's Hill, for instance, where they spent the second and third days of the battle, nearly all of the trees within 300 yards of the Federal line were riddled with bullets; clotted blood still stained the ground and trampled leaves where wounded and dying men had lain. "Paper, envelopes, bits of letters, shreds of clothing, pieces of photographs, muskets, bayonets, ramrods, knapsacks, haversacks, caps, old shoes and blankets" were scattered everywhere. At the spot where Confederates had charged a battery of Union guns double-shotted with canister, men "had literally [been] blown to atoms. . . . Corpses strewed the ground at every step. Arms, legs, heads, and parts of dismembered bodies were scattered all about, and sticking among the rocks, and against the trunks of trees, hair, brains, entrails, and shreds of human flesh still hung, a disgusting, sickening, heartrending spectacle." From shallow graves hastily dug while the battle raged on the first day emerged body parts and faces. Throughout the battlefield, birds frightened by the noise and smoke were eerily absent although flies swarmed everywhere.[36]

Later in the year, when the new national cemetery was being prepared for its late November dedication, an official from Pennsylvania reported to the military secretary for Wisconsin that he had witnessed the removal of bodies from the battlefield to the new cemetery, including those who fell near the Railroad Cut. "Most of the bodies had been buried as they fell and nothing being found on them to identify their Regiment, they were placed in the mass grave assigned to the 'Unknown'" in the "fine lot" assigned to Wisconsin troops.[37]

A Battle Annihilates Time

Of course, the end of any battle is a gradual thing, at least for the men enduring painful treatments for wounds; they either lived or died, returned to their regiment, or went home. As during the aftermath of the battle autumn of 1862, some of the wounded returned to the regiment quickly, others after months in a general hospital. Even those who came back no doubt went through a period of recovery and for some time remained vulnerable to infections. Men clearly too badly injured to continue as soldiers had to wait in a twilight of pain and doubt until they were well enough to make the strenuous journey back to Wisconsin. Some endings came faster than others.

Although his comrades thought Levi Stedman had been killed outright during the charge at the Railroad Cut, he in fact lingered in a Gettysburg hospital for over two weeks before dying what can only be called a typical "good death." Stedman—at forty-eight, one of the oldest men in the regiment—had been shot through the chest, with the bullet exiting near his spine. To the correspondent of the Boston *Recorder* who approached his bedside, he "had the look of a man who had never known fear, nor asked for help,—he could suffer without a groan and die without a complaint." Their conversation turned to spiritual concerns when the stoic Wisconsinite admitted that he had "received no religious education" and asked the visitor to "teach me, and tell me what I must do to be saved." The visitor prayed with the wounded man and later that day brought witnesses so the dying man could be baptized properly. The next day he found Stedman "suffering the greatest pain" but remaining "evidently peaceful." When asked "Do you still trust in Jesus?" he replied, "Oh, yes, I lean on him; I hope in him alone." He died two days later, and when the correspondent asked, "How did he die?" one of the attendants confirmed that "he was sensible and peaceful to the end, and prayed much that God would not judge him for his sins, but would show him mercy for the sake of Jesus." The account ended with the prayerful "May we not hope that the repenting soldier, like the dying thief, was received that day into the paradise of God?" The way in which the reporter framed Stedman's painful death, although perhaps hard to take at face value, matches the narrative that would give comfort to surviving comrades and family members.[38]

At least forty-one members of the Sixth were killed or mortally wounded at Gettysburg, although the total number continued to rise during 1864 as men finally succumbed to infections or pneumonia brought on by their wounds. Ten would be discharged by early 1864; two of the wounded men would desert, while four more would be discharged for illness. Twenty-four men of the Sixth would transfer to the Veteran Reserve Corps during the last few months of 1863; seventeen had been wounded, most likely at Gettysburg. In all, eighty-one men would leave the regiment sometime during the months after they charged the Railroad Cut, leaving it with no more than 170 men.[39]

A few months after Gettysburg, a member of the Sixth wrote a letter that appeared in the *Baraboo Republic*. "It's getting chillier," he wrote prosaically, but then with more feeling he added, "Winter takes but the leaves; war takes the forests, and the modest little rivulet, concealed and protected by the strong branches of luxuriant oaks is stripped of its guardian giants and laid bare to the unshrinking gaze of the sun." The bloody summer just passed seemed to have flown by. "Very often you can hear some one ask: 'Why, where has the summer gone?'" The answer: "Half of it was swallowed by Gettysburgh [*sic*]. A battle annihilates time." He was counting the days until his three years were up.[40]

An Uphill Business

In just over ten months, the Sixth Wisconsin had lost over 70 percent of its men—and the other regiments in the Iron Brigade had suffered even heavier casualties. Indeed, regiments in I Corps had been so diminished by deaths and discharges that its divisions were merged and sent to the reorganized V Corps early in 1864. The survivors somehow had to process that astonishing fact in their own ways. Back home, the obvious need for additional recruits once again thrust the issue of duty and sacrifice back into newspaper head-lines and family conversations. Around the time the Sixth made their mad, bloody dash toward the Railroad Cut, Wisconsin was coming to grips with the first Federal draft.[41]

Most of the public conversation revolved around commutations, the price of substitutes, and strategies for meeting local quotas. Eligible men organized "draft clubs" and "draft insurance associations" in a number of the towns and cities from which the Sixth had been drawn. The *Appleton Crescent* noted that "nearly every Western city and town have formed these organizations for mutual security against the hardships of the forthcoming draft." They were "calculated to exempt those whose means are limited, or whose circumstances are such that they could not leave home without making great sacrifices."[42]

The responses of the communities represented by the Sixth Wisconsin to the draft perfectly fit Brian Luskey's recent study of labor and military recruitment. Luskey places the scramble for recruits in the context of the aftershocks of the Panic of 1857; the extraordinary growth of government spending, leading to an equally impressive growth in opportunity for graft; and the increasingly misleading rhetoric about the dignity of "free labor," even as laissez-faire economics left laborers more rather than less vulnerable to market pressures. Soldiering came to be seen as a form of wage labor, as volunteers had to adjust to a dependent status and restricted freedom.[43]

The fall 1863 draft went off with far less controversy and violence than in 1862, although minor forms of resistance flared up throughout the fall. An 1880 history of Fond du Lac County—home to nearly five dozen members of the Sixth—offered a rather lighthearted account of the county's 1863 draft, when 20 percent of those drafted simply refused to turn up, citing a "sudden onset" of mysterious illnesses and news of deathly ill relatives. Twenty men allegedly stole away from the city of Fond du Lac for Canada in a single night, along with a couple of dozen others from Ripon and Waupon.[44]

Recruiters continued to promote the ever-expanding bounties. An ad that appeared multiple times in a number of newspapers informed readers that veteran volunteers who reenlisted for three years would receive $402 in installments and a month's pay in advance; nonveteran recruits would receive $302 and a month's pay. Full bounties would be paid even if the war ended before the term of service was up and to legal heirs if the recruit died. "Premiums" of up to thirty dollars would be paid for those bringing in acceptable recruits and for turning in deserters. "There is no moonshine about the large bounties offered by Uncle Sam," declared a newspaper from southwestern Wisconsin. "Every dollar will be paid. . . . Hurry up boys and enlist." Ultimately, a total of just over $750,000 was paid out in bounties to Wisconsin veterans and recruits in 1863.[45]

Capt. D. K. Noyes, still recovering from his wound in the famous shell explosion at Antietam and needing two canes to get around, was back in Wisconsin recruiting at about the same time. The federal draft had been held, but he doubted that it would provide much relief to the Sixth, or to the army for that matter. He predicted that only one drafted man out of twenty would actually serve, with most paying the $300 commutation fee or hiring a substitute (he was just off—about 6 percent of the 15,000 Wisconsin men actually drafted were mustered into service, and 5,000 bought their way out of the army). Indeed, 1863 saw only fifty-three volunteers and no draftees join the Sixth.[46]

The Iron Brigade would keep its name, and the name would continue to mean something to soldiers and civilians alike. But its extraordinary losses on the first day at Gettysburg—1,200 men, over 60 percent of the total who went into action—all but destroyed it as a fighting unit. It would see major changes in its regimental lineup in the last two years of the war. Only the Sixth and Seventh Wisconsin regiments would serve through Appomattox.

Despite Abner Doubleday's gracious compliment in his after-action report, the Sixth's contribution to the Union victory at Gettysburg was, according to a letter to an editor by James Sullivan twenty years later, "forgotten by all except a few veterans and cripples and the wives and mothers who lost all they held dear." But that fateful hour at Gettysburg would forever remain their most triumphant—and their most tragic—moment of the war.[47]

5

News Tonight, from the Field of Battle

"The men are cheerful, proud of Union deeds, and ready to fight again when necessary," wrote Edward Bragg to his wife Cornelia in late September 1862. He spent several paragraphs complaining about generals and politicians. "So long as our Governors waste their time & the Peoples money in pleasure trips . . . and talk about the Negro, and do nothing but talk and resolve— so long [will we] lie idle." Bragg was homesick and "tired of lying about in the dirt." His wounded hand and arm were sore but not badly injured. He had visited the hospitals, where the men were "doing <u>well</u>, and are in good spirits—which is everything." His military legacy never far from his mind, Bragg wrote that his coat, now bloodstained and ripped by a bullet, "was a new one, and I can hardly afford to keep it as a relic—but will have it repaired for now—the pieces will show where the ball passed through." His vanity extended to his children: "How are the babies all? Does my brave soldier boy put on airs, because Papa has been in four real battles?" His confidence in his immortality, or at least temporary immortality, had only grown since Second

Bull Run, and he even entertained an image of what would after the war become a familiar symbol of honorable sacrifice: "I don't believe I am going to be killed—I may lose that left arm in some fight, but I guess nothing more."[1]

It is probably not surprising that Bragg kept the gruesome truth from his wife and children; perhaps it took that kind of irrational confidence for him and other men of the Sixth to keep fighting. But the chatty tone and optimism of his letter are oddly jarring in the face of the reality of the regiment's troubling casualties and terrifying experiences on the battlefields of 1862 and 1863. Even those men who survived the battle without wounds were shattered by what they had witnessed at Antietam. Two days after that battle the regiment marched past "frightful . . . piles of dead" along the Hagerstown Turnpike. Rufus Dawes would later write that this site was what he compared every other battlefield to for the rest of the war—"the 'angle of death' at Spotsylvania, and the Cold Harbor 'slaughter pen,' and the Fredericksburg Stone Wall. . . . My feeling was that the Antietam Turnpike surpassed all in manifest evidence of slaughter." The "scene was indescribably horrible. Great numbers of dead, swollen and black under the hot sun"—Union and Confederate intermingled—"lay upon the field. My horse, as I rode through the narrow lane made by piling the bodies along beside the turnpike fences, trembled in every limb with fright and was wet with perspiration."[2]

The pioneering historian of Civil War battlefield photography, William A. Frassanito, identified as Louisianans a dozen or more Confederates lying dead along the fence at the side of the Hagerstown Pike in one of the best known of Matthew Brady's photographs—one man twisted onto his side, an arm frozen hauntingly in the air, as though he died while reaching for help or comfort. They belonged to the brigade that attacked the Sixth as it advanced along the road early in the battle, near the Miller farm, and just before the brigade redeployed and the Sixth entered the Cornfield. Although the photographs—included among those featured in the famous exhibition at Brady's studio in New York a month later—were taken two days after the fighting, and the bodies had already been disfigured by decomposition, they still show a scene with which men of the Sixth would have been familiar: bodies jumbled together, heads lodged against splintered fence rails; arms akimbo or clutching at wounds or personal belongings. Indeed, dead and wounded members of the Sixth would sprawl along a similar fence in a field west of Gettysburg less than a year later.[3]

The men of the Sixth usually refrained from describing the worst of the carnage they witnessed and rarely commented on the damage done to their dead and wounded comrades. Yet, like all Civil War soldiers, they witnessed unimaginable assaults on the human body. Edwin Brown's face and head must have been ravaged when he was shot in the mouth. The picturesque descriptions of Capt. Werner von Bachelle lying peacefully on the ground, arms crossed, failed to note the ways in which the dozen bullets that struck must have torn apart his clothes and body. The tragic story of friendship and sacrifice of two boyhood friends, William Black and Franklin Gerlaugh, immediately captured the romantic imagination of their hometown of Freedom and of Wisconsinites ever since. But Black had been shot through the forehead—the bullet might have exploded out a different part of his skull—and Gerlaugh was shot through the throat, no doubt drenching his uniform and anyone near him with blood.[4]

No civilian could imagine the grime and gore of a field hospital. Yet those in Wisconsin receiving news of the dead and injured among the Sixth became enmeshed in fear, grief, and desperation for more information that would be repeated after every battle for every regiment in every state, north and south, until the end of the war. For the Sixth Wisconsin and its communities at home, the last months of 1862 and much of 1863 would be dominated by an ever-growing list of the dead and wounded, each new loss tied to new suffering.

This suffering was rooted in more than grief and fear for the fate of Wisconsin's fighting men. Soldiers' families had to adjust not only to the absence of loved ones but to uncertain incomes, tightened belts, and, for some, genuine poverty. The women left behind by spouses or sons had to figure out how to feed their children and maintain farms or businesses. In addition to the emotional toll of the absence of breadwinners, coparents, dutiful sons, or other family members, those dependents found housing and feeding themselves to be a fundamental challenge.

It May Not Be So Bad as We Give

During its first year in Virginia, news from the Sixth Wisconsin encompassed entertaining stories about camp life and inspiring vignettes of patriotism. That would change during the Sixth's autumn of battles. The first notice of combat in Virginia in the *Baraboo Republic* appeared a few days after Gainesville, although it did not mention the battle itself. Headlined "Gallant Conduct of Some Invalid Wisconsin Soldiers," the front-page article described the successful effort by a ragtag group of guards and men on the sick list to defend a wagon train from Confederate raiders. The editors seemed to know that a bigger fight had occurred, however; on an inside page the editor called for ladies to come to the post office to prepare bandages, lint, and other medical supplies to send to the army. A week later, the *Republic* had a better grip on what had happened and amplified its call for assistance. "Our brave boys of Co. A, in the 6th Regiment, were probably in the recent battles near Washington, and . . . if a single life of that company could be saved by our utmost exertion, who would hesitate to make it?"[5]

In mid-September, as more detailed news of the fighting in late August would have begun drifting back in personal letters and notices in papers all over the state, and three weeks after Gainesville and Second Bull Run, an original poem by "Elizabeth" appeared in the *Appleton Crescent*:

> . . . News tonight, from the field of battle!
> Have ye not heard it?—quick and tell.
> From the far-away plains where the cannon rattle,
> And our brave ones stand 'mong the shot and shell.[6]

Learning that a family member was dead or wounded was just the beginning of a long process of certification—the accuracy of published casualty lists was famously unreliable, and the effort by well-meaning comrades, bureaucrats, and editors to inform families promptly could lead to heartbreaking mistakes. One newspaper admitted that "we know not what reliance can be placed in the list of killed and wounded which we publish today. The names in many instances were very indistinct—not being spelled rightly, and in our endeavor to give a full list, we may be in error. We would advise the friends of the annexed list to hope, it may not be so bad as we give."[7]

Most local newspapers would publish overviews of the battles—usually copied from eastern newspapers—but the Sixth and its companies would be mentioned only in passing in official accounts. Letters from soldiers tended to fill in the gaps, although, again, they tended to be focused on one man's vantage point or one company's experiences. Indeed, one of the first casualty lists published in Wisconsin after the Sixth's initial battles came in the form of a letter from one of the wounded, Company A's Capt. D. K. Noyes. Taking up two full columns, his account included his reaction to the shock of battle—"It was terrible. The cries and groans of the dying and wounded, oh!"—and a rushed but straightforward list of the casualties in Company A:

> John Starks, in leg, pretty bad; Philip Hoefer, in neck, bad; Peter Stackhouse, in leg, not bad; Harvey Clay, in arm, arm amputated at shoulder. I fear he may not survive as he was left at Manassas, as he could not be moved, and is cared for by the enemy, I presume. Dayton

Hedges was there the last heard of, and he may be able to take care of Clay. Clay was a brave soldier.—Wm. L. Lively, wounded in lg, not bad; Phillip Nippert, wounded in hips, bad, and missing, probably a prisoner; Wm. Klyne, wounded in leg, slightly.[8]

Noyes's account appeared on September 17—the same day that the Sixth charged into the Cornfield at Antietam. A week later, reporting that Company A had been "fearfully cut up," the *Republic* published a list of the fallen at South Mountain and Antietam. There was also no attempt to sugarcoat the cost.

George C. Miles, dead
J. C. Langhart, dead
John C. Weldman, dead
Capt. Noyes, foot amputated
A. H. Young, both arms amputated

And so on. Newspapers would report the status of soldiers still hospitalized from wounds suffered in the fall of 1862 from time to time through spring 1863.[9]

The most complete version of the wreckage left by the battles fought between August 28 and September 17 appeared on October 8, when Norman Eastman, the secretary of the Wisconsin Soldiers' Aid Society, published a "list as of September 26 of Wisconsin soldiers in hospitals in Frederick, Middleton, Boonsboro, and Keedysville, Md." It was filled with the names of Iron Brigade soldiers, along with each soldier's company and type of injury, and the location of the hospital where he was being treated. Forty-nine members of the Sixth appeared on the list. It also included the grave sites of men who had died just after the battle or in the hospital: two were in Boonsboro; nineteen were "buried on the road between Sharpsburg and Hagerstown" (this includes Captain von Bachelle, so these are probably the men buried under the locust tree near the Dunker Church); and another half dozen were buried "on Blue Ridge, one half mile from the Tavern facing Middletown, MD," a village on the road to Frederick.[10]

Months later, after most of the wounded had died, been discharged, or returned to the regiment, a soldiers' aid representative from Wisconsin reported on the scattered resting places of more men, including several who had died of their wounds days or weeks after the battle. In a graveyard near Keedysville, the bodies of the two childhood friends Franklin Gerlaugh and William P. Black, who had died at almost the same moment in the fighting along the Hagerstown Pike early in the Battle of Antietam, were buried in the same grave under a marble slab featuring their names and ages and the epitaph "Rest, Brave Soldiers, Rest." Abraham Fletcher had died at a private residence and was buried in its yard; there was no gravestone, but if one asked, the "grave will be pointed out by Mr. Lantz." Ten or twelve additional graves of men from the Sixth had "nothing whatever to distinguish them," although family members could purchase marble slabs for sixteen dollars each from a local man. Other soldiers were buried near the sites of makeshift hospitals in Smoketown and Boonsboro.[11]

Learning that in less than a month 80 of the men in the Sixth had been killed or mortally wounded, with nearly 150 more badly injured, must have been a tremendous shock. Families in fifty-four different communities throughout Wisconsin and in Iowa, Illinois, Minnesota, and Michigan would eventually receive the dreaded news, sometimes months afterward, as men gradually succumbed to their wounds. It would take months, even years, for the true cost of Gainesville, Second Manassas, South Mountain, and Antietam to be known. The army would eventually discharge ninety-eight men from the Sixth for disabilities caused by wounds suffered at one of those battles, mostly in the fall of 1862 or winter of 1863, but others—as some men no doubt tried to stick it out with their companies and others needed extended treatment in hospitals—did not receive their discharges until 1864 or even early 1865.[12]

The intense fighting in Virginia spurred aid societies into equally intense action. Surgeon General William A. Hammond called for "the loyal women and children of the U.S." to replace the exhausted supply of lint used to pack wounds. Any woman or child could scrape lint, "and there is no way in which their assistance can be more usefully given than in furnishing us the means to dress the wounds of those who fall in defence of their rights and their homes." The women of Madison and the surrounding region were encouraged to bring to the post office "such articles as they can from their own homes, to aid in preparing a box of these necessary things." Instructions for making bandages—the kind of cloth (washed cotton, sturdy enough to "bear a hard pull") and the proper dimensions—were also published.[13]

Reports on Sixth Wisconsin men in eastern hospitals drifted back to the state until well after the first of the year. By then, however, men who had survived their wounds but were not fit to take up arms again were being discharged and sent home. During the first four months of 1863 alone, the descriptive roll shows that at least eighty-one men were discharged from the Sixth. Forty-seven had been wounded; the rest were apparently discharged for illness. Some could pick up normal lives. About a fifth of them returned to wives and children; several married over the next two or three years. At least three died before the war ended.[14]

From these returning men, close friends and families no doubt heard the stories about the nighttime attack up South Mountain and the exhilarating and horrific fighting in the Cornfield. By the late fall and winter of 1862, "the Iron Brigade" and "Bragg's Sixth" meant something back in Wisconsin. But 1863 was also the year that the home front really had to come to grips with casualties in the Sixth Wisconsin. This was especially true for those wives and mothers who had to care for men worn out by war or too sick to work or who had to change the bandages as wounds took months and even years to heal. Although the gulf between the soldiers and civilians would never close completely, this intimate exposure to the wages of war brought some of the latter a bit closer to the experiences of the former.

The Most Lonesome Day I Ever Spent

One aspect of the soldiers' experiences that civilians could have learned only from the wounded men returning home was the extraordinary system of medical care that evolved during the war. Neither soldiers nor civilians had any conception of a hospital when the war began. There had been hospitals in the United States before the Civil War, but most were small affairs, devoted to orphans, paupers, and pregnant women. Without technology or medicines to guarantee routine treatments, most actual medical care took place in the home, with nursing provided by midwives and other women and a few poorly trained doctors. Early hospitals, in the words of one historian, served "a vague population of individuals incapacitated by illness, disability, mental impairment, senility, and social isolation . . . as well as lack of money." A few people might have recalled tales of military hospitals during the War with Mexico, but they would also have been much smaller and far from the eyes of worried family members or civilians living nearby. And it would not have mattered much to the men and families of the Sixth, since only a handful of men or relatives of men in the regiment had fought in Mexico. There were no hospitals in the state's largest city, Milwaukee, until the local Roman Catholic bishop brought in French nuns from the Sisters of Charity to create St. Mary's Hospital in 1848 on the County Poor Farm. The second hospital appeared in 1863, when Milwaukee Lutheran was established on the western edge of the city.[15]

But most Milwaukeeans, let alone Wisconsinites, would have had little if any conception of a hospital of any kind, much less one with a mission of healing. The war would begin to change all that. The term "hospital" suggests the organization and cleanliness carefully photographed in general hospitals far to the rear. But wounded and sick soldiers had a long and painful journey before they reached those tidy havens. The places to which the wounded of the Sixth were taken after South Mountain and Antietam, for instance, in small towns or hamlets like Sharpsburg, Keedysville, and others, were damaged houses and barns, if they were lucky, tents, or blankets thrown over tree branches and ropes, surrounded by battered cornfields and trampled pastures, overlain with smoke and the growing stench of dead men and horses. "All the houses, barns, outbuildings, stacks and the rail fences were used to shelter the wounded," recalled a veteran. "Operating tables everywhere. It was not an uncommon sight to see wagons drawing off loads of legs and arms to be buried." He had gone several days in the hospital without food, and "hundreds died for lack of attention." James Sullivan, shot in the foot at South Mountain, laid for one or two nights on a straw pile in a barnyard, where his wound was bandaged by another man from the regiment. He was offered but refused a shot of brandy, and he lay next to a man whose arm and part of his torso had been shot away by a cannonball. Although local civilians and doctors rallied and saved untold lives at these makeshift "hospitals," the wounded were taken "as fast as possible . . . to the general hospitals all over the country."[16]

Wounds were complicated by exposure, as men roasted in the sun or froze in the dark, lay in the rain or sleet, fouled themselves because they were unable to move, and became dangerously dehydrated. An infection could begin long before they were brought into a field hospital, where only the most basic and sometimes heroic (in a medical sense) measures could be performed. As a result, diarrhea, respiratory ailments, and other conditions complicated the recovery of many wounded soldiers. It did not help that some treatments caused more vomiting and diarrhea—sometimes encouraged by the medical theories of the day—and further dehydrated patients, who were often plied with various alcoholic mixtures. Treatments prescribed by surgeons at Fairfax Seminary Hospital—where at least two men of the Sixth died and from which another deserted—were no doubt used in other hospitals. Doctors prescribed various kinds of gruel (cereal boiled in milk or water), eggs (raw or soft-boiled), dried beef and crackers, chicken and potatoes, and even stewed oysters and custard. What seems particularly odd to modern

Americans is the amount of alcohol doctors prescribed. Virtually everyone received brandy for days or weeks at a time, in a "milk-punch," mixed with eggnog, or even straight up. A milder alcoholic concoction was "wine-whey," made of milk and white wine. The central place of alcohol in Civil War–era medicine is reflected in the fact that, when a young surgeon headed out to a Virginia hospital in August 1862, he took with him 4,800 bottles of whiskey, brandy, and sherry and 2,600 blankets. If one assumes one patient per blanket, that would mean that each patient was expected to consume well over a bottle and a half of an alcoholic beverage in a matter of days![17]

Because of its proximity to Washington and Baltimore, its location on a rail line, and its excellent sources of water and gas lighting, Frederick, Maryland, emerged as a major medical center for the Union army. After South Mountain and Antietam, the medical corps took over churches, schools, private homes, and other buildings and erected a number of temporary structures. Eventually there were at least twenty-nine hospitals that held a number of men from the Sixth.[18]

A constant stream of ambulances made the twenty-mile journey from the temporary hospitals near Antietam to Frederick, each carrying up to six men. Even a fortnight after Antietam more than 100 ambulances arrived every day. Soldiers able to walk made the journey on their own. A large percentage of the men stayed in Frederick for only a few days before being sent on to larger, better-equipped hospitals in Washington, Baltimore, or Philadelphia. Yet one local resident estimated that there were 6,000 to 8,000 patients in Frederick for weeks after the fighting; on any given day, one would meet scores of them, including amputees, wandering the streets.[19]

Men from the Sixth were scattered through nearly a dozen of Frederick's hospitals. Ten were assigned to the largest, General Hospital No. 1, a rambling collection of stone buildings, hurriedly constructed and drafty barracks, and miscellaneous other structures. Among the thousands of wounded who passed through this hospital were about 200 with compound fractures of the thigh bone and severe wounds to the knee. These were among the most dangerous wounds; many resulted in amputations, and many others resulted in deadly infections. Indeed, a number of the Wisconsinites treated there suffered from injuries to their knees and thighs. Other men were housed in churches, schools, and a fire hall. Among those in Hospital No. 6 was Sgt. Jasper Chestnut of Company C, who was shot in the lower right arm at Antietam. His wound never healed correctly; a partial amputation was performed in early December, but he "wasted away gradually" and died in late January 1863. Several seriously wounded Wisconsinites remained in Hospital No. 3

for many months; E. B. Cornish, for instance, did not receive a discharge until March 1863.[20]

The road to recovery for the most seriously wounded men of the Sixth would have been long and littered with dangers. In addition to poor Chestnut, several men from the Sixth suffered amputations after Antietam, including Ariss Young, who lost both arms; D. K. Noyes, who lost a foot; Henry Brady, who lost his left arm; John W. Frodine, who lost a leg; and William Darling, who lost his left foot. Although exact treatments obviously varied for different kinds of amputations, some of the shared experiences after the initial amputation (either soon after the wound occurred or after other treatments failed) may have included receiving painkillers in the form of morphine, which was sometimes applied directly to the wound prior to bandaging but taken orally afterward. After amputating a limb, a doctor smeared flaxseed poultice on the stump to stave off inflammation, then packed it in lint and wrapped it in several yards of linen bandages. Hanging out of the ends of the bandages would have been at least several—and perhaps as many as twenty—silk strings. Each was attached to a ligature, or knot, used to tie off arteries. When the arteries had rotted away and no longer carried blood, the ligatures could be pulled off. A constant worry was that the ligatures would come loose, causing dangerous bleeding and forcing surgeons to reopen the wound and repeat the procedure. Many patients had to be rebandaged, and a number died when the ligatures failed. Indeed, Frodine's stump developed a necrosis that caused his wound to hemorrhage, killing him a month after the battle.[21]

At least some of the Sixth's wounded developed "hospital gangrene" when a major outbreak spread through the hospitals in Frederick. The famous Union surgeon Silas Weir Mitchell described its sudden and horrific appearance: "A slight flesh wound began to show a gray edge," which could widen at the rate of half an inch an hour. The infection caused skin to lose definition, become discolored, form ulcers, and literally sag away from the bone and muscle. It was one of the most commonly mentioned conditions described by army surgeons. Their only recourse was to cauterize the affected area by, according to the leading manual for military surgeons at the beginning of the war, "mopping the affected surface freely with strong nitric acid," which would have caused intense burning and pain and turned the skin yellow. The death rate in any given hospital could reach nearly 50 percent.[22]

The Roster of Wisconsin Volunteers in the War of the Rebellion, 1861–1865, two different newspaper reports, and hospital records reveal that at least 151 different members of the Sixth Wisconsin were sent to hospitals in the days or weeks after the battles of August and September. This does not count those men who either died in field hospitals nearer the battlefield—primarily at Antietam—or were only slightly wounded and returned to duty soon after. Of those 151 men, half eventually returned to duty. Five more died, seven eventually ended up in the Veteran Reserve Corps, and fifty-two were discharged from the army. These sources do not tell us how long the men who returned to duty lingered in one hospital or another before rejoining their comrades, but at least thirty-one men who did so stayed for a time in general hospitals in Washington, Baltimore, or Philadelphia, so their absence was probably a matter of weeks rather than days.

Virtually all transfers from hospitals in Frederick were completed in ten days or fewer. Five men from the Sixth apparently too badly injured to travel remained in Frederick hospitals for between 73 and 239 days. Of the fifty-three men of the Sixth who were discharged from the service, about 60 percent were discharged straight from Frederick hospitals; others were discharged much later. Some seem to have been sent home to Wisconsin to await discharge. From the limited evidence available, and discounting two men who spent 515 and 309 days, respectively, in hospitals before leaving the service, it seems that for wounded men from the Sixth, the average number of days between being admitted to a hospital—not counting time spent in field hospitals—and discharge was 108 days.

Although soldiers might not have thought about it at the time, the ways in which medical care was administered to them was on the cusp of a major change. Wounded and sick members of the Sixth would have noticed the appalling lack of organization, at least early in the war, the overwhelmed and undertrained surgeons, and the sometimes nearly sadistic treatments. But their suffering would pave the way for a modernization of military medicine that would leave a legacy lasting into the twentieth century.

US Army surgeons, determined to learn from the carnage, produced the *Medical and Surgical History of the War of the Rebellion, 1861–1865*, a massive six-volume compilation and analysis of scores of thousands of cases of wounds and illnesses, broken down by type. Army surgeons submitted reports and, when possible, actual specimens of shattered bones, amputated limbs, necrotic organs, and every other kind of sample imaginable. Many of the specimens collected by surgeons in the field and sent to Washington were exhibited in the Army Medical Museum, which was intended as a teaching museum but also welcomed thousands of curious visitors every year—including some soldiers who came to visit the limbs they had lost on southern battlefields, now preserved by carbolic acid in glass jars.[23]

Men from the Sixth provided a number of specimens, and several dozen of them appear in the *Medical and Surgical History*'s many tables of various wounds and treatments that listed the names, regiments, and dates of wounding and discharge or death of thousands of soldiers. A few appear in more elaborate descriptions of cases, including treatments and outcomes, which provide details about what individual men actually experienced. These were the stories that their families would have come to know in late 1862 or 1863—from survivors or returned comrades—but told with dispassionate jargon. The most extensive accounts of the experiences of men from the Sixth were of Jasper Chestnut, the man who had "wasted away" after being shot in the wrist at Antietam, and of John Crawford of Company K, who was shot in the knee at Gettysburg and captured. Confederate surgeons amputated his leg above the knee. His case got a long paragraph in the *Medical and Surgical History*. For months he suffered from diarrhea, fever, loss of appetite, and extensive pain. An abscess developed near the exposed bone; another surgery removed more of Crawford's leg. Surgeons performed yet another surgery in early 1864, and after surviving one of those often-deadly hemorrhages, Crawford was finally discharged a few months later. Two specimens of his bones were sent to the museum. Most other wounded members of the Sixth received shorter notices, although images of bits of their bones, submitted as specimens, were published as lithographs.[24]

Portraits of two men of the Sixth, both wounded late in the war, were featured in the *Medical and Surgical History*. Chauncey Winsor was shot in the right shoulder at Gravelly Run; surgeons removed the head of the humerus but left the arm. A photograph was taken of Winsor, shirt pulled down to his waist, showing the still healing bullet hole and gash stretching five or six inches below the wound that was the result of the surgery. At about the same time, a shell took away part of the lower jaw of draftee Ferdinand Lauersdorf; in a photograph taken after his treatment ended, the wound is healed, and a beard has begun to obscure his partially missing lower jaw and the deep scar running from just under his left cheek to his throat.[25]

We can usually only surmise the deeper feelings of wounded men—they often simply described their experiences, however appalling. But one member of the Sixth, George Fairfield, left what seems likely to have been a common response of men to the immediate aftermath of being wounded and sent to a hospital. Fairfield was wounded at South Mountain and ended up in a hospital in Washington. In his diary he recorded the depression that fell over him when he had the chance to think about his experiences. It was "the

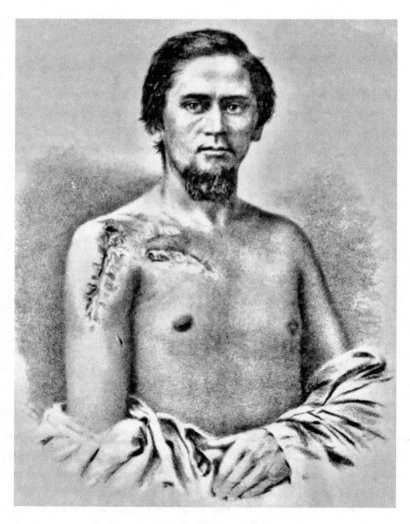

Chauncey Winsor. From Otis, *Medical and Surgical History of the War of the Rebellion*, pt. 2, 2:544.

most lonesome [day] I ever spent," thinking about "earlier days, the many kind friends that are far away[,] the remembrances of happier days" and of "schoolmates and teachers. I always loved school and books and will cease to love and think of them when I cease to breathe. I tried to sleep upon my bed but could do no more than . . . look about upon human misery and distress." Although "an old comrade was by my side who had braved the hardships of march and the dangers of battle with me . . . to converse with him was now no relief. I wanted to turn to some old Schoolmate or friend and hear the

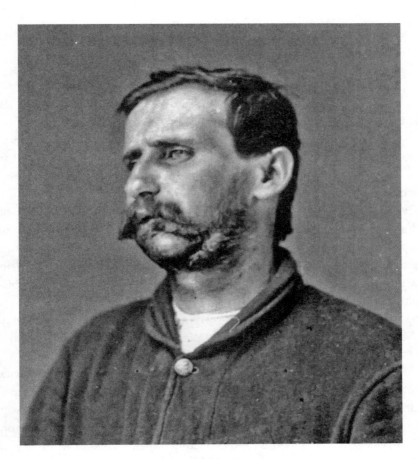

Ferdinand Lauersdorf. Otis Historical Archives, National
Museum of Health and Medicine, Silver Spring, MD.

milder tales of civil life. My wishes could not be gratified and I worried along till about twelve when I fell asleep."[26]

Fairfield's mournful account of his stay in the hospital—he would recover and fight through the expiration of his term in 1864—highlights the gulf that soldiers felt between their prewar lives and wartime existence. Of course, there are no lonelier places than a hospital, however busy, but Fairfield's longing to talk to someone who had not experienced war, who could not imagine the blood and pain and fear that were a soldier's companions, shows how precious those memories could be to soldiers and how far away they actually were.

Shall They Suffer While Their Brave
Ones Are Battling for the Union?

Sadly, the voices of the families of the Sixth Wisconsin are difficult to find in the archives. But some surely expressed the fears and frustrations that appeared in the letters written by the wives of men in other regiments. For instance, Margaret Patchin, whose husband Augustus was a sergeant (and later lieutenant) in the Tenth Wisconsin, frequently expressed her regret that he had enlisted and often urged him to resign or at least get a furlough. She achingly communicated her love for him and kept him up to date on their several children. Margaret also worried a great deal about finances. It helped that Augustus was earning more than a private's thirteen dollars a month, especially when he was promoted to lieutenant halfway through the war, but she fretted about his irregular paydays. She had to hire neighbor boys to help with the harvest, and the timing of Augustus's wages likely had practical implications as well as an impact on her pride in being able to pay her debts. Yet by fall 1863, despite her frequent expressions of concern, between the money she took in from the harvest and what Augustus was able to send home, she assured him that they were doing well financially, if not emotionally.[27]

When Morris Waldo joined the First Wisconsin Cavalry, his young wife Ann and their baby moved in with her parents, like many other wives, especially those with young children. Ann wrote Morris often, keeping him up to date on their daughter's development but also worrying about "living on charity" in her family's home and collecting unpaid debts for work he had done for other farmers prior to enlisting.[28]

An overview of public generosity—and the limits of that generosity—appears in local newspapers, which chronicled the needs of soldiers' families through the reporting of ad hoc efforts to help. A Madison man offered to provide milk at half price to the families of volunteers, while a Mauston doctor provided his services to soldiers' families free of charge and a meeting of citizens in Dodgeville began a subscription to raise money to buy firewood for soldiers' families.[29]

The most consistent aid came from the state government, which began offering five dollars per month for the families of volunteers in the summer of 1861. In addition, local and county governments regularly set up relief funds to be administered by existing or ad hoc agencies. A typical process had several steps, beginning with aldermen or county supervisors creating lists of the wives of volunteers and their young children and their likely needs in the coming year. The city council tightly controlled aid in Appleton, requiring recipients to be recommended by aldermen. Milwaukee's Office of the Relief Committee hired an agent to visit soldiers' families and report on their "precise condition and wants," which would guide the committee's apportionment of benefits. The Milwaukee Soldiers' Aid Society branched out to assist soldiers' families to get state payments, find jobs for soldiers' wives and mothers and for partially disabled soldiers, and provide for widows and orphans.[30]

Although a great deal of time and energy were, indeed, poured into campaigns to aid soldiers and their families, it was never enough. Less than a year into the war, Governor Alexander Randall's annual message to the legislature noted that, although there were currently at least 700 outstanding applications for aid from families of volunteers, the war fund was exhausted. "It will not answer to let these matters remain as they now are much longer," complained Louis Harvey, who succeeded Randall in early 1862. "The mails are coming loaded down with letters setting forth the wants and sufferings of the families of volunteers. . . . And what answer can I make to them?"[31]

Politics marred the state's program to aid soldiers' families. There was more than a little of the traditional concern that recipients of public aid would become too accustomed to it, and that somewhere, somehow, someone was taking advantage of the system. Democrats demanded that captains of military companies in the field be required to provide lists of men still serving their country—they worried that discharged, deserted, and dead soldiers' families were still receiving aid—and that local justices of the peace check to make sure women who applied were actually married to soldiers. Those rules failed to pass, but Democrats were able to block temporarily a continuation of the war fund in 1862, although it survived and expanded so that during the fiscal year ending September 30, 1864, the payouts to those families was the largest single expenditure in the state budget, at $615,693.68, which dwarfed the next highest line item by more than half a million dollars. Over the course of the war the legislature would also fund various kinds of medical care, protect soldiers in active service and their families who fell behind in their taxes and mortgage payments, and expand and define more carefully aid to soldiers' families.[32]

And yet, at the local level, a certain kind of war-weariness crept into local campaigns on behalf of soldiers' families. In a late 1863 editorial warning of the dire need that would threaten many families during the coming winter, the *Appleton Crescent* reported that "some of these suffering and helpless have not seen a pound of meat or a cup of tea or coffee for weeks!—Some have to saw their own wood" or scrounge for downed branches. "Shall they suffer from cold and hunger while their brave ones are battling for the Union, or sleeping in a Soldier's Grave?" the *Crescent* asked. How "can you expect men to volunteer while Soldiers' families starve at home?"[33]

At least some counties tried to bridge the gap between need and public responsibility by folding aid for soldiers' families into antebellum forms of poor relief. Only a few months' worth of the records of the Soldiers' Relief Commission in Milwaukee County survive; during that time the county awarded a total of $13,653. About two dozen soldiers in the Sixth and their dependents appear in the "Descriptive Roll of Milwaukee County Volunteers & Drafted Soldiers" that listed the soldier by company and rank, name and residence of the person receiving the money, and the amount awarded. The amounts given out over the course of the year ranged from twelve dollars to as much as sixty dollars. Unlike state aid, which was cut off when the soldier left the service for any reason—including death—several of the soldiers on Milwaukee's list had died prior to 1864, but their dependents seemed to have remained on the rolls for at least a few months.[34]

Recognizing that many men hesitated to enlist out of concern for their families' welfare, the government awarded bounties to the enlistees of 1863 and 1864; by early 1864, the families of men who reenlisted would receive four quarterly payments of $100. One newspaper argued that the bounty, together with a soldier's monthly salary and sixty dollars a year in state aid, would give a soldier's family a total of $652 for the year. The message: taking carefully calculated risks would net significant benefits to men shrewd enough to take advantage of the government's desperation. And men, assuming they were able to get that money into the hands of their families, could rest assured that most of life's necessities would be provided.[35]

Only those soldiers who enlisted in the fall of 1863 or after, or who survived long enough to become veteran volunteers in 1864, would receive enough in wages and bounties to replace their prewar income. Although price information is not available for the war years, we can get an idea of the cost of living by taking a look at the average cost of basic food items immediately after the war. The amount of food consumed by individual families would vary greatly, of course, but US Army rules for soldiers' rations may give us a (very) rough baseline for the amount of money families might expect to pay for the most basic of food items. In 1861 the army established as a daily ration twelve ounces of pork or bacon or twenty ounces of fresh or salt beef and twenty-two ounces of flour or soft bread. Assuming that women and children would consume somewhat less than a soldier, and using a table of prices for a long list of foodstuffs in Wisconsin from just after the war, we can offer the following monthly estimate of the cost of these staples for a family of four:

- three pounds of beef per person, per week,
  at fourteen cents per pound: $1.68
- a bushel of flour every two weeks, at $9.66 per bushel: $19.32
- perhaps 2.5 quarts of beans per person, per
  month, at ten cents per quart: $2.50

Add a dozen eggs per week, per family, which would cost eighty-four cents, and a cup of coffee each morning, which might cost seventy-two cents per month, and the monthly total for the most basic of diets consumed by a family of four (which would cover a large majority of Sixth Wisconsin families) comes to just over twenty-five dollars—far above the funds available to a private prior to the 1864 bounties. Families who needed wood for cooking and warmth—at least one cord per month (probably more in the winter)— would need an additional $5.25 for the cheapest, fastest-burning wood.[36]

Of course, a majority of the men in the Sixth Wisconsin were farmers, much of whose income would be measured in bushels of wheat or heads of cattle rather than wages; virtually all would also have raised at least some of the food consumed by their families. But a very—*very*—rough way to estimate how far the available resources could be stretched is to compare them to the average wage of unskilled and agricultural laborers, which nationally hovered a few cents on either side of a dollar per day in the 1860s, or maybe something over $300 a year. A skilled craftsman—a carpenter, for instance— working in Wisconsin might make an average of $1.73 per day, or $10.38 for a six-day week. The five-dollars-per-month state stipend would cover roughly a week's wages for an unskilled laborer or farmhand; it would replace less than a week's wages for a skilled laborer.[37]

But only a tiny minority of families had to endure more than a year without their men (aside, of course, from those who died). A total of 573 married men entered the Sixth Wisconsin. Of the 240 in cohort 1 (the men who enlisted in the summer of 1861), a third had left the regiment within a year (five had died), another forty-four left in 1862 (twelve by death), and over sixty left the regiment in 1863 and 1864 (thirteen by death). None of the men who belonged to cohort 2 (the group enlisting in late 1863 and early 1864) served more than eighteen months; moreover, these families would have benefited from fairly substantial bounties. Finally, of the 290 draftees who were married, none were absent more than eight months.[38]

Length of absence was not the only factor shaping families' experiences. Edward Bragg's wife Cornelia could draw on the resources represented by her husband's $5,000 in real property and $3,000 in personal property, while Mary Marnell was no doubt at least partly supported by her husband Luke's $5,000 grocery business; both men served for four years, but their relative prosperity would have eased the financial burden on their families. Yet laborers' spouses like Sarah Metcalfe (with a three-year-old child) and Mary Langhoff (with three children and no property) would have had to rely on "state money" and their husband's private's wages. Perhaps eighteen-year-old Pearl Spooner, married to Cyrus just as the war was starting, went to live with his parents, who lived nearby; perhaps Margaret Powderly continued to work as a domestic and boarded with the family that she and husband Owen had lived with in 1860. Just over half of the married soldiers owned land—ranging in value from under $100 to several hundred or even thousands of dollars—that should have provided families with at least some rental income.[39]

From the available evidence, it seems that roughly fifty wives lived for at least three years without their husbands; their circumstances and resources varied widely. Just under half, like Ann Waldo, were basically newlyweds with no children or one very young child. It's likely that a number of them would have lodged with parents or other relatives. Some had substantial property or businesses that could, perhaps, have continued to operate with hired help. Several of the most experienced men would become sergeants or even junior officers; the rise in pay from enlisted man to second lieutenant was nearly ninety dollars per month—more than enough to cover expenses.[40]

Of course, some absences were permanent. The war made over eighty wives of the Sixth Wisconsin into widows. They could immediately apply for an eight-dollar monthly pension, although few did so with as much dispatch as the young wife of John Ticknor. Married less than a year, Kate Ticknor got the news of John's death at Gettysburg in July 1863; her application was submitted a fortnight after the battle. The extent to which the war had forced them to the edge of survival—especially those with young children—may be revealed in the speed with which some of them remarried. Frederick Bunzell was drafted in October 1864 and killed in action five months later; his wife Sophia married another veteran before the year was out. Ann Scott, only nineteen and the mother of three children under the age of three when husband John died at Hatcher's Run, was married in just over a year. Perhaps the quickest marriage occurred when Dutch immigrant Elizabeth, wife of another immigrant, draftee Arnoldus Zweerink, married yet another immigrant two and a half months after Arnoldus died in the regiment's last battle.[41]

One gets an even better idea of the desperation of some families—and the pittances that they were forced to live on—in the pension applications by dependent parents. Most applicants were mothers and widows, although some women applied because their husbands were unable to work. The Pension Bureau required these applicants to prove the level of support provided by their sons prior to the war; they viewed more kindly the cases in which sons had maintained their parents before entering the army. According to Jane Bates, her son Asbury had delayed enlisting until January 1864, at least partly because before entering the army his wages as a farm laborer were "entirely expended to the support of his parents." Old and sick, they were "very needy." With a bounty and his private's wages, Asbury would have made half again as much as he had earned before the war. He was shot in the neck at Petersburg and died in June 1864. Dennis Johnson had supported his mother on about $100 per year before enlisting as a substitute late in 1864; he died of typhoid less than three months later. Jane Russell seems to have needed even less to live on; a witness in her pension application declared that the eighty dollars her son Sylvester was able to provide each year kept her in flour, tea, butter, sugar, lard "and other necessaries."[42]

For a majority of the families of the Sixth Wisconsin, home-front economics would create problems that were never fully resolved.

However, in the end, it was the anxiety of waiting for news from the battlefield that animated the home front, where the fog of war and unreliable sources of information—in newspapers and personal letters alike—would raise an insurmountable barrier between the men of the Sixth and their families.

This was demonstrated in the misidentification of one of the regiment's prominent casualties at Antietam. A few days after the battle Cornelia Bragg received a telegram that brusquely said, "Your Husband was shot Yesterday," and indicated that his body was on its way home. Preparations were made for a hero's funeral—until another telegram arrived from Chicago, where a party of locals had gone to meet the body. It was, of course, not Bragg but Edwin Brown, whose corpse was too badly disfigured by his wound or too badly decomposed to be shown at the funeral that was held immediately after the escort brought the coffin to Fon du Lac.[43]

Bragg soon became aware of the mistake. Mrs. Brown "must feel the loss of her husband severely," Bragg wrote in his September 28 letter to Cornelia. "I wrote her a letter of condolence, a day or two since—it was difficult for me to do—but I thought it would be soothing to her feelings and gratifying to the family." Also gratifying were the compliments directed toward Bragg when he was thought dead: "By the way, I read my obituary in the *Madison Journal*, it was quite complimentary." The "obituary" he referred to may have been a paragraph that called him "a man of brilliant abilities" whose "life is not one of the least of the costly sacrifices" required by the war. "Long will the memory of the gallant soldier, the genial friend and warm hearted man survive him."[44]

Typically, Bragg had a hard time sticking to the tragedy at hand, focusing more on his own emotions and fantasies. He seemed captivated by the thought of a glorious death: "Only think of all the honors of a death & funeral." But he acknowledged in a later letter "how badly you must have felt, and how terribly [you] suffered." To "my little chicks" he wrote, "Did you really think poor papa was gone? And that you would never see him again? How bad you felt I know & and it almost makes Papa cry to think how you mourned for him. But how happy you were, when you heard he was not hurt much and was alive to come home again!"[45]

Of course, the relief felt by Cornelia Bragg and her "little chicks" was more than balanced by the sorrow that devastated Ruth Brown and her three young children, who were now part of the ever-increasing community of bereaved family members and friends whose lives were forever changed by the battles of 1862 and 1863.

6

Carnivals of Blood

1864

"We are in the midst of grand events," Rufus Dawes wrote his fiancée in mid-December 1863, "and the men who carve their names as representatives of the triumph of right in a struggle of such magnitude, will have a proud distinction in history." Having the chance to take part in "grand events" seemed decidedly unattractive to men who had yet to "carve their names" on enlistment papers. Capt. D. K. Noyes, out of commission since being wounded at Antietam, was on recruiting duty in Wisconsin. All but one of the seventeen men he had recruited had chosen to go into the cavalry; "I have tried them all for the Sixth, but it is no use, they must ride." He added with some bitterness, as a soldier missing out on the boom times in Wisconsin, that "the merchants are all getting rich."[1]

At the same time that their former comrade was leaning into the recruiting headwinds back home, the men of the Sixth were considering whether a thirty-day furlough and hundreds of dollars in bounties were worth committing to another three-year term. A lull of sorts in the fighting during the fall had given the regiment a chance to ponder the government's offer of a $402 bounty and a month at home, which would also come with the honor of remaining together as a "veteran" regiment. The term of enlistments for the Sixth Wisconsin and tens of thousands of other men in the Army of the Potomac would expire in the summer or early fall of 1864, and the War Department desperately worried about the loss of so many experienced officers and men. The reenlistment plan was floated in late summer 1863, and the regiment spent the autumn debating the question. There was a lot to think about. With the victories at Gettysburg and Vicksburg in July, the war seemed to be going better. No doubt many men wanted to see the war through, to live up to the pledges they had made back in 1861. Of course, $402 was real money, more than their total pay during their first two and a half years in the army. There may have been a cold calculation that, whether or not they reenlisted, they would have to fight what *might* be the climactic campaign of the war once the Virginia roads dried in May—three months before their enlistments were up. They might as well get the bounty and the furlough and take their chances. Finally, although the often-copied image, "A Soldier Dreams of Home," which they would have seen on patriotic stationery and Currier and Ives lithographs, was a cliché, the sentiment was real and the notion of spending a few weeks with friends and loved ones, sleeping in warm beds, and eating soft bread must have been a powerful selling point.[2]

In any event, as late as New Year's Eve, Dawes was still twenty-three men short and doubtful that the Sixth would become a veteran regiment. He complained that those who had risked less—or were at least out of harm's way in the fall of 1863—were least willing to extend their service. Dawes seemed somewhat disgusted that "nearly all" of the sixty-eight men on detached duty as cooks, teamsters, clerks, and so forth declined to enlist, while nearly all of the men "who have stood day after day in the presence of death, who have endured every sort of privation and suffering," had reenlisted, "present[ing] an example that should bring a blush of shame to the brows of the young men who have failed their country at this crisis."[3]

Perhaps one of the men at whom Dawes scoffed was James Schultz (or Shults) of Company B. Years later, when Schultz applied for a pension, nearly a dozen comrades filed affidavits that testified, almost to a man, that Schultz had been a terrible soldier who had escaped combat by feigning illness (he was also overweight and, one man said, "could not climb a hill without stopping" to catch his breath). One man said Schultz was "generally considered the only coward we had in Company B" and even accused him of inflicting his own wound and "trying to make it worse" in the hospital, although his accuser admitted "that was only talk and no one could prove it." Another remembered with a sneer that Schultz "was the Co[mpany]'s washerwoman," doing other men's laundry for pay. No one mourned Schultz's decision not to reenlist.[4]

His men proved Dawes wrong; just enough of the 290 eligible men re-enlisted for their unit to earn the title of a "Veteran Volunteer Regiment." Overall, about a third of the Army of the Potomac's soldiers reenlisted. The Seventh Wisconsin also reached the minimum, but the Second, which had suffered greater casualties than the rest of the brigade, did not, and many of its survivors would muster out in July 1864. A few score men from the Second with later enlistment dates were turned into an "independent" battalion, which in fall 1864 would be folded into the Sixth. The Nineteenth Indiana also failed to be recognized as a veteran regiment and would leave the brigade. Although the Iron Brigade would still exist, it would be in name only by summer 1864. It had already lost its cohesion as a "western" brigade when a Pennsylvania unit had joined it after Gettysburg; other eastern regiments would come and go during the rest of the war.[5]

One of the great questions of 1864 was why these men reenlisted. His-torians have tended to focus on ideology, comradeship, bounties, and the furlough. Lt. Earl Rogers thought that "three years should be sufficient in active service for any one," but "encouraged by bounty and the love of the excitement, many have reenlisted."[6]

Decades later one old soldier offered a hint that some deals had been made. Cyrus Spooner, who in late 1863 was worn down and suffering from a severe case of piles (hemorrhoids), claimed in his application for an in-crease in pension that he reenlisted only when the officers promised that he would be put on detached duty. If the deal was in fact offered, the officers kept their part of the bargain. Spooner spent the rest of the war at division headquarters or as a teamster for the commissary department. Eugene Hardy made a very different kind of bargain. Inspired by his abolitionist father and Edward Bragg's dramatic speech at the public meeting in Fond du Lac in 1861, Hardy had been one of the first volunteers in Company E. However, in 1863, after "some real or fancied insult from one of his officers," he deserted, "put on citizen's clothes," and traveled through New England and New York for a few months. He was eventually arrested and court-martialed but was not convicted when he agreed to reenlist. Taken prisoner in 1864, he died in Andersonville.[7]

Continuity of leadership, or at least familiarity with their leaders, may also have spurred reenlistments in some companies. Three of the companies with significant numbers of reenlistments enjoyed a certain comfort level with their officers. Thirty-one men from Company F—the German-dominated company from Milwaukee—reenlisted. Although the company had gone through three different captains in a year and a half—including Werner von Bachelle, killed at Antietam—its captain from fall 1862 through the summer of 1864, Otto Schorse, had joined the company as a sergeant and risen through the ranks. It seems reasonable to speculate that the elevation of one of the company's own contributed to a morale boost for the enlisted men.

Companies D and K reenlisted twenty-eight and twenty-six men, respectively. Company D was led by Thomas Kerr from the first day at Gettysburg through summer 1864, when he was promoted to major. He had been a corporal, sergeant, and lieutenant during his three years with the company. K was Rufus Dawes's company, of course, and although he was promoted to major before the company's first battle, he had led the regiment through two of its biggest fights and remained a major presence in the company even after he was promoted. Moreover, an original member of the company, William Remington, took the place of the beloved John Ticknor, killed at Gettysburg, and commanded the company for more than a year, including throughout the reenlistment period.[8]

The losses suffered by any given company (deaths from combat or disease, wounds, and illness severe enough to earn a discharge) may have also played a role. Heavy casualties among comrades and friends no doubt affected individual decisions differently. Virtually every company had lost about 50 percent of its men, and several had lost many more; those losses could have demoralized individuals or, on the contrary, inspired them to go on fighting so their comrades would not have died in vain. For instance, the company with the highest number of reenlistments, Company F, had suffered the fourth highest number of casualties, with sixty-six. The third lowest number of reenlistments occurred in Company A, with twenty; it had suffered the most casualties, with seventy-two. Almost exactly half of the veteran volunteers had been wounded at least once prior to reenlisting.[9]

Dora L. Costa and Matthew E. Kahn's study of soldiers' motivations does not explicitly address the choices of veteran volunteers in 1864, but their work provides useful insights. They focus on the social networks that influenced soldiers' decisions—to enlist, to desert, not to desert—which could override purely practical, even rational decision-making. A homogenous community—a regiment, or a company for that matter—is more cohesive and more likely to make similar decisions. Virtually all of the fewer than 300 veterans of the Sixth who had survived into the fall of 1863 came from the 1861 cohort. Many still identified with their core communities, their regiment, and their brigade, and that, as much as anything else, might have inclined them toward reenlisting.[10]

Men of the Sixth rarely talked about their decisions to reenlist, but it is easy to imagine their letters to family members in which they explained their reasoning, resisted or responded to pressure from home, implored wives and mothers to accept their decisions, reluctantly or enthusiastically accepted pleadings from children, and grimly made the calculations of betting their lives on surviving the dangers to come for the $402 bounty. One can also imagine soldiers sitting around campfires and shivering on picket lines, laying out their arguments for and against reenlisting, as men desperate for the money and the furlough encouraged more hesitant comrades, as officers explained the process yet again, as the damp weather, bad food, and more intimate longings offered very tangible disincentives.

Fifty years later, the men who talked about it may have preferred to believe that they reenlisted out of higher motivations than a bounty and a furlough. That was certainly the case with the historians of the Sauk County Riflemen: "Re-enlisted after two and one half years of suffering and privation; weary marches and disastrous campaigns; after passing through seven of the hardest fights and bloodiest battles of the war. Re-enlisted for three years more to fight in defense of the Union and to maintain the integrity of this nation. . . . Where is recorded a more exalted example of patriotism and loyalty!"[11]

Quiet, Peaceful Scenes

Warm welcome, soldiers, howsoe'er you come.
Whether you keep step to the stirring drum,
Or maimed and feeble, faltering and slow,
Sad victims of the conflict and the foe. . . .
We bid you welcome, oh ye valiant braves,
To happy lives or honorable graves.[12]

Although Park Benjamin's "To the Returned Soldiers" actually honored the three-month regiments returning in the early fall of 1861, his sentiments fit the homecomings of hundreds and thousands of men since then who had limped back from the front, crippled by wounds or disease. And it seemed appropriate to at least two Wisconsin newspapers to publish it in late January

1864, as the families and friends of the Sixth Wisconsin awaited the regiment's return on a thirty-day furlough.[13]

For the original cohort of Sixth Wisconsin men, the February 1864 furlough must have been a dreamlike interlude between nightmares. It was also no doubt disorienting to be among civilians who would have a limited understanding of what the men had been through. Perhaps the furlough gave the veterans a chance to tell their friends and families about a war that civilians could not imagine; perhaps they preferred to shield their loved ones from the truth.

It took the regiment two days to travel from Virginia to Wisconsin. They paused in Washington, DC, where they picked up new uniforms and Colonel Bragg retrieved the Second Mississippi battle flag from the War Department to show off back in Wisconsin. The men of the Sixth must have had mixed feelings of joy and relief, along with an awareness that this interlude of peace and quiet and warm embraces would be all too brief. Gen. Lysander Cutler had urged the Milwaukee Chamber of Commerce to throw "such a reception as is due to such a body of men." When their train arrived in Milwaukee at midnight on January 13, a large number of citizens greeted it "with vociferous cheering" and led them to their temporary quarters a few blocks away. The official reception at noon the next day included an escort from a local military company and the Thirtieth Wisconsin. Commanded by Col. Daniel J. Dill, the original captain of the Sixth's Company B, the Thirtieth had for a year and a half performed garrison duty in Wisconsin and St. Louis and in the Dakota War farther west. The reception featured a welcome from ex-governor Edward Salomon and "a brief and pithy" response from Colonel Bragg, who also led three cheers for "the bright eyes, sweet lips and loyal hearts that welcome us to-day." Local dignitaries gave speeches, and a glee club called Uncle Sam's Boys sang songs, including "All Hail to the Sixth," an original piece set to the tune of the "Battle Hymn of the Republic." A "sumptuous dinner" for 400 soldiers and civilians followed at the Newhall House hotel, which was decorated with the national colors and, again, featured patriotic music by the band. "Take it all in all," a local newspaper predicted, "this reception was an occasion that will long be remembered by all who took part in it."[14]

The men quickly scattered to their hometowns to be feted and pampered. Prescott greeted the survivors of Company B with a supper and "other things accordin'"; the list of members of the various organizing committees included at least one former member of the company, the wife of a former officer, and family members of several other current or former members of the company. Baraboo invited all members of the Sixth and Fourteenth Wisconsin (also home on furlough) to an "Oyster Supper and Festival." The crowded court-room was decorated with garlands, wreaths, and evergreen boughs framing flags, a copy of the Emancipation Proclamation, and "the (photographic) Record of the great battles of the Iron Brigade." A leader of the local soldiers' aid society welcomed the men, acknowledging "the vast contrast between the life in camp and on the battle field, and these quiet, peaceful scenes mid which we live," but hoped that their "visit will be so filled with pleasant and inspiring occasions . . . as to strengthen and encourage your hearts in lonelier hours."[15]

Viroqua and the vicinity pulled out all the stops for the men of Company I. An Oconto woman—supposedly a niece of the novelist James Fenimore Cooper—wrote a poem in honor of the Iron Brigade: "What makes Wisconsin's giant heart / Bound in her breast with joy and cheer, / And down her woman's lovely cheek, / Steal silently a glittering ear?" Why, "the *brave* have come, the *Iron Brigade*, / Home from the bloody field of death." The highlight was a grand ball in Ontario; seven wagonloads of "Co. I boys and their ladies and other friends" traveled the twenty-seven miles over snow-clogged roads to dance to the music of the Sparta Cotillion Band and enjoy a supper "put up in good style." The dancing lasted until morning. A "Farewell Ball" was given at the courthouse in Viroqua just before they headed back to Virginia.[16]

Although the furlough saw one man die of smallpox and another desert, there were also happier occasions.[17] At least eleven members of the regiment got married. Earl Rogers wed Amanda L. Williams in Viroqua on February 3, with many friends in attendance. "The happy couple and their friends took sleighs for Sparta, shortly after the knot was tied. The brave deserve the fair." Michael Bowler married Margaret Powderly—perhaps the sister of comrade Owen Powderly (also married to a Margaret)—in Milwaukee, while John Miles hurried out to Grant County to marry Lucretia Pittenger.[18]

One more member of the Sixth took advantage of the furlough to marry. Rufus Dawes left the regiment in Pittsburgh and hurried to Marietta, Ohio, where he married his longtime correspondent, Mary Gates. They left immediately for Milwaukee, where they visited friends and honeymooned in the Newhall House. In his memoir, Dawes wrote that while in Milwaukee he and Mary came across a room where, before leaving for their homes, the men had stacked their muskets, with belts and cartridge boxes hanging from them. Mary "never saw more than this of the Sixth Wisconsin." He seems to have begun a thought that he never finished—this organization in which he had come of age and had come to lead, that meant so much to him, would never be more to her than a room full of hard-used equipment. That short moment must have been for Dawes one more reminder of the vast distance between battlefront and home front.[19]

Surely there were tears and regrets when the time came to pick up their equipment in Milwaukee and return to the grim work awaiting them in Virginia. The *Baraboo Republic* reported that Company A had "left Baraboo on Monday last, in the best spirits. . . . Although still small in numbers, they are strong in the belief that the back-bone of the Confederacy is in a bad fix." Perhaps the men had intimated their motivations for reenlisting, or perhaps the editor was projecting his own thoughts when he concluded, "Having attentively watched its progress thus far, they desire to be 'in at the death.'"[20]

The furlough winter would be the last time that the folks back home would see these particular men as the Sixth Wisconsin; by the time the regiment returned home for good more than a year later, it would be made up of an almost entirely new set of men. Of the 227 who reenlisted, thirty-eight would die of wounds received in combat—including four of the grooms in the roll-the-dice furlough weddings—six would die of disease, and three would die in Confederate prison camps. Twenty-nine more would be wounded.[21]

Upon reaching Washington, Colonel Bragg gave a little speech just before the men boarded the train that would take them back to their camp near Culpepper Court House. "Men of the Sixth," Jerome Watrous remembered Bragg saying, "nearly three years ago you responded to your country's call for soldiers. How well you have done your duty the history of your part . . . written in blood, plainly tells." When their country needed more from them, "without hesitation you raised your right hands and gave a new pledge." He turned and pointed his sword at the US Capitol building. "For that flag, that capitol, and the nation they represent, we have done the best we could these past three years, and we here and now pledge anew our devotion to flag and country as long as our services are required." He then led the regiment in three cheers to the republic.[22]

As the echoes of their cheers died down and the Sixth filed into the cars, at least some no doubt drew comfort from memories of the last three or four weeks when they could force from their minds thoughts of demoralizing marches, degrading camp diseases, bad rations, and wounded comrades. Of course, our knowledge of the terrible cost of the war's last year lends the story of the veterans' furlough an exquisite poignancy. But even without the benefit of knowing the future, the thoughts of the inevitable summer campaign must have begun crowding out the more recent, happy memories of home as soon as they stepped out of the cars and trudged into camp.

Chapter 6

Not long after the Sixth Wisconsin arrived back in Virginia, Lt. Gen. Ulysses S. Grant took command of the Union armies. His blunt determination changed the conduct of the war and, with it, the fate of the Sixth—a regiment substantially changed from the one that had arrived in Virginia some eighteen months before.

The Transformation of the Sixth Wisconsin

Soon after they returned to camp, the men of the Sixth finally benefited from the bounties offered by the Federal government and by towns and cities across Wisconsin. Dawes reported the arrival of two different contingents of about 100 men each between January and April 1864. This was the largest group of reinforcements to reach the regiment since the war had begun.[23]

These groups of recruits—cohort 2, for the purposes of this study—differed from the 1861 cohort in several ways. They were on average two to three years younger, but more significant is that far more of them came from outside the county that provided the kernels of the original companies. Only 21 percent of the original men in Company A came from outside Sauk County, but 94 percent of its sixteen recruits in cohort 2 came from other counties. In only two companies—E, from Fond du Lac County, and I, from Vernon County—were the percentages of out-of-county recruits even close. In addition, fewer men in cohort 2 were known to be immigrants (16 percent to cohort 1's 20 percent) and fewer were married (21 percent compared to 28 percent). The overwhelming majority came from the more rural central and western parts of the state.[24]

One result of the arrival of the new men, according to Lance Herdegen, was that as early as spring 1864, with "strangers in many ways, serving in each company" and a massive turnover in officers, "the veterans, distrusting the new men, clung to themselves." The Sixth would experience this disruption most severely in the fall of 1864, but that summer would foreshadow the nearly complete transformation of the regiment. Veterans appreciated the presence of the new recruits as a practical matter—the burdens of warmaking were dispersed among more men, obviously—but they seemed not to have been interested in the newcomers. Few actually remarked on the reinforcements during the war; indeed, the separation of the old from the new men would become most evident long after the war, when the soldiers who joined the regiment in 1864 and 1865 found it difficult to find senior officers and sergeants to support their claims for pensions. Most of the regiments in the Army of the Potomac shared in this jarring transition; the arrival of new recruits and draftees, the breaking up of old brigades and corps, and the departure of the surviving members of the volunteers of 1861 transformed the army and erased the identities of some of its most vaunted units.[25]

As the regiment looked toward the spring campaign, its official strength was around 450 men. But, as always, many of those men were not actually present for duty. One reason was the number of detached soldiers required by the increasing specialization, size, and complexity of a nineteenth-century army. Two examples offer a hint of this expansion: by the eve of the Overland Campaign, the V Corps ambulance corps and train consisted of seventeen officers and 550 enlisted men, while Gen. George G. Meade ordered the Army of the Potomac's Pioneer Corps to equal 2 percent of the "effective strength" of any given brigade.[26]

Just under 300 men were detached from the Sixth for at least a month or two at some point during the war, with thirty-five of them on duty with US Battery B, which fought alongside the Iron Brigade throughout the war. The rest generally served at division or brigade headquarters as clerks, guards, orderlies, or adjutants; in the provost marshal force; as teamsters; as hospital nurses and attendants or ambulance drivers; in construction or pioneer units; and as recruiters. Seventy-eight men were detached to work at one headquarters or another, while thirty-nine performed medical service (occasionally after or even during their own stays in the hospital), thirty-seven worked as drivers, thirty-one worked with the provost, and twenty-eight each worked in various construction details. Twenty-eight more were assigned to what must have been the favorite work of all: recruiting back in Wisconsin. The latter assignment usually lasted two to four months. Most other detached duties lasted between a month and six months, although a handful of men worked in the pioneer corps or as teamsters for much of the war, and Calvin Hubbard was on detached service throughout his three-year term, serving as a mail carrier and clerk for the division.[27]

In the case of the Sixth, the number of men detached at any one time grew in almost linear fashion, from only five for all or part of the fall of 1861 to ninety-five during the spring of 1865. In between, each six-month period saw an increase in the number of men detached for at least a month or two, from nineteen in the first half and thirty-one in the second half of 1862, to eighty-nine in the first half of 1864. Even in fall 1864, when the regiment had dwindled to less than 100 men, sixty-one were on detached service, although not necessarily at the same time.[28]

Not surprisingly, the overwhelming majority of the detached men came from the cohort of men who enlisted in the summer of 1861: 214 out of 252 (not counting those in Battery B who were on more or less permanent assignment—although they, too, all came from cohort 1). They had served the longest, of course, and may have been chosen as a reward for their long and hard service. The process seems to have been fairly subjective—officers were probably asked to assign men to meet immediate needs—and it is difficult to assign specific characteristics more or less conducive to being detached. Some had wives and families while others did not. Some had been sick or wounded once, twice, or even three times, but that did not necessarily correspond to being detached as some kind of reward. No obvious link existed between prewar occupations and rear-echelon responsibilities.

The number of detached men varied widely from company to company. There may have been a rough correlation between the number of men on detached service and the casualties the company had suffered and the extent to which the company had enjoyed continuity of leadership. In some cases, companies with higher-than-average casualty rates and less turnover in their commanding officers saw more men on detached duty. For instance, Company E had only twelve men on detached duty for any length of time during the war; it had suffered the fewest casualties of any company in the regiment (sixty-two) and went through five captains, with its founder, Edward Bragg, leaving the company early on and, apparently, not exerting his influence as a senior officer to assign his old comrades to detached duty. On the other hand, Company F suffered the second-most killed and wounded, with ninety-nine, but had only twenty-nine detached men. However, the company, which at least early in the war was made up of a majority of native German speakers (in itself a likely reason that fewer men were assigned to headquarters), went through six captains. Company K, with thirty-six, had the third-most detached men. Company K was Rufus Dawes's old company, and as he rose through the ranks, familiarity and a certain amount of protectiveness might have influenced his choices for detached duty. A whopping twenty of Company K's men, for instance, served at one time or another in brigade or divisional headquarters, double the number of men from any other company.

The number of Sixth Wisconsin men available for duty was significantly less than the official number of men in the regiment, with dozens in the hospital recovering from wounds or in camp or on restricted duty due to illness and another score or two on detached duty. As a result, although the regimental roll boasted more men in May 1864 than at any time since at least early 1863, that number was misleading. Moreover, Confederate shot and shell would soon dramatically reduce the number of men able to fight.

That Dreary, Desolate Wilderness

Bragg would take command of the Iron Brigade early in the summer campaign, leaving Dawes in charge of the Sixth. In the meantime, Gen. Lysander Cutler had moved up to divisional command. The Sixth would spend the rest of the war in V Corps under the command of Maj. Gen. Gouverneur K. Warren.

Historians have imposed an order on that summer of combat, describing Grant's strategy of exploiting his advantage in men and material by luring Robert E. Lee into open ground and, when that failed, forcing Lee to respond to his insistent flanking movements around the Confederate right. Historians have organized the Overland Campaign and its aftermath into discrete battles named the Wilderness, Spotsylvania Court House, North Anna River, and Petersburg (which in turn is divided into several separate offensives).[29]

That is not how the men on the ground saw it. The battlefields they fought over in the summer of 1864 were unlike anything they had experienced before. As soon as they marched into the Wilderness their war was transformed; they had largely fought out in the open in set piece battles that had beginnings and endings and in which they could identify their specific role and contribution. Battlefields are, of course, notoriously confusing, as smoke, noise, topography, and vegetation make it hard to see or hear. It was much worse during the fighting in early May 1864. And by the time the Sixth had slogged into their position on the Petersburg line several weeks later, the nature of their war would change again. They would rather suddenly find themselves in a campaign that would be fought over the same few square miles for many months, with the only variable the level of violence and the amount of risk they faced on any given day. There would be no winter quarters, as such, in 1864–65, and although they had often fought from behind or against quickly thrown up breastworks, they, like the rest of the Army of the Potomac, would learn that this new form of warfare was almost as much about digging as it was about dying.

The Wilderness and Spotsylvania area, in particular, took on a dreadful mystique. Closed in, opaque, forbidding, the area forced the armies to fight at close range. Adding to the physical limitations of the topography was the fact that many of the men were nearing the end of their three-year terms, while many others may have been regretting their decisions to reenlist. Their reluctance to take chances clashed with the resolute determination of their commanding general to bring the full force of the army to bear on the out-numbered Confederates. As Carol Reardon has written, what set this campaign apart from all others was "the seemingly endless quality of its fighting, for its constant reminders of the nearness and randomness of death, and for its relentless physical and emotional stress." Heat and dust followed by humidity and mud created alarmingly poor personal hygiene, adding to the general misery of the soldiers. The enhanced use of entrenchments at Petersburg gave rise to the "sharpshooter mystique" that added to the sense that fighting skill had nothing to do with survival; soldiers' dogged reluctance to give up breastworks led to increased hand-to-hand fighting, with all of its terrors.[30]

The disturbing fighting that would dominate the summer of 1864 was fought through a fairly narrow swath of central and southeastern Virginia; it was roughly ninety miles as the crow flies from the Union starting point north of the Rapidan to the area east and south of Petersburg where the advance ground to a halt. The battles would run together and the narratives produced in letters and other documents by members of the Sixth would reflect the confusion and ignorance of men who could relate only events and images that occurred within eyesight.

All of this lay in the near future for the men of the Sixth. They knew nothing about the strategy being formulated by Grant and his generals, although by April it was clear that preparations were underway to move south. "We expect to make a move in a week or ten days," wrote new arrival William Ketner to his mother in early April. "The Sutlers have been ordered back to the rear. The women and children have been removed." Later in the month, Governor Edward Salomon visited the Wisconsin troops, who were called out on parade. "It was a . . . sight to see . . . the whole work as a piece of machinery," Ketner marveled. He also reported another sign of imminent action; the men were told no mail would go out for thirty days. A week later the Sixth crossed the Rapidan at Germanna Ford with the rest of its division and camped for the night.[31]

Everyone came to see that river crossing as a turning point. Writing several weeks after the fighting, J. C. Moody sharply divided the regiment's experiences that summer into two phases: before and after the Wilderness. On May 4, "we halted, tired and foot sore, there being a nice creek near we made no delay in taking a general bath. After we had all got our supper and laid down to rest, the brigade bands began to play their sweet notes which seemed to have unusual sweetness as the gentle breeze wafted those beautiful soul cheering national airs to our ears." They were asleep by ten o'clock, "little thinking that ere another setting of the sun many of them would offer up their life's blood on the altar of liberty, in that dreary desolate wilderness." They woke the next day to a nightmare that would last the rest of the summer—for those who survived.[32]

On the morning of the fifth, the Sixth left the Orange Turnpike, deployed into line of battle, and plunged into an area of straggly second- and third-growth forest, over uneven ground thick with the moldering leaves of the previous autumn. It would have been difficult for the men to go more than a few steps without ducking under a branch or around a bush; the thorny underbrush tugged at their uniforms. The spring foliage would have limited visibility to no more than fifteen to twenty steps. They knew that their job was to push aside the Confederates in their front, but they had no precise idea of the location of that front.

In another marker of the monumental change that would occur on May 5, Capt. John Kellogg was called to General Cutler's tent to receive orders for the brigade skirmish line that Kellogg would command. Gathered around were a number of other captains, "evidently pleased," Kellogg wrote later, that the order had "come to some one besides themselves." They covered up their relief and guilt with black comedy, teasing one another about what they should write to widows and girlfriends and offering to shake hands with Kellogg, "for it's the last we'll ever see of you." Kellogg retorted, "I expect you fellows will all be wiped out before I get back" and "Look out you don't get run over by the line of battle, when they follow me in."[33]

It was a moment when the good-natured if nervous joking among long-time comrades reminded them that, at least for now, they still belonged to a community of soldiers called the Sixth Wisconsin, with a reputation and set of assumptions that had sustained them for three years. But by the end of the day Kellogg would be a prisoner of war and in a few weeks at least two of his friends would be dead.

Kellogg led his skirmishers forward. His experience that morning—and the experiences of the Sixth and the entire brigade—represent perfectly the confounding disorientation of the fighting in the Wilderness. They soon made contact with their Confederate counterparts and drove them back. The brigade came up but was soon flanked and forced back in disorder. Kellogg and others were briefly caught up in hand-to-hand fighting, and the captain was knocked out by a blow to the head. He came to a few minutes later, foggy-headed, bleeding from his nose and ears, and too dizzy to stand up straight. Although he had lost all sense of direction, he staggered off to find his regiment—and promptly stumbled into a Confederate unit whose commander also had no idea where he was. "Not being in the humor just then to 'surround them,'" Kellogg wrote years later, "I surrendered." What followed may have been one of the oddest conversations held on this or any battlefield. The Rebel colonel asked:

> Do you know where [Confederate general John B.] Gordon's brigade is?
> *Yank.* Gordon's brigade! Why, I don't know where I am myself.
> *Confederate.* Then there are two of us in the same fix. To tell the
>   truth, I am lost. I got through an interval in your lines, I think;
>   at all events, I found myself in your rear without knowing how I
>   got there, and was trying to get back when you uns run over us
>   [apparently the panicked retreat of the Iron Brigade]. We just lay
>   still, and the Yanks passed us.
> *Yank.* In which direction did they go?
> *Confederate.* Out yon.
> *Yank.* Then it strikes me that your rear is in an opposite direction.

That made sense to the Confederate, and Kellogg was sent off with other prisoners. Countless other soldiers on both sides would be equally confused by this new brand of fighting.[34]

J. C. Moody's narrative of the first few days of the Wilderness captured the difficulty of knowing the location of either army at any given time, as well as the oppressive volume of fire produced by the armies and the distress that could overwhelm even the steadiest soldier. Just as their initial attack failed and the regiment was ordered to retreat,

> a ball passed through my left thigh about 4 inches from my body, it
> knocked me off my pins, but I jumped up and run to the rear, stopped
> to bind my leg up; here our lines passed me in retreat the balls flew so
> thick that I thought it safest to lay down. I did so and as soon as the
> fire slackened I tried to follow our men, but the rebs fired a volley at
> me one ball passed through my coffee pail . . . one lodged in my haver-
> sack, two struck my knapsack, [and] one struck my hand," [inflicting a
> very bloody wound].

He took cover behind a tree as the Confederates advanced; the main line of Confederates passed over him, "yelling like demonds [*sic*]." As the second line passed over Moody, some of the Rebels took him prisoner and robbed him of most of his equipment and clothes. Then they left him "nearly dying of thirst, and bleeding so fast that I expected to bleed to death." For the first time his courage began to fail. Eventually some Georgians took charge of the prisoners and, "kind as brothers," carried him back to a hospital, where a surgeon "tied up the artery in my leg." Moody witnessed the next day's fighting from behind Confederate lines. Despite his wounds, he would escape a month later and finish the war as a brevet captain.[35]

Fearful Perils

Rufus Dawes, as commander of the regiment, had a somewhat clearer view of the big picture than most, yet after the first week of fighting in the Wilderness and Spotsylvania, he wrote his wife Mary a letter shaded with hopelessness: "Through God's blessing I am yet alive. . . . The perils of the last week have been fearful. I cannot hope to pass thus safely through another such." The blood and horror "of the last week make my heart almost like a stone." From Spotsylvania he wrote, "Day after day we stupidly and drearily wait the order that summons us to the fearful work." Some of the regiment's dead and wounded burned in the fire that broke out in the battlefield's dry grass and leaves. At one point the regiment endured 120 hours of continuous fire and movement. On a single day and night they took heavy losses in a "manifestly hopeless" attack on Confederate breastworks and then, in a driving rain, fought for eighteen hours before the Confederates pulled back. Men slept with their heads on the bodies of dead comrades.[36]

At one point the regiment was pulled off the front line, and Dawes could write, "It does seem pleasant to get even for a few hours out of the presence of death, suffering, and danger. . . . It is impossible for one who has not undergone it, to fully understand the depression of spirits caused by such long, continued, and bloody fighting and work."[37]

In the official report he submitted several weeks later, Dawes provided a somewhat more organized version of the fighting, with only hints of the despair that seeped from his personal letters. The Sixth had already been fighting for two days in the Wilderness when he assumed command of the Sixth. At eight o'clock in the evening of May 7 they began to march toward Spotsylvania Court House in the first of Grant's redeployments to the left. "Taxed by the exertion of two days' battle, the march, continued throughout the entire night, was very trying upon the strength and energies of the men." Yet there was virtually no straggling. "It gives me great satisfaction to say that when, on the morning of the 8th, the brigade was placed in order of attack, the ranks of my regiment were full."[38]

Ordered to attack the Confederate left flank on a slight ridge called Laurel Hill, they moved forward just "a few rods" before halting and firing. As Confederates came around the Sixth's right, and the Union units on its left "retreated in confusion," the Sixth wavered and, eventually "pressed by the enemy from all sides ... broke in disorder" for the second time in three days. "By the great exertion on the part of many officers of the brigade"—including General Bragg—a line was established about 200 yards to the rear. Dawes admitted that at this point—he must have been writing his report from notes taken closer to the events described—the casualties "of my regiment in this affair I have no means now of accurately stating."[39]

The regiment skirmished for the rest of that day and all of May 9. On the tenth they advanced with the rest of the brigade; after again retreating and regrouping, the Sixth got to within 200 yards of the Confederate line, where they fought all day, taking "severe" losses. The regiment's next attack came on the twelfth. "The men sprang over the breastworks with great alacrity," but after advancing only 100 feet or less found themselves isolated in thick timber, with no support on either flank. He halted and ordered the men to fire until the rest of the line caught up. "After a few minutes of rapid firing, suffering meanwhile severe loss, convinced of the futility of striving without support to advance through the abatis of sharpened stakes in our front, while to remain longer was wanton sacrifice of life," Dawes withdrew his men to their original breastworks.[40]

Several days of bloody but inconclusive fighting at Laurel Hill were followed on the thirteenth by orders to move four miles to the left to support Hancock's VI Corps at the famous "Mule Shoe" (later called the "Bloody Angle"), a looping protrusion of the Confederate line that seemed a likely weak point to Union commanders. The Sixth eventually relieved the Seventh Wisconsin on the firing line. They spent the rest of the night "firing upon the enemy's works." Dawes's description of the unimaginably awful night resembled the testimony of countless others: "The mud was near 6 inches deep, the night dark and stormy, and the hardship of this service to men exhausted by the battle, marching, and work of the day before, can scarcely be appreciated."[41]

There was a few days' lull in the fighting, at least for the Sixth. Dawes believed that the previous ten days of fighting had been the "most exhaustive to the energies of the men, and perhaps most trying to their morale of anything in the experience of the oldest in service, but the hardships and dangers were undergone with fortitude, and the men were always ready to put forth their best efforts in the most perilous undertaking." The "Third Epoch" of the campaign, as Dawes put it, began with the crossing of the North Anna River at Jericho Ford. On the evening of May 23, the regiment fell into a confusing fight in "thick and tangled brush." Unable to see the enemy clearly, but under constant and heavy fire, they changed their front two or three times. The unit on their left suddenly "fell back in great disorder, running through my ranks and breaking the regiment. My men, however, rallied promptly around their color, and reforming, I moved to the right in the open field" and continued the fight.[42]

In almost constant fighting or skirmishing, the Sixth could enjoy no sense of regimental or brigade accomplishment other than, eventually, a vague notion that their sweat and blood had somehow helped push the Confederates back to Petersburg. One thing they knew for sure was that they had suffered appalling casualties. The regiment had crossed the Rapidan just under three months earlier with 380 men; since then they had lost 227 killed, wounded, or missing.[43]

By late June the regiment was moving in and out of the trenches near Petersburg in a six-day rotation.

One of Dawes's sergeants later described the "labyrinth of ditches and Forts" stretching from east of Petersburg toward the south and west of the city. "A stranger going in to it, cannot find the same way back again." A dull but dangerous routine had developed: "Our duty is so near alike every day, be on the alert in the Breastworks, Picket duty, and digging in regular Rotation. A third of the men have to be under Arms during the night, when the rest lay down and sleep, then in the day time there is no thoughts of sleep, the heat and flies are insufferable and are our greatest Enemy at present." The vast, confusing trench system, and the seemingly aimless and repetitive nature of their experiences, became a physical manifestation of a war in which it was hard to tell who was winning or losing.[44]

Dawes gained an insight into how the campaign had affected the army when in July he was assigned to the board examining the conduct of officers in V Corps. Many had wilted under the pressure, and the board would decide how to punish officers who had failed to do their duty. "During this unexampled campaign of sixty continuous days," he recalled, "the excitement, exhaustion, hard work and loss of sleep broke down great numbers of men who had received no wounds in battle." Dawes had managed to hold himself together, but "some who began the campaign with zealous and eager bravery, ended it with nervous and feverish apprehension of danger."[45]

Dawes understood completely. He reported sympathetically that the men whose terms were up on July 15—the men who had not reenlisted in fall

1863—had become understandably nervous, as stories circulated about regiments forced into battle on the eve of their termination, or even after terms had expired. The few dozen men in the Sixth who had not reenlisted "are nearly wild at the prospect of seeing once more their long-separated families." Dawes was equally anxious to get home to his new wife and turned down the chance for a colonel's commission and the command of a regiment comprising survivors of the Second, Fifth, and Sixth Wisconsin, mostly because it would have required him to reenlist for three years. The war had devolved into a swirl of dust and blood, and Dawes—and no doubt many other soldiers who had been in it from the beginning—could actually imagine that it might go on for another three years.[46]

Personal tragedy shadowed Dawes's last few weeks in the regiment. In June, Dawes learned that his nineteen-year-old brother-in-law, Charley, had died from injuries suffered in a train accident on his way to join the army. Dawes seems to have felt guilty, writing later that the younger man "was not prepared for the stern hardships of war." Yet when Dawes had tried to talk him out of going, Charley would have none of it. "You belong to the Iron Brigade," he protested. "How do you think I will feel to take no part in the war, and be in the same family?" Rufus and Mary would name their first son—a future vice president of the United States—after him. Dawes also received word that his younger brother Ephraim, who was an officer in an Ohio regiment at Shiloh and was with Sherman in Georgia, had lost most of his lower jaw to a Confederate bullet.[47]

The Sixth remained largely out of combat from late July through Dawes's departure in early August, although the regiment went into battle soon afterward. In a September 1 letter announcing his safe arrival in Washington, he told Mary, "I am fairly heart-sick at the stories of blood I hear from the old regiment." There had been much fighting since he left. "It seems almost certain to me that I could never have lived through another such carnival of blood. Only eighty men are left in the ranks for service."[48]

A few weeks before he left the regiment, Rufus Dawes had encountered Edward Bragg, now a brigade commander, who said to him, "Of all I have gone through, I cannot now write an intelligent account. I can only tell my wife I am alive and well. I am too stupid for any use."

The kind of stupor that Bragg described emerges in the letters and reminiscences of many of the men in the Sixth, who described combat and behaviors unfamiliar to longtime members of the regiment. Each man had a different point of view and set of experiences, and thus their writings reflect distinctive personalities and priorities. Even as some focused on the behavior of their comrades in battle, others restricted their commentary to a narrow set of circumstances. For them, the minutiae became the narrative: the regiment changes camps, gets paid, mans the picket line. Yet even as the letters written by members of the Sixth show how disorienting the summer campaign was, they still show men struggling to retain their personal dignity and the regiment's reputation.[49]

The letters of Sgt. John O. Johnson of Company H provide a glimpse of the hard, demoralizing combat grinding down the Sixth. Johnson was a German immigrant and original member of the regiment who had been wounded at Gettysburg. He began the summer 1864 campaign as first sergeant but often acted as commander of Company H after Capt. John Hauser resigned in March. Johnson kept Hauser up to date on the company with letters that described in great detail the company's role in the fighting. Although he did not begin the first letter until the regiment was camped "near Petersburg" on July 2, he began his narrative on May 5, when the fighting started for the Sixth.

Old-timers like Johnson feared that the regiment was at risk of losing its reputation. He freely expressed his disdain for men who shirked their duty, including members of his own regiment and company. When Union lines broke at one point on May 6, the fleeing Yankees "came running right into us." He pushed against them with his musket but to no avail. The retreat was stopped when Colonel Dawes and General Bragg appeared; Bragg "made a little speech here exhorting the men not to disgrace the name we had so nobly won for the Iron Brigade." Some men did disgrace it, unfortunately. He had "hard work to keep Wm. L. Johnson in his place, he was a great annoyance in the Company." He and another man would "skedaddle ... out of the company" later in the day. However, the new recruits "proved noble boys," except for one man who had gotten a pass to go to the hospital "and that is the last I have heard of him."[50]

The regiment's old invincibility had vanished. Johnson reported the unsurprising "hesitance" of the Wisconsin men to charge Confederate breastworks that were only sixty yards away. Eventually they attacked into a heavy fire and suffered many casualties; Johnson saw four men hit at virtually the same time. Johnson continued to list the men who fell. Ten of the company were killed or wounded that day alone. Everyone retreated, although Johnson dashed back with a few other men to get a wounded comrade—"this was a bad job but we could not leave him there." Two of the men who went with him were wounded, and the man they rescued, John Moy, died two days later after his leg was amputated.[51]

Perhaps the most compelling theme to emerge from soldiers' correspondence was a general sense of pessimism—the men did not see the point of individual maneuvers that often seemed tragically pointless. At times, it was difficult to recognize the old Sixth on the messy battlefields of 1864. Men wrote more about failures than successes, and the focus turned from heroic action to the meager satisfaction of doing their duty in the face of weariness and death. The men were quite aware of the changes that had occurred in the nature of the war and in their own attitudes and at times expressed a sadness about the way in which the regiment had been whittled away.

In late June Earl Rogers wrote his brother Clayton—the letter would later appear in the local newspaper—with news of Company I during the previous six weeks of fighting. The brothers had joined the regiment in June 1861, with Clayton resigning after Gettysburg. Apparently describing their initial attack in the Wilderness, he wrote, "no one could live to reach their works. We scattered and went back to the starting place." He listed the dead and wounded; ten men in the company had been killed in the campaign's first few days. "Antietam had no place where the dead were as thick." Rogers had been shot in the leg and was in the hospital, where in the relative peace and quiet he could reflect on the "nearly three years [that] has passed since we filed through the gates of Camp Randall, an akward [sic] and green company of Soldiers, stepping on the heels of the file leader, Sachel in hand, and loud with huzzahs, throats sore and hoarse with cheers." It seemed like a lifetime ago. Like many of his comrades, Rogers kept score of their appalling losses. "Our Co. has but four in the field."[52]

Men found different ways of coping with the violence and despair. Frank Waller had been with the regiment since the beginning of the war and had earned the Medal of Honor for his part in capturing the flag of the Second Mississippi at Gettysburg. That day at the Railroad Cut must have seemed like a different war to Waller, whose flat, unemotional diary entries reflect the disjointed nature of the campaign—at least to the common soldier. The curt sentences or phrases present the campaign as a jumble of marches and picket duty, volleys fired into the night, retreats conducted on the run, and sweat and exhaustion and constant movement. Waller did not focus on the losses, although he mentioned a few specific casualties. Only a few place names appear—they meant nothing to most common soldiers, at least at the time—limiting his commentary to "right" and "left." It is entirely likely that Waller's personality lent his diary entries their taciturn quality, but it is hard for a modern reader not to sense the effects of the numbing, soul-crushing violence. Waller found mild and intermittent solace in putting on the occasional clean shirt, getting an envelope of medicinal powder when he felt ill, and sitting in the shade. As the siege of Petersburg took shape, boredom set in, although Waller reported winning twenty-five dollars in a poker game one day and ten dollars in another.[53]

Some took refuge in the recent past. Although he would not become a member of the Sixth until fall—having enlisted in January 1864, he would be among the Second Wisconsin men who came to the Sixth late in the year to finish his term—Alcinous Stratton wrote to his wife Emma on July 4 from breastworks opposite Petersburg. The day brought back a treasured memory of the previous year's Independence Day, several months before he enlisted. While his future comrades in the Sixth were burying bodies at Gettysburg he had been with Emma "at uncle John's to a dance dont you recolect it Emma but things has changed since that hant they." Inevitably he turned quickly to the future, and then back to the present: "I hope that a year will make a change again and bring me back again to the place where I was one year ago to day and then I will be satest fide to live the rest of my days with my little famley." He asked Emma to have their little boy, Albert, "say hurrah for the union if I was there I would learn him to say most every thing I would have him say shit ask him if he can say shit and if he can then kiss him fore me a half a dozen times."[54]

Sometimes the regiment itself brought forth reminders of past heroics. Late in August the regiment took part in a battle to capture the Weldon Railroad, and for at least a day Sergeant Johnson felt like the regiment was its old self. Although forced back at first, the men soon rallied. They "turned about, gave one Hurrah, and went forward as fast as men could run. This was the best piece of work I have ever seen the sixth perform," and it was "to[o] much for the Rebs. I see them get up, and skedaddle, as I have never sent them do before." Things did not go so well the rest of that day and beyond, and it was hard to watch. Johnson ended his last letter to Hauser plaintively: "There are now only about 73 muskets left in the Regt and . . . all I loved in it has gone hence." Johnson asked Hauser to try to get him a position in one of the new regiments being formed in Wisconsin. He seemed anxious to start anew, where the ghosts of dead comrades did not haunt him. "There are unpleasant memories. All my old friends dead mostly." Johnson left the regiment in September with a lieutenant's commission in the newly formed Forty-Fifth Wisconsin, which was stationed near Nashville and never fought a battle.[55]

Even the cheerful youngster Henry Matrau found it difficult to maintain a good face. Like a number of other comrades, as the months ground on, he reported on the deterioration of the Sixth. Following one particularly foolish attack, he promised his younger brother he would bring home a musket ball shot at him by a "Johnnie Reb" but also wrote, "Our reg't lost 50 men killed & wounded in 15 minutes in this disastrous & useless affair." At the end of June, Matrau reported a detail not mentioned by anyone else: with only "134 muskets," the regiment had been consolidated into just four companies. Almost exactly a month later he complained that the war would be over and 100,000 lives saved if they had enough men; alas, "there are thousands of young men in the north that are either too cowardly or too selfish to shoulder a musket like a man and help fight for their native country." A few weeks later he was promoted to orderly sergeant. "I have a big company, too," he wrote bitterly. "One Lieut., 2 privates, & one Sergt comprises all that remains for duty in Co G, which formerly had an aggregate of over 100 men." By late August, "the old sixth Wis has been terribly decimated in these fights and we now number 75 men, rank and file, in the reg't."[56]

As Though We Had Won a Victory

That the war had changed irrevocably is apparent from the evolving definition of "victory" for the common soldiers, which had become less a matter of defeating the Confederates or taking territory and more a matter of surviving with limbs and dignity intact. During the rainy night that followed the Battle at the Weldon Railroad, James Sullivan and a small squad of survivors gathered around a fire and drank coffee from a giant coffeepot. Brigadier General Bragg stopped by for a cup. "The boys felt good and were as jubilant as though we had won a victory, for they felt that though we had been overpowered and compelled to run it was better than to lie down and surrender and partake of the noted hospitality . . . of the confederacy at Libby, Belle Isle or Andersonville."[57]

Many of the men fighting in the summer of 1864 betrayed greater or lesser degrees of strain, fear, and regret, as well as a palpable sense of weariness of being burdened with the inevitability of pain or death. This emerges clearly in the case of Nathan Burchell, who suffered three wounds during the war: A bullet damaged his left hand and another ripped through his face, exiting from his neck. The third, according to his former colonel, Rufus Dawes, Burchell had caused himself by slicing off the tips of the first, second, and third fingers of his right hand with a butcher's cleaver while cutting up beef. Dawes was adamant when interviewed by a special pension examiner in 1894. His description of the scene was specific and striking: Burchell came to the assistant surgeon, John Hall, and held up his left hand in my presence showing that the four [*sic*] fingers had been cut off just below the second joints and he held up the stubs for the surgeon to see and he said to the doctor, "Doctor I have met with an accident" or words to that effect. I then said, "Burchell that is no accident. . . . You did that on purpose." He then admitted that he had done it himself. I knew of many cases of self inflicted injuries in the service and that fact was what aroused my suspicions in this case. Burchell was an excellent soldier and had taken part in many battles, and in view of that fact I decided not to prosecute him although we had strict orders to prosecute offences of that kind. He remained with the command until mustered out at the expiration of his term and did good service. I considered him one of our best soldiers. He explained to me that he cut his fingers off with the butcher's cleaver, and the only excuse that he offered was that he had a presentiment that he would be killed. . . . We were right in the midst of that terrible campaign, and I ordered no investigation and none was held. He expressed great regret at having cut off his fingers. I then considered it a hasty act. We were under a very great strain and excitement at that time. It was an insane act, I am sure, but I cannot tell whether his mind was affected or not when he did it.

When he applied for a pension in 1868 Burchell had changed his story; he claimed he had been injured while cutting timber. In a later affidavit he testified that he had hurt himself cutting tent stakes with an axe.[58]

Burchell had been a good soldier for three years, having already survived an extremely close call and some of the worst fighting of the war. But at least temporarily he lost his will to fight. His effort to extricate himself from the violence failed, and regaining his composure he could never admit to himself that he had actually succumbed to what, horrifically, seemed an "easy" way out.

There were no easy ways out for the men of the Sixth Wisconsin. By September 1864 the overwhelming majority of their original officers were dead, disabled, or gone home. As Jeffrey D. Wert writes, "The Iron Brigade lost its identity" during the summer of 1864. The few dozen survivors available for duty knew they would face at least one more season of hard fighting. But probably they did not know that the regiment would be reborn before their very eyes when late in the year hundreds of new men appeared: the product of the war's last levy of conscripts.[59]

7

Off to the War

1865

After dwindling to a few dozen men available for duty in the fall of 1864, the regiment swelled to over 700 with the addition in the late fall and early 1865 of over 450 draftees, as well as dozens of substitutes, a few survivors from the Second Wisconsin, and a dribble of regular enlistees. Their commander would be Col. John A. Kellogg, the lawyer who had been one of Rufus Dawes's lieutenants back in 1861. Kellogg's story must have impressed the raw recruits; he had served as a company commander with the Sixth through all its battles until his capture at the Wilderness. He escaped twice—once jumping from a moving train—and, with help from enslaved people in South Carolina, he eventually made it to Union lines. After a brief furlough in Wisconsin, he returned to Virginia with, as he wrote later, "enough drafted men to fill our regiment to the maximum."[1]

Kellogg would lead the regiment—and eventually the brigade—through the last frenzy of marching and fighting in 1865. Although the term "Iron

Brigade" would still appear in reports and newspaper articles, both the brigade and the Sixth Wisconsin had undergone astonishing transformations. Relatively inexperienced officers had to manage companies that had not been this large since before Gainesville; the men would be thrust into combat after no more than two months of drill; and most of the draftees were no doubt much more comfortable speaking German than English. Yet this would be the regiment that finished what the old Sixth Wisconsin had begun nearly four years earlier.

The casualties suffered by the Sixth had led to this transformation. By the end of the war the regiment would lose 149 men killed in combat. Another 159 died of disease, but eighty-one of the men who died of disease had also been wounded, so it is likely that many died from complications from their wounds—pneumonia, for instance—so the number of deaths related to combat is probably much higher. Fifteen men were listed as missing in action and presumed dead. These add up to 323 deaths, or 16.3 percent of the total number of men who served in the regiment. Another 509 men were wounded, some multiple times (not counting men who were *both* wounded and died of disease or went missing), or 25.7 percent of the total number who served. If we add to our list of casualties the number of men discharged due to illness—314 men were discharged for reasons other than combat injuries—there were a total of 1,146 casualties killed, wounded, died of disease, or discharged for disease. This brings the effective casualty rate of the Sixth Wisconsin to 57.6 percent. By late 1864, well under 200 of the original 1861 enlistees were still with the regiment, and it is likely that a majority of them were on detached duty or in the hospital.[2]

As in all Civil War regiments, on any given day illness kept scores of men off the duty lists. The total number of men noted as absent due to sickness in the descriptive roll was only 511, which is clearly too low. The fact that the number of men who were even listed on sick rolls varied quite a bit by company—from a high of 92 men in Companies B and I and 78 in Company I to a low of 25 in Company D—suggests that there might have been an ethos of simply not going on the sick list in certain companies or a habit among some company commanders of not allowing men to report to the surgeon. Company D never had more than a half dozen on the sick list in any given six-month period, but Companies H and K each had at least ten men absent due to sickness in five of the eight six-month periods examined. Memoirs and pension files show that men frequently fought through illnesses and even minor wounds without reporting to the hospital or were treated informally "in camp" by the regimental surgeon. Indeed, pension files are replete with examples of frustrated applicants who cannot provide evidence of poor health from their time in the army because they had simply ignored it. As a result, it is likely that the ravages of dysentery, diarrhea, camp fever, and other chronic illnesses kept many more men off duty or at least functioning at a reduced capacity than the records suggest.[3]

Dozens of men were missing for weeks and months due to sickness or wounds. For instance, 655 of the 1,095 men in cohort 1 (59.8 percent) were absent from the regiment for anywhere from a week to several months, with just under half of the sick and just over half of the wounded gone for eighteen weeks or more. Most of the long-term absentees survived (less than 10 percent died); those gone for six weeks or less died at much higher rates (44 percent of wounded men, 17 percent of sick men). This is not surprising—the most grievously wounded and seriously ill would simply have succumbed more quickly than the less severely injured or sick. But even those who survived the first few weeks were quite likely to be sent home.

During the first two years of the war, many long-term absentees received discharges—about 60 percent of the sick men and 93 percent of the wounded. This changed later in the war. The number of discharges for disability declined after May 1863, due to manpower needs, a tightening of the rules regulating medical discharges, and the establishment of the Invalid Corps (later the Veteran Reserve Corps). After this time, disability discharges went only to amputees or men with other major conditions or to those whose recovery would take longer than the amount of time left on their enlistments. This certainly holds for the Sixth, where the seriously sick and wounded of the cohort that enlisted in late 1863 and early 1864 received discharges at a rate of only about 20 percent.[4]

Desertion played only a small role in the comings and goings of the Sixth. A recent estimate suggests that 200,000 is likely a serious undercount of the number of actual deserters from the Union army. That would put the rate of desertion for the Union army as a whole at roughly 10 percent. That was decidedly not the case with the Sixth. Although several score appeared on various lists as deserters, only a fraction seem to have actually deserted. Eliminating those men who seemed to have left the army in good standing—they mustered out with the regiment at the end of the war, later received veterans' benefits like pensions or places in a soldiers' home, or participated in the Grand Army of the Republic or other veterans' activities—it seems quite possible that there were only thirty-seven deserters from the Sixth Wisconsin, which comes to just 1.9 percent of the total number of men who served. Just under half (eighteen) deserted before the first battle, including three before they reached Virginia. Most were without wives or children, suggesting that if family ties *were* a compelling motivation for deserting, they were to elderly or destitute parents. At least nine deserted after being wounded or sick, often after an extended stay in the hospital.[5]

All but three had enlisted in 1861; those three were substitutes who had been with the regiment for only a month or two and seem to have simply walked away while the regiment was waiting for mustering out. Running counter to the poor opinion of conscripts held by senior officers, not one of the Sixth's draftees deserted.[6]

There is no record of anyone from the Sixth receiving severe punishments for desertion. Indeed, despite several dozen men being listed as deserters in *The Roster of Wisconsin Volunteers,* few are reported to have received any punishment other than loss of pay. Even the incorrigible Charles Mevis seems to have gotten off lightly. He had deserted from the Second Wisconsin in 1862; by the time he was "returned from desertion" the survivors of the Second had become part of the Sixth. He deserted again, returned to be tried, then deserted yet again in June 1865. Andrew Tuttle of Company E deserted in January 1863 and was captured and sent back to the army seven months later. Although he was court-martialed, his sentence was "remitted," and he came back to the regiment in time to reenlist as a veteran and enjoy the winter furlough with his comrades. He survived the war and was discharged as a sergeant.[7]

Old Abe Is the Man

As the regiment began to absorb—or, perhaps more accurately, be absorbed by—the new recruits, most members of the Sixth welcomed the reelection of President Abraham Lincoln. Although constitutional issues, war policy, and practical politics loomed large in the election, by late 1864, every man in the regiment, every voter in Wisconsin, and every person in the United States, for that matter, would have at least temporarily decided how they felt about slavery and the enslaved. Available evidence from men of the Sixth does not indicate strong feelings for or against emancipation as an issue in the election.

It is reasonable, however, to assume that soldiers' attitudes roughly mirrored Wisconsin's rather ambiguous attitudes about slavery and race. Although prior to the war the rise of the Republican Party in Wisconsin—one of the places that claimed to be the "birthplace" of the party—indicated a great deal of angst over the *issue* of slavery, *racial justice* seemed less vital. A mob had staged a famous rescue of a fugitive slave named Joshua Glover at

Milwaukee's federal courthouse in 1854, and the state legislature had challenged the infamous Fugitive Slave Act—which forced states to aid federal authorities in recapturing escaped slaves—by passing a "personal liberty" law in 1857. Yet most antebellum Wisconsinites were not overly concerned with actual enslaved people. Aside from a few prominent abolitionists like Milwaukee's Sherman Booth, most opponents of the institution were aligned with the Free Soil movement, which sought to limit the expansion of slavery into western territories. Republicans dominated statewide offices and held majorities in the legislature from the late 1850s through the war years, but, despite the firmly abolitionist attitudes of some leading politicians, as a party they tended not to promote emancipation or equality for former slaves. Even in 1860, as the sectional conflict dominated the national election, in Wisconsin temperance and the ongoing financial crisis were more important political issues than slavery. By the end of the war, however, the state had accepted the notion of emancipation and would quickly ratify the Thirteenth Amendment.[8]

We can capture a sense of the contours of the issues of slavery and freedom in Wisconsin by focusing on the two major newspapers published in Appleton, where the core of the Sixth's Company E was formed: the Democratic *Crescent* and the Republican-leaning *Motor*, which provide useful examples of the attitudes that must have animated farmyard, street-corner, and tavern debates throughout the communities from which the Sixth had been recruited, as well as similar conversations around army campfires.

The *Crescent* dismissed talk of emancipation and racial equality. When Booth lectured to a "half-full Adkins Hall" in early 1862, the *Crescent* admitted that he "is a smart man" but had become "a confirmed monomaniac on the subject" of abolition. The editors never let up in their criticism of abolitionism, abolitionists, and African Americans. The lurid headline "AMALGAMATION!" introduced a brief entry in early 1864 that foreshadowed decades of racist portrayals of race relations. "On Tuesday night, while standing in front of the Post Office, a tall 'American of African de *scent*' passed by, as full of style as a Country Doctor, and with him, hanging to his arm in loving embrace, was a *pure(?) white woman*! . . . Was this a forerunner of coming events?" A brutal expression of Darwinian racism appeared at about the same time. Democrats must simply accept that "slavery is dead to all practical intents." But that should not worry any white man. "If one-fourth of the slaves are used up by the Union and another fourth by the Rebel Army, and two-thirds of the remainder die of filth, starvation and disease occasioned by being deprived by their masters, it is no concern of yours: it is the Destiny of the Negro."[9]

The *Appleton Motor* provided the antislavery counterpart to the *Crescent*, excitedly printing the preliminary Emancipation Proclamation in every issue during the weeks leading up to the off-year elections late in 1862. In mid-October, a front-page article urged soldiers to vote for candidates dedicated to emancipation: "Can any gallant volunteer in the field deliberately vote to prolong the war by paralyzing the arm of the President?"[10]

The *Motor*'s approval of emancipation seems at first to have been more a matter of using it to cudgel the Confederacy than as a matter of achieving social justice. Yet its sympathy for African Americans grew as the war went on. It eagerly supported the use of African American troops and admired their performance. "In all the recent battles in which negroes were engaged," the *Motor* declared, "they fought nobly." A few months later the *Motor* expressed outrage over the massacre of surrendered Black soldiers at Fort Pillow and by Wisconsin Democrats' failure to "disapprove . . . of this atrocity" and their galling effort to blame President Lincoln for the murders. Yet at no time during the war did the *Motor* address the issue of the status of freed people once released from the bonds of slavery.[11]

As they had during earlier elections, Democratic newspapers once again assumed soldiers would vote Democratic in 1864, largely because their old commander, Gen. George McClellan, was the party's candidate for president. A few men in the Sixth expressed their support for "Little Mac"—perhaps simply as a default reaction to a choice between a military man with no political record and the far more complicated incumbent. An anonymous letter from a "Captain of the Sixth" Wisconsin predicted that "the old Iron Brigade is as ready and willing to fight for the restoration of the Union under the constitution to-day as at any former period." Another correspondent writing from "the Trenches on the Weldon Railroad" urged his civilian friends and neighbors to vote and declared his support for the Democratic candidate: "We, for our part, will stand by Little Mac as bravely as we stood by him on the battle-fields of South Mountain and Antietam." Support for their former commander seemed to hinge on his inspiring leadership style rather than the Democratic Party's promise to end the war.[12]

As the election results would show, in the end a large majority of the men in the Sixth could not bring themselves to vote for McClellan. Perhaps opinion among the soldiers changed at the last minute. "Many of the men in the Iron Brigade regiments were for McClellan until just before the balloting," a soldier in the Seventh Wisconsin wrote. Then Confederate and Union soldiers got into a cheering match one evening—the Rebels yelled for Jefferson Davis and then joined the Yankees when they shouted for McClellan. "We all agreed that what the Rebels liked was just what we had no right to like," he wrote, "and if it was going to do them so much good to elect McClellan, we just wouldn't do it." Afterward, "you hardly [heard] McClellan's name mentioned in our regiment." It may have been that simple: the friend of my enemy is my enemy. The soldiers' vote for Lincoln should not be read as a mandate for emancipation. Although soldiers did vote overwhelmingly for the president and the Union Party, the results may have stemmed from anger at Democratic efforts to limit soldiers' voting, the departure of many Democratic soldiers from the army when their terms expired in 1864, and the boycott, in effect, of perhaps 20 percent of the Democratic soldiers who remained.[13]

But at least some members of the Sixth had made up their minds in favor of Lincoln and his policies long before the call-and-response between the trenches. The reenlisted veterans of the Sixth trumpeted their strong support for Lincoln, the restoration of the Union, and emancipation in a letter to a Racine newspaper, and from a New York hospital, one of their comrades wrote, "I hope soon to recover and return to my regt. and help finish this rebellion, and elect Old Abe this fall." Another Lincoln supporter in the Sixth reported to his parents that a September straw vote in the regiment had gone overwhelmingly in favor of Lincoln. The kind of men who would vote for McClellan, he continued, were "the soldiers that have gone back on their fallen comrades and are willing to forget their suffering, and hard ships they have endured and to give up [their] honor." But those who support Lincoln "still retain the memory of the battle field, and the fall of [their] comrades."[14]

"Old Abe is the man," Francis Waller happily reported after the election. Company I had voted unanimously for Lincoln, and the hero of the Railroad Cut celebrated with two canteens of whiskey. Although the *Daily Milwaukee News* asserted that chicanery had suppressed the Democratic vote in the Iron Brigade, it had to report that the Wisconsin regiments had voted over-whelmingly for the Union ticket, including 127–36 in the Sixth, just under the percentage of Lincoln votes among all Wisconsin soldiers and far above the 51.5 percent for the state as a whole.[15]

The huge gap in the votes between the veterans of the Sixth and the vot-ers back home may seem to indicate another distinction between soldiers and civilians. But a closer look shows that the counties that sent many of the original cohort to the Sixth—Juneau, Rock, Vernon, Grant, and Win-nebago—cast majorities for Lincoln of at least 50 percent and as high as 90 percent. The counties that provided many of the votes for McClellan—Washington, Ozaukee, Sheboygan, and Manitowoc—were the counties along Lake Michigan where draft resistance had been most visible in 1863 and from where many of the Sixth's draftees came in 1864.[16]

The War Is Being Thoroughly Closed

As if to sanction the rising consensus in favor of prosecuting the war to a just close, the drafts in the spring and fall of 1864 caused little disruption in Wisconsin. More important, the Sixth would finally benefit from a major influx of recruits. Newspapers issued the familiar calls for men to use the military emergency to their advantage. In May 1864, the *Wood County Reporter* compared the financial benefits of collecting a bounty and six months of army pay to having a decent job—a willful piece of wishing away the oceans of blood that would actually be spilled during those six months. A few months later, the *Reporter* invited men from other counties to help local communities meet their quotas: "Come in, boys, and get your greenbacks."[17]

Lincoln's reelection meant that the war would go on, and the draft scheduled for spring 1865 animated much conversation, as likely draftees and editors alike scrambled to find men willing to be paid to go to war. In February, Milwaukeeans voted on a $120,000 tax "to aid in clearing the city from the draft." That language—that the draft was an external force bearing down on the community and that only united action could defend the community from its evils—had been part of the conversation about the draft since 1862, especially in Democratic newspapers and communities, where resistance to emancipation continued to sharpen resistance to the draft. A few days earlier, a notice had called residents of the Fourth Ward to a meeting "to complete arrangements to Free the Ward from [the] Draft"—by which they meant encouraging enough men to volunteer willingly so that other men would not be forced into the army unwillingly. "It is hoped," commented the *Daily Milwaukee News*, that "the large majority of our citizens, including those who are exempt from the draft will nobly come forward and show their willingness to contribute something to relieve the people of the heavy burden imposed upon them." Indeed, Milwaukeeans passed the tax by a large majority, which to the *Daily News* reflected the city's "patriotism, and her determination to protect her citizens from the oppression resulting from a draft." Under the headline "Declining Patriotism," the *Crescent* noted the irony that "two years ago the object of all the war meetings was to procure men for the war. Now the object of all the war meetings is to devise means for not going to the war."[18]

On the other side of the state, a Viroqua newspaper urged men to consider enlisting rather than waiting to be drafted. "There was never a better time to enlist. The war is being evidently and thoroughly closed," and men should take advantage of the government's offer while they could. Volunteers would receive a "$400 Bounty and $16 a month, and Board, Clothing and Medical Attendance." And, in fact, a few men did go to the Sixth in the spring of 1865: thirty-one substitutes (about half of the regiment's total number of substitutes) and fourteen recruits. Most arrived during the third week of March or after and two dozen showed up in April. A few drifted in after Appomattox and as the Sixth prepared for the Grand Review. For these few dozen men, the payoff was definitely worth the mild risks they faced.[19]

But the hard but necessary campaign that would end the war would largely be fought, at least in the case of the Sixth, by the conscripts who had not "escaped" the autumn 1864 draft. They would serve only a few months, but the percentage of killed, wounded, and discharged for illness among them would rival the casualties among the volunteers of 1861.

How I Hate the Whole Thing

A rare account shows just how different the experiences of the draftees coming to the Sixth in late 1864 were from those of the men who enlisted earlier in the war. J. B. Ingalls, a Waushara County blacksmith in his late thirties with a wife and four children, kept a diary of his first few months after being drafted in mid-November 1864. A devout Christian, Ingalls hoped to be assigned to a noncombatant role, perhaps as a nurse (and was encouraged to think that by a provost marshal in Wisconsin). He continually complained about the rough ways and foul language of the other draftees at Camp Randall. "I tell you this is a hard place, lots of dutchman [Germans]—Jabber, jabber all the time," he sighed. "I look around me" and ask, "Can I stand it a year[?]"[20]

After three weeks of bad food and cold weather, the draftees entrained for the front on December 7 and learned for the first time that they would be joining the Sixth. Although Ingalls had his own particular thoughts about the next few weeks—the men would finally reach their regiment on December 17—no doubt all of the men in his group witnessed the sensory overload that assailed them as they journeyed to the war.

Ingalls noted that "from the time we left camp Randall we have been strictly guarded. The officers were martinets, and guards observed their eating, washing, and "tend[ing] to the calls of nature." By December 11 they were at Fortress Monroe at the tip of the Virginia peninsula, where they spent hours at a time standing in the rain and cold, waiting for orders or food or any kind of attention.[21]

The war became even more real for the westerners at City Point, the Army of the Potomac headquarters and site of a massive supply depot and general hospital located at the confluence of the James and Appomattox Rivers. At least 100 vessels crowded the bay, where the masts of ships sunk by the CSS *Virginia* two years earlier still jutted out of the water. Men and horses were in constant movement; Ingalls and his fellow westerners were just a few among thousands of new recruits passing through the bustling port on their way to the army. Held in a "bull pen with a guard around us," on December 13 they heard their first cannon fire in the distance and saw five deserters who had been sentenced to death. When one of the draftees got too close to a pen of Confederate prisoners, a Rebel stabbed him.[22]

Ingalls—and no doubt many of his comrades—was appalled by the casual cruelty they witnessed, to horses and men alike, including a man hanged by his arms so his feet barely touched the ground as punishment for some unknown offense. At one point 2,000 men waited in line for meager rations— next to the latrines. "You cannot imagine the stench that is there & all on an empty stomach." The last phase of their journey to the Sixth took place on the top of railcars packed with hay followed by a four-mile march. They passed through fields of tents, ruined plantations, and wrecked houses.[23]

When they finally arrived at the regiment, Ingalls was assigned to Company E. Ingalls decided to take the bull by the horns and begin his campaign to be detached to noncombatant duty. It did not go well. He went to the adjutant—probably Jerome Watrous, who had taken over that job in the fall—who with another officer "called me everything that they could turn their toung to & swore that if they could do as they wished . . . they would hang me." He had no better luck with Colonel Kellogg.[24]

Ingalls gave up, accepted a gun, and with the other draftees began learning how to be a soldier. By the first of the year they could hear distant firing almost every day. In mid-January they went out on picket duty. On the first night a couple of shots rang out; "this made the boys begin to look kind of corner ways as the old chaps said that if they fire again we should have to 'fall in' & go & see what the trouble was." The newcomers were held to the same high standards as the veterans—perhaps higher—earning punishments for such violations as blowing their nose on dress parade. "Another was made to stand on a board for half a day for putting a brass button into a wound so as to keep it from healing so he could get his discharge" and "had a paper pinned on his back stating his crime." Ingalls's diary ends in disgust: "I have to get me a hat with a bugle 6 & E & a feather. O how I hate the whole thing. From beginning to end." How times had changed from the days when that *6* was a source of pride to the men marching below it.[25]

A total of 475 conscripts served in the Sixth Wisconsin—incredibly, that was slightly more than 1 percent of the total number of draftees who served in the Union army. By comparison, the next highest number of draftees in regiments from the Badger State, 292, went to the Third Wisconsin, which had seen heavy fighting in the Shenandoah Valley, Gettysburg, and Georgia. Their Iron Brigade twin, the Seventh, received only 71. The other regiments receiving significant numbers of draftees fought in the West. Three-fourths of the regiments organized in 1861 and 1862 (most of the others enlisted men for 100 days or one year) received fewer than 100 draftees, and half of those regiments received only one or none at all.[26]

The cohort of draftees differed from the first and second cohorts in important ways. As we have seen already, virtually none came from the "home" counties of any of the companies in the Sixth. More than a quarter came from the eastern counties of Sheboygan, Washington, and Milwaukee, where some of the most virulent resistance to the draft had occurred in 1862 and 1863. Half the draftees were immigrants—almost double the percentage in the regiment as a whole—with most coming from Germany, Prussia, or other Germanic countries. They also trended older than any of the other cohorts, with the median birth year falling between 1830 and 1831, fully eight years earlier than that of cohorts 1 and 2 and a decade earlier than that of the enrolled substitutes (more on them below). The draftees had a wide range of backgrounds and experiences, although they were generally more settled and, as a result, had more to lose than many of the other new recruits.[27]

In the end, twenty draftees were killed outright or died of wounds and a dozen more died of disease, while eight were wounded, six went missing in action, and thirteen were discharged for illness. This amounted to a casualty rate of 12.4 percent—fairly high, considering they only served for roughly seven months.[28]

Not surprisingly, a sampling of draftee casualties shows that they produced the same sad stories as earlier volunteers. James Eastland apparently injured his back while in camp in Madison. By the time he and the other draftees joined the Sixth in December, he "gave out" and had to be helped into camp. He was discharged in January and never really recovered. A photograph included in his pension file shows a dignified, elderly man with a white beard, trouser legs pulled up over his knees to reveal alarmingly thin, deformed legs and feet—"shrunk and to some extent withered," as one witness testified—the result of many years of rheumatism, cramps, and other problems. Since the war, he had been unable to walk without difficulty, much less do a full day of manual labor. He spent the last three years of his life in the National Home for Disabled Volunteer Soldiers in Milwaukee.[29]

Henry Hohenstein was a forty-five-year-old farmer with six children and another on the way when he was drafted; he survived the harsh winter of 1865 and all of that spring's battles but sickened and died in May. He was buried in Arlington National Cemetery. Tragedy followed German-born Frederick Bauer to the army; he and his wife Catharine had already lost three of their six young children in 1862. Frederick was killed at Gravelly Run and his body was never recovered. Not surprisingly, draftees were among the regiment's last casualties. The forty-year-old brewer Gottfriend Winsch left a wife and at least one child when he was killed on April 2, while another German immigrant, August Fredrick, who was also married and had three children, died of disease shortly after being mustered out in June 1865.[30]

A draftee was also the only member of the Sixth known to have died by suicide during the war. Perhaps it was the harsh conditions the regiment faced in February 1865, but Martin Judas, a German immigrant who had arrived as a thirty-one-year-old in the United States in 1861, "committed suicide by shooting with musket," according to regimental surgeon John Hall.[31]

Sixty-seven "enrolled substitutes" also joined the regiment, thirty-seven before the spring campaign began (mostly in a large group that must have come to the regiment with the draftees late in 1864), with almost two dozen being assigned to the regiment in April 1865 or later. Substitutes could not be eligible for the draft—which applied to men between the ages of twenty and forty-five—so it is not surprising that they were on average far younger than any other contingent in the Sixth, with their median birth year falling between 1845 and 1846. Well over 60 percent had been born in 1843 or after; half were born in 1845, 1846, or 1847. One gets the sense that many were teenagers who had simply bided their time until they turned eighteen or received their parents' permission to sign up. Only four are known to have been married; fifty-five are known to have been single. Only ten reported occupations other than "farmer" or "laborer," but most of them—even the ones who claimed "farmer" when reporting their occupation—were actually still living on their parents' farms in 1860. Although information is relatively scarce in some of the categories (for instance, although we can establish with certainty that fourteen substitutes were immigrants, with at least four having arrived in the United States in 1860 or later, that seems low), it is safe to say that few of these young men had established themselves in an occupation or family before entering the army. One enlisted under an alias, three came from other states, and just one had already served in another regiment.[32]

The substitutes, more even than draftees, were untethered to any of the companies' counties of origin. Of the sixty-four for whom locations were noted, only three came from their company's home county, with most coming from substantial distances away. Company H was organized in Buffalo County, along the Mississippi River; it received fourteen substitutes, the most of any company, virtually all from counties along the Illinois border, on Lake Michigan, or in the more urban southeastern part of the state. The thirteen substitutes in Company G, which had been raised in Rock County in south central Wisconsin, came from every part of the state, from Kewanee in the far northeast to Grant in the southeast and Wood in the state's north central lumbering district.[33]

Of the thirty-five substitutes who reached the regiment in time for the fighting in spring 1865, four died in combat or of disease, five were wounded, two were taken prisoner, and one was discharged due to illness—for a casualty rate of more than 33 percent![34]

Although hardly representative, Hans Rasmussen, who came to the regiment in late 1864, provides a rare narrative of a substitute's journey. His pension file contains a somewhat rambling affidavit that, along the way, described the process by which he ended up in the Sixth. "Now about my enlistment you must understand that I don't talk any English when I enlisted," Rasmussen's original affidavit began. "I was just from the old country, Denmark, where I had been in the war with Russia—the Schleswig-Holstein war and I come to America to get in the war here. I suppose I was a substitute I don't know. I didn't get any money for it and I don't know who I went for as substitute." However, during a second day of questioning, Rasmussen recalled that he had, in fact, received $400 for going into the army. His lack of facility with the English language no doubt contributed to his hazy memory. He could not remember any officers' names, although "Grant was the general over them all." During "the last battle we had" his captain stood next to him and said, "'Do you see those men over there—You must kill 'em.' I raised my gun and fired and then I saw the man fall." This happened "two or three days before the war ended but I can't tell you where it was."[35]

Two other groups also came into the regiment in the fall of 1864 or spring of 1865. At about the same time that the contingent of draftees arrived in late November 1864, the 113 survivors of the Second Wisconsin were folded into the Sixth. They had been operating as a two-company "independent battalion" since the summer, mainly serving as the provost guard. Six of the Second's remaining officers filled similar roles in the Sixth; Thomas Kelley and Henry Naegely came as first lieutenants and were the last commanders of Company H and G, respectively, while Dennis Daily came as captain and eventually became a major. Five former members of the Second died in the spring fighting. But many seem to have never actually seen duty with the regiment. The terms of ten men expired early in the spring, and a number were already in hospital or in the process of being transferred to the Veteran Reserve Corps when they received their official transfers. The entries for absent and detached soldiers in the descriptive roll suggest that at least twenty-five of the men from the Second spent their entire time as members of the Sixth in the hospital and twenty-seven on detached service (as teamsters or as members of various provost guard units), while eight transferred to the Veteran Reserve Corps before the spring campaigns and five were on furlough, received other discharges, or were absent without leave.[36]

Finally, regular enlistees—also attracted, no doubt, by the ever-increasing bounties but also by a sense of adventure or patriotism, or after finally coming of age—continued to drift into the regiment during the war's last few months. A total of forty-eight men enlisted between April 1864 and May 1865, with eight coming to the regiment in both September and October, five in November, eleven in December, and another six just before the last spasm of fighting began in February 1865. Of the thirty-seven known years of birth, the median was 1837. Their geographic origins resembled the draftees'; virtually all came from outside the original county—indeed, virtually all came from noncontiguous counties. There are huge gaps in our detailed knowledge of this group, for some reason, but they seem to have been married at a slightly higher rate than enrolled substitutes, and they seemed to have been slightly more likely to be established, independent men than the substitutes. Four died of wounds or disease, five were wounded, and one was discharged for illness. Only one appears on the rolls as a deserter.[37]

Over 1,500 men volunteered to wear the tall black hats with the brass 6, and although it is simplistic to say so, there were probably 1,000 different motivations or combinations of motivations for enlisting. Adventure, patriotism, and community spirit may well have been the guiding sentiment for the men who enlisted in the feverish summer of 1861—although ambition certainly propelled some, and hard economic times others—but we can assume that the calculations made by the late war volunteers and substitutes involved money; nothing else can explain the hard choices some made to leave behind vulnerable family members. Dennis Johnson, according to neighbors, had been his parents' main support for several years prior to volunteering as a substitute late in 1864. Belinda, Dennis's mother, had done some "weaving and spinning for other people" after Dennis's departure, but in her late fifties she was "about past labor" and her husband Oliver had been unable to work for years. They did not own the small farm they lived on, and their fourteen-year-old daughter could not yet contribute to the family income. Dennis had been paid something for being a substitute—the going rate in Madison was $100 that season—and with his army pay he would have made more than the $100, the amount he had been able to devote to his parents' care before he left for the army. Unfortunately, Dennis took sick with typhoid fever and died in the hospital less than three months after arriving in Virginia. His mother successfully obtained a twelve-dollar pension, which helped support her until her death in 1889. If Stanley Vanderwalker had intended to support his twenty-year-old wife Sarah and two small children more securely when he enlisted in early 1864, his plan backfired spectacularly. Sarah died a month after he departed, and his children became orphans when he died in March 1865 after being released from a Confederate prison.[38]

By the end of 1864 the Sixth Wisconsin had been substantially reconstituted. At least three-fourths of its members were draftees, substitutes, or survivors of the Second Wisconsin. A number of factors made it a less cohesive group than the original cohort. The old soldiers—along with the native-born draftees—may have been separated from many of the draftees by language; all of the recent arrivals differed from the more experienced comrades in that they had watched the war from afar for over three years while hundreds of the first wave of soldiers had suffered and died. Of course, the original cohort that gathered at Camp Randall in 1861 were hardly homogenous; they, too, were separated by geography, occupation, and ethnicity. But those ten companies had had a year to grow into a well-functioning and unified regiment. The new men would not have that chance, and the Sixth would go into battle in the late winter of 1865 as a fractured regiment with relatively little training and limited knowledge of the men standing beside them. Yet the newcomers would eventually earn the respect, if not the friendship, of the experienced soldiers.

Good, Strong, Healthy Fellows

The draftees and substitutes were part of a massive reorganization and reinforcement of the Army of the Potomac as it recovered from the 68,000 casualties suffered during the summer. Throughout the fall, Ulysses S. Grant and his generals had fretted about the readiness of the new recruits. They frequently reorganized units and, on occasion, delayed operations until a time when more battle-ready men were available. In early October, Maj. Gen. Gouverneur K. Warren, commanding V Corps—the Sixth's home since the previous spring—urged Gen. George G. Meade against extending the Army of the Potomac's line too far to the left. "We need time to get our new levies in order," he warned, "and no matter how great the pressure, we cannot succeed with them till they have at least acquired the knowledge of the rudiments of their drill and discipline." Some of Gen. Nelson Miles's regiments "are mainly composed of substitutes who have recently joined, and the frequency of desertions among this class of men renders it necessary that they be placed in positions where they can easily be watched and guarded." Devoting so much of the new recruits' time to building entrenchments worried Maj Gen. Winfield Hancock: "There are a good many recruits in the command whom we are trying to drill, and I have not allowed them to be worked within the last few days on that account." And the constant construction work was not without risk. The Sixth's Frederick Wion had his head laid open by an axe while building breastworks late in the war. He blamed the accident for the dizziness and an intolerance of heat that plagued him for the rest of his life.[39]

As the top brass sought the right balance between digging and drilling, the Sixth had to accommodate hundreds of untrained and untested new comrades. In a letter to his parents in December 1864, Winslow Loring described an encounter between Gen. Edward Bragg—now commanding the brigade—and the green reinforcements flooding into his command. Bragg, wrote Winslow, "is rather hard on our recruits. He came down to see them drill yesterday and seeing one in his shirtsleeves went up to him jerked him out of the ranks and told him to go & get his coat." Another was smoking and Bragg stepped up to him and "pulls the pipe out of his mouth [and] threw it away. He is worse on them than he was on us probably because there [sic] drafted and so Dutchy."[40]

The new men of the Sixth would not have the luxury of a year of training before their first battle, nor would they enjoy the leadership of professional soldiers like John Gibbon or ambitious young officers like Rufus Dawes—or any of the dozens of captains, lieutenants, and first sergeants who had been killed or discharged or chosen not to reenlist. Moreover, some of the surviving officers were in terrible shape. Alexander Lowrie, captain of Company I, had lost two fingers and the use of another to a shell fragment way back in 1862, while a slice had been taken out of Capt. Andrew Gallup's right arm at the Wilderness and soreness from a chronic liver complaint forced him to wear his sword belt over his shoulder rather than around his painful waist.

Kellogg, their new commander, had returned from prison "much emaciated and somewhat feeble," according to regimental surgeon Hall, and complained "mostly of cerebral trouble," including vertigo, dizziness, and severe head-aches, which continued through the end of the war.[41]

Others coming into positions of authority were noncommissioned offi-cers who had risen through the ranks. In a letter to the departed Rufus Dawes in which he called the draftees "a good strong, healthy set of fellows of the right age, and altogether the best lot of recruits I ever saw," surgeon John Hall marveled at the extraordinary turnover of officers and chuckled that "even little [Henry] Matrau" had become a lieutenant. Despite suffering his third or fourth major wound in the summer of 1864, James Sullivan was promoted to sergeant in the badly diminished Sixth. One of his duties was to turn them into soldiers. Because they were hopeless in company-level drills—where they vastly outnumbered the handful of remaining veterans—they were bro-ken up into smaller squads. Chaos ensued, represented in Sullivan's reminis-cences of a diminutive Irishman and a six-foot German. His account—full of imaginative spellings of their thick accents, as men bickered and snarled at one another—suggested it was difficult for the new men to understand such simple ideas as the need to step off with their left feet. Simple maneuvers were literally painful to perform and to watch, but the newcomers eventually "proved to be good soldiers."[42]

One of three German immigrant brothers drafted into Company E, Got-tlieb Torke, wrote earnest letters to his wife and two young children filled with sincere piety, expressions of affection, and homely advice about turnips and cattle. Like most new soldiers, he reported on the long days and plain food, hard drilling and daily cutting of firewood, the unfamiliar weather and sandy soil. His instructions for keeping the farm running were clear, detailed, and loving. He urged her to do a particular chore "on a nice warm day, so that you don't freeze on the way." She should also "keep yourself away from the sheep that they don't butt you." He seemed to keep thinking of new bits of advice to give her, almost as if he wanted to extend this moment of personal contact with her. "I remain your true husband," he finally wrote, "until death." Three weeks later Gottlieb wrote Elizabeth of picturing his young children sleeping as he walked the midnight shift at guard, of missing Christmas and praying for peace, of worrying that she was working too hard and perhaps tormenting the oxen, and of drilling "very hard now. . . . As soon as something happens here at Petersburg, then we will have to go off to the war."[43]

The sudden immersion into the harsh late winter weather (the winter was wetter than in Wisconsin, and of course, they were living rough rather than

Off to the War

in comfortable farmhouses), the unfamiliar food, and hard drilling weighed heavily on the new men. A draftee in Company A, according to one of those veterans, became in February 1865 "somewhat despondent and demoralized by reason of the hardships endured, gave up in despair and was ready to die. He longed for his wife and nice quiet home.... In short, he was homesick; he neglected personal cleanliness ... and would soon have died if the boys had not put up a job on him." He was eventually convinced by the experienced men to take better care of himself.[44]

A number of men traced their chronic illnesses later in life to those early days of February 1865, when, in the words of one pension claimant, the regiment experienced "excessive and unavoidable exposure, without tents or proper shelter, during sleeting & freezing weather." The regimental surgeon did what he could for them in camp, but only a few were treated in a hospital, which later led to some problems when they applied for pensions. In his testimony on behalf of a comrade, Manfred Bump swore that they slept in cold so severe that their "clothes would freeze to the ground." It was cold and rainy from that time on through the "gravely run fight" (March 31); "we had to sleep in the mud & hadn't any thing for a shelter but a little piece of tent cloth."[45]

The arrival of the new soldiers inspired a surge of optimism in the regiment. A cheerful letter from "the Veteran Sixth Wisconsin" published in early January 1865 indicated that the army was in good spirits due to several bits of good news from other battlefields and the president's recent call for 300,000 additional men. Another reason for optimism: the regiment now had nearly 700 men, more than at any time since the Battle of Gainesville more than two and a half years earlier. "They are mostly drafted men, and with a few exceptions, a fine, robust lot of fellows, well suited for soldiers." The regiment would enter the spring campaign "with good round numbers, and will doubtless sustain its former well earned reputation."[46]

However good a face they put on it, though, it was clear that the veterans missed the old days. "Our Brigade is broken up," complained the newly commissioned Henry Matrau. By February the Nineteenth Indiana was long gone and the Twenty-Fourth Michigan had been reassigned. The Second Wisconsin no longer existed; all that was left were the Sixth and Seventh Wisconsin. A few units from New York and Pennsylvania had been in the brigade between August 1864 and February 1865, but they had also been transferred. John Kellogg felt the loss personally. He had "found many changes" since he returned. "Nearly every officer on duty when I left the regiment the previous May, was either promoted, killed, or mustered out. It seemed lonesome." He figured that many of the newcomers wondered who "that white-headed old fellow" was.[47]

Drafted Men Can Fight

This lightly trained and rather sickly regiment would fight the Sixth's final battles. Most generals seemed to have dismissed their fighting qualities. John Gibbon, who commanded a corps by early 1865, spoke for many when he later wrote of the wearing down of the "old soldiers" and the poor performance of the draftees and substitutes. "It became a recognized fact amongst the men themselves that when the enemy had occupied a position six or eight hours ahead of us, it was useless to attempt to take it," he wrote years later. "This feeling became so marked that when troops under these circumstances were ordered forward, they went a certain distance and then lay down and opened fire." Some of the severest losses in the spring occurred among the new troops, "who had not had sufficient experience in attacking breastworks" to fight as effectively "as the old soldiers."[48]

Yet most of the new men of the Sixth seem to have done their duty, at least as far as their limited skill and experience allowed. Although they did not necessarily get to know them well, none of the old-timers criticized the new men's performance in battle. About halfway through the hard fighting in early 1865, one officer reported that the Sixth had lost 175 killed, wounded, and missing in the recent fighting. Yet "our reg[iment] did remarkably well considering that we had nearly 400 drafted men in the fight."[49]

In early February, elements of the Union V and II Corps pushed west toward the Boydton Plank Road. In two days of hard fighting, the new recruits and draftees finished their journey "to the war." The inexperienced draftees saw the fighting through a terrifying haze. Gottlieb Torke's letter to his wife was simple but oddly eloquent: "I could think of you only a little. I directed my thoughts to the heavenly father above, to whom many thousand prayers were rising." When the battle finally started in midafternoon on February 6, "we all looked at the world through tears, and I had given myself over completely to dear God. Then we had to attack the Southerners."

The fighting surged back and forth. "The shooting was so heavy as if a great thunderstorm were thundering an hour long. . . . The bullets always flew past my head, I thought to myself that here I must die, but the dear God had protected me." After a cold and rainy night, the fighting started again. Torke's account, free of military verbiage or jargon, captured what must have been a blur of images, sounds, and fears for men experiencing their first fight:

It was a hard day for us, we were quite wet and freezing. We had to fight the Southerners again and had driven them back a piece again. There we made a good trench where the bullets would always fly over our heads, and then when we had finished making the trench, we went out again against the Southerners [who] stayed in their trenches, and we stood in the woods. Then we lay down on the ground and fired at them. We had been firing a half-hour, then we sprang up again and ran back again in our trenches, as we wanted to draw the Southerners out of their trenches so that they would come near our trenches. And so we tried to decoy them but they wouldn't come, so then we went out again toward them. They were firing very much at us with cannons.

This time a shell fragment struck a glancing blow to his head. His brothers carried him to the hospital, but his injury was minor. "Dear God had surely placed his almighty arm on my head."[50]

The Sixth took heavy casualties in this first scene of the war's final act. Although the men might have begun to believe that the war was entering its last phase, it remained deadly, and no one was immune. It was especially hard when original members of the regiment fell. Sgt. Allison Fowler, for instance, had already survived three wounds; he was shot in the head and killed instantly. By this time Kellogg commanded the three-regiment brigade, now including the Ninety-First New York, a heavy artillery unit that had just been converted to an oversized infantry regiment.[51]

After a few weeks' lull, the Sixth Wisconsin fought their last battles at Gravelly Run and Five Forks on March 31 and April 1, respectively, just before the Confederates evacuated Petersburg on April 2. The battles cost the regiment at least 100 men. Once again the drafted men did well; veterans from Company A recalled that their initial success against the Confederates was threatened when the regiment was outflanked. But the Sixth recovered and drove back the Rebels. "Company A proved that drafted men could fight. . . . The work they did was entitled to great praise and they received it from the Commander of the regiment."[52]

Kellogg's report of the brigade's last two battles sounded like the reports of old, when the Wisconsinites held firm as other units fell apart, gave ground grudgingly, and ultimately did what they needed to do. In his account of the action on March 31, he described his men forming a line of battle when the troops in their front collapsed. After some initial confusion, once the retreating men were through, the Wisconsinites closed intervals and fired on the advancing Confederates, who soon flanked them on both sides. Some got behind the Yankees, who retreated across Gravelly Run "in as good order as possible." Kellogg's report on the operations of April 1 indicated a far more successful day of fighting, when his men drove the enemy from their entrenchments, attacking "across an open field, pursuing them closely about three-quarters of a mile, taking many prisoners and killing and wounding many of the enemy."[53]

The Confederates pulled out of Petersburg the next day, and the Sixth raced westward with the rest of the Army of the Potomac as it tried to cut off the Confederates' desperate attempt to reach supplies and rail connections west of Richmond. The next few days saw a great deal of marching and preparing for battles that never came, yet the "tired but gallant column pushed on." Kellogg claimed that the "long forced march" that the brigade made on April 8 was "the most tiresome I believe ever made by troops." The draftee Robert McMinn later claimed that he had been "greatly overtasked and prostrated" during the march, "causing nervous debility and physical prostration, and a disease of the nervous system causing epileptic symptoms" that worsened as the years went on. Conrad Bates, another conscript, blamed his lifelong struggles with his health and with the Pension Bureau on the march to Appomattox. He spent a number of weeks in the hospital at the front and in Wisconsin; a close neighbor claimed years later that Bates was unable to work for at least a year after returning from the army and "that he has never been a sound and healthy man since his return."[54]

No one could predict those outcomes, but as the regiment spent the night of April 8 in line of battle, they anticipated at least one more fight, even as rumors and signs that the Confederates might surrender multiplied. The next day, wrote Kellogg, "the enemy, tired, dispirited, harassed, and surrounded, surrendered."[55]

After their V Corps accepted the formal surrender of the Army of Northern Virginia, the regiment got some well-earned rest. Maj. Lewis Kent—a Virginian who as a student at Beloit College four years earlier had cast his lot with the Union and the Sixth Wisconsin—helped with the surrender process. He had the unique experience of gathering the weapons from a regiment from his home county; some of the grizzled Confederates were surprised to find a familiar—if older—face among the Yankees. "What are you doing here?" one Confederate asked. "Just now I am busy taking the guns of your regiment," Kent replied in good humor.[56]

Henry Matrau wrote that the men had finally started to imagine a life beyond the war: "I think our hard fighting is over & the boys are beginning [to] plan what they will do for a living when the war is over." He asked his parents to tell his younger brothers to be good and assured them that his brother Hank, serving in a different regiment, "will if he lives, be at home to stay a while pretty soon."[57]

Should Our Country Be Again in Danger

According to the published *Roster of Wisconsin Volunteers*, there were still 854 men in the Sixth Wisconsin on April 9. Of course, many were detached, in hospital, or otherwise occupied. The number of men actually on duty declined throughout the remaining three or so months of their service. By the end of May, the official roll was down to 772; eleven men—all from the original 1861 recruits—had died, and ten had received disability discharges during the previous two months. Sixty-one had been mustered out, including a dozen from the original cohort and almost four dozen draftees and substitutes who had joined the regiment in late 1864 or the spring of 1865.[58]

The march back to the Rebel capital after the surrender was punishing, especially to the unseasoned draftees, substitutes, and new recruits. Many years later, surgeon John Hall commented in an affidavit for a veteran's pension that the claimant "was one of the many men of the 6th Wisconsin who broke down in the rapid march of the troops from 'Appomattox' to Petersburg after the surrender of Lee." By May 12 the brigade was camped outside Washington, DC, where the men received new uniforms and continued drilling in preparation for the upcoming Grand Review. It's likely that between 600 and 650 men marched with the regiment on May 23. Following the cavalry, provost marshal, and engineering units, the IX Corps, and the divisions of US Colored Troops, the Sixth Wisconsin's V Corps finally stepped off for their turn before the cheering crowds and somber generals and politicians. Although it was a memorable day for the old soldiers—and no doubt for the newcomers who had been with the regiment for only a few months or even weeks—it seems to have been more of an annoying delay to members of the Sixth than something worth writing about at the time or afterward.[59]

Even as the regiment anticipated its impending return home, casualties continued to whittle away at the survivors. Seventeen-year-old Madison Brower had joined the regiment as a substitute at the end of March. He was relieved that he had survived the march north; "I thought I would melt, but I stood it." The heat was followed by rain—"the hardest I have ever saw in my life"—and freezing temperatures. Even the "old soldiers . . . say it was the hardest time they ever saw." It was the last letter Brower would ever write. A few days later he went to the hospital with "intermittent fever" and died on the day of the Grand Review. He was buried in Arlington National Cemetery.[60]

Brower had been with the regiment for only two months. We sometimes carelessly imagine men serving together through four years of war, with the survivors limping home, grizzled and diminished. Yet only about 166 men actually served for the entire war (this includes twenty-six men who transferred from the Second Wisconsin to the Sixth in the fall of 1864). How did they survive? Information gleaned from the *Roster* and the Descriptive Roll can suggest the main—and fairly obvious—reason a soldier in one of the hardest-fighting units in the Union army could last the entire war: he managed somehow to miss significant campaigns. In the end, it seems, only thirty-three men can be assumed to have been present at virtually all of the battles fought by the Sixth. For the purposes of this exercise, prisoners of war—facing their own set of risks—are not counted as "absent."

Sixty-nine were detached from the Sixth for months or even years, allowing them to miss key battles and campaigns. Although some were detached for only two or three months, those assignments caused them to miss all of the first four weeks of fighting in the fall of 1862 or the entire spring campaign in 1865. The next largest group—forty-one—were sick, wounded, or on furlough during at least a few crucial months. Another ten served in the Veteran Reserve Corps for the last year or two of their terms, while seven had deserted or been absent without leave for significant amounts of time before returning and finishing the war.[61]

Four-year men differed from the rest of the regiment in two not particularly surprising ways, considering the additional wear and tear their longer service must have inflicted (even on those who missed some campaigns). Thirty (18.1 percent) would end up in a soldiers' home for at least some time, significantly more than the regimental average of 11 percent. They also lived shorter lives. Twenty-two died before the age of fifty-two, with at least eight dying at the age of forty or younger. Their median age at death was sixty-seven—several years below the median age at death of all three cohorts.[62]

But most of the men mustering out in the summer of 1865 had served for much shorter periods; the majority were, of course, draftees. Others had just arrived in Virginia as the Sixth prepared to leave. Seven recruits joined the regiment on June 1 at Ball's Crossroads near Arlington—having missed not only the fighting but the hard march north from Richmond and the Grand Review! These five teenaged substitutes and two married draftees spent nearly as much time en route to Virginia and back to Wisconsin as they actually spent in camp. Nevertheless, four received pensions for their brief service and at least one would join the Grand Army of the Republic.[63]

The Sixth was kept in camp near Washington for more than three weeks— idle, hungry, and waiting for pay. Oddly, many of the drafted men were sent home before the veterans; of the 160 who left the regiment in late May and the first two weeks of June, 115 were draftees. Matrau complained that while the men who had fought for years cooled their heels near Alexandria, "men who have never seen a battle or smelled gun powder" were heading back to Wisconsin.[64]

They finally left for home by rail and then steamer on June 16, only to be held in camp across the Ohio River from Louisville, Kentucky, for another three weeks, delayed at least partly by a shortage of blank discharge papers. Nevertheless, a little over five dozen additional men were mustered out while in Indiana—again, mainly draftees and substitutes.[65]

Officially, 473 men were mustered out and ordered to Wisconsin on July 14. Two days later they reached Madison, where they stayed briefly at Camp Randall, where former colonel of the Second Wisconsin and soon-to-be governor Lucius Fairchild greeted the regiment before a large crowd of civilians. He delivered a short speech that included a rather bombastic passage that might have sounded like a bit of bluster to those few survivors who had begun the war on these grounds four long years before: "Should our country be again in danger, we'll raise another 2nd, 6th, and 7th, Indiana will furnish another 19th and we'll send to Michigan for a 24th and we'll have another Iron Brigade." After one last, short march, flags flying, bayonets fixed, fifes and drums playing, the regiment was finally dissolved, the last original regiment from the Iron Brigade to be dismissed.[66]

Aside from the ceremony in Madison, there were no parades or major celebrations to welcome home the Sixth Wisconsin. A few score members of the regiment had arrived by steamer in Milwaukee a month earlier and were treated to a breakfast by local supporters. The remaining members of Company A were feted by "our kindred, loyal friends and the ladies of Baraboo" with a "most royal" reception, followed by a party hosted by an old comrade, Maj. D. K. Noyes.[67] "Discharged soldiers begin to arrive home in goodly numbers," the *Appleton Motor* remarked in mid-June. "In a very few days now," declared the *Motor*, "we shall have nearly all our boys home from duty. They will receive a hearty welcome." Perhaps, but most of those welcomes were made in the privacy of family homes or in churches, lodges, or other small gatherings. Indeed, rain forced the cancellation of a July Fourth parade in Appleton intended to feature Company E and other local veterans.

Otherwise, few other men of the Sixth reported much of a fuss being made over them.[68]

Even as Fairchild released the regiment from duty, there were still fifty-six men to be mustered out, most still hospitalized with wounds. A number of them were in the Harvey US Army General Hospital in Madison, a 300-bed facility that had opened in 1863.[69] Most of the patients from the Sixth were draftees who had fallen ill or been wounded during the last few months of the war, but some had been with the regiment from the beginning. Before departing Madison after being mustered out, the survivors of Company A visited the hospital to bid Elon Wyman farewell. "He was very low and fast passing away," wrote one. "His desire to live and enjoy the comradeship of those just returned from the fields of battle, camps and weary marches of four long years of service . . . was intense. We bade him farewell, as parting from a loved brother, realizing full well that when we next met . . . it would be in that final bivouac on the other shore." Wyman died shortly after this somber visit.[70]

There were other casualties in the weeks and months following the surrender. Henry Jones was mustered into Company K as a draftee less than a month before Appomattox and mustered out with his regiment in July, but in the meantime he had come down with "malarial disease, chills & fever," and diarrhea. He was barely able to make it home to Ridgeway, in Iowa County. Colonel Kellogg noted that when the regiment arrived in Madison, Jones was too weak to complete any of the forms required to muster out. Believing Jones "could not live long," Kellogg paid his passage to his home in Mazomanie, where he went to bed and died less than a month later. Frederick Fischer, a late enlistee, fought through the spring of 1865 and witnessed the surrender at Appomattox; he was sent home a few weeks early with diarrhea and fever and died of typhus in August, leaving a wife and three children. Another man died in the soldiers' home run by women in downtown Milwaukee. Others would die of wounds or disease, surrounded by family, in the next year or two.[71]

Among them would be their old colonel Lysander Cutler, who joined them in "the final bivouac" within a year of returning. Just after the war, John Kellogg happened upon the general on a Milwaukee street. Cutler's last words to Kellogg before the younger man was captured a year earlier in the Wilderness had been to "report frequently." They had not seen each other since, and when they finally met, Cutler's "usually stern face became more stern, his chin quivered, [and] he grasped my hand more firmly. At length he blurted out: 'You've been a terrible long time reporting!'" Cutler did not survive long after this bittersweet reunion. According to his doctor, the fifty-eight-year-old had returned from war in a "shattered condition of health." He "continued declining" until July 1866, when a series of "apoplectic shocks" caused his entire right side to palsy. He died two weeks after the first attack.[72]

— — — — — —

Although families and friends no doubt noted these aftershocks of the great war, there is a sense that civilians wanted to get on with their lives. The Appleton Soldiers' Aid Society formally declared its work over in mid-May. Even before the Sixth had returned to Wisconsin the *North Western Times* declared, "Wide awake is the word in Viroqua." Residents "seem to feel sure of better times. They seem to foresee great prosperity for themselves and the citizens of the county generally." Stores were filling up "with stocks of New Goods—Mechanics are busy—and building and repairing have commenced three months earlier than usual." Now that "glorious peace has come . . . industry and energy must prosper." Veterans certainly hoped to benefit and to be remembered during that glorious peace.[73]

8

Heroes and Marauders

Government Aid and the Ambiguity of Disability

Peter Mohrbacher, an eighteen-year-old substitute, was one of the last men to join the Sixth Wisconsin in April 1865. He never fought in a battle, probably did not march in the Grand Review, and actually spent most of his service on the sick roll. Yet by 1891 he was receiving a quarterly pension from the federal government for rheumatism and kidney disease that would reach $100 by the 1930s. In addition, for twenty years he lived at least part-time at the Iowa Soldiers' Home, and when he finally died, his stepdaughter was reimbursed $329.60 for his funeral. Mohrbacher apparently did not join the Grand Army of the Republic (GAR) or attend Iron Brigade reunions, but when his long life finally came to an end, few men in the Sixth Wisconsin had benefited more from the pledge by federal and state governments to care for veterans of the war.[1]

Mohrbacher's record suggests a beneficent government living up to the commitment expressed in the famous Second Inaugural promise of Abraham

Lincoln "to care for those who shall have borne the battle." But that is a dramatic oversimplification of the role of the government in the lives of the many survivors of the Sixth Wisconsin who came out of the war with lasting wounds or chronic illnesses.

Wisconsin's new governor, the one-armed former Iron Brigade colonel Lucius Fairchild, wanted his constituents to know about some of the challenges facing veterans and their families. In his first message to the state legislature in early 1866, he proposed creating a state agency to help veterans and their survivors collect back pay and to facilitate federal pension applications, called attention to the plight of the state's 6,000 orphans or "half orphans" (children with one living parent), and recommended allocating funds to help the State Historical Society collect the "narratives of our gallant Wisconsin soldiers" and to help create the new Antietam National Cemetery, where at least twenty-five Sixth Wisconsin soldiers were buried. The legislature accepted most of Fairchild's recommendations and continued to address veterans' issues for years after the war. They ranged from paying for the treatment of "indigent Wisconsin soldiers suffering from the diseases of the eye or ear" and giving preference for state employment to "maimed soldiers" to providing funds for the burial of indigent veterans and urging Congress to pass "an adequate pension law." The legislature also approved a number of bills related to war monuments, the GAR, and other commemorative activities.[2]

These state programs and policies joined local and federal efforts undertaken on behalf of veterans. In the end, the federal government would create a massive pension program and a system of soldiers' homes, the first federally funded social welfare programs. At the state level, most legislation created short-term or very specific programs for veterans or their survivors; the state's most significant contribution was taking over the GAR's Wisconsin Veterans' Home shortly after it was built in the late 1880s. Very little public money went toward veterans' needs at the local level until the legislature eventually prodded communities to provide cash assistance to the neediest veterans and widows.

Many of these programs were unprecedented—and expensive—and they inevitably attracted criticism. Like their comrades from other regiments, veterans of the Sixth would no doubt take notice of the distrust toward veterans that, for one reason or another, seeped into popular notions about them in the decades after the war. Veterans' programs had become so politicized by 1889 that a Wisconsin veteran could write to a local newspaper about "professional old soldiers" who were being used by their friends and enemies alike. He accused all three groups of making "merchandise of patriotism, honor and glory." They took "extreme views of everything that pertains to the rebellion or the soldiers who survived," turning every veteran into "either a hero or a marauder." Each group had its own motivations: "The professional friend plays his part for political reasons, the professional enemy for partisan reasons, and the professional old soldier for mercenary reasons."[3]

These attitudes swirled around Union veterans in Wisconsin and elsewhere. Even as veterans grappled with crippling disabilities and reduced health, they were forced to deal with the always laborious and sometimes demeaning process of assembling proof of financial need and physical impairment. As the boundary between individual duty and government responsibility blurred and conversations about pensions, especially, lapsed into controversy over deserving and undeserving applicants, the lifelines offered by soldiers' homes and pensions complicated the efforts of men from the Sixth Wisconsin trying to build new lives in the decades after the war.

The pensions and soldiers' homes on which many veterans of the Sixth depended bound them to hundreds of thousands of other Union soldiers. This ever-expanding community of the maimed and the destitute represented every possible kind of disability and illness. Some, like the empty sleeve or prosthetic leg, marked the veterans as clearly—and perhaps proudly— disabled. Other forms of disability were far less obvious, even hidden, and facing a federal bureaucracy that demanded evidence became one of the major challenges facing the disabled men of the Sixth Wisconsin.

Disabilities, Hidden and Revealed

No one would ever doubt that Frank Hare was disabled—he had survived imprisonment and the loss of a leg at the hip at the Wilderness. Likewise, poor Arris Young, who lost parts of both arms when the shell exploded over his company at Antietam, would never be questioned about whether he deserved aid. Many other survivors of the Sixth suffered from similarly visible disabilities or limitations.

But many others suffered from disabilities that were often, for lack of a better word, invisible, or at least too subtle to be noticed by casual observers. Many such men may have chosen to hide their conditions for practical reasons—getting a job, for instance—or out of pride. Until they were sick or weak or poor enough to go into the soldiers' home or to finally apply for a pension, few people would have known of their conditions or that they were caused by exposure and hard service twenty or thirty years before. Perhaps they had earned good livings as farmers, salesmen, or mechanics for a decade or two after the war. They may have been active in churches or local GAR posts and turned out for community functions as apparently healthy men. But eventually their health had failed, and some combination of rheumatic or digestive or respiratory problems—the unholy trinity of old soldiers' maladies—would force them to reveal their distress and seek help.

For these men and virtually every other veteran, the notion of a "long Civil War," rather than a clever turn of historiographical phrase, would have been a fact of life. They would never have used the term, of course, and here it does not suggest unresolved political and racial issues. Rather, it encompasses the lived experiences of the men who fought the war and of their families. For them—or at least a significant number of them—the effects of the war were permanent. This does not mean that they all sank into depression and substance abuse or could not find satisfaction and joy in their work or families. But it also means that we cannot simply assume that they transitioned easily to "normal" lives or that the war did not from time to time, perhaps increasingly as the years passed, shape their realities.

The postwar lives of the men of the Sixth cannot be categorized neatly. We cannot say whether Civil War soldiers were generally successful or generally unsuccessful. Some men adapted well to peacetime; some never adapted. Most fell somewhere on a rather wide spectrum between success and failure. And it is likely that many veterans could identify phases of life during which they slid from one to the other.

A few survivors of the war wrote memoirs; a somewhat larger proportion gave a talk at a GAR campfire. But the best chance for most men to explain the ebbs and flows of their lives was through a pension application. The myriad affidavits, letters, examination reports, and other pieces of evidence in a typical file were produced for specific reasons; framed as legal documents, they were also highly performative. But they were the only opportunity most common soldiers would have to narrate their war and postwar experiences. Often gathered over the course of many years, they show the ways in which veterans could fade in and out of crises and the ways their families and the communities in which they lived understood veterans' issues.

One of the most obvious—and most damaged—category of survivor consisted of the eighty members of the Sixth Wisconsin who had been prisoners of war. At least a dozen died while imprisoned, and two more died shortly after being released. Sixteen, mostly wounded men left behind during the retreat from Seminary Ridge, were captured at Gettysburg. Over two dozen fell into Rebel hands during the confusing fighting during the summer of 1864, while another sixteen were captured and held briefly during the last few weeks of fighting between February and April of 1865.[4]

By the end of the war, the suffering of Union prisoners had become infamous, not only for the appalling conditions in the camps but for the permanently ruined health with which many survivors came home (the same could be said, of course, for Confederate prisoners in northern camps). The long-term effects of imprisonment clearly emerge among the prison camp survivors in the Sixth: eleven (18 percent) spent at least a few months in soldiers' homes, compared to 11 percent for the regiment as a whole, and their median age at death was three years lower than that of enlistees as a whole and seven years lower than that of draftees. Not surprisingly, former prisoners were often held up as particularly worthy of admiration and sympathy. In some cases, that translated into community support, particularly when a former prisoner returned to his hometown and his condition became known.[5]

This was the case for Levi Tongue, whose experiences and physical condition seem to have been well known throughout Hillsboro, the village in west central Wisconsin where he lived. Although it was almost impossible to prove that his terrible treatment at Andersonville caused it, he suffered from epilepsy throughout his postwar life. The local sheriff employed him out of sympathy for his condition, whose symptoms included poor memory and slowness of speech. Tongue faced other, non-war-related, trials: a threshing accident damaged his ankle, an infection claimed part of a hand, and a year before he died he was run over by an automobile.[6]

In 1868 Tongue's initial affidavit claimed that "through starvation and exposure while in prison and especially in Andersonville, his nervous system was so effected [sic] and his health so impaired that he has never recovered, but is still subject to 'Epilepsy' and to nervous debility and is wholly unable to procure his living by manual labor." In a rare display of community support for a pensioner—perhaps because of his status as a prison camp survivor—neighbors in 1880 submitted a petition supporting an increase in Tongue's pension. "Mr. Tongue was one of those unfortunate men who endured the horrors of 'Andersonville' for a protracted period with a fortitude born only of genuine patriotism. . . . He has not and in all human probability never will recover." Everyone knew that "his mental capacity is weakened by long and protracted suffering." One of Tongue's former commanders, Earl Rogers, estimated his disability as worse than losing a leg.

Interestingly, Tongue apparently presented as a fairly healthy person, and surgeons who did not know him had difficulty finding physical evidence of his symptoms. Although they recommended a fairly small pension, Congress saw fit in 1886 to raise it to twenty dollars per month. The report from the House Committee on Invalid Pensions added a detail to his story; after being treated in a hospital for nine months after his release, he was given back pay and discharged "but was so demented that he did not remember that he had been a soldier, and in that condition was robbed of his pay." The corresponding Senate committee ended its report with "Thus this brave soldier, who was conspicuous for his brave acts, is now almost an imbecile."[7]

To his friends and neighbors, Tongue's status as a survivor of Andersonville granted him special status and elicited pity that, while perhaps somewhat grating to him personally, ensured that he would have their support when he applied for a pension.

A more typical example of hidden disabilities was the case of John Kellogg, an original member and longtime captain of Company K, who had been wounded and captured at the Wilderness, only to return to command the regiment and the brigade. A Confederate soldier had knocked him unconscious in the fighting on May 5. When Kellogg came to, "my hat was gone"—as was his regiment—and his "head was swollen very badly, especially on top of the head. I was bleeding from both ears & from the scalp. I was partially blind & in this condition I was taken a prisoner by the enemy." A Rebel surgeon bound up his head, but he received no other medical treatment. He escaped a few months later and fought through the war's last spring. In the late 1870s he told his thrilling story in a series of articles in the *La Cross Leader*. He had finished a book-length manuscript by the time he died about a decade later. It remained unpublished until the Wisconsin History Commission issued it in 1908 as *Capture and Escape: A Narrative of Army and Prison Life*.[8]

Although he had a successful postwar career as a lawyer, legislator, and US pension agent, for the rest of his life Kellogg suffered nearly debilitating pain and dizziness. Yet he did not apply for a pension until 1879, believing other men were in greater need. Kellogg's pension file offered a narrative unavailable in his memoir. When he returned to the regiment, surgeon John Hall recalled, he was "much emaciated and somewhat feeble" and complaining of "cerebral trouble," including vertigo, dizziness, and severe headaches, which continued through the end of the war and, indeed, for the rest of his life. Another doctor described his frequent attacks of pain, partial blindness, and unsteadiness. He could not stoop over to pick up objects without having an attack. One physician, believing that Kellogg's skull had actually been fractured, worried that the condition was "liable to terminate fatally." Kellogg died four years later at the age of fifty-five, from the "effects of neuralgia," according to the surgeon who tended him during his last few years. The pain had spread from his injury to his neck and shoulders and eventually to his heart; it was so intense that painkillers were useless and he became delirious. Just a few months earlier, Kellogg had vainly applied for a life insurance policy, which had, not surprisingly, been rejected.[9]

Kellogg's disabilities might have been concealed from many people because he had managed to build a more or less normal life. Even more difficult to prove were the psychological effects of trauma on some men. Although it is difficult—and dangerous—to diagnose historical figures with modern-day pathologies, such diagnoses nevertheless provide insights that help us better understand Civil War veterans. Historians have found plentiful evidence of psychological distress among survivors of the war, including sleeplessness, anxiety, the desire to be alone, flashbacks, "melancholy" (crying spells, trembling, inability to concentrate, and apathy), anxiety, mania, violent behavior, irritability, depression, and alcoholism.[10] All of these symptoms appear in the pension files, obituaries, and other records produced by and about veterans of the Sixth Wisconsin, sometimes individually, sometimes as a slate of related conditions. Specific evidence of mental debility is rare, but we can say with confidence that four men died of drug or alcohol abuse, at least five died by suicide (including Edward Moore, who killed his wife Mary and then himself), and eight spent at least a few years in mental institutions.[11]

These numbers are no doubt undercounts, perhaps dramatically so. For instance, according to a recent study, 3.6 percent of Massachusetts veterans died by suicide during the decades after the war. Although reporting processes and policies can blur the statistics, these numbers are nevertheless shocking. Using the number of men of the Sixth who survived the war—1,635—the five men of the Sixth who definitely died by suicide comes out to only 0.3 percent. That is far below the fifty-nine suicides that we would predict using the Massachusetts model. Four of the known suicides and all of the possible suicides among the survivors of the Sixth had been wounded or discharged for illness during the war. Although the sample is small, the experience shared by virtually all of these men of being wounded or seriously ill hints at a possible, if partial, cause of suicide.[12]

Although the pension files and other documents certainly chronicle numerous cases of mental distress and decline—for instance, the 1890 veterans census taker simply wrote "head affected" in the notes section for Joseph Denman—a few were specifically diagnosed with mental illness. Thomas Case died in the Minnesota State Hospital in Rochester. William Winkleman and Nicholas Clumb resided in county insane asylums in Wisconsin, while Thomas Hobbs died at the Westboro Insane Hospital in

Massachusetts. James Burrell, Richard Corcoran, Herman Langhoff, and Reuben Pettit all ended their days in the Elizabeth Insane Asylum in Washington, DC, where residents of National Home for Disabled Volunteer Soldiers (NHDVS) branches were transferred if they were believed to be too mentally disabled to be treated locally. Pettit, officials reported, died of "chronic melancholy." Four of these eight men had been wounded or discharged for disability.[13]

Virtually all of the men on this admittedly short list spent at least some time in a soldiers' home—mainly the NHDVS Northwestern Branch in Milwaukee—before being sent to Washington. Although he was not speaking specifically of men from the Sixth, one resident of the Milwaukee home had a "good deal" to say "about the men here." Testifying before a congressional committee investigating the NHDVS in 1886, he asserted that residents "were all dissatisfied, every one of them. . . . We are not comfortable. We are unhappy. I would venture to say—in fact, I know it to be the case—that [the] petty persecution" that he claimed to be chronic at the home "has caused men to commit suicide. I know this to be a fact, because I know my own feelings, and I can judge others by those. Often I wish I was in the penitentiary; that I was hanged or dead, or in some other place."[14]

The stories of sickness, decline, and hardship flow from the pension files and records of soldiers' homes; although all are as unique as the individuals at the heart of their narratives, these representative samples show the numerous shades of gray spreading from revealed to hidden disabilities.

Upon the Same Level as Paupers

The vast majority of Union veterans would be awarded federal pensions, although many would not begin receiving pensions until the 1890s. In the meantime, some towns and counties extended aid to veterans and their families as part of their regular poor relief programs.

Wisconsin mandated local aid in 1887, when the legislature required county boards of supervisors to levy a property tax for the purpose of "creating a fund for the relief of indigent union soldiers, sailors and marines" and their families. The law promised that no "honorably discharged soldier, sailor or marine of the late war shall be sent to a poor-house in the state of Wisconsin."[15]

While perhaps noble in concept, the Soldiers' Relief Commissions (SRCs) thus established were hardly generous. The actual amounts initially granted to individuals ranged from as little as three or four dollars to ten dollars, money that was meant to last at least a month. Most commissioners sought to highlight the positives of the program, even as they acknowledged its limitations. "The money has done a great deal of good," the secretary of the Portage County SRC reported in spring 1888, after the program had been in operation for only three months. "It has kept quite a number of the old boys from going hungry to bed during the long cold winter." Still, "more worthy soldiers" went without help, and he recommended additional funding in future budgets.[16]

Americans had always resisted providing too generous support to the needy. "Outdoor" relief—meaning the recipient did not live in a poorhouse or other institution—had, since colonial times, provided something like a subsistence level of support, at least for short periods, to the absolutely destitute. But village, county, and state governments constantly worried about poor people becoming a "public charge" and fretted that the charitable impulse could easily be exploited by the "unworthy poor." The pension system for volunteer soldiers would be shaped by exactly that fear, and SRC administrators were even more determined not to burden public treasuries by funding laziness, irresponsibility, and "vicious" habits. A number of communities cut regular poor relief to veterans and their families who received SRC funds; no one wanted to extend *additional* aid to those in need. The expansion of the pension system in 1889 also reduced support for the SRC. In fact, in the wake of the passage of the Dependent Pension Bill in 1889, there was a brief effort in the state legislature—led by an assemblyman, Robert Lees, who had served in the Sixth Wisconsin—to cut SRC spending. The idea sparked outrage among veterans, and the bill was tabled.[17]

The danger of giving aid too freely was expressed most directly in 1897 by a western Wisconsin newspaper. "There seems to be a general misconception as to the purpose" of the relief fund, warned the chair of the Eau Claire County Commission in a circular to county officials, "that it is a kind of pension, free to all poor soldiers, etc., whether they are in actual need or not." Grant County commissioners responded to criticism of their policy of giving money only to actual "paupers" with a sharply sarcastic "Oh no! no applicant has ever tried to impose on the committee and get something out of the fund when not entitled to it."[18]

It was nearly impossible for Wisconsin officials to accept that veterans and their families were really any different than other poor people. "There is a sentimental side to the case," an editor wrote in 1901, "and that is the fancied odium of placing an old soldier and his family upon the same level as other paupers, but in a legal point of view this is correct."[19]

The SRC process that most resembled previous forms of poor relief was the practice of publishing the names and towns of recipients as well as the amounts they received. This was a particular kind of public shaming, seemingly designed to hold recipients accountable, perhaps even to encourage them to avoid their neighbors' pity and contempt by refusing aid despite their desperate need. Virtually every county in the state published these lists—usually in the regular minutes of the Board of County Supervisors—well into the twentieth century.

Recipient lists from Grant County include several men from the Sixth. Urias Reed, a draftee from Company A, received at least thirty dollars in 1894, while another draftee from the same company, Madison Turner, received sixteen dollars in 1909. In addition to the dozens of widows given relief in Grant County in 1912 were Company C draftees William Morris (eighteen dollars just as winter approached) and Bernhard Hurst, who received nearly thirty dollars over the course of the year. James Pigg, a once-wounded enlistee, only needed a single payment of eight dollars to tide him over at Christmastime.[20]

Surviving applications from men of the Sixth to the SRC in Milwaukee County—chaired for a number of years by one of their comrades, the ubiquitous Jerome Watrous—reveal the difficulties faced by veterans' families living on the margins of the Gilded Age economy. Abraham Brill, who served a few months as a draftee in Company H, was an unemployed laborer; he reported $200 in household effects and $400 in real estate but no family members to help support him in his "old age" and "infirmity." The wife of James Riley, who had been wounded in the regiment's first battle and eventually transferred to the Veteran Reserve Corps, requested aid due to Riley's illness. A common laborer, he had found little work in recent months. The couple's total income per month was six dollars; rent was three dollars, and they had four children between the ages of three and eleven. Mary Herdeg, apparently the wife of John Herdeg, a twice wounded veteran of Company H, reported a family income of eight dollars per month against four dollars' rent and the need to care for three children, including a baby, a toddler, and a "small for [his] age & sickly" teenaged boy. Alexander Johnston, who had been imprisoned for a time after Gettysburg, declared in his application that despite his pension of twelve dollars per month, he was "out of work and money" and needed help supporting his wife and himself. Finally, Mary Halls, whose husband George had served in Company D, was wounded at Gettysburg, and had worked as a hack driver, pled for relief for her and her four children, all under the age of thirteen—because George had deserted them.[21]

This was the best local authorities could do for their veterans: a few dollars now and then to keep them from starving. For more substantial aid, the neediest men of the Sixth would have to turn to the federal and state governments, where they would also be exposed to the similar, if more nuanced, ambivalence of administrators and the public.

A Place to Call Home

The federal government and most northern states founded homes to provide more comprehensive care for disabled veterans, although financial need remained an important criterion for admission, especially at the state level. Congress established the National Asylum (later Home) for Disabled Volunteer Soldiers in 1865. By the end of the decade, branches had been established in Milwaukee (the Northwestern Branch); Dayton, Ohio (Central); Togus, Maine (Eastern); and Norfolk, Virginia (Southern), with several more added in subsequent years.[22] Most states followed suit, including Wisconsin, which in 1888 established the Wisconsin Veterans Home near Waupaca.[23] In 1910, 31,830 veterans—about 5 percent of those still alive—resided in federal or state homes; it has been estimated that just under 100,000 Union soldiers eventually entered a federal or state facility.[24]

The 180 men of the Sixth Wisconsin who at least temporarily resided in a state or federal home comprised just over 11 percent of the 1,635 men who survived the war. That was almost double the roughly 6.7 percent of Union soldiers who spent at least some time in homes. Not surprisingly, the men who volunteered in 1861—who had seen longer and presumably harder service—were far more likely to end up in a soldiers' home than draftees (14.9 percent versus 3.3 percent). Soldiers' home inmates from the Sixth were also less likely to be immigrants and much more likely to have been noncommissioned officers than the population as whole. Finally, slightly more residents of soldiers' homes among the Sixth Wisconsin survivors participated in veterans' activities than the Sixth's average; nearly 40 percent joined in at least one form of veteranizing, including the just-under 25 percent who belonged to the GAR.[25]

Home records, although hardly complete, can tell us more about the men who lived there. The twenty veterans of the Sixth who lived at the Wisconsin Veterans Home had to declare themselves unable to support themselves or their families. In addition to the typical questions about birth date, dates of military service, occupation, family makeup, and property, they were asked whether they were under the care of a guardian, whether they were "addicted to the use of intoxicants," and whether they had previously lived in a state or federal home or had ever been refused admission to one. They were asked "Will you without question obey all orders given to you by the officer of the Home?" and whether they were willing to work at the home if physically able. They also had to agree to turn over their pensions. In short, applicants were expected to be destitute and to surrender voluntarily any income they might earn. Local GAR officials, "two taxpayers," or officials with knowledge of the applicant's financial status had to vouch for the applicant.

It is easy to fall into certain assumptions about the residents of soldiers' homes: that the populations were somewhat static and that a man entered a home and stayed there for years or decades. That comfortable image fails to capture the experiences of most residents of soldiers' homes from the Sixth Wisconsin. Although most men lived in just one home, it was relatively easy to transfer between branches of the NHDVS, and residents of state homes need not have served in a regiment from that state. As a result, men of the Sixth resided in a dozen different NHDVS branches from California to Maine, Virginia to Kansas, Tennessee to the Black Hills of South Dakota, and Arkansas to Ohio (these included state homes later converted to federal facilities). Most of the Sixth's men (63.1 percent) who lived in an NHDVS facility chose the Northwestern Branch in Milwaukee, but a significant number also resided in Sawtelle, California (twenty-three), and Leavenworth, Kansas (nine). In addition to the men (and several women) who lived in the Wisconsin Veterans Home in King, thirty-one survivors of the Sixth Wisconsin lived for months or years in state homes in Minnesota, Iowa, Nebraska, Montana, Idaho, Washington, and Oregon.

In addition to the geographical mobility that many men displayed in moving from home to home, there was also a certain temporal mobility. Of the 139 men of the Sixth for whom we can establish dates of residence, almost 34 percent stayed in a home for a year or less; the average length of stay was 6.8 years. Relatively few men entered a home and simply stayed until they died. Even the forty or so men who lived in a home for at least ten years (28.8 percent of the men for whom we have dates) usually came and went two, three, or more times, depending on their health, the economy, and the capacity of family members to offer them a room. For instance, Norwegian immigrant Andrew Arneson was in and out of the Pacific, Northwestern, Southern, and Mountain Branches of the NHDVS at least fifteen times between 1895 and 1918, staying for no more than four years at a time and sometimes for just a few months. Yet another man, despite officially being listed as "dishonorably discharged" from the army, spent decades flitting from one home to another, being admitted, released, or readmitted at least forty separate times![26]

About one-fifth of the Sixth Wisconsin home residents spent only the last weeks or days of their lives in a soldiers' home, brought there by desperate kin or GAR comrades in the forlorn hope for a last-ditch cure or, more likely, to find a comfortable place for their loved one or friend to die. That was certainly the case for Philip Schardt, who died on the very day he entered the Northwestern Branch. Many veterans of the Sixth outlived their families or were cut off from them or never had families in the first place. Of the seventy-eight men from the Sixth who died in a soldiers' home, seventeen died without a family member listed on their admission record (James Blue noted his local GAR post as his next of kin). Twenty were widowed. Others drifted away and never reappeared in the home system, while six were reported as absent from the home without leave or as "deserted," and four were dismissed to make their way in a sometimes unfriendly world.[27]

Although a relatively small percentage of Sixth Wisconsin survivors ever lived in a soldiers' home, they, like the tens of thousands of other residents, represented to many Americans all veterans. Their importance as symbols of sacrifice—and pity—transcended the actual proportion of veterans living in homes, and they were generally seen by the general public as deserving of government largesse. That would not be the case for the far larger proportion of men who received veterans' pensions.

Respectable and Entitled to Credit

A large majority of veterans of the Sixth Wisconsin would eventually receive a pension from the federal government. Aside from their actual military service, the pension process would become the veterans' primary engagement with the federal government, and even for nonveterans the Pension Bureau would become the most visible federal agency aside from the Postal Service. While local aid was intended to be short-term and limited, and state aid narrowly provided for only the neediest of veterans, the federal pension system for Civil War volunteers was breathtakingly ambitious and perhaps understandably controversial. Although pensions were a godsend to many veterans who would otherwise have been thrown on the uncertain mercy of states and communities, the demands of the pension system became a major challenge facing many veterans of the Sixth and their families.

Three main laws shaped the government's commitment to veterans. The General Law, first passed in 1861, established pensions for widows and orphans of soldiers and for soldiers disabled as a direct result of military service. In 1879 Congress passed the Arrears Act, which changed the start date for pensions from the day a pension was approved to the day a soldier received his discharge or, for widows and other dependents, the date of the soldier's death. The major systemic revision of the General Law came with the Act of 1890, which extended pensions to any disabled man who had received an honorable discharge after serving at least ninety days. His disability need not have been incurred during his military service, but it could not be caused by "vicious habits."[28]

In 1885, a quarter of a million men—nearly 17 percent of all Union veterans—were receiving federal pensions, and the percentage continued to climb until 1915, when over 93 percent of all living veterans—just under 400,000—were on the rolls. By comparison, at least 49 percent of the survivors of the Sixth had received pensions by 1885, and eventually 60 percent of the men of the Sixth who survived the war received a pension.[29]

Despite the impressive proportion of men receiving pensions, the process would have been perceived by many to be exacting, if not capricious or even demeaning. This was particularly true, it seems, when veterans already on the pension rolls applied for increases on the basis of late-emerging disabilities.[30]

A few examples from the men and families of the Sixth illustrate the laborious and fraught application process. Veterans or their surviving family members—wives, parents, or children represented by a guardian—would have begun by completing a claim and assembling a number of supporting documents, usually with help from an attorney or pension agent. Besides surgeon's reports, most evidence came in the form of affidavits sworn before a judge, clerk of court, or notary public. All such testimony began with the official stating that the witness was a person "whom I certify to be respectable and entitled to credit, who being by me duly sworn." A widow had to swear that she was "still a widow; and that she is the identical person she represents herself to be." Mothers of dependent children had to swear that they had not "abandoned" them or "allowed them to be adopted" by anyone else and that they had not "aided or abetted" the rebellion. In most cases, court officials seemed to take the notes more or less verbatim (at least in parts of the documents) or had someone else take notes.[31]

Once a file was completed, caseworkers set out to prove or disprove the facts of the case. Investigators sometimes provided more nuanced judgments about the reliability of witnesses, especially for illiterate or elderly people. The crux of the pension system was trust: Did the judges, clerks, or notaries taking evidence believe the witnesses? Were copies of marriage or birth certificates available? Although obvious, it is worth noting that, lacking a nationwide database of births and deaths, or a register of identification numbers, or even uniform methods of preserving official documents, there was a natural suspicion of any evidence. The burden of proof fell entirely on the applicant; the extent to which exact information was required often far outstripped the capacity of individuals, churches, and local governments of recovering that information.[32]

The bureau granted pensions only to men who could not support themselves through manual labor. As a result, although not every witness used the exact words, implicit in the testimony, even from the most sympathetic witnesses—comrades, neighbors, physicians—was the idea that claimants were unable to perform their natural and expected roles as *men*. One witness stated simply that illness kept the Sixth's Mathias Steinmetz from being "able to do a man's work" and that "we used to go and help him out, as he could not do his own work." Two neighbors were so insistent that William Douglass was "wholly incapacitated from performing any manual labor" that the notary public taking down their testimony underlined it. Douglass's own affidavit repeated exactly the same words—the notary dutifully underlined them, too—and went on to admit that "he has no trade, and had none at time of volunteering into the army, and has no business occupation, and can do no labor whatever toward earning a living or subsistence for himself."[33]

Others tried to quantify the loss of manhood. Isaac Fort's personal physician reported that the forty-eight-year-old could "do no more than one third the work of an able bodied man," while varicose veins "as large as eggs" and rheumatism had rendered Silas Morrison unable to "do more than half the work a man should be able to do." One of Martin Hull's oldest friends declared he had "never been a sound man" since returning from the army and estimated that Hull was "perhaps able to do one fourth of a man[']s work." A witness for another claimant stressed that "he has been disabled to such an extent" during the three years that he knew him that "at no time has he been able to fully provide for himself and his family." One veteran's neighbor called the fifty-seven-year-old claimant an "old man, and a cripple."[34]

The pension process could grind to a halt over confusing or missing information. Margaret Powderly's widow's pension was held up for two years because her name appeared as "Mary" in one document, she had not provided proof of death for her husband's first wife, and there was confusing information about her children's birth dates. Although Margaret eventually received the pension, in other cases the failure to prove particular claims permanently sidetracked an entire application. When Seth Morey died in

1913, his sixty-eight-year-old wife Mary could not prove that she had actually been divorced from her first husband over forty years earlier. "I can prove ever thing but my divorce," Mary wrote in her letter to the bureau. She never received the pension; her file was stamped "abandoned."[35]

When Martha Barrett gave birth three months after her husband George was killed on the North Anna River, she named the little girl Georgia. Because of the circumstances of their 1855 marriage—her parents had been "bitterly opposed" to the union, the couple had moved away immediately after the wedding, and the elderly minister had died a few days after the ceremony, before he filed the necessary paperwork—it was impossible to prove they had actually been married. A witness to the wedding was finally located and Martha received her pension.[36]

Throughout the extraordinarily labor-intensive process, veterans and their families were reminded that the bureau was at least as interested in limiting government liability as it was in easing the way for families. But as the recipients of the first federally funded entitlement of any kind, veteran-pensioners were set apart from other Americans, and the surprisingly public process of being pensioned and the political acrimony that eventually colored the entire issue actually resegregated them from their communities. Moreover, many of the biases of bureaucrats, policy makers, examiners, and surgeons could affect the outcome of any given pension claim.[37]

Other complications for applicants ranged from the existential to the ridiculous. Thomas Lalor's widow Mary could not actually prove that Thomas had been killed at the Wilderness. At one point, Mary testified that no one saw him die or saw his dead body, although she swore that she "has never heard from her said husband since the said 5th day of May 1864 and has no doubt of his death." Lalor's captain had been killed in the same fight, but John Kellogg—also injured and captured on the first day of fighting—had learned from other captives that Lalor had died while a prisoner of the Confederates. Clearly annoyed by the bureau's attitude, Kellogg pointedly used language often reserved for illnesses and underlined it in disgust and bitter humor: "The origins of the disease which caused his death was a rebel bullet fired by some enemy of the U.S. on the day and at the place aforesaid; and that the cause did not exist at the time of his enlistment."[38]

Predictably, faulty memories also posed problems. Regimental surgeon John Hall testified in countless cases, but by the 1880s, he told one applicant, "I should be very glad to give you my affidavit, if I could remember your case. . . . After so long a time it is next to impossible to recall cases I treated in the army." James Rhoades was just one of a number of Sixth Wisconsin veterans to find Hall a willing but unhelpful witness. The normally reliable Norman Bull, who as a sergeant and a file closer had a good vantage point for witnessing battle wounds, admitted that "I can sit down and recall eighty names of men out of my Company, sent to hospital for wounds, but to swear to times and places I could not now recall . . . without sitting down and talking with them or others."[39]

Drafted men and other short-timers had the hardest time getting witnesses. As one examiner stated, "I find as a general thing that the old members of the company had very little to do with the drafted men." Marcella Kota had enlisted in early 1864 but was often sick or on detached duty. "I have made every effort possible to obtain evidence from my company officers or from my comrades," he protested. Many letters were returned undelivered, while in other cases the recipients "seemingly do not remember me. I was on detached service and while on such service I was sick [so] that most of my comrades of my own company" never really knew him. The lack of evidence hurt; although he received a tiny four-dollar pension in 1887, his application for an increase was rejected in the 1890s.[40]

The peripatetic John Coughran was discharged from the Sixth late in 1862 for, among other things, severe hemorrhoids. He never got over them, but when he applied for a pension in the 1880s, he was unable to provide evidence from doctors, comrades, or neighbors that his condition was related to military service. "I was on the move from place to place"—he lived for varying periods of time in Wisconsin, Michigan, Kansas, Arkansas, Texas, and California—"and did not form acquances [sic] sufficient for them to remember so long ago." Moreover, "I sought to hide my disability rather than to call attention to it." That simple statement no doubt represented a number of men who preferred not to call attention to particularly delicate conditions.[41]

Like Coughran, a number of applicants had after the war avoided doctors, choosing instead to self-medicate, thus negating any chance of creating a paper trail that would support their claims. A longtime friend and comrade reported that Henry Revels "took medicine" to try to deal with his chronic diarrhea, while Frederick Klinehaus treated his shattered shinbone with "liniments or domestic remedies." Despite being plagued by epileptic fits, Charles Taylor never employed a physician, using instead patent medicines and other remedies. When he was finally pensioned, one of his witnesses was his longtime supplier. None of the many doctors Charles Bohn consulted cured the diarrhea he had acquired during the war, so he turned to "Uncle Tom's Syrup." A patent medicine salesman actually provided "expert" testimony for Martin Hull. A fellow veteran and member of the same GAR post and Odd Fellows lodge, the salesman swore that as an agent for the "Elixir of Life," a patent medicine for diseases of the kidney and liver, he had consulted with Hull. Identifying "all the Symtomes indicative of Liver complaint," he sold him several bottles of the medicine, "which has been of grate benifit to him." "Too poor to hire physicians," William Hartman treated his chronic diarrhea "with liniments" or patent medicines "when I had to." Tucked into the scores of pages of Silas Morrison's pension file is a surgeon's affidavit reporting that for many years after the war Morrison "was not under the care or treatment of any physician but doctored wholly by means of patent medicines."[42]

Although doctors normally supported applicants, they could become major obstacles when they doubted a claimant's story. Jerome Hall had been a prisoner for a number of months in 1864, and as a fifty-nine-year-old in 1901 was clearly not in the best of health with, he claimed, the typical old soldiers' complaints of rheumatism, heart trouble, and chronic diarrhea. Yet when he applied for an increase, the surgeon's report went further than most in assessing reality and motivation. The doctor actually did not doubt that there were times when Hall found it difficult to work. At other times, however, the doctor noted, "he could undoubtedly perform some labor, perhaps more than he does." Hall had "convinced his friends"—several of whom attested to his weakness and truthfulness—"and very likely himself, that he is absolutely unable to work. Some men with his disabilities but with stronger will power would no doubt perform considerable manual labor without derogation of health." The doctor recommended only a modest increase to ten dollars.[43]

Missing documents, poor memories, and lapsed relationships gave Pension Bureau examiners pause, but they also seemed naturally suspicious of all but the most obvious cases of disability. Until a case was proven, in fact, the bureau described all illnesses as "alleged," an unfortunate use of a word normally used to describe suspected criminal activities.

An Ungracious Thing

Opponents of the pension system—particularly Democrats who believed Republicans bought veterans' votes by constantly increasing pensions—savagely attacked the system and veterans alike. As Theda Skocpol argued decades ago, "Many elite and middle-class Americans viewed Civil War pensions as a prime example of governmental profligacy and electorally rooted political corruption." In addition to political partisanship, opposition also came out of the prevailing distaste for publicly funded social welfare programs. By the nineteenth century, most Americans—at least those not marginalized by poverty, ethnicity, or disability—believed opportunity was available to all, the poor were responsible for their plight, and public charity would only pauperize recipients. The demeaning and rather demoralizing workhouses and other forms of "indoor relief" that emerged in the nineteenth century were intended, in fact, to "deter people from becoming paupers." Most Americans were able to distinguish between truly disabled veterans and the unworthy poor, but as the pension system expanded its definition of disability and its causes, it came under attack for encouraging less deserving former soldiers to exploit their government's generosity.[44]

"Coffee coolers" became a popular target for critics. It became a catch-all for those men who had either come to the army too late to get into the actual fighting, who had been on relatively safe detached duty during key battles, or who had somehow shirked their duty as soldiers. Although in the Sixth enlistees of 1861, enlistees from late 1863 and early 1864, and draftees all received pensions at about the same rate (around 60 percent), a large percentage of new pensions granted after 1890—at the height of the pension controversy—went to draftees and short-timers who bore the brunt of the vicious attacks by Democrats.[45]

Two members of the Sixth were prime examples of the kind of men highlighted by opponents of the system. In what must have been one of the angriest, even contemptuous, reports by an examiner, the application of the Danish substitute and immigrant Hans Rasmussen failed miserably: "This is about as unsatisfactory a case as I have ever had to handle. The claimant is not intelligent and it is the hardest kind of work to get anything out of him." His claim that a spent bullet struck his chest and caused permanent damage "appears to me to be ridiculous. I have no doubt that he was hit by a spent ball but that it should have left any disabling effect for a quarter of a century is to me, incredible." The examiner was furious that surgeons had rated him as totally disabled. If Rasmussen was told "that he was that bad off . . . he would be more surprised than any one else."[46]

A special examiner also visited the farm of Ole Rosenwater, a draftee who had served for about nine months with the Sixth. Ole had submitted a claim for a pension based on rheumatism, although some witnesses suggested that Rosenwater's complaints predated his service (he was drafted at the age of forty-three). The examiner found the claimant stacking hay with his son, "pitching and raising 'fork-fulls' that only an able bodied man could." There was no sign of lameness—"till he got in the house & found what I was there for when he became quite lame & . . . put his hand on his hip keeping it there whenever he thought of it." The examiner had formed quite a strong opinion of Rosenwater, who had "accumulated quite a large property . . . & has a great deal of influence among his class"—neighbors and immigrants, apparently. He as much as admitted that a related heart complaint predated his service. In building his case against Rosenwater, the examiner had found that he "has always been a hard drinker & his condition is beyond doubt in my mind the result of hard work while young & hard drinking since." Although his initial claim was rejected, in 1895 he received a six-dollar pension for "rheumatism and resulting irritable heart."[47]

Veterans of the Sixth Wisconsin fell into a surprisingly savage debate over pensions when, in 1887, a small group sought to replace Gen. John Gibbon as president of the Iron Brigade Association because he was so rarely able to join them in person. This would have made Edward Bragg, the perennial vice president and practical head of the association, the likely successor. Yet Bragg had recently made enemies when, as a Democratic congressman, he had come out strongly against expanding the pension system—a heretical position for a prominent veteran. Bragg called his speech "Pensions for Soldiers, but No Pay to Coffee-Coolers and Substitutes," and in it he had warned that "we [must] not bankrupt the country in order to obey the behests of claim agents and of coffee-coolers, laggards, deserters, bounty-jumpers and substitutes." Even worse, he had been one of the nominators at the 1888 Democratic National Convention that chose as their candidate President Grover Cleveland, the notorious opponent of pensions.[48]

The fight over pensions within the association embroiled the veterans of the Sixth in particular; Jerome Watrous apparently supported his fellow Democrat Bragg, while Earl Rogers headed the opposition. At the 1889 meeting, "the wildest scene ensued" when Bragg was once again nominated as senior vice president. Even the mention of his name "was met with shouts of derision." The crowd shouted one of Bragg's supporters off the podium, and "for a time perfect pandemonium prevailed." When Bragg was finally voted down, "a yell" went up "that nearly took the roof off the hall." Never, one newspaper reported, was a man "ever more completely shelved, buried and covered up out of sight by his fellow men with whom he had so recently held close fellowship."[49]

A correspondent to the *Whitewater Register* who defended the so-called coffee coolers wrote, "It was an ungracious thing . . . [Bragg] did . . . when he denounced the soldiers who joined the army during the closing years of the war as being mere scum and riff-raff." The men "who entered the service in the early months of 1861 thought that the service would be short and, without serious danger." However, men who enlisted or submitted to the draft later in the war "knew that they were facing death and the worse horrors of the prison pens." Language condemning the latter "may be pleasing to the high official whom he is so anxious to serve, but the day will come when he will care more for the kindly good will of his lowliest comrade in the great contest than for the favor, purchased or unpurchased, of any president."[50]

Although Bragg's former subordinate Rogers did not mention Bragg by name in a column-and-a-half editorial, he attacked President Cleveland, the Democratic Party, and the "rich newspapers" who opposed pensions. "The veto of the dependent pension bill measures the president's sympathy for the unfortunate poor." Later in the year Rogers wrote another editorial defending the right of all veterans to receive pensions. "The Grand Army, on each memorial day, strews flowers alike on all without questioning" their date of enlistment. "The mother's or wife's grief is none the less for the boy or husband killed" late in the war rather than early. "It was the enlistments of 1864 that strengthened the army," he reminded readers. The Sixth was "not 'ashamed' of them but rejoiced that they had come to lift the burdens even though it was the 'eleventh hour,' and they who came at the last call bore their part equally with those who came before them, fought as bravely, suffered wounds and died." There is no reason to doubt Rogers's sincerity—he closed his editorial with "Fraternity, Charity, Loyalty," as though to wrap veterans of all kinds in the rhetoric of the GAR's famous motto—but there is some dissonance between the support of draftees as a class in the 1880s and the indifference shown them as individuals in 1865.[51]

The feud within the Sixth eventually blew over—revealing the strength of the bonds developed during the war—but the controversy demonstrates the difficult path that pensioned Union veterans sometimes had to follow, particularly when their disabilities and their actual service fell below the arbitrary bars set by the government and many Americans.

In Sickness and in Health

Edward Bragg, not known for his sensitivity and an opponent of too-generous pensions, nevertheless movingly stated in an 1884 speech that every fallen soldier "was missed from some circle, humble or great; each name was a treasure of some hearthstone, and as each fell, some other life was darkened." The ever-expanding pension system recognized this and, in fact, the federal government had during the war basically told volunteers not to worry about their wives and children if they were killed or maimed. An 1862 cartoon in *Harper's Weekly* showed Uncle Sam waving marching soldiers on to Virginia, surrounded by women and children, and calling, "Go ahead, Boys: I'll take care of the Wives and Babies. God bless you!"[52]

Our understanding of any regiment's history must also take stock of social connections and impacts at home—including the long-term effects of deaths, wounds, and diseases on soldiers' family members. Of the more than 300 members of the Sixth Wisconsin who died of wounds or of diseases during or just after the war, at least eighty-six left widows and at least three "orphans," and 162 left "half orphans."[53]

As a result, one of the striking aspects of the pension system was the long-term care provided for wives, children, and parents of men long dead—those lives "darkened," to use Bragg's words, by the loss of a husband, father, or son. Few men probably anticipated having to—or being able to—support their wives, children, or parents in death. Although the amounts sound small by our standards, the four, eight, or sometimes as much as twenty dollars per month awarded by the Pension Bureau to widows, minor children, and dependent parents provided a basic minimum that provided a margin between subsistence and disaster.

The pension files for dependents of the Sixth Wisconsin are filled with examples of surprising, moving, and sometimes astonishing extensions of financial support by dead soldiers. Martha Hyatt married Jabez Hyatt at the age of eighteen two years before the war began. He joined Company G in the war's first summer and was killed at Gainesville. After having lived with Jabez for less than two years, Martha received a widow's pension, never remarrying, never moving from Beloit, for nearly sixty-two years. Two widows diagnosed by doctors as "insane" and "incompetent" (the latter was consigned to a poorhouse for a time) were likewise supported by widows' pensions for many decades.[54]

Despite lasting only a few months, at least two of the furlough marriages shaped the lives of young widows for decades. Caleb C. Wright married a sixteen-year-old named Emma. During the fighting that summer, Caleb was shot in the head; he lingered for a few weeks and died in Washington, DC. Emma was still receiving a pension when she died more than half a century later. Milo Sage died of wounds received near Petersburg six months after marrying Frances. She received a widow's pension, which she gave up when she married another veteran. Her second husband died fifty years later, after a long and happy marriage, but his death left her destitute and sometimes unable to heat her home. An article or advertisement in the *National Tribune* had led her to inquire about the possibility of "renewing" her pension from Milo—which Congress had begun to allow in 1901. She did not want to be "found by the town as a pauper." Memories of her short-lived first marriage seemed to have faded a bit; she was unable to say in what battle Milo had fallen, although she certainly remembered that he belonged to the Iron Brigade. She received a twenty-dollar pension into the 1920s.[55]

These and other stories give new meaning—or embody the original meaning—of the marriage vows that many of these men and women would have taken. An 1860 example of those vows from the Methodist church asked grooms, "Wilt thou have this woman to thy wedded wife, to live together after God's ordinance, in the holy estate of matrimony? Wilt thou love her, comfort her, honor, and keep her, in sickness and in health; and, forsaking all other, keep thee only unto her, so long as ye both shall live?"[56]

Although bound to dead soldiers by a different kind of commitment, a number of mothers and children also found themselves depending for support on absent sons and fathers. In some cases, those pensions rescued aging women from disastrous marriages or economic catastrophes. George W. Atwood of Whitestown had, with his brother, supported his mother Jemima and father Alonso before the war—but both were killed, George in the Cornfield at Antietam. Their parents lived in a simple log cabin on a largely unimproved—and apparently unimprovable—farm. Their father was unable to work, and Jemima received a small pension. But in 1893, after Alonso died, Jemima lost the pension at the age of seventy-three when she married a Nebraska man named Hatfield. As it turns out, at least according to a neighbor, the new husband was "shiftless and . . . wholly unable to support her having no property or other sources of income." As Jemima wrote in the request to renew her pension, her new husband "proved an adventurer and deserted her." The bureau did, indeed, reinstate the pension, which she received until her death in 1904.[57]

Dependence, as well as marriage vows, worked both ways. The postwar records of the men of the Sixth Wisconsin are filled with hints of spouses who inevitably had to devote substantial time and energy to caring for disabled husbands, helping amputees get around, administering medications, and preparing special meals. Those stories of the ripple effects of the long Civil War on loved ones are poignant, perhaps heartwarming, but ultimately sad, as exemplified in the case of Maria Lauersdorf. A shell sliced off a portion of her husband Ferdinand's lower jaw on March 31, 1865. Ferdinand had been drafted a few months earlier, less than a year after their wedding. The wound was devastating: Ferdinand never ate a solid meal again, which eventually led to all kinds of digestive problems and kidney failure. He had difficulty talking and his breath stank. He frequently went to the doctor, who could only give him prescriptions of medicines that he used "continually," including morphine—the only way he could stand the pain and get a little sleep. He rarely left the house, and from time to time he was confined to bed. He developed heart trouble and lost the sight in his right eye. In short, according to his physician, he was "a constant sufferer" and, as another said, "a used up man." He apparently never worked again after the war.

The most melancholy element of the Lauersdorfs' story is that Maria had married a healthy twenty-eight-year-old harness maker. A year later she was married to a disfigured and completely disabled man who would live for another thirty-six years. By 1898, and likely for much longer, she spent half her time "caring for the personal and bodyly wants of her husband," frequently having to "attend to him at the night time," when he usually rested "uneasy." His death four years later must have come as a bitter relief.[58]

Life Has Been Very Hard Indeed

In a letter to the Pension Bureau the barely literate Thomas Sweet ended his short and sassy note with a kind of PS: "Iff [sic] you cant read this come out hear and I will read it for you." That tone offers a glimpse at another thread that emerges from the pension files. Despite their poverty, their desperation, or even their exaggerated debility, pension applicants often discovered a certain freedom of expression. The veterans, widows, and offspring who challenged the authority of bureaucrats, pension commissioners, and even presidents would have said they were simply standing up for themselves in a way not available to most Americans. They pleaded their cases directly to the government for the benefits they believed they deserved; they entered a dialogue with government officials at a time when that kind of communication was extremely rare; and they posed questions about right and wrong, justice and injustice.[59]

One of the more remarkable examples of a woman engaging the government came in a case she could not possibly win. Hiram B. Merchant and his wife Elizabeth—married during the veterans' furlough in 1864—divorced in 1884. He died in Arkansas in 1904. A few years later Elizabeth began a concerted campaign to receive a widow's pension—even though officials repeatedly told her that her divorce had rendered her ineligible. In 1910 she wrote President William Howard Taft: "I take the liberty of writing you in Regard to a pension as I am in need of one badly." She had already been rejected, but she wanted the president to know the circumstances of her disastrous marriage—apparently hoping to soften the hearts of the bureaucrats standing in her way. Hiram "became very dissipated, and cruel to me without a cause and in fear, of my life I left him. . . . I had very little worldly goods, and my son that helped me died with pneumonia" in the same year as her former husband. "Since [then] I have gotten along as best I could." The sixty-nine-year-old was "badly crippled with rheumatism and would be very glad if in your kindness of heart you would help me. I feel I am as deserving as thousands who are getting one." She closed with another plea: "Neither of us ever married again and why should I not get one. I am leaving this to your kindness of heart, to help an old lady, who needs the money badly." Taft naturally turned this over to the commissioner of pensions, who curtly responded that "there is no law providing pension for a divorced woman as widow of a soldier." Yet two years later Elizabeth wrote Taft again, taking "the liberty of addressing you, reading in the papers your many acts of kindness to others." She repeated her story of abuse and divorce. Since the death of her son, "life has been very hard indeed." She provided Hiram's war records—mentioning "the iron Brigade," just in case its fame made a difference—and closed with "If you want any reference I can easily furnish it." Despite several increasingly angry attempts to get someone to agree with her, Elizabeth never received a pension. Perhaps she considered it a moral—if hollow—victory to have spoken what she believed to be truth to power.[60]

Even people who had received pensions found reasons to complain, particularly when the bureau became especially exacting about evidence in considering increases. James Sullivan was wounded several times—including an incident when a ramrod struck him in the back during a ceremonial salute—during his three different stints with the regiment. Although by the 1880s he had become a rather prolific writer on the regiment's history for the *Sunday Telegraph* and had passed the Wisconsin state bar, he never really prospered—and he never believed he received enough aid from his government. When he was yet again denied an increase in 1904 (just two years before his death), he got someone to type his letter to the commissioner of pensions. After cataloguing his complaints, he wrote, "I think that President [Theodore] Roosevelt should clean out the whole gang in the Pension office and put in men like General [John C.] Black who was a soldier himself and understands and realizes what it is to suffer from old gunshot wounds if I could possibly get along without it I would tell you to keep your munificent $14 a month and give it to some 'Coffee Cooler,' who seem to be the favorites of the pension office."[61]

Sometimes a claimant simply wanted to state that enough was enough. Chauncey Green washed his hands of the Pension Bureau in 1894 when it demanded that he undergo another physical examination. He had apparently been examined sometime prior to the beginning of Cleveland's second administration in 1893. "I have been examined once, and I am willing to stand or fall by the report of that Examination," he wrote in a sharply worded and untidily typewritten letter. "The Board that made the Examination were true to their business, and knew their business, they were appointed [by] a good loyal Administration"—the Republican Benjamin Harrison preceded Cleveland in the White House—and "I see no reason why I should be compeled [*sic*] to spend my time and money to be reexamined." He would wait until an administration more sympathetic to old soldiers came back into power. "Do with my claim as you please." He added a handwritten PS: "I have not done a days work for over two years—I will try & stand it."[62]

Some veterans exerted their rights and bolstered their self-respect by maintaining constant contact with the Pension Bureau, especially as new laws were passed—not just the major overhauls in 1879 and 1890 but smaller revisions to the system that Congress approved every few years—and as their conditions worsened. Perhaps the best example of this kind of perseverance was Darwin Kinney, who aggressively sought increases in his pension due to worsening or new conditions. His original pension covered a gunshot wound to his left hip at the Weldon Railroad in 1864. Forced to use crutches or canes when he returned home in 1865, witnesses recalled that he had been lame ever since. The bullet remained in his pelvic cavity for a few years, then migrated into his thigh, causing frequent abscesses until it was removed six years after the war. The Pension Bureau recorded at least eight applications for increased pension payments due to this injury. Kinney also claimed disability from rheumatism—which pension examiners accepted up to a point, although they blamed his pain and lameness (which he claimed "has increased from year to year") on the gunshot wound rather than rheumatism—and from lung trouble dating to sleeping on the ground and without blankets on Arlington Heights in the war's first autumn. Although the symptoms were specific—including frequent colds and hacking coughs as well as deafness—the causes were harder to pin down. Yet Kinney submitted at least seven requests for new or increased pensions for those conditions between 1868 and 1896. Not all were approved; his pension seems to have topped out at fourteen dollars per month in the 1890s.[63]

These expressions of anger, confusion, and entitlement show that at least some Civil War veterans and their survivors believed they were owed something for their misfortune and that the government seemed to be the only plausible source of relief—even when it was unclear that the source of their plight was the war. Moreover, the government became a surrogate for all the people and institutions that had wronged them, for all the bad luck they had experienced, and even for the degrading ravages of old age. As these and countless other pension files show, the testimony of claimants and of witnesses are tinged with nostalgia, for that time before events outside their control had intervened in futures that for many were not yet set, when limitations had not been imposed on them by violent chance, bad generals, or ignorant doctors. Their agency consisted, in a way, of articulating somehow their grief at lost years and lost chances, at the sad and constrained lives forced on their families.

These emotions confronted a giant government agency that tried to impose strict bureaucratic rules and medical standards at a time when those rules and standards could not be sustained by social norms, technology, or medical science. The pension files that proliferated over many decades are difficult for historians to understand completely and no doubt reflect a process that was confusing for bureaucrats and applicants alike. They are extraordinarily sloppy, with many layers of paperwork of different sizes and types and evolving forms that mirrored changes in the role of government and the grindingly slow modernization of technology. They feature horrific handwriting from county clerks and justices of the peace working in local, state, and federal courthouses and from agents and their secretaries in the Pension Bureau and in pension agencies, with frequent cross-outs and abbreviations that meant something to someone at some point but a century later seem lost to history.

———   ———   ———   ———   ———   ———

Receiving a federal pension or living in a soldiers' home became an important common denominator linking survivors of the Sixth Wisconsin. They created another layer of identity to the Union veterans who benefited from them. Applying for a pension gave voice to men who would never have thought to put pen to paper in a diary or a memoir, who had no need to write letters, and who never spoke at or even attended a veterans' reunion. Perhaps even more important, accepting a pension or filling a bed at a soldiers' home placed veterans in a new category of American: those who relied on the federal government to maintain a certain standard of living—and, in some cases, simply to survive.

9

When I Die I Shall Be Dead a Long Time

The Life Cycle of Soldiers' Memory

Levi Tongue had nearly died in 1864 while imprisoned in the notorious Confederate prison camp at Andersonville, Georgia. In a December 1901 letter to his old comrade J. S. Driggs, who had made a home for himself in northwest Georgia not far from Andersonville, the experience remained vivid as he shared what he remembered of the locals. "I am glad to hear that you are well—Yet trying to subdue the unsubdued part of the South," Tongue kidded. He wondered particularly about how Driggs was finding the women in his adopted community, whom he remembered as "some of the worst . . . that ever tread Gods [sic] Green earth." Although he admired the "pluck-Vim-courage-endurance" of Southern women in general, he remarked to Driggs that "if they feel half as bad as many of them talked and acted while we were down there, I think they would have to be run through some kind of machinery to ever become sufficiently subdued to have peace."

Tongue spent the rest of the letter catching Driggs up on comrades living and dead, particularly those in Hillsboro, to which he had returned after the war. William Van Wie "looks and acts about the same as he used to only he is older & I think lazyer." He had also seen John M. Goodwin, who "looks just about the same only . . . his hair is white as snow." Over the last three years "we have buried 8 of our company. We can't hold out like that many years." Recently two had been buried on the same day. "We had [Grand Army] members enough of our Company for Pall bearers, one to carry the flag & one to march in the ranks."

In a previous letter Driggs had mentioned mistakenly thinking he had seen two dead comrades—one had been killed during the war, and one had died just a few months earlier. "You say I may think you some what loony. . . . You certainly are & I think your wife had better procure a place in some workshop [asylum, perhaps] before you get clear gone." Tongue was collecting the addresses of surviving members of Company I. "As long as I am alive I am going to keep tract [sic] of them, & I am going to live as long as I can for when I die I shall be dead a long time." There were only two of the original cohort left in Hillsboro. Tongue rambled on a bit, finally closing with a pensive "How I would like to be able to go down South & look some of them old fields over."[1]

Whether counting the deaths of their elderly comrades, teasing boyhood friends with whom they'd gone to war, or expressing surprising nostalgia for the places they had served, fought, and survived, veterans insisted on keeping their stories alive—not just the accounts of leaders and grand strategies but also those of privates, whose tales were granted the same dignity as those of their commanders. For most veterans of the Sixth, the stories they told were the most natural means of embracing the passage of time and commemorating the war. They appeared mainly in newspapers and magazines—some published with a soldier audience in mind, others for the general public. Yet there were many other ways the men of the Sixth remembered and *were* remembered by their families and communities. They ranged from joining formal organizations, attending reunions large and small, and eagerly scanning soldiers' newspapers for news of old friends. Of course, they also died, were memorialized, and buried.[2]

A life cycle of Civil War memory emerges from the personal letters and memoirs, official reports, soldiers' and veterans' missives to hometown newspapers, minutes of Grand Army of the Republic (GAR) meetings, and countless other sources. The memories constructed by the men of the Sixth Wisconsin, their families, and their communities tended to look inward rather than outward. They seemed to have shared the general impulse to reconcile with the South, while at the same time nodding vaguely toward emancipation and usually restricting their rhetoric to pride in having saved the Union. It was most important to them that *their* particular legacy—of the regiment, of the Iron Brigade—be protected.[3]

The performance of memory effectively reconstituted the Sixth Wisconsin. It did not matter whether a man had enlisted in 1861 and been discharged for chronic diarrhea nine months later, or if he had been drafted and served for only a few months at the end of the war, or if he had managed somehow to survive through four long years of fighting. Once the regiment became a memory rather than a functioning military unit, anyone who had followed its banner could once again march behind it, at least figuratively. This version of the Sixth would live far longer than the fighting regiment itself.

Letters home and diaries kept in the moment would become important to the remembered war, but perhaps the first stories were constructed and told at wartime funerals where comrades and families, as people do in these moments, reminisced about the past and mourned futures that would never be. For the Sixth Wisconsin, these original markers of memory would have been the small but formal military ceremony held by the comrades of Homer Lillie, the teenager who drowned in summer 1862; the closed casket funeral in Fond du Lac for Edwin Brown, mistakenly identified as Edward Bragg after being shot in the mouth at Antietam; or the fine, crowded Milwaukee funeral for young Philip Shields, who died in a Philadelphia hospital but was sent home for burial.[4]

Another source of early stories were the battle flags the Sixth had carried into countless fights, as well as the flag captured from the Second Mississippi at Gettysburg. For years after the war, Republican governors—usually former generals—displayed them as part of their "Bloody Shirt" attacks on Democratic opponents. When the Democrats captured the legislature in 1875, they forbade anyone from removing the flags from their cases at the Wisconsin Historical Society. The law was later amended to allow the flags to be displayed during the 1876 centennial and at soldiers' reunions. They often appeared at gatherings of Iron Brigade veterans.[5]

But for many decades the most basic version of veteran storytelling took place at the GAR "campfire," a ritual that ended virtually every local, state, and national encampment. The campfire allowed veterans to revisit a sanitized and safe version of their army service and to tell tales of battles and marches and friendships cemented or riven by combat. A description of a Milwaukee GAR post's campfire was typical of the genre: "A genuine old-time meal of soldier fare was attacked in true army style, and bacon and beans, hard-tack and coffee, all on tin dishes, disappeared in a manner that showed the members to be very valiant trenchermen as well as old soldiers." Later, the men sang war songs, told stories, and smoked pipes "to the memory of old times."[6]

Every regiment had its own favorite stories. The Sixth Wisconsin's most repeated story offered a satisfying mix of courage and pathos. Frank Hare's three-page biography in a local history from the 1890s related the harrowing tale of his being wounded and captured in the Wilderness, where a Confederate surgeon took off his leg. But it also included the story of another captive, Capt. Rollin Converse, who had been shot in the stomach and in the leg. Understanding that his wound was mortal, Converse wanted to avoid the unnecessary suffering caused by the amputation that Confederate surgeons seemed anxious to perform. He had hidden a small revolver in his coat pocket. He gave it to Hare and whispered that he should "prevent if possible his being disturbed before he died." Pointing the gun at the Confederate guards, Hare declared, "What do you suppose I care for my life with my leg gone? Kill me if you will, but that man is my captain . . . and so long as I . . . have strength to shoot it will be dangerous for any man to touch him while he lives." A Rebel officer ordered the guards to stand down, then remarked wistfully, nodding toward Hare, "I would like a regiment of such men." Converse responded with defiant last words: "I had the honor to command a hundred such men; the North is full of them, and sooner or later we shall triumph, and your rebel flag will be trailed in the dust."[7]

It is impossible to verify the accuracy of this dialogue, but the confrontation certainly occurred. It appeared from time to time in various newspaper accounts and most notably in the narrative of John Kellogg, another witness who wrote about the incident, ending his version with a dramatic flourish that made Converse into a sacrificial victim of the rebellion: "With these brave, prophetic words he breathed out his young life. At the instant he expired the sun broke through a rift in the battle cloud, and glancing down through the shimmering foliage of the forest tree, illumined the face of the dead."[8]

The central character of the other most repeated story was decidedly less Christlike, as suggested by the Dickensian headline of its central character's obituary: "Little Ed Brooks is dead." Thus began the obituary of Edward

Brooks, who had joined the Sixth as a teenager in the summer of 1861. He rose quickly to sergeant, then to lieutenant, and then to adjutant, partly, some believed, because his uncle and employer, David Atwood, was a founder of the Republican Party, editor of the *Wisconsin State Journal*, general in the Wisconsin militia, state legislator, and acquaintance of President Lincoln. James Sullivan described Brooks as "rosy-cheeked," "boyish," and needing hair dye to make his wispy mustache visible. He took soldiering seriously—perhaps a little pompously—and "although a most gallant son of Mars, he was no less a worshipper at the shrine of Venus," always on the lookout for pretty girls. "I know not how many dark-eyed daughters of the south were smitten by his handsome, pleasant face."[9]

Yet he served well, gaining the notice of higher-ups as a staff officer during the Second Bull Run campaign and making a notable contribution to the regiment's charge at the Railroad Cut. He was captured late in 1863, only to be exchanged after President Lincoln asked Gen. Benjamin Butler to intervene.[10]

The story that featured Brooks, told over and over by men of the Sixth—with implied aspersions and more than a little contempt—came out of a seriously ill-fated mission conceived and led by the young officer. Veterans were generally uncritical of other veterans unless they had committed some unpardonable sin in their military or postwar lives. Lt. Edward P. Brooks had done exactly that.

In the summer of 1864, as the Army of the Potomac ground its way through Virginia, Brooks had boldly proposed to Gen. Ulysses S. Grant a lightning raid behind Confederate lines by a small, select band of mounted infantrymen to burn key railroad bridges. (In "an exceedingly unmilitary act," as Brooks put it, he had written to the commanding general directly.) Grant quickly approved the mission and a few days later Brooks and the thirty men he chose from the Iron Brigade rode south from Petersburg. They went out with a much larger force—the also ill-fated Wilson-Kautz raid—but soon peeled off on their own.[11]

The unlikely expedition quickly spiraled into fiasco. After capturing and releasing a Confederate officer home on leave on the first night out, on the second night that same officer, with seven shotgun-armed farmers, surprised the entire patrol and forced their surrender without firing a shot. Having failed to put out guards, Brooks had been fooled into thinking he was surrounded. The *New York Times* picked up the story from a Richmond newspaper, using the same snide headline—"A Gallant Affair"—and related the embarrassing denouement, after which, the correspondent reported, "the commanding officer shed tears" and the Yankees were "all safely shipped to prison."[12]

The most detailed account of the raid came from Thomas Newton, who recalled over twenty years later that Brooks had sworn the men to secrecy before they set out. "We of course had all confidence in him, as a true and brave officer." Brooks claimed to have spent the night scouting for a route through Rebel lines, but finding Confederate units in every direction, he believed "fighting would be useless." Here Newton made the bold claim that they had somehow been betrayed—perhaps by Brooks, perhaps by some other traitor: "We were sold; bought for a price, but as we could not prove it, all we could do was to suffer the consequences, of which tongue cannot describe or pen portray." The rest of Newton's lengthy memoir, published in the *Milwaukee Sunday Telegraph,* was a graphic account of the cruelties endured in the infamous Andersonville prison camp and of the numerous physical maladies that he traced to his months in prison.[13]

The lifelong suffering of the men who went out with Brooks provided the grim undercurrent to the story. At least two members of the regiment died in prison, but several others returned home in ruined health. Samuel Waller survived and became a preacher after the war but died in 1880 at the age of thirty-seven, while Company B's Silas Lowery was forced to spend the last several years of his life in the Minnesota Soldiers' Home, and John St. Clair of Company K died some time before 1890, when he would have been only fifty-three.[14]

From time to time correspondents to the *Milwaukee Sunday Telegraph,* a newspaper devoted to veterans' interests, revisited the incident. "We all know the unfortunate result," wrote one in 1881, "how the command was surrounded and captured." A longer reminiscence mentioned the wretched health in which prison left two of the raiders, criticizing Brooks along the way: "On the second day out the poorly officered command surrendered, and the raiders were taken to Andersonville." Passing over most of Brooks's postwar life, the article reported that he "landed in Washington where he has since conducted the *National Republican,* better than the raid." The details of the story and tone of the telling got worse as time went on. A few years later the *Telegraph* asserted with some exaggeration that "less than half of the thirty picked men ever returned. Some of them died at Charleston, others were starved to death at Andersonville, and others still were run down and killed by bloodhounds while trying to escape. Two or three of them became insane, but have since recovered their reason."[15]

Like many of the men he led, Edward Brooks seems never to have regained his health. He made three failed escape attempts—once by cutting a hole in the floor of a railroad car—and finally succeeded on the fourth try. After the war, Brooks worked as a *New York Times* correspondent, edited Republican and African American newspapers in North Carolina and Washington, DC, and served as US consul in Cork, Ireland. He began receiving a pension for rheumatism in 1884; at one point, a pension examiner had to go to his home to interview the bedridden Brooks. He was never able to perform manual labor after the war, he testified, and "for weeks and months at a time" was unable even to perform the "mild labor" of being a journalist. Asthma and heart troubles followed, and Brooks died at the age of fifty, living with his mother, in 1893.[16]

The *Telegraph's* obituary oozed ambiguity. After a brief summary of his military career and a reminder that most of the thirty men with him "died in prison, or have been wrecks ever since," the piece ended with the dismissive "Poor little Ed. Brooks. His life was not what he expected it to be, and was in some respects, a disappointment to his friends."[17]

There is no evidence that any of Brooks's comrades encountered the man himself after the war, but the story became a set piece narrative for and about the Sixth. It seemed to reflect an ambivalence about Edward Brooks the man but also framed the classic narrative of prison-camp cruelty. No greater failure could be imagined than allowing your men to be captured and subjected to those conditions. It also hints at the nature of the war as it had developed in the summer of 1864: the promise of the raid—men on horseback turned loose into the countryside, leaving behind the grinding violence and drudgery of the previous six weeks—turning into yet another poor ending for soldiers who had already survived three years of war. It might have begun as a freewheeling moment in which the Sixth could have claimed a specific contribution to the war effort, but it ended as a powerful, if peculiar, example of men's lives and health being thrown away with seemingly little thought. It was, indeed, a metaphor for the war of attrition in which the Sixth found itself.

We All Have History

It was no doubt gratifying to tell tales to other soldiers, but an important element of the life cycle of memory was, of course, telling those stories to nonveterans, often through so-called soldiers' newspapers. The *National Tribune* and the *American Tribune* were especially prominent nationally; the latter also became a platform for its publisher's side hustle as a pension agent.

The heyday for veterans' publications came in the 1880s and 1890s, when a number of soldiers' newspapers were published in the North and West.[18]

In Wisconsin, the first newspaper to proclaim its devotion to soldiers' interests was the aptly named *Soldiers Record*, published in Madison from 1867 to 1873. Other attempts to bring Wisconsin war veterans together were the *Grand Army Sentinel*, a monthly published briefly in 1874, and a column of soldiers' reminiscences called War Memories in the *Boscobel Dial* that lasted only a few months in 1887.[19]

The *Milwaukee Sunday Telegraph*, edited by the Sixth's own Jerome Watrous, became the premier publication for Wisconsin soldiers. Watrous had been a twenty-one-year-old newspaperman when he joined Company E. He served through the war as a commissary sergeant and adjutant and returned to Wisconsin with the brevet rank of lieutenant colonel. He continued in the newspaper business, publishing papers in Black River Falls and Fond du Lac before settling in Milwaukee to edit the *Sunday Telegraph*. Along the way he served a term in the state assembly and became perhaps the most visible member of the state's GAR, serving as state commander in 1894–95 and giving literally hundreds of talks at state and local encampments and campfires.[20]

Watrous aimed to "set a table around which the thousands of soldier readers can assemble with pleasure." That sense of building a community of like-minded veterans animated all soldiers' newspapers. An admirer once described the *Telegraph* as "a messenger from one old soldier to another" that "conveys tidings that relight the camp-fires and seem to bring the survivors of the dark and bloody days once more within hailing distance of each other." A one-legged veteran explained the attraction of the *Telegraph*: "We all have a history; why not let it be known, even though it does not affect the political or financial condition of the country now saved."[21]

Letters from or news about soldiers in dozens of Wisconsin regiments appeared in the page or two dedicated to soldiers in each issue, frequently from men of the Sixth. Former captain D. L. Quaw of Company K wrote from Tennessee that "I get more of the particular kind of news I want from your paper than I get in all the balance of from four to five papers I get. . . . It is like a good, long letter each week, and is sure to have a word from some soldier friend." Another old soldier of the Sixth living in Dakota Territory declared, "I can get along without my meals better than I can without the *Sunday Telegraph*."[22]

The *Telegraph* reminded readers of old times—from funny stories to notable deaths—but also alerted readers to comrades' accomplishments, life changes, and in a few cases, financial need. A cheery tone tended to dominate, especially, of course, for men who had prospered. Philip Gaubatz of Company F "is a pleasant knight of the road," traveling northern Wisconsin on behalf of a tobacco company. Capt. A. L. Roberts wrote expansively from Wahpeton (in current-day southeastern North Dakota) that he was "engaged in the grocery and provision business." Prosperity had found Jake Stackhouse of Company A in Pittsburgh, where he had moved shortly after the war to work in the steel industry. He "puts in about 312 days of good service a year and that each day counts him $25. . . . He is getting rich, owns lots and houses and is happy." Back in Wisconsin, Capt. J. H. Marston was memorialized by having a steam barge on Lake Winnebago named after him.[23]

As far as we know, no one else had a vessel of any kind named after him, and not everyone shared good news. Two other migrants to Dakota complained of hard times in 1880, chiefly due to a recent grasshopper plague. The same year, it was reported that popular Maj. John Hauser "has had a hard time of it" and had entered the soldiers' home in Milwaukee. Some old comrades gave him a subscription to the *Telegraph* for Christmas in 1881, and when he died a number of officers and men from the regiment sent money to help his widow.[24]

Frequent contributor Earl M. Rogers provided haunting anecdotes of the dead in one of his offerings. "The bones" of the five Company I soldiers who died at Gainesville "laid where they fell, watched only by the vultures, till one year later," when they were finally buried in a single grave. Two years later, several men from the company never "came out" of the Wilderness; "the army marched away and the pine trees of that gloomy woodland moaned the requiem over the fallen that lie coffinless."[25]

From time to time, a veteran would attempt a comprehensive, if brief, history of a regiment or company, along with a summary of survivors' postwar lives. An 1880 article provided reminders about the men who had formed Bragg's Rifles, the original core of Company E. Sometimes pathetic, sometimes humorous, the article suggested the wide variety of postwar lives built by the company's survivors. "Edwin C. Jones, the only man of the kind the world has produced, returned to Wisconsin at the close of the war. He died about twelve years ago. Jones was EMPLOYED AS A SPY a portion of the time. He was the readiest public speaker in the regiment and by all odds the most awkward soldier on drill or parade; but perfectly fearless in a fight." H. W. Durant, "the quiet, scholarly man, who wrote three letters a day, was INSTANTLY KILLED AT GETTYSBURG," while after the war Lucius Murray "removed to Missouri and was killed in a quarrel in which he was not a participant." Henry

G. Garfield, Company E's last captain, "met with indifferent success after the war. The last heard of him he failed as a saloon-keeper at New London." On the other hand, Peter Steenis lost a leg and returned to Appleton, where he "bought a poor horse and rickety wagon and commenced draying. He would load and unload goods as rapidly as the best of men with two limbs. He is now a prosperous liveryman, worth eight or ten thousand dollars." The where-abouts of Nathan Malloy had been a mystery since 1864; "slightly injured in a railway accident while returning to the army" after the veterans' furlough, he went to the hospital, "since which time no member of the company or regiment has been able to get track of him. It is presumed that he died on the way and in the hurry and confusion no record was preserved."[26]

Every issue of the *Telegraph* featured one or more notes about the Sixth. Under Watrous's editorship, it became one or the most reliable sources of information for survivors who sought comfort in the comradeship of the past, as well as a vehicle for knitting together a community of veterans who had spread throughout the state and the nation.

The Duty of Every Soldier

The *Telegraph* and other publications provided a venue for one of the favorite and most basic forms of commemoration performed by old soldiers: making lists. Stephen Berry has shown, using the example of Clara Barton's efforts to record the names of the Civil War dead, that producing lists was an "instinc-tive response" to witnessing the unimaginable scale of death experienced by soldiers. "Make a list. Count the dead. Record the names." Men of the Sixth shared that instinct and with Barton and others "had hit upon one of the simplest and most effective ways to render simultaneously the twin scales of human catastrophe: the list." That is, of course, the reason the Vietnam Vet-erans Memorial, simple as it is, is so powerful: those names are an accounting of loss and regret.[27]

The lists kept by men of the Sixth ranged from the mundane to the moving—but all entailed recording for posterity the names of dead and living comrades. Among the more inveterate list makers was James "Mickey" Sulli-van, one of Rufus Dawes's original Company K recruits. In one of the several articles he wrote for the *Telegraph*, the thrice-wounded Irishman listed all of the original members of Company K, as well as those who joined later in the war—at Arlington Heights, at Fredericksburg, and during the veterans' furlough, along with the drafted men and substitutes who came to the com-pany in 1864 and 1865. A week later he listed all the men who had been killed or wounded during the war, including those who died of disease and one, Harrison Edwards, who had died of a "broken heart" in 1861.[28]

The lists made by survivors signaled grief for their dead comrades and respect for those still alive. Although not a list keeper himself, Edward Bragg articulated the fundamental reasons old soldiers did so in an 1884 speech: "It is the duty every soldier owes to his comrades, living or dead" to preserve "the individuality of each soldier, that the record of his bravery, of his endurance, of his privations and sufferings, shall be a part of his children's knowledge, and his name a household word at our firesides."[29]

A preliminary effort to provide a comprehensive roster of Wisconsin volunteers was inspired by the 1880 reunion in Milwaukee, which welcomed men of all military branches from every state. Promoted by Watrous and his *Sunday Telegraph*, among others, it helped spark the revival of the GAR. The massive *Reunion Roster* honored those comrades who had died during the war but also listed survivors' residences and occupations. It reflected a yearning for remembrance that betrayed old soldiers' concern that they would be forgotten, that public memory of their contributions and sacrifices would dissolve into ashes and dust as they themselves surely would.[30]

The compilation of reliable lists of soldiers coincided with the massive effort to organize and publish the military records of the war in the 128-volume *War of the Rebellion: The Official Records of the Union and Confederate Armies*. The Sixth Wisconsin had a close connection to the project: Company E's Leslie Perry. A twice-captured four-year man who ended the war as a captain in the commissary department, after the war he published newspapers in Wisconsin, Kansas, and Michigan. But he also spent a number of years on the staff of the *Official Records* project as "Chief Proof Reader," according to his obituary, although he is cited as a member of the three-person Board of Publication through most of the 1890s.[31]

Federal and state officials had other pragmatic reasons for compiling official lists of soldiers, the most important of which was helping to locate the officers, surgeons, and comrades whose testimony was necessary for successful pension applications. In Wisconsin, the state censuses of 1885, 1895, and 1905 compiled names and units of veterans and whether they were receiving a pension, while the only surviving schedule from the 1890 federal census was the special enumeration of Union veterans, which collected an old soldier's name, residence, regiment, company, length of service, and rank.[32]

The "list of all lists" for the Sixth and every other Wisconsin regiment was *The Roster of Wisconsin Volunteers in the War of the Rebellion, 1861–1865*. Overseen by the adjutant general of Wisconsin, Chandler P. Chapman, the

Roster appeared in two volumes, in 1886 and 1888. Most states published similar volumes in the 1880s, partly to commemorate the service of the men who fought and died for the Union, partly to make sure the state got credit for doing its duty in the nation's time of crisis, but also partly to help veterans build their pension cases.[33]

Chapman's office was the official repository for all documents related to Wisconsin's war effort. It was also the agency charged with helping veterans compile the necessary proofs of service for pension filing. As many as fourteen clerks, all of them veterans, and a number of them amputees, worked through bales of fragile, stained, and erratically completed records, ranging from recruiting documents and monthly and sometimes daily muster rolls to monthly and quarterly surgeon's reports, quartermaster reports, discharge papers, and regimental descriptive books. The preliminary results were recorded in massive ledgers called the "descriptive roll," which are nearly two by three feet, with each weighing upward of ten or twelve pounds; each regiment filled at least two volumes. Inside, beginning with the field officers and staff (surgeons, adjutants, musicians, etc.) and then proceeding through each company alphabetically, all the information available for every soldier who ever served was entered in tiny, meticulous handwriting.[34]

Chapman was an honorary veteran of the Sixth; he appears in the *Roster* as a teenaged hospital steward under his father, Dr. Chandler B. Chapman, who was surgeon of the Sixth for the first few months of the war. The younger Chapman became active in the fledgling National Guard movement in the 1870s and 1880s and served for several years as the state adjutant general. In his 1884 annual report, Chapman wrote, "As time passes and the memory of active participants in the war becomes more and more unreliable," the records preserved in Madison "will soon be the main, if not the only," source for the proof required in "the settlement of claims against the United States." Chandler estimated the need might continue for at least fifty years—"hence the *imperative necessity* of putting these records and files into proper condition for daily examination and use." Moreover, "many a veteran's heart would be cheered by the thought that the state had not forgotten his service and sufferings in its behalf."[35]

Veterans no doubt did take comfort in that knowledge. The lists that soldiers and veterans alike insisted on keeping or having made—from lists of dead and wounded scribbled into hurried letters in the aftermath of battle to the more formal casualty lists that soon appeared in newspapers, from the partial records of men who attended various reunions after the war to the massive undertakings of compiling reliable lists with basic information—all reflected a compulsion to impose order on the memory and significance of their service. In commemorating and logging their experiences, sacrifices, and contributions, soldiers hoped to inspire continuing respect and patriotism in others.

Days Long Gone By: Veteranizing

Although the GAR would become the best-known example of organizational commemoration, associations had sprung up almost as soon as the fighting ended. Survivors of the Sixth could choose several formal organizations to join, from the local to the national, and although only a minority did so, veterans' associations became the most visible part of the life cycle of soldiers' memory. The writer Sherwood Anderson, the son of an Ohio veteran, called these activities "veteranizing," and although his own feelings were ambiguous, the term happily captures the many ways in which the men of the Sixth commemorated their experiences.

In 1866, veterans in Wisconsin formed fourteen Soldiers and Sailors Leagues—all local, all reflecting veterans' interest in continuing their comradeship and recognition through organized, institutional commemoration. Jerome Watrous, D. K. Noyes, and Earl M. Rogers of the Sixth were very prominent in the 1867 reunion of the Army of the Potomac in Madison, with Noyes giving one of the keynote speeches. Watrous and John Kellogg were also heavily involved with the soldiers' reunion held in conjunction with the state fair in Milwaukee in September 1870. The *Daily Milwaukee News's* report of the grand review of the 3,000 veterans in attendance described their "marching past the reviewing officers and then breaking ranks, probably never again to re-assemble under the old flag."[36]

The writer could not have been more mistaken; there would be many more parades of old soldiers in Wisconsin's towns and cities in the coming decades. When the GAR formed in Illinois in spring 1866, Wisconsin veterans quickly formed their own local posts. The first state commander would have been well known to the survivors of the Sixth: he was Lucius Fairchild, the Iron Brigade veteran and newly elected governor of Wisconsin. Fairchild would be a power in the GAR and in Republican politics for decades.[37]

In a little more than a year fifty-six posts had formed in Wisconsin towns. By the 1870s, however, membership lagged and posts started to close due to a lack of orderly business practices, a too-close attention to wartime rank, and overly complicated rituals and hierarchies that, for some, may have too closely resembled the Masonic order. Partisan politics inevitably infiltrated the organization—it leaned heavily toward the Republican Party—and the 1873 depression made it difficult for some men to pay their dues. The "Great Falling Away," as it was known in GAR circles, led to the closure of most of the Wisconsin posts; only six remained in 1874.[38]

The 1880 "soldiers and sailors" reunion in Milwaukee helped spark the GAR's extraordinary renaissance, along with an easing of membership rules; congressional approval a year earlier of the Arrears Act, which sparked a new round of applications for pensions among veteran volunteers; and the growing popularity of fraternal orders like the Independent Order of Oddfellows and countless others. In Wisconsin, membership in the GAR rose to 2,500 by 1882. That doubled in the next year, and nearly again in 1884. By 1889 there were just under 14,000 comrades in Wisconsin. Much has been written about the GAR at the national level and some at the state level. But we know much less about the participation of individual regiments in the GAR or, for that matter, any other form of veterans' activities.[39]

Men of the Sixth left their mark on the GAR in many different ways. Many were charter members of posts; their comrades were remembered when posts were named after them. Seventeen different local chapters were named after members of the Sixth—far more than the other two Wisconsin regiments in the Iron Brigade (the Second had thirteen and the Seventh, seven). Some had died during the war, including Maj. Phil W. Plummer, killed in the Wilderness; Edwin A. Brown (his friend Edward Bragg was the first post commander); Henry Didiot, the man who had written the farewell song for the Anderson Guards, killed at Brawner's Farm; Frank Haskell, killed at Cold Harbor; and Rollin P. Converse, the subject of the famous story at the beginning of this chapter. Another notable name was Lysander Cutler Post in Wausau, where one of the charter members was the last commander of the Iron Brigade, John A. Kellogg. In turn, after his death in 1883, the veterans of Antigo named their new post after Kellogg. Several veterans of the Sixth were regularly elected to statewide leadership, including department commanders Philip Cheek Jr. and Jerome Watrous. They were joined in prominent positions by Earl Rogers and Daniel J. Dill.[40]

The Sixth tended also to be well represented at state and national encampments, with at least two dozen veterans of the Sixth attending the massive fiftieth-anniversary reunion of the Battle of Gettysburg in 1913. This was probably the most famous—and one of the largest—of the so-called Blue and Gray reunions that welcomed veterans of both armies. For many this was the first time back at the scene of the regiment's most heroic and heartbreaking action; although they had been called "old soldiers" since the 1860s, these soldiers were truly old, and at least some must have seen this as a chance to relive this remarkable moment in their long lives one last time.

Most came from Wisconsin and Minnesota—including one who was granted leave from the National Home in Milwaukee—but five came from California, another from Washington, and yet another from Kansas. They probably were able to take advantage of the reduced fares offered by most railroad companies; once they arrived in Gettysburg they would have walked a mile in the 100-degree heat to the great encampment, picking their way through what one historian has described as a "vibrant bustling, albeit well-organized carnival," complete with refreshment stands, souvenir booths, and sideshows. One of their first stops would have been the Iron Brigade tent, where they signed the reunion register that was eventually preserved in Watrous's papers.[41]

A fairly short walk would bring the men to the Wisconsin section in the northwestern part of the "Great Camp," between Confederate Avenue and the Emmitsburg Road—where half a century earlier the Sixth's triumphal march into Gettysburg, flag flying and drums drumming, was interrupted and they double-quicked into history. The seminary around which they had fought was just up the hill from their camp. The Sixth Wisconsin men could make a hike of perhaps 1,000 yards to the now-finished railroad cut, near the monument to them erected a quarter century before the reunion. Less spry men could hire an automobile or buggy to take them around the battlefield. The recommended route would take them very close to the monument and within a short walk of their position on the second and third days at Culp's Hill.[42]

How many times did the grand old man of the Sixth, Jerome Watrous, hold forth with what was probably his favorite story of the battle? As an ordnance sergeant he was ordered to resupply the brigade during the first day's fighting; he led the ammunition wagons in a mad dash through town, past the seminary, and to the rear of the hard-pressed regiments. Under fire, he and his crews hacked open the ammunition boxes with axes and then, wagons empty, made another dash back into town—perhaps the battered Sixth saw the wagons careening by—and on to safety. He had published the story of "The Mule Train Charge at Gettysburg" in the *Milwaukee Sunday Telegraph* thirty years earlier but probably told it again to anyone who would listen, now that they were camped so close to the place where it happened.[43]

It is pleasant to think that the five survivors of Company K in attendance—all still living near the same small town—traveled to Gettysburg together, smoking pipes and swapping war stories as they swayed in their

The Sixth Wisconsin monument (*far left*) looks over the Railroad Cut at Gettysburg a few years after its dedication. Also shown are monuments to the Ninety-Fifth New York (*center*) and the Fourteenth Brooklyn. The monuments were moved early in the twentieth century. Library of Congress, Washington, DC.

discounted passenger seats. Or that the several members of soldiers' homes in attendance compared the food, availability of cheap beer in neighborhood dives, and other facets of home life.

The Gettysburg reunion was a once-in-a-lifetime experience for these old men. Mostly they had to be satisfied with the smaller, cozier forms of commemoration and veteranizing in more intimate settings, like the monthly post meetings where there were rituals to perform and business to conduct but also stories to tell at virtual campfires.[44]

The primary occasion at which most Wisconsinites would have encountered soldiers performing Civil War memory came once a year, on Decoration Day, when veterans became the centerpiece of public veteranizing. Veterans of the Sixth participated in the holiday in large and small ways. J. H. Marston, always at the forefront of veterans' activities in Appleton, was the point man for gathering the names of former soldiers buried in Outagamie County to be published—as a list, of course—in the *Appleton Crescent*. In a "novel" addition to the regular exercises, the 1886 celebration in Fond du Lac featured the reading of resolutions prepared by former officers of the Sixth "expressing the sentiments of the Grand Army on the recent triumphal march of Jeff Davis through the South." Jerome Watrous spoke at countless Decoration Day events, and in 1894 he distributed a circular to GAR posts that was published widely around the state. In it he urged educators, ministers, and public officials to encourage and help schools and churches to sponsor appropriate ceremonies and asked veterans to keep the question before the public. Thus would patriotism and citizenship be strengthened.[45]

Members of the Sixth also took other opportunities to "veteranize," often in events and with organizations that operated parallel to the GAR. Although many Wisconsin regiments held reunions more or less annually, the Sixth seems to have held only one. "Shall We Have a Re-union?" asked an 1869 article originally appearing in the *Badger State Banner* in Black River Falls—the paper published by Jerome Watrous. The reunion was eventually held in March 1870, in the Newhall House in Milwaukee—the site of the reception for the veteran volunteers during their 1864 furlough. Officers for a permanent organization—including Bragg, Earl Rogers, John Kellogg, D. K. Noyes, and other prominent members—were chosen and a date was set for a second reunion, but it seems not to have materialized.[46]

The Sixth may not have held their own reunions because, often due to the leadership of men from their regiment, they had many other chances to reunite. In the 1880s a number of men of the Sixth attended a series of reunions of the La Crosse and Lemonweir Valley Veteran Association in Viroqua sponsored by the local GAR post, named after the Sixth's Capt. Alexander Lowrie. Very late in the century, another group of veterans from the Sixth formed an organization of former members of Company K at a two-day meeting in the GAR Hall in Mauston. Some had not seen others of their old company for thirty years, and they filled the hours "with stories of their careers, past experiences and reminiscences."[47]

Grant County hosted one of the most successful annual reunions outside of the GAR. The survivors of the Sixth's Company C—including the diarist George Fairfield—called a reunion in September 1879 to be held in Boscobel. This one-off gathering evolved into an annual reunion of all Grant County veterans under the name of the Grant County Veteran Soldiers' and Sailors' Association. Over eighty men had come to the regiment from Grant County, and the lists of attendees—which could include as many as 500 veterans and thousands of family members and friends—always included a number of men from the Sixth.[48]

Dozens of men of the Sixth belonged to an alternative to the GAR: the Iron Brigade Association (IBA). Relatively few Civil War–era units identified more closely as brigades than as regiments, both during and after the war— John B. Hood's Texas Brigade comes to mind, for instance. The Wisconsin, Indiana, and Michigan regiments shared a nickname and a reputation; most members of these hard-fought regiments knew that their service carried more weight—more meaning, to themselves and to the people at home— because they were part of the Iron Brigade of South Mountain, Antietam, and Gettysburg fame. Even as men of the Sixth could appreciate their separate contributions at Fitzhugh's Crossing and on the field west of Gettysburg, they knew that their true fame grew out of the larger organization. Many attended the annual reunions that began in 1880, often, especially late in its history, in conjunction with a national or state encampment of the GAR.[49]

Aside from the bitter fight over the pension issue in the mid-1880s, their meetings were boisterous, happy affairs, with the active participation of hundreds of men, including many members of the Sixth, at least seventy of whom seem to have chosen to attend IBA reunions rather than GAR encampments. The two-day 1883 reunion in La Crosse—held just three years after the organization was founded—was representative. The local reception committee met the 150 attendees at the train depot and escorted them to headquarters, where they registered and pinned on their badges, amid "hearty handshaking and fraternal greetings." A formal procession of the old soldiers, with bands, local militia companies, GAR representatives, and disabled soldiers in carriages, proceeded to a local hall, which was decorated with a giant floral flag, displays featuring the names of Iron Brigade commanders, and the names of the men who had died in battle. The afternoon business meeting included recitations and a glee club singing the wartime ballad, "The Vacant Chair," while "the evening was passed at the Germania Garden, which was beautifully illuminated with electric lights and Chinese lanterns." The next year's reunion was somewhat unusual in that General Gibbon was able to preside with his usual dash of humor—accepting the "surrender" of the city of Lancaster from the mayor, who turned the town over to the military for twenty-four hours—and because Rufus Dawes had traveled all the way from Ohio. The program was packed with battle reminiscences by Gibbon; several members of the Sixth, including Dawes, Philip Cheek Jr.—current commander of the state GAR, who also sang the humorous army song "Army Beans"—and Watrous. Highlights from the next year's meeting was a "Bean Banquet" and a band playing the "Iron Brigade Quickstep"—one of the few times the tune was ever mentioned![50]

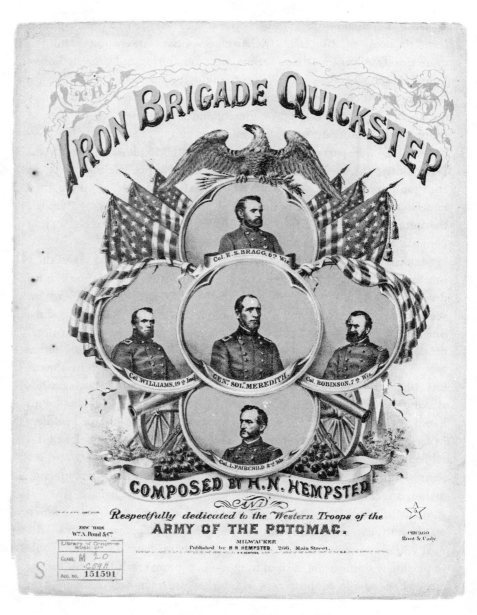

Commissioned late in 1862 by a member of the Sixth Wisconsin, the "Iron Brigade Quickstep," while forgettable as a piece of music, reflected the pride in the regiment's fierce performance in that fall's battles. Library of Congress, Washington, DC.

Gibbon's long association with the IBA marked an unusual relationship between a brigade and the man who had led it for less than a year—and may have been one reason some men chose the IBA over the GAR. He was elected president without opposition year after year; the annual invitation to all known survivors went out over his name. And although as an active-duty officer in the West he was usually unable to attend—he commanded one wing of the campaign that ended with the Battle of the Little Big Horn and was later seriously wounded during the campaign against the Nez Perce—he frequently sent letters to be read at reunions. One of the major efforts undertaken by the association was raising money to erect a memorial over the general's grave in Arlington National Cemetery when he died in 1896. Led by Bragg and Watrous, the organization commissioned a monument featuring a bas-relief head shot of the general on one side and the familiar Maltese cross symbol of the Union V Corps on the other with the inscription "The Iron Brigade Rears This Block of Granite to the Memory of A Loved Commander."[51]

Time caught up to the IBA, as it does for all organizations founded to honor a single generation. Long after most men of the Sixth were dead, a young boy named Frances Peterson attended the 1924 reunion of the Iron Brigade. He was the nine-year-old great-grandson of the long-dead Edward Bragg, and he went around the room shaking hands with the two dozen or so old men in attendance. When someone asked young Frances "if he realized who he was shaking hands with he answered, 'Yes, sir, I do; with the best soldiers of the war.'"[52]

A rough but suggestive estimate of the extent to which veterans of the Sixth Wisconsin participated in Gilded Age veteranizing can be gleaned from the various records embedded in the Sixth Wisconsin Demographic Database. There are three main categories: (1) belonging to the GAR (appearing on a membership list or attending an encampment, having a GAR funeral, or being mentioned as a member in an obituary); (2) attending reunions of the IBA; and (3) attending other reunions or events unrelated to either organization. All of the numbers that follow should be considered minimums, of course, given the impossibility of obtaining all of the necessary records.

Among the 1,635 men of the Sixth Wisconsin who survived the war, 359 (22 percent of the total number of veterans) seem to have been members of the GAR. At least ninety-two (5.6 percent) of the total attended at least one Iron Brigade reunion. Another twenty-eight appeared on lists of ad hoc or local reunions and other events. Altogether, 479 (29.3 percent) of the Sixth's veterans were definitely participants in one or more kinds of "veteranizing." The limited information suggests a number of key differences;

officers participated in veterans' activities at a much higher rate than enlisted men—52.5 percent to 27.5 percent. They were also somewhat more likely to participate in both GAR and Iron Brigade reunions than the lower ranks. Among the latter, 31.4 percent participated, while only 18.6 percent of the draftees and 10.9 percent of the substitutes participated. Interestingly, well over 40 percent of former prisoners of war and an incredible 81 percent of amputees participated in veterans' activities. This may indicate that their unique experiences not only caused them to be held up as particularly admirable but also that their personal sacrifices caused them to be more invested in its commemoration.

Although only about 60 percent of all Sixth Wisconsin survivors received pensions, 75.4 percent of men who participated in some kind of veterans' activity collected pensions. This suggests two things that are not necessarily mutually exclusive: receiving pensions encouraged men to engage in veterans' activities, and engaging in veterans' activities encouraged men to apply for pensions and gave them the chance to renew friendships with comrades who could serve as witnesses in their applications.[53]

"Veteranizing" no doubt provided a core experience for a significant minority of survivors, but the reasons they decided not to participate must have varied widely. As in any voluntary association, much would have depended on who else belonged or whether certain cliques controlled local posts, on the possibility that membership would bring with it social or economic advantages, and on practical issues like distance to meeting places or whether an old soldier was healthy enough to make the effort or affluent enough to pay the dues. Unmeasurable, of course, is the extent to which men chose not to remember their service in any public way.

Elbow to Elbow down the Sunset Slope

More than a half century after the war ended, a report from Madison's Lucius Fairchild GAR post remarked that there were now more members of the post who had died (164) than were currently alive (98). Yet, he wrote, "we old comrades . . . are glad because of the peace and harmony in our ranks as we march elbow to elbow down the sunset slope."[54]

Of course, death was the last passage in the life cycle of Civil War veterans' memory. In a very important sense, the lives of the veterans of the Sixth Wisconsin were typical for Americans of the Gilded Age. Some prospered more than others and most died in the mundane, random, and sometimes tragic ways in which all American men died. Ener Birum of Company A survived eleven battles and became a prosperous flour miller in Minnesota but was killed in 1893 when he fell while trying to catch a train in Minneapolis. August Schwanke died of a brain hemorrhage while cutting his grass; Simeon Mortimer broke his neck falling out of a buggy. But mostly, like other men of their time and place, they seemed to have died of heart disease, cancer, and the cumulative maladies common to the late nineteenth and early twentieth century—often hurried along by the long-term effects of wartime wounds and illnesses.[55]

Yet the obituaries published after their deaths captured often moving if impressionistic glimpses of how the communities in which veterans lived and died viewed these aging heroes. Of course, those memories were shaped by the veterans themselves. If a man preferred not to talk about his days in the Union army, it was less likely that that service would be remembered by others. On the other hand, if he wore his patriotism and sacrifice on his sleeve—especially if that sleeve was empty—memorialists would naturally be drawn to the stories the veteran had told over and over. The most thorough obituaries were for men who had returned to the towns from which they had marched in the 1860s or had been pioneers in new communities in northern Wisconsin, the Great Plains, or the West Coast. Men who held public office or ran their own businesses would obviously have been noticed. And during its zenith, membership in the GAR and the participation of their comrades in their funerals would draw attention to men's service. More obscure veterans, like the other anonymous men and women who lived quiet, unassuming lives during the Gilded Age or any other age, received the briefest of obituaries—a few dates, names of spouses and children, perhaps a reference to place of birth and occupation. Many others were far better known as pioneers, philanthropists, or church men than as soldiers.

Yet the available obituaries of veterans of the Sixth Wisconsin still suggest certain useful elements of the process of remembering the Civil War. Many appeared under headlines that mentioned some aspect of military service or veterans' activities, especially in towns where the spirit of commemoration meant something, and where the local GAR camp was or had been a source of pride and leadership. Typical headlines in this genre were "Well Known Veteran Passed Away," "War Veteran Dies in the East," "One More Comrade Has Stepped from the Rapidly Thinning Ranks of Remaining Civil War Veterans," "Civil War Veteran Is Called," "Prominent Civil War Vet Dies," "An Old Soldier Gone," "Responds to Roll Call," and "The Old Veteran Is Mustered Out." The Gilded Age fondness for wordplay usually failed to obscure the sincerity of the sentiments the obituaries expressed.[56]

Obituaries varied dramatically in length, from short paragraphs to full columns. Some left military service out altogether; some simply mentioned it briefly. Others, especially if the deceased had remained in Wisconsin, mentioned the Sixth Wisconsin and the Iron Brigade. Indeed, phrases along the lines of "the famous Iron Brigade" or sometimes "Gen. Bragg's Iron Brigade" assumed that readers would still remember at least the name of this hard-fought unit and its best-known commander. But many obituaries, especially for officers, included a much more detailed account of the man's military service, including dates, battles, injuries, and other pertinent details.

The more elaborate obituaries tried to capture unique aspects of their subjects. "Wash" Force was a carpenter and milkman, who "in his younger days . . . played for dances in all parts of the country . . . and as a caller for the old-time square dances was regarded without an equal in this section." After homesteading with his wife Rachel in Kansas, Will Gardner was remembered as a "lover of children," although six of his and Rachel's eight sons and daughters had died in infancy. "Every youngster who ever met him remembered his kindly laugh and jokes." Christian Koelsch lived in Neenah, Wisconsin, for fifty years after the war, where he was a member of the GAR and "never tired of telling of his experiences during his time in the army."[57]

Others praised men who had suffered bravely for decades from injuries or illnesses incurred during the war or highlighted character traits that reflected their continued patriotism, courage, and commitment to the public good. "His love for his adopted country has been manifested on eleven battlefields of the Civil War," wrote a local paper of Ener Birum. "Like other mortals," James Deery "had his failings, but his virtues which were many overshadowed them. He was honest and detested all that was gross and impure." Although others "would have thought themselves incapacitated for active life," the *Galesville Republican* wrote about the amputee and former prisoner Frank Hare, "this was not the case with Mr. Hare. His land . . . was improved to a fine farm." Although he had served for just under a year, David Lombard, according to his obituary, "has lived a long and useful life serving his country in her time of need and filling his place in the great scheme of life always to the best of his ability."[58]

Obituaries would mention the loss of limbs in combat, of course, but would also occasionally catalogue other medical conditions that stretched back to their military service. "For nearly thirty years before his death," Atwell Cook "had been so crippled with rheumatism, contracted in the service of his country, that he was unable to engage in manual labor." The *Appleton Crescent* noted that Frank Delaglise had been "sent home to die" after being wounded at Antietam but recovered to live another thirty years and cofound the northern Wisconsin town of Leopolis. Although never wounded in battle, Charles Eichler hurt his back in the service and "was compelled to walk with a stoop for the remainder of his life," while Will Gardner, wounded at Gettysburg, "never returned to soldier duty, in fact, never fully recovered from this injury."[59]

Finally, a few obituaries acknowledged the passing of a generation set apart. Of course, every death is an inevitable life passage, for the dead and for their survivors, but there is a sense from the obituaries of the Sixth that the death of one more old soldier provided a somber opportunity to reflect on the generation who had saved the Union and on the struggle itself. It almost seemed as though local editors—perhaps themselves veterans or the children of veterans—were counting down the last few witnesses to the most dramatic era in American history, not unlike the twenty-first-century devotion to tracking the shrinking number of veterans of the Second World War through heartwarming honor flights and inspiring newspaper stories about their sacrifices at Normandy and Okinawa.

"The "remaining members" of James Flynn's GAR post attended his 1924 funeral, while only two veterans attended John Hacker's military funeral in Black Earth, Wisconsin, which nevertheless was "one of the largest ever held" in the small town. One of the last Civil War veterans in Sawtelle, California, passed away at the National Home for Disabled Volunteer Soldiers in 1935; he was Daniel Alton of the Sixth, who had been living at the home for a year. When William L. Riley died at age ninety-eight, he had been not only one of Milwaukee's four remaining Civil war veterans but the last member of the Sixth to die.[60]

Obituaries were simply the last chapter of larger narratives, but burial rites punctuated lives lived in the shadow of the long war. Soldiers had always feared that they would go unrecognized if they were killed. Men of the Sixth Wisconsin tried to ensure that hastily buried dead comrades could be found and buried with more respect and dignity. John Costigan of Company D put a board with the name of the well-respected sergeant Dick Montgomery on the battlefield at South Mountain, "that his friends may find him easily should they seek his remains."[61]

George Johnson's friends managed a more meaningful and permanent farewell. He had kept mementos of his four years of service, perhaps tucked away in a dresser drawer. The twenty-seven-year-old mustered out as a lieutenant in the summer of 1865 and returned to his hometown of Shawano but died in November 1866, leaving neither a family nor a will. Among his meager possessions was one of the ornate, suitable-for-framing "memorials" commemorating a soldier's service; perhaps he hung it on the wall of his rented room. Otherwise, the propertyless former "lumberman" owned household items, clothing, a little cash, and a government bond worth $200 (perhaps purchased with his reenlistment bounty). But objects related to his military service peppered the inventory: in addition to the "Soldiers Memorial," he had twenty-seven dollars of Confederate money; a pocket looking glass; two volumes of infantry tactics; one corps badge; and two lieutenant's epaulets. Other items may have been part of his military baggage or related in other ways to his service, including a satchel and a trunk, a tobacco box, an "old pocket book," a package of envelopes (perhaps featuring the patriotic slogans and images popular during the war), and a black hat that might have been the one he received with the new uniforms in which the regiment marched in the Grand Review.

Another Company E survivor, Julius Murray, acted as executor and hosted an auction of Johnson's belongings. Aside from the government bond, which was sold separately, the auction brought in $28.86. The epaulets and soldier's memorial each earned a nickel, while the corps badge and infantry tactics went for twenty-five cents each. Murray's report of the auction and disposal of the assets included the cost of the funeral (seventeen dollars), Johnson's coffin (twenty-five dollars), the cemetery plot (five dollars), and expenses for decorating and erecting a picket fence around the grave (eleven dollars).[62]

Not all veterans of the Sixth had such devoted friends, and not all could afford a proper grave or marker. Many years later, the government began providing the elegantly simple tombstones familiar to anyone who has visited Arlington or any other national cemetery. But they also, often in designated lots or groupings, appear in the huge, park-like cemeteries in cities and in small burying places on windswept hills outside small towns. Pension files often contain copies of the form, completed by a family member or, much later, representatives from American Legion posts, requesting free tombstones.

Hundreds of men of the Sixth are buried under those plain grave markers that list only their names and units; many dozens are also buried in the mass graves in national cemeteries holding the "unknown" dead, usually organized by state. The largest single gathering of the regiment's honored dead—aside from the national cemeteries near the great battlefields in Pennsylvania and Virginia—are the forty-five men of the Sixth who lie among the more than 30,000 men and women buried at Wood National Cemetery on the grounds of the Clement J. Jablocki Veterans' Administration Medical Center near the historic buildings of the National Home for Disabled Volunteer Soldiers near Milwaukee. The men are scattered through fifteen of the cemetery's oldest sections in the northwest corner of the vast space. Most were privates; Maj. John Hauser, however, lies in one of the oldest sections of the cemetery, buried there in 1883 after a long struggle with his health and finances. The four men of the Sixth in section 12 lie a short stone's throw from the alert sentinel guarding the cemetery from the top of the towering 1903 Soldiers and Sailors Monument, whose shadow marches across their graves like a martial sundial on fall and winter days.[63]

Most of the men from the Sixth are buried far from their comrades, although the five men in section 18—one of the most pleasant areas in the cemetery, with plenty of shade—who all died within a few months of one another in 1911 and 1912, could easily carry on a conversation if they were aboveground. The two members of the Sixth in section 20 are surrounded by Wisconsin veterans from other regiments, many belonging to the old Iron Brigade.

An Abundant and Sufficient Reward

The short lives and bloody deaths of the men who had died in the war haunted the survivors of the Sixth Wisconsin. They would have felt a twinge of survivor's guilt, no doubt, of sincere grief, of soldierly respect, and of patriotic gratitude. Most failed to record those intimate thoughts and feelings, so Rufus Dawes's moving tribute to his dead comrades will have to represent them all.

Dawes had become a successful businessmen in his hometown of Marietta, Ohio, after the war, surviving typical Gilded Age ebbs and flows of prosperity but generally living a contented life with his wartime bride Mary and their five children. His three sons would become prominent businessmen, lawyers, and politicians; his oldest, Charles, would serve as vice president of the United States. Rufus served on boards of several institutions, including his beloved Marietta College, and enjoyed having some of his grandchildren—including a grandson named Rufus—nearby. He wrote articles for newspapers and other publications about the war, worked on his memoirs, and served as commander of his local GAR post in the late 1870s and in the US House of Representatives for a single term in the early 1880s. Although he was never wounded, by the 1880s he nevertheless suffered from rather delicate health that he blamed on the war. Although only in his early fifties, in 1893 he reported being "used up" after speaking and marching in the procession on Decoration Day. He often complained about his legs, periodic attacks of indigestion, and exhaustion.[64]

He noted the thirtieth anniversary of the day "I commanded the Charge at Gettysburg—How far and yet in memory how near." Yet deeply appreciative of having survived that moment and all the other battles he had fought, he continued, "It is thirty years of contentment joy and peace for the most part and my gratitude goes to the giver of all good for it." He died six years later at the age of sixty-one.[65]

The war had never been far from Dawes's thoughts. In late 1881, taking a break from his duties at the Capitol, Congressman Dawes visited Arlington National Cemetery to "worship at the shrine of the dead." His mission was to find the graves of "my friends and comrades . . . who followed my enthusiastic leadership in those days, followed it to the death which I by a merciful Providence escaped." He located those two dozen gravestones among the 16,000 already in the cemetery, including several who had pledged their lives to the Union on that spring evening fraught with excitement and danger twenty years earlier. But the occasion also made him reflect on the past, on his youthful enthusiasm, on the ways in which the war tempered that enthusiasm and shaped his ambition—both as an officer and as a civilian. His regiment had camped nearby when they first reached the war, and as a young captain his "ambitious imagination," looking out over the Potomac River at Washington City and its unfinished capitol, had "builded castles of the time when I might take my place there." Now, "at middle age, with enthusiasm sobered by hard fights and hard facts," he stood with "uncovered head" at each of the graves of his old comrades, and considered ambition and service differently. Their deaths—their lives, actually—had inspired him to run for Congress, "to stand for all they won in establishing our government upon freedom, equality, justice, liberty, and protection to the humblest. . . . For what they died I fight a little longer."

Dawes was all of forty-two when he penned this powerful letter to Mary, yet he felt old. "The shadows of age are rapidly stealing upon us," he wrote in a section of his memoir directed toward his old comrades, whose "generous courage" and "ambitious hope" had helped save "the most beneficial government ever established." Now, however, "our burdens are like the loaded knapsack on the evening of a long and weary march, growing heavier at every pace." As a kind of benediction, he urged the old soldiers to remember that "this is your abundant and sufficient reward."[66]

By almost any standards Rufus Dawes lived an extraordinarily successful and happy life. But even he could not let go of the war—or, perhaps, the war would not let go of him. Although he did not seem to be wracked by guilt over the deaths of the men under his command, he felt compelled to remember them in concrete and meaningful ways, to remind others of their sacrifice. He had transformed from a somewhat callow youth into a conscientious leader and, in the fullness of time, into a thoughtful, mature man who reflected seriously about the Civil War and his part in it.

That was Rufus Dawes's long Civil War.

Epilogue

The journalist Orlando Burnett discovered a profound truth when he visited Milwaukee in 1898 to do a piece on the Northwestern Branch of the National Home for Disabled Volunteer Soldiers. A guide showed Burnett through the bustling facility; with 2,000 residents and a sprawling, idyllic campus with shaded drives and three ponds, it was one of the jewels of the soldiers' home system and a point of pride for the flourishing city. The guide gushed over the home's 1,400-seat theater, well-stocked library, spotless kitchen, and antidrinking Keeley club.

Burnett would faithfully report all of these wonders, but his article took a turn when he and his guide paused at the foot of a hospital bed. As his host droned on about the convenience of having a card with the patient's medical and personal information attached to the bedpost—"when he dies we have here all his record"—Burnett noticed that the patient "stirred uneasily." The oblivious guide went on to talk about the man as though he were already dead. Burnett could not shake the image of the old soldier, who he learned had served with the Iron Brigade. "The man on the bed must have been somebody once. . . . Women had once admired his fine-lined face and kissed it." The man had once been "young and full of fire. He had marched from home with cheers in his ears, and he had seen the foe. He had thought great thoughts on picket duty under the stars, and he had done a man's work in the world." But now he was so weary that he could not close his mouth, and he cared little about what people thought when they looked at him. "He was rather a tired child—this big, old man, who once marched with Gibbon and Bragg. And as he lay on his pillow, the white bed clothes wrapped about his thin, gaunt frame, he . . . seemed to want nothing of God but a chance to sleep for ten million years." Burnett admitted, "It knocks a man's theological systems into little pieces to see an old man who fought for a nation on his death bed." As anyone who has visited a nursing home knows, despite even the highest quality of care, there is, as Burnett sighed, "a pathos to it all."[1]

Perhaps the poor, slack-jawed veteran of the Iron Brigade was Stephen Bennett of the Sixth Wisconsin's Company B, a former sailor without a family who died and was buried at the Northwestern Branch in 1898, the year of Burnett's visit; or James Haynes, the hostler; or the draftee from the Netherlands John Piron, who, like Haynes, also died at the home in 1898. In any event, few contemporaries captured better than Burnett how the long Civil War ended for many.[2]

The experiences of the men of the Sixth Wisconsin ricocheted through time and families, destroying and creating communities, forcing—allowing—men and women to forge new institutions and traditions, and ending or irrevocably altering hundreds of lives. Over 300 men died in combat or from disease during the war, leaving over 250 widows and children. Scores of others were so physically disabled by their war experiences that they sought and received pensions within a few years of leaving the army or needed to enter a soldiers' home at some point in their lives. The war seems to have shortened the lives of countless men; at least sixty-five of the Sixth Wisconsin's survivors of the war died before their fiftieth birthdays.[3]

All of these life passages find their way into biographies of regiments, much as they do in biographies of men and women. It seems that every biography ends with decline and declension, with flaws exposed, old alliances collapsed, and accomplishments eclipsed by disillusion. That holds true for those individual members of the Sixth Wisconsin who struggled with health and economic vulnerability, family tragedies, and all the other ways in which the long Civil War could affect its survivors. When they returned from the war—on that surreal 1864 furlough, perhaps, but certainly at the end of their service—they sought to fit in, and their loved ones and communities desperately wanted them to be the same men or boys grown to manhood who had marched off to war. Only the veterans knew how many emotional and physical obstacles stood in the path of that dream. This was true for men who had served four years and for men who had served six months; some of the former managed to shrug off the horrors of the war, while some of the latter had difficulty recovering physically or psychologically from their one big battle or one long stay in a tawdry army hospital.

But a biography should also root their subjects in larger contexts and offer ways in which they are remembered and the legacies that they left.

Some members of the Sixth left their marks as public servants. At least ninety men of the Sixth—just over 5 percent of the survivors—went on to some sort of public service at the local, state, and even national level. The most prominent were the three congressmen, the Democrat Edward Bragg and the Republicans Rufus Dawes and John Jenkins. Another thirteen men served in state legislatures, seventeen served on town or county boards, and twenty-two accepted appointments as postmasters. Among the others were a sprinkling of sheriffs and deputy sheriffs, district attorneys and county judges, and clerks of court and justices of the peace, as well as a county coroner, a street commissioner, a register of deeds, and a town assessor. Chandler P. Chapman, who had been a hospital steward with the Sixth, spent many years as adjutant general of Wisconsin, while former private Theodore Kanouse served as Wisconsin's state superintendent of schools and warden of the South Dakota penitentiary and later ran as the Prohibition candidate for governor in both South Dakota and California.[4]

Men of the Sixth also joined one of the signature movements of the late nineteenth century by migrating to other states or territories. Americans were famously on the move during the Gilded Age, as immigrants poured into the country, as easterners flocked to the West, and as country folk relocated to towns and cities. Civil War veterans helped power the extraordinary geographical mobility in Gilded Age America, and a large percentage of the Sixth Wisconsin also sought other—if not necessarily greener—pastures. It must be said, however, that virtually all of the men in the Sixth had already made at least one move in their lives, either as children accompanying their parents to the Wisconsin frontier, as immigrants, or as young men on the make.

The postwar diaspora of the Sixth Wisconsin did not happen overnight, however, as many of the men who moved did so after returning to Wisconsin for a time, and only moving on after reuniting with family, recovering from wounds or illnesses, and returning to old jobs or trying new ones. About half of the men for whom we know postwar residences left Wisconsin for at least a time. The largest single group—just over 150, or more than 20 percent of all migrants—relocated to the Great Plains (one veteran lived in a Nebraska town named for his old commander John Gibbon, while another joined 200 other veterans who named their central South Dakota community Gettysburg). Others followed or joined family members seeking business opportunities or warmer climates, including a couple who moved to "soldiers' colonies" in Florida. Eventually some retired and went to live with or near children, especially after the deaths of spouses or a stay in a soldiers' home. Some moved around from one soldiers' home to another. A few lived elsewhere for years, even decades, but retired back to Wisconsin or were brought home to be buried or to spend the last few months of their lives near loved ones.[5]

In many cases, the Sixth's legacy found expression in marble, granite, and limestone. The most important formal monument to the Sixth Wisconsin, appropriately enough, stands west of Gettysburg, near the Railroad Cut, through which trains still rumble on their way to towns and cities on the Eastern Seaboard and in Canada. It dates back to 1887, when a quartet of Sixth Wisconsin veterans—Philip Cheek Jr., Earl Rogers, J. H. Marston, and Howard J. Huntington—helped lead the effort to erect the monument that was dedicated in 1888, in time for the quarter-century anniversary of the battle.[6] At the local level, the names of men of the Sixth Wisconsin appear on monuments throughout the state, some erected shortly after the war, others decades later, some on smooth modern monuments dedicated to the communities' war dead from all of America's conflicts.[7]

Some legacies are tongue in cheek; at the Blue and Gray Bar and Grill in downtown Gettysburg, tourists can order a chicken wrap with spicy "Iron Brigade Sauce." On a grander scale is US Highway 12, officially named the Iron Brigade Memorial Highway. And on Interstate 90/94, a rest area between Madison and Eau Claire features a historic marker offering a pocket history of the Iron Brigade.[8]

Just as it stood apart from the brigade at Fitzhugh's Crossing and Gettysburg, the Sixth is honored separately in various museums and other venues around Wisconsin. Rufus Dawes and his men burst out of Antietam's Cornfield in a life-sized diorama at the Wisconsin Veterans Museum in Madison; a small plaque on a large stone honors Jerome Watrous in a Milwaukee County park; exhibits at the Kenosha Civil War Museum quote pithily from the writings of Dawes, Watrous, and James Sullivan; a short video on the Lemonweir Minutemen can still be streamed on the Wisconsin public television website;

the names of four members of the Sixth appear on a marble plaque listing the forty-six former students at Beloit College who gave their lives for the Union; and over on the Mississippi River, the Fort Crawford Hospital Museum at Prairie du Chien features Maj. Phil W. Plummer, killed at the Wilderness, and a photo of several early twentieth-century Grand Army of the Republic members, including three men from the Sixth. In the 1960s and 1970s, a target-shooting team calling itself the Sixth Wisconsin competed in black powder tournaments around the country and took part in reenactments in Wisconsin and elsewhere. Its founders included the historians William Beaudot and Lance Herdegen, whose books have been valuable sources for this one. Finally, in the 1980s, Rufus Dawes's old hometown of Mauston held a four-day celebration around Memorial Day called Company K Days, which featured reenactments, parades, and a Blue and Gray Ball.[9]

But a more substantial way to honor the Sixth Wisconsin's legacy is to articulate what its biography can teach us about the Civil War. Studying the nearly 2,000 men of the Sixth—and their hundreds of wives, children, and parents—helps us understand the long Civil War as it played out in a representative sample of Union soldiers and families. Including the communities from which they came and to which they returned provides concrete knowledge of the distinct experiences of soldiers and civilians and the tensions that could divide them. They help us better understand the challenges of a massive, modern conflict that forced them to invent new ways of mobilizing, fighting, surviving, and explaining the war. Exploring the life cycle of memory within a single regiment uncovers the contours of commemoration and understanding; examining the complicated relationships formed by disability, soldiers' homes, and the pension system fleshes out the tensions that could develop between and among veterans, communities, and policy makers. If a biography of Abraham Lincoln or Ulysses S. Grant can offer meaningful reflections on antebellum society or the development of the American way of war—even as they highlight the unique characteristics of their subjects—so can the biography of a single regiment of Union soldiers reveal much about the time and place in which they fought and died, survived and remembered.

The most moving monument to Civil War soldiers in Wisconsin greets visitors to Rienzi Cemetery, a few miles outside of Fond du Lac, home of many original members of Company E. Rather than depicting a young man in a typically generic, martial pose, this modest statue features an old soldier standing comfortably on a short pedestal—mustache trimmed, neatly attired

The unique monument to Civil War soldiers in Rienzi Cemetery in
Fond du Lac, Wisconsin, features an old soldier, hat in hand, offering
a wreath to his departed comrades. Author's collection.

in a Grand Army of the Republic uniform, hat in hand, offering a wreath to
his dead comrades.

A small cluster of veterans' graves stretches to his right, including that
of Harrison Buchanan of Company D, who died in 1917. Farther into the
cemetery, along a narrow path over the hill rising gently beyond the statue,
is Edward Bragg's grave, flanked by two American flags. One side features a
bas-relief profile of Bragg in uniform, framed with laurels; on the other side

is the V Corps Maltese cross, with Bragg's name, rank, and the phrase "In the end peace." Other veterans' graves are scattered throughout the cemetery, including, a few hills away, that of the man mistaken in death for Bragg, Edwin Brown. On his tombstone is carved a sword and the awkward but strangely evocative inscription "Edwin A. Brown Capt. Co. E 6th Regt. Wis. Vols. WAS KILLED at the battle of Antietam Sept. 17, 1862 IN THE 31YR. OF HIS AGE."

Unlike the stone soldiers on eternal duty in countless other cemeteries and courthouse lawns, the graceful sculpture greeting visitors to the graves of the first two commanders of Company E shows a man in the late autumn of his life. His battles are in the distant past; he comes as a friend and comrade to visit the men who have gone before him. His pride in serving his country is evident, as is his sorrow that so many comrades have preceded him to the other side. Most of the other 2,000 men who had gone to war under the banner of the Sixth Wisconsin failed to reach that kind of self-aware, if bittersweet, contentment.

It is easy to assume that the Civil War not only was the most interesting thing that ever happened *to* the men of the Sixth Wisconsin, but it also was the most interesting thing *about them*. But this careless assumption ignores qualities and experiences and conditions that are necessary to fully understand the war they fought and the peace they tried to achieve when the guns fell silent.

A NOTE ABOUT DATABASES AND CITATIONS

Much of the research for this book is contained in two major databases, which were drawn from the published *Roster of Wisconsin Volunteers in the War of the Rebellion, 1861–1865*, the descriptive roll, and numerous other sources. The first simply recreated the *Roster* in an Excel spreadsheet; it contained each soldier's name, company, residence, entrance and exit date, whether he enlisted or was drafted, information about casualties, beginning and ending rank, and a "remarks" section that often provided information about where a man had been wounded, residence in soldiers' homes, and so forth. It provided a jumping-off point for the second major database, the Master Sixth Wisconsin Database, which contains twenty-six data points on the soldiers' prewar and postwar lives. In addition to the data from the *Roster*, the Master Sixth Wisconsin Database includes cohort 1: 1861 enlistees; cohort 2: 1863–64 enlistees; and cohort 3: draftees); service in the Veteran Reserve Corps; prewar and postwar occupations and residences; family makeup; dates of birth, death, marriage, and pension applications; immigration status; postwar political activities; veterans' activities, including Iron Brigade reunions and Grand Army of the Republic membership; and residence in state or federal soldiers' homes. Although some of the information in the database came from newspapers, pension files, and other sources, much of the research consisted of combing through the vast resources made available through Ancestry.com. Ancestry's algorithms can sometimes produce puzzling search results, but the sheer volume of available records makes it an indispensable resource for researching records that would otherwise take years to consult. The most important sources available through Ancestry are manuscript censuses from

1860 through 1920; the Civil War Pension Index: General Index to Pension Files, 1861–1934; records of federal soldiers' homes; marriage and death records produced by federal, state, and local governments; the 1890 veterans' census; and rosters of Grand Army of the Republic members and veterans compiled by Kansas, Iowa, and a few other states. Complementing Ancestry was the Find a Grave website. Although results were somewhat hit or miss because of its crowdsourced data, the site also filled in many blanks regarding birth and death dates, family members, residences, and on a few lucky occasions, obituaries for the old soldiers. Also useful were the "Soldier Personals" and lists of attendees at various veterans and Grand Army of the Republic functions published in the *Milwaukee Sunday Telegraph* in the 1880s. Although an effort was made to locate all of the men listed on the roster, that was not possible (although all were searched for). Having said that, we obtained information on the overwhelming majority of men. For instance, the Master Sixth Wisconsin Database contains both birth and death dates for 80 percent of them, prewar occupations for over 80 percent, postwar occupations for over 60 percent of the survivors, and postwar residences for just under 80 percent. Several other databases were created for particular groups—some drawn directly from the master database, others containing information not in the master—and are cited separately.

Although it is not surprising to anyone who has used these sources, it must be stated that they were produced by countless, anonymous recorders: census takers, government clerks, recruiters, newspaper correspondents, officers and soldiers, pension agents and investigators, genealogists, and historians and research assistants, for that matter. As a result, although most names and places are fairly clear cut, a certain inevitable drift away from accuracy sets in for some men, as misspelled names and mistaken dates are passed along and eventually fossilized into the records. The men and women creating the original documents relied on the spoken word, which means that they heard unusual names spoken in thick German, Scandinavian, Irish, and Welsh accents by the hundreds of immigrants who served in the Sixth. Other names seem to have been simply too hard to manage, while no one thought to record dates of birth—rather, ages at the time of enlistment were provided or estimated, which means that setting a birth year requires admitting that one will be at least a few months off for half of the men. The military records were produced in noisy training posts, as recruits stood in line, or in dreary, wet camps, or just behind ghastly battle lines. Once a mistake was made, it tended to carry down through the ages, making the search for reliable information for a small minority of the men in online platforms an adventure.

A Note about Databases and Citations

And, inevitably, some recorded names are simply too inaccurate to be searchable, or the men themselves lived such short or such anonymous lives that they escape formal detection in census returns or other written records.

Read-only versions of all databases featuring the raw material on which the text is based can be found at https://epublications.marquette.edu/marten_2024.

The other principal set of primary sources were pension records for veterans, widows, and other dependents. Information drawn from these rich although often frustrating sources is sprinkled throughout the book, although the files are most thoroughly examined in chapter 8. I consulted a total of 259 pension files: 151 at the National Archives in Washington (which often include the files of both the soldiers and their widows); ninety-eight on the Fold3 military records website (these are entirely related to widows, minor children, and dependent parents); and ten photocopies from the Beaudot Archival Collection in the Kenosha Civil War Museum archives. I selected files to represent—very roughly—the men's geographical origins (by choosing about the same number from each company) and in proportion to the percentage of men from each of the three cohorts. Pension files from the National Archives are cited by soldier's name and certificate number, followed by "NARA"; dependent pension files are cited as they are organized online, by soldier's name, company, and widow certificate number, followed by "Fold3"; files from the Kenosha Civil War Museum are cited as other documents in that archive are cited.

NOTES

ABBREVIATIONS

Co.   Company
DA   Dawes Arboretum, Newark, Ohio
DSR   Digital Scholarship Repository, Raynor Memorial Libraries, Marquette University, Milwaukee, Wisconsin
Fold3   Fold3 Military Records Database
GNMP   Gettysburg National Military Park Library, Gettysburg, Pennsylvania
KCWM   Kenosha Civil War Museum, Kenosha, Wisconsin
NARA   National Archives and Records Administration, Washington, DC
OR   *War of the Rebellion: A Compilation of the Official Records of the Union and Confederate Armies.* 128 vols. Washington, DC: Government Printing Office, 1880–1989. All references are to series 1.
VCHS   Vernon County Historical Society, Viroqua, Wisconsin
WC   widow's certificate
WHS   Wisconsin Historical Society, Madison
WVM   Wisconsin Veterans Museum, Madison

INTRODUCTION

1. Current, *Civil War Era*, 260–96.
2. *Wisconsin State Journal*, April 15, 1861.
3. Zimm, "'On Wisconsin!,'" 28–37.
4. "A Note about Databases and Citations" at the end of this book explains the various sources that went into the massive databases that provide the foundation of this book. There is at least some information on each of the nearly 2,000 men who served in the Sixth; perhaps 1,000 appear in most of the data points in the Master Sixth Wisconsin Database. For comparison, Joseph T. Glatthaar's acclaimed *Soldiering in the Army of Northern Virginia* drew on a sample of 600 Confederate soldiers.
5. Aside from Lance J. Herdegen and William J. K. Beaudot's stirring account of the

Sixth Wisconsin's pivotal role on the first day at Gettysburg (*In the Bloody Railroad Cut at Gettysburg*), the histories of the Sixth and of the other two Wisconsin regiments in the brigade appear most notably in Nolan, *Iron Brigade*; and Herdegen, *Iron Brigade in Civil War and Memory*. See also Herdegen, *Men Stood Like Iron*; and Nolan and Vipond, *Giants in Their Tall Black Hats*. For the other Iron Brigade regiments, see Dunn, *Iron Men, Iron Will*; and Donald L. Smith, *Twenty-Fourth Michigan of the Iron Brigade*.

6. Smith and Arsenault, *Long Civil War*, 2. For exceptions, see Gordon, *Broken Regiment*; and Pinheiro, *Families' Civil War*.

7. Wiley, *Life of Johnny Reb*; Wiley, *Life of Billy Yank*; Lindermann, *Embattled Courage*; Hess, *Union Soldier in Battle*; Carmichael, *War for the Common Soldier*.

8. Jordan, *Marching Home*, 3; Lindermann, *Embattled Courage*, 267.

9. Master Sixth Wisconsin Database, DSR; Cimbala, "Officers of the US Army Veteran Reserve Corps," in Smith and Arsenault, *Long Civil War*, 54–74.

10. Mitchell, *Vacant Chair*. Useful analyses of home-front and military communities include Etcheson, *Generation at War*; and Keating, *Shades of Green*.

11. Catton, *Glory Road*, 218, 141. Jeffrey Wert simply called the westerners "the finest combat brigade in the army." Wert, *Heart of Hell*, 70.

CHAPTER 1

1. Hardgrove, "General Edward S. Bragg's Reminiscences," 285.

2. Current, *Civil War Era*, 296–301.

3. Thwaites, *Civil War Messages and Proclamations*, 55, 62, 63.

4. Fish, "Raising of the Wisconsin Volunteers," 258–73, quote 263.

5. Fish, "Raising of the Wisconsin Volunteers," 261; Glazer, "Wisconsin Goes to War," 146–64; Quiner, *Military History of Wisconsin*, 52.

6. Herdegen and Beaudot, *In the Bloody Railroad Cut*, 52–53, 61–62, 65; William Fiske Brown, *Rock County*, chap. 16; Master Sixth Wisconsin Database, DSR; Fitch, *Echoes of the Civil War*, 17–22. Michael Fitch would be appointed adjutant of the Twenty-First Wisconsin in July 1862; he would end the war as a brevet colonel of volunteers after hard service in the western theater.

7. For this and the preceding paragraph, see Cheek and Pointon, *History of the Sauk County Riflemen*, 1–12; Tucker diary, June 10, 19, 1861, Personal Papers, WVM.

8. Herdegen and Beaudot, *In the Bloody Railroad Cut*, 53–54; *Daily Milwaukee News*, June 25, 1861.

9. Hardgrove, "General Edward S. Bragg's Reminiscences," 286; *Milwaukee Sunday Telegraph*, August 6, 1882.

10. *Appleton Motor*, June 27, 1861.

11. *Appleton Motor*, July 4, 1861.

12. Dawes Diary, vol. 2, June 25, 1860, WHS.

13. *Mauston Star*, April 24, May 1, 1861.

14. Dawes to his sister, May 4, 1861, Dawes letters, DA.

15. Dawes to Ephraim Dawes, June 10, 1861, Dawes letters, DA; Master Sixth Wisconsin Database, DSR.

16. *Wisconsin State Journal*, June 26, 28, July 1, 3, 8, 1861.

17. Master Sixth Wisconsin Database, DSR.

18. *Prescott Transcript*, June 29, 1861; Master Sixth Wisconsin Database, DSR. The departures of the Prescott Guards and other units reflected the sentimentalism eloquently described in Carmichael, *War for the Common Soldier*.

19. *Appleton Motor*, July 4, 1861.

20. Tucker diary, June 22, 1861, Personal Papers, WVM; Cheek and Pointon, *History of the Sauk County Riflemen*, 14–15; *Baraboo Republic*, June 27, 1861.

21. Herdegen and Beaudot, *In the Bloody Railroad Cut*, 57.

22. *Wisconsin State Journal*, May 28, June 17, 1861; Dawes, *Full-Blown Yankee of the Iron Brigade: Service with the Sixth Wisconsin Volunteers*, 10; Cyrus Spooner pension record, no. 171265, NARA.

23. *Wisconsin State Journal*, June 27, July 18, 1861.

24. *North Western Times*, July 17, 1861.

25. Amorin Mello, "They Called Him 'Gray Devil,'" Chequamegon History (blog), January 21, 2015, https://chequamegonhistory.wordpress.com/2015/01/21/they-called-him-gray-devil; *Aroostook War*, 22–23.

26. *Wisconsin State Journal*, July 11, 17, 1861.

27. *Wisconsin State Journal*, July 17, 1861; *Prescott Transcript*, July 31, 1861.

28. Mattern, *Soldiers When They Go*, viii, quote xi–x.

29. Chandler, *Chandler's Tactics*, 3–5.

30. Marten, *Children's Civil War*, 68–100; Bragg to Cornelia Bragg, July 10, 1861, Bragg Papers, WHS.

31. Mattern, *Soldiers When They Go*, 5; Cheek and Pointon, *History of the Sauk County Riflemen*, 15.

32. *Wisconsin State Journal*, June 12, 28, 1861.

33. Quiner, *Military History of Wisconsin*, 439–42; *Wisconsin State Journal*, July 23, 1861.

34. *Wisconsin State Journal*, July 24, 1861.

35. McPherson, *For Cause and Comrades*, viii; Gleeson, "Immigrant America and the Civil War," 178–79; Glatthaar, "Tale of Two Armies," 315–46.

36. Sixth Wisconsin Geography Database, DSR.

37. Cohort 1 totaled 1,096 men, cohort 2 totaled 202, and cohort 3 totaled 475.

38. Bledsoe, *Citizen-Officers*, xii, 4–6, 32–40, 64–67, 41; Officers Database, DSR.

39. John H. Cook, "Cook's Time in the Army," unpublished manuscript, Cook Papers, WHS.

40. Russell L. Johnson, *Warriors into Workers*, chap. 1. Johnson provides an excellent summary of soldiers' motivations for enlisting in 1861 (pp. 104–17).

41. Merk, *Economic History of Wisconsin*, 17–18, 210–30; Huston, *Panic of 1857*. Russell L. Johnson distinguishes between "independent soldiers" and "soldier-sons"—those whose economic status depended on family or was masked by living with family. See Russell L. Johnson, *Warriors into Workers*, 123–25.

42. Herdegen, *Iron Brigade*, 211.

43. Master Sixth Wisconsin Database, DSR; Glatthaar, "Tale of Two Armies."

44. Herdegen, *Iron Brigade*, 71–72.

45. Quoted in Donald L. Smith, *Twenty-Fourth Michigan*, 237.

46. *Wisconsin State Journal*, July 24, 27, 1861; quoted in Mattern, *Soldiers When They Go*, 24.

47. *Wisconsin State Journal*, July 27, 1861.

48. *Mauston Star*, July 31, 1861.

CHAPTER 2

1. "Searching for the War of 1812 in Patterson Park!," Baltimore Heritage, accessed November 15, 2022, https://baltimoreheritage.org/patterson-park-archaeology/history.

2. Rufus Dawes to E. G. Dawes, August 1861, Dawes letters, DA. Accounts of the early months of the war in Baltimore do not mention mob attacks on Union troops; the exception is the more famous and deadly riot against the Sixth Massachusetts. See, e.g., Ezratty, *Baltimore in the Civil War*.

3. Rogers, "Autobiography," 14, VCHS; Henry Matrau to his parents, August 15, 1861, in Reid-Green, *Letters Home*, 13.

4. Benjamin Campbell pension record, Co. D, WC no. 13991, Fold3; Matrau to his parents, August 1, 1861, in Reid-Green, *Letters Home*, 1–3, 9.

5. George Moser pension record, no. 123356, NARA.

6. Nathaniel D'Lamatter pension record, Co. E, WC no. 82671, Fold3; Benjamin Campbell pension record, Co. D, WC no. 13991, Fold3; *Daily Milwaukee News*, August 18, 1861.

7. *Grant County Herald*, August 28, 1861; Matrau to his parents, August 15, 1861.

8. Chandler B. Chapman to "My Dear Wife and Daughter," August 20, 25, 1861, Chapman Papers, WHS.

9. *Milwaukee Sentinel*, November 11, 1861.

10. Dawes to E. G. Dawes, August 24, 1861, Dawes letters, DA.

11. *Mauston Star*, September 4, 1861.

12. *Wisconsin State Register*, September 21, 1861.

13. *Appleton Crescent*, October 19, 1861.

14. Huntley to his wife, November 21, 1861, Huntley Papers, WHS.

15. Bragg to Cornelia Bragg, November 21, 1861, Bragg Papers, WHS.

16. Bragg to Cornelia Bragg, December 11, 1861, Bragg Papers, WHS.

17. *Appleton Motor*, July 11, 1861.

18. *Appleton Crescent*, September 7, 1861.

19. *Grant County Herald*, May 9, 30, 1861.

20. *Wisconsin State Journal*, August 27, September 2, 1861; *Appleton Crescent*, October 26, 1861. For an excellent short summary of Civil War–era panoramas, see Marsh, "Drama and Spectacle by the Yard," 581–92.

21. *Madison State Journal*, May 1, 4, 11, 7, 9, 1861.

22. *Appleton Crescent*, November 9, October 26, 1862.

23. Dawes, *Full-Blown Yankee of the Iron Brigade: Service with the Sixth Wisconsin Volunteers*, 41 (hereafter cited as Dawes, *Service with the Sixth Wisconsin Volunteers*). The most useful account of the experiences of formerly enslaved refugees and their fraught relationship with Union soldiers is Taylor, *Embattled Freedom*.

24. Dawes, *Service with the Sixth Wisconsin*, 200.

25. Dawes, *Service with the Sixth Wisconsin*, 58, 109, 110.

26. Dawes, *Service with the Sixth Wisconsin*, 199.

27. Dawes, *Service with the Sixth Wisconsin*, 242, 314–15. William returned to Marietta with Dawes, who helped find him work; he eventually became a successful businessman.

28. Herdegen, *Iron Brigade*, 515–18, 524–26.

29. Fairfield diary, January 13, 1863, Personal Papers, Beaudot Archival Collection, KCWM; Cheek and Pointon, *History of the Sauk County Riflemen*, 25–26.

30. Beaudot and Herdegen, *Irishman in the Iron Brigade*, 39–41.

31. Beaudot and Herdegen, *Irishman in the Iron Brigade*, 82–84.

32. See Manning, *What This Cruel War Was Over*.

33. *Wisconsin State Journal*, November 27, 1861.

34. *Appleton Crescent*, September 27, 1862; *Wisconsin State Journal*, September 13, 1862; Adam I. P. Smith, "Beyond Politics," 145–69.

35. Current, *Civil War Era*, 405.

36. *Appleton Crescent*, November 7, 1863; *Appleton Motor*, May 21, 1863.

37. James Conklin record, Co. D, Sixth Wisconsin Regimental Muster and Descriptive Rolls, WHS.

38. Report of A. Collyer, August 20, 1861, Series 7, US Sanitary Commission Records, Rare Books and Manuscripts, New York Public Library. Margaret Humphreys calls the Civil War "the greatest health disaster that this country has ever experienced." Humphreys, *Marrow of Tragedy*, 77.

39. Camp inspection return, Sixth Wisconsin, August 19, 1861, US Sanitary Commission Records, Rare Books and Manuscripts, New York Public Library.

40. "Report of Sick and Wounded, September 1861," MAD 3/21/R1-V6, folder 1, box 28, Adjutant General Records, WHS.

41. George Andrew, camp inspection return, US Sanitary Commission Records, Rare Books and Manuscripts, New York Public Library.

42. W. M. Chamberlain, camp inspection return, Sixth Wisconsin, February 10, 1862, US Sanitary Commission Records, Rare Books and Manuscripts, New York Public Library.

43. Benjamin Smith pension record, no. 6613; Lorenzo Pratt pension record, no. 98657; William H. Matthewson pension, no. 191720; Adolph Sulzer pension record, no. 292767, all NARA.

44. Washburn, *Life and Writings of Jerome A. Watrous*, 51; Bragg to Cornelia Bragg, November 29, 1861, Bragg Papers, WHS.

45. Cheek and Pointon, *History of the Sauk County Riflemen*, 21; *Vernon County Censor*, April 30, 1862.

46. Edwin Brown to Ruth Brown, December 20, 1861, Brown letters, Personal Papers, Beaudot Archival Collection, KCWM.

47. Tucker diary, September 29–30, 1861; May 11–14, 24, 27, July 7, August 29, 1862, Personal Papers, WVM.

48. George Andrew, camp inspection return; W. M. Chamberlain, camp inspection return.

49. *Prescott Journal*, December 18, 1861.

50. Dawes, *Service with the Sixth Wisconsin*, 26–27; *Annual Report of the Adjutant General of the State of Wisconsin, for the Year 1861*, 26–27.

51. Gamble, *Fiery Gospel*, 42–45, 88–89; Dawes, *Service with the Sixth Wisconsin*, 34–35.

52. John Harland, letter, n.d. [1862], box 4, folder 11j, Manuscript Small Collections, WVM.

53. *Mineral Point Weekly Tribune*, March 19, 1862 (copied from *Washington Chronicle*).

54. Gibbon, *Personal Recollections of the Civil War*, 12–14, 39. See also Lavery and Jordan, *Iron Brigade General*.

55. Quote in Wert, *Brotherhood of Valor*, 104; Herdegen, *Iron Brigade*, 117–30, 142–43.

56. Ainsworth Saunders to David Saunders, June 17, 1862, Archives and Special Collections, Davee Library, University of Wisconsin–River Falls; and Brown to Ruth Brown, July 16, 1862; and to his father, July 16, 1862, both in Brown letters, Personal Papers, Beaudot Archival Collection, KCWM. For the traditional thirst for action among American soldiers, see Royster, *Revolutionary People at War*; and Lang, *In the Wake of War*.

57. Dawes to his sister, July 10, 1862, Dawes letters, DA.

58. *Baraboo Republic*, June 25, 1862.

59. *Grant County Herald*, July 16, 1862.

60. Warren C. Garwood to S. S. Cooke, February 16, 1862, in *General Orders*, February 2020, 4.

CHAPTER 3

1. *Appleton Crescent*, August 20, 1862; Rogers, "Autobiography," 25–28, VCHS; Hartwig, *To Antietam Creek*, 15. The biblical passage Rogers parodied goes like this: "And it came to pass, after the year was expired, at the time when kings go forth *to battle*, that David sent Joab, and his servants with him, and all Israel; and they destroyed the children of Ammon, and besieged Rabbah. But David tarried still at Jerusalem" (2 Sam. 11:1).

2. "Report of Sick and Wounded, September 1862," MAD 3/21/R1-V6, folder 1, box 28, Adjutant General Records, WHS.

3. See Hess, *Union Soldier in Battle*, 1–20. Jeffry Wert notes the same response to the repulse on the peninsula in the Army of the Potomac. Wert, *Sword of Lincoln*, 121–25.

4. Fairfield diary, June 2, July 22, 1861, Personal Papers, Beaudot Archival Collection, KCWM.

5. Cutler to Capt. J. P. Wood (assistant adjutant general, Gibbon's Brigade), August 9, 1862, *OR* 12(2):123–24.

6. Fairfield diary, August 5, 6, 9, 1862, Personal Papers, Beaudot Archival Collection, KCWM.

7. Master Sixth Wisconsin Database, DSR. For a unique account of the effects of weather and terrain on the health of the men fighting in Virginia in 1862, see Shively, *Nature's Civil War*, esp. chap. 2.

8. Peter Hansen pension record, no. 277390, NARA.

9. Stephen M. Long pension record, no. 21141, NARA.

10. Samuel Birdsall pension record, no. 99557, NARA.

11. Birdsall pension record.

12. Huntley to his wife, August 13, 1862, Huntley Papers, WHS; *Appleton Crescent*, August 9, 1862.

13. Dawes, *Full-Blown Yankee of the Iron Brigade: Service with the Sixth Wisconsin Volunteers*, 56 (hereafter cited as Dawes, *Service with the Sixth Wisconsin*); Cheek and Pointon, *History of the Sauk County Riflemen*, 31. For more detailed narratives of this campaign, see Gaff, *Brave Men's Tears*; Herdegen, *Iron Brigade*, 161–213; and Hennessy, *Return to Bull Run*.

14. Dawes, *Service with the Sixth Wisconsin*, 57; Cheek and Pointon, *History of the Sauk County Riflemen*, 32.

15. Gaff, *Brave Men's Tears*, 56, 59; Dawes, *Service with the Sixth Wisconsin*, 58–59.

16. Gibbon to Adjutant General, US Army, December 4, 1863, OR 12(2):380–82.

17. Cheek and Pointon, *History of the Sauk County Riflemen*, 37; Beaudot and Herdegen, *Irishman in the Iron Brigade*, 44. Years ago, Alan Nolan made a convincing case for calling this first battle "Brawner's Farm." Nevertheless, I will use the name adopted by the Iron Brigade: Gainesville. Nolan, "John Brawner's Damage Claim," 1–12.

18. Cheek and Pointon, *History of the Sauk County Riflemen*, 38; Henry Matrau to his parents, September 13, 1862, in Reid-Green, *Letters Home*, 33.

19. Dawes, *Service with the Sixth Wisconsin*, 61.

20. Beaudot and Herdegen, *Irishman in the Iron Brigade*, 45; Dawes, *Service with the Sixth Wisconsin*, 61.

21. Cheek and Pointon, *History of the Sauk County Riflemen*, 38–39; Fairfield diary, August 28, 1862, Personal Papers, Beaudot Archival Collection, KCWM; William W. Hutchins, letter to the editor, *Brandon Monitor*, October 10, 1862; Dawes Diary, August 28, 1862, WHS.

22. Cheek and Pointon, *History of the Sauk County Riflemen*, 39.

23. Dawes, *Service with the Sixth Wisconsin*, 62; *Daily Milwaukee News*, October 15, 1862.

24. Dawes, *Service with the Sixth Wisconsin*, 63.

25. Gibbon, *Personal Recollections*, 58; Fairfield diary, August 29, 1862, Personal Papers, Beaudot Archival Collection, KCWM.

26. Matthew H. Kinsey pension record, no. 15537, NARA.

27. Dawes, *Service with the Sixth Wisconsin*, 68; Fairfield diary, August 28, 1862, Personal Papers, Beaudot Archival Collection, KCWM.

28. Huntley to his wife, ca. August 31, 1862, Huntley Papers, WHS.

29. Catton, *Mr. Lincoln's Army*, 24, 23; Hennessy, *Return to Bull Run*, 191–92.

30. Gaff, *Brave Men's Tears*, 95.

31. Dawes, *Service with the Sixth Wisconsin*, 71; Sgt. William W. Hutchins, letter to the editor, *Brandon Monitor*, October 10, 1862.

32. Cheek and Pointon, *History of the Sauk County Riflemen*, 44.

33. Quotes in Herdegen, *Iron Brigade*, 202.

34. Hennessy, *Return to Bull Run*, 463–72.

35. Dawes, *Service with the Sixth Wisconsin*, 68; Bragg to Cornelia Bragg, September 13, 1862, Bragg Papers, WHS; Brown to Ruth Brown, ca. September 1, [no year], Brown letters, Personal Papers, Beaudot Archival Collection, KCWM.

36. Quiner, "Quiner Scrapbooks," 3:262, WHS.

37. Dawes Diary, 1:29–31, WHS.

38. Lucius Murray, letters, September 6, October 1, 1862, in *Blackhat*, no. 6, p. 11, Beaudot Archival Collection, KCWM; Dawes, *Service with the Sixth Wisconsin*, 64.

39. Bragg to Cornelia Bragg, September 13, 1862.

40. Herdegen, *Iron Brigade*, 215; Dawes, *Service with the Sixth Wisconsin*, 78.

41. Quote in Hartwig, *To Antietam Creek*, 415.

42. *Daily Milwaukee News*, October 15, 1862; Hartwig, *To Antietam Creek*, 415–27, quote 424.

43. Lt. Col. Edward S. Bragg, reports on the Battles of South Mountain and Antietam, September 20, 1862, *OR* 19(1):254.

44. Brig. Gen. John Gibbon, reports on the Battles of South Mountain and Antietam, September 20, 1862, *OR* 19(1):248; report of Gen. George B. McClellan, *OR* 19(1):52.

45. Herdegen, *Iron Brigade*, 235–37; *Milwaukee Daily Sentinel*, September 27, 1862; *Mineral Point Weekly Tribune*, October 1, 1862. There was a surprising amount of confusion about the name. Oddly, a member of Company C recalled for the *Milwaukee Sunday Telegraph*'s January 15, 1888, issue that he received a silver shield inscribed with his name and company and "Iron Brigade, war of 1861." He distinctly remembered receiving it while they were camped at Arlington Heights in late 1861. *Milwaukee Sunday Telegraph*, January 15, 1888. A November 28, 1895, story in the *National Tribune* suggested that Confederates had started calling the Black Hats "the Iron Brigade" after Gainesville, but it also repeated the McClellan version of the story.

46. Herdegen, *Iron Brigade*, 243, 245.

47. *Milwaukee Free Press*, September 22, 1912, quoted in Herdegen, *Iron Brigade*, 242.

48. Herdegen, *Iron Brigade*, 242–47.

49. Dawes, *Service with the Sixth Wisconsin*, 87; de Thulstrup, *Battle of Antietam*.

50. Bragg to Cornelia Bragg, September 21, 1862, Bragg Papers, WHS; "Exhibit A," Bragg to Ezra Carmen, December 26, 1894, photocopy, Iron Brigade at Antietam Papers, Iron Brigade Files, Beaudot Archival Collection, KCWM; "Colloquy Under Fire," Unassociated Civil War Documents, American History, 1493–1945, from the Gilder Lehrman Institute of American History, accessed August 31, 2024, http://www.americanhistory.amdigital.co.uk/Documents/SearchDetails/GLC06181.

51. Dawes, *Service with the Sixth Wisconsin*, 88, 99; Herdegen, *Iron Brigade*, 252. An excellent account of the Sixth Wisconsin's role in the battle can be found in a book that borrows for its title Rufus Dawes's post-battle thoughts; see Hartwig, *I Dread the Thought of the Place*, 71–83, 86–96, 143–54, 160–61.

52. Dawes to Ezra Carmen, March 4, 1898, photocopy, Iron Brigade at Antietam Papers, Iron Brigade Files, Beaudot Collection, KCWM; Herdegen, *Iron Brigade*, 252–74.

53. The preceding two paragraphs rely on Hartwig, "'I Dread the Thought of the Place.'"

54. Dawes, *Service with the Sixth Wisconsin*, 92–3; *Milwaukee Sunday Telegraph*, October 10, 1880; Dawes to Carmen, March 4, 1898.

55. Bragg to Cornelia Bragg, September 21, 1862; Herdegen, *Iron Brigade*, 276.

56. Faust, *This Republic of Suffering*, 77; "Exhibit A," Bragg to Ezra Carmen, December 28, 1894, Iron Brigade at Antietam Papers, Iron Brigade Files, Beaudot Archival Collection, KCWM; Rogers, "Autobiography," 50, VCHS. The 1864 Elliott map of the battlefield

marking where bodies had been buried indicates several possibilities for this site. "Burials on the Antietam Battlefield," Antietam on the Web, accessed August 31, 2024, https://antietam.aotw.org/burial_maps.php?map_number=main.

57. Buell, *"Cannoneer,"* 35.

58. Col. Edward Bragg, report on the Battle of Antietam, September 21, 1862, *OR* 19(1); Bragg to Cornelia Bragg, September 21, 1862.

59. *Manitowoc Herald*, September 4, 1862; *Appleton Crescent*, September 6, 1862. The first line of a 1920 account of the state's response captures its slapstick nature: "That masses of human beings are subject, no less than the lower animals, to sudden outbursts of wild, unreasoning panic and hysteria is a matter of common knowledge." Quaife, "Panic of 1862 in Wisconsin," 166.

60. *Wisconsin State Journal*, May 13, 1861; "Wisconsin Civil War Regiments," Wisconsin Genealogy Trails, accessed July 14, 2024, http://genealogytrails.com/wis/CivilWarIndex .html.

61. *Wisconsin State Journal*, December 31, 1861.

62. *Appleton Crescent*, August 16, 1862.

63. *Milwaukee Daily Sentinel*, September 15, 1862.

64. *Manitowoc Herald*, September 11, 1862; *Baraboo Republic*, September 24, 1862; *Appleton Crescent*, September 20, 1862.

65. *Appleton Crescent*, August 23, 1862.

66. See Gallman, *Defining Duty in the Civil War*, 252–53. Although perhaps more life-and-death than in the North, where manpower was relatively plentiful, Confederate conscription, like its Union counterpart, forced the military, government, and civilians alike to define loyalty and duty in the contexts of conflicting needs on the home front (including families) and battlefront. See Sacher, *Confederate Conscription*.

67. Quote in Carr, *Such Anxious Hours*, 92; *North Western Times*, November 20, 1861.

68. *North Western Times*, July 30, 1862, copied from *Milwaukee Sentinel*.

69. *Appleton Crescent*, October 4, November 15, 1862; *Milwaukee Daily Sentinel*, November 21, 22, 1862.

70. Klement, *Wisconsin in the Civil War*, 29–31; Quiner, *Military History of Wisconsin*, 146–47.

71. Quiner, *Military History of Wisconsin*, 140, 141; "Wisconsin Civil War Regiments," Wisconsin Genealogy Trails.

72. Beaudot and Herdegen, *Irishman in the Iron Brigade*, 65.

73. *Milwaukee Daily Sentinel*, October 8, 1862.

CHAPTER 4

1. Dawes to his sister, December 1, 25, 1862, Dawes letters, DA. Dawes's disgust and letters are featured at the beginning of Conner and Mackowski, *Seizing Destiny*.

2. Herdegen, *Iron Brigade*, 296–333.

3. Dawes, *Full-Blown Yankee of the Iron Brigade: Service with the Sixth Wisconsin Volunteers*, 97, 105 (hereafter cited as Dawes, *Service with the Sixth Wisconsin Volunteers*).

4. Rogers, "Autobiography," 54, 62, VCHS.

5. Rogers, "Autobiography," 43, VCHS; George Cassidy record, Co. B, Sixth Wisconsin Regimental Muster and Descriptive Rolls, WHS.

6. Report of Col. Lucius Fairchild, February 16, 1863, OR 25(1):16–17.

7. *Baraboo Republic*, March 25, 1863. The actual passage (Ruth 1:16) in the King James Bible is "And Ruth said, 'Intreat me not to leave thee, or to return from following after thee: for whither thou goest, I will go; and where thou lodgest, I will lodge: thy people shall be my people, and thy God my God. Where thou diest, will I die, and there will I be buried: the Lord do so to me, and more also, if ought but death part thee and me.'"

8. Fairfield diary, April 13, 23, 1863, Personal Papers, Beaudot Archival Collection, KCWM.

9. *Appleton Crescent*, May 23, 1863.

10. Beaudot and Herdegen, *Irishman in the Iron Brigade*, 77; *Appleton Crescent*, May 23, 1863.

11. *Appleton Crescent*, May 23, 1863; Fairfield diary, April 29, 1863, Personal Papers, Beaudot Archival Collection, KCWM.

12. Bragg to Cornelia Bragg, May 8, 1863, Bragg Papers, WHS; report of Col. Edward Bragg, May 10, 1863, OR 25(1):271–72.

13. Bragg to Cornelia Bragg, May 8, 1863; Cheek and Pointon, *History of the Sauk County Riflemen*, 66.

14. *Daily Milwaukee News*, June 26, 1864.

15. Holford diary, June 3, 1863, GNMP; *Appleton Crescent*, May 23, 1863.

16. *Baraboo Republic*, July 1, 1863.

17. Dawes, *Service with the Sixth Wisconsin*, 156.

18. Holford diary, June 27, 28, 1863, GNMP.

19. Dawes, *Service with the Sixth Wisconsin*, 157; C. J. Johnson, "Personal Recollections," GNBL. Johnson's account was heavily edited by his son.

20. Buell, "*Cannoneer*," 20, 63–64.

21. Beaudot and Herdegen, *Irishman in the Iron Brigade*, 93; *Paddy's Wedding*.

22. *Milwaukee Sunday Telegraph*, April 27, 1890, quoted in Herdegen, *Iron Brigade*, 360.

23. Holford diary, July 1, 1863, GNMP; Dawes, *Service with the Sixth Wisconsin*, 164–84.

24. Reports of Maj. Gen. Abner Doubleday, US Army, Commanding Third Division of, and First Army Corps, December 14, 1863, OR 27(1):244–45. Doubleday refers to all other brigades in the traditional manner by their commanders' names. Herdegen provides an excellent account of the brigade's fighting west of Gettysburg in *Iron Brigade*, 359–76.

25. Reports of Maj. Gen. Abner Doubleday, 245. One of the finest pieces of combat narrative in the historiography of the Civil War is in Herdegen, *In the Bloody Railroad Cut*, 168–211. I have relied heavily on Herdegen as well as on Dawes, "With the Sixth Wisconsin at Gettysburg," an article he published as a stand-alone piece but later included in *Service with the Sixth Wisconsin* (160–84).

26. Herdegen, *In the Bloody Railroad Cut*, 188–89.

27. C. J. Johnson, "Personal Recollections," GNMP.

28. Pfanz, *Gettysburg*, 103–8; Herdegen, *In the Bloody Railroad Cut*, 186; Steplyk, *Fighting Means Killing*, 90–118; Herdegen, *Iron Brigade*, 376–89.

29. Herdegen, *Iron Brigade*, 390; Dawes, *Service with the Sixth Wisconsin*, 169–70.

30. Herdegen, *In the Bloody Railroad Cut*, 211.

31. Herdegen, *In the Bloody Railroad Cut*, 218.

32. Herdegen, *Iron Brigade*, 422–23. A plausible route of the regiment from Seminary Ridge to its eventual post on Culp's Hill has been plotted by the longtime historian at Gettysburg National Military Park, Scott Hartwig, who provided it to the author via email on June 6, 2022.

33. Dawes, *Service with the Sixth Wisconsin*, 158; *Baraboo Republic*, July 15, 1863.

34. Excerpt from Kerr to his wife, July 4, 1863, published in *Semi-weekly Wisconsin*, July 17, 1863, transcription, GNMP.

35. Excerpt from Kerr to his wife, July 4, 1863, 73. For burial processes and their horrors, see Faust, *This Republic of Suffering*, 66–79.

36. Faust, *This Republic of Suffering*, 62–66, 71.

37. "Report on the Removal of Bodies to the Cemetery," GNMP.

38. Coco, *Killed in Action*, 15–17; Faust, *This Republic of Suffering*, 3–31.

39. Master Sixth Wisconsin Database, DSR.

40. *Baraboo Republic*, October 7, 1863.

41. Herdegen, *Iron Brigade*, 465, 470.

42. *Appleton Crescent*, August 1, 1863.

43. Luskey, *Men Is Cheap*, 79. William Marvel argues in *Lincoln's Mercenaries* that economic motivations played a crucial role in enlistments throughout the war.

44. *History of Fond Du Lac County, Wisconsin*, 552.

45. *Boscobel Broad-Axe*, December 3, 1863; *Final Report Made to the Secretary of War, by the Provost Marshal General*, 222–23.

46. Current, *Civil War Era*, 325–26; *Annual Report of the Adjutant General of the State of Wisconsin* [. . .] *for the Year Ending December 31, 1864*, 399–400; Dawes, *Service with the Sixth Wisconsin*, 232.

47. Quote in Herdegen, *In the Bloody Railroad Cut*, 277.

CHAPTER 5

1. Bragg to Cornelia Bragg, September 28, 1862, Bragg Papers, WHS.

2. Dawes, *Full-Blown Yankee of the Iron Brigade: Service with the Sixth Wisconsin Volunteers*, 95 (hereafter cited as Dawes, *Service with the Sixth Wisconsin*). For the ways in which the aftermath of Antietam affected Union soldiers, see Jordan, "What I Witnessed Would Only Make You Sick."

3. Frassanito, *Antietam*, 126–37.

4. Cal Schoonover, "Death at Antietam: Friends to the End," Emerging Civil War, April 22, 2021, https://emergingcivilwar.com/2021/04/22/death-at-antietam-friends-to-the-end.

5. *Baraboo Republic*, September 3, 10, 1862.

6. *Appleton Crescent*, September 20, 1862.

7. *Baraboo Republic*, September 24, 1862; Faust, *This Republic of Suffering*, 102–36.

8. *Baraboo Republic*, September 17, 1862.

9. *Baraboo Republic*, September 24, 1862.

10. *Baraboo Republic*, October 8, 1862.

11. *Wood County Reporter*, April 16, 1863. For a brief account of the many aftermaths of Civil War battles, including burial practices, the evolution of military policy regarding the dead, and the creation and continued relevance of national cemeteries, see Groeling, *Aftermath of Battle*.

12. Master Sixth Wisconsin Database, DSR.

13. *Baraboo Republic*, September 3, October 1, 1862; *Wisconsin State Journal*, September 1, 1862.

14. Master Sixth Wisconsin Database, DSR. Stephen Berry has written in his typically incisive prose about the loneliness of wounded Civil War soldiers in "When Metal Meets Mettle," 16.

15. Greer, "Health Care Delivery."

16. Cheek and Pointon, *History of the Sauk County Riflemen*, 52–53; Herdegen, *Iron Brigade*, 239.

17. Woolsey, *Hospital Days*, 72–74, 19; Rutkow, *Bleeding Blue and Gray*, 154–55, 151; Keen, *Surgical Reminiscences of the Civil War*, 103. Megan L. Bever explores the myriad issues surrounding alcohol's uses and abuses in Civil War armies in *At War with King Alcohol*.

18. Reimer, *One Vast Hospital*, 12–13, 114.

19. Reimer, *One Vast Hospital*, 14–18.

20. Reimer, *One Vast Hospital*, 83–90, 47–48; Otis, *Medical and Surgical History of the Civil War*, pt. 2, vol. 2, p. 1005.

21. Keen, *Surgical Reminiscences of the Civil War*, 103–4; Bollet, "Amputations in the Civil War," 64; Figg and Farrell-Beck, "Amputation in the Civil War," 454, 459.

22. Devine, *Learning from the Wounded*, 96–98; Rutkow, *Bleeding Blue and Gray*, 234–35; Gross, *Manual of Military Surgery*, 93–94; Smart, "On Hospital Gangrene," 178.

23. Devine, *Learning from the Wounded*, 179–83.

24. Otis, *Medical and Surgical History of the War of the Rebellion*, pt. 3, vol. 2, p. 241.

25. Otis, *Medical and Surgical History of the War of the Rebellion*, pt. 2, vol. 2, p. 544; pt. 1, vol. 2, p. 366.

26. Fairfield diary, September 28, 1862, Personal Papers, Beaudot Archival Collection, KCWM.

27. Margaret Patchin to Augustus Patchin, July 12, August 2, 1863, in Carr, *Such Anxious Hours*, 142, 124, 132.

28. Ann Waldo to Morris Waldo, December 4, 22, 1861, in Carr, *Such Anxious Hours*, 38–39, 44.

29. *Wisconsin State Journal*, November 25, 1863; *Dodgeville Chronicle*, December 24, 1863.

30. *Appleton Crescent*, July 6, 1861; *Milwaukee Sentinel*, May 2, 1861; Hurn, *Wisconsin Women in the War*, 54–55.

31. *Journal of the Assembly of Wisconsin, Fourteenth Annual Session for the Year A.D. 1862*, 72, 409.

32. Trattner, *From Poor Law to Welfare State*, 44–71; *Wisconsin State Journal*, September 25, 1862; *Boscobel Broad-Axe*, December 28, 1864; Quiner, *Military History of Wisconsin*, 170–71, 172–74, 186–87. Although as a relatively young frontier state Wisconsin's situation was quite different from Philadelphia's, some of the same tensions and processes

nevertheless emerged. See J. Matthew Gallman's classic study of the home front, *Mastering Wartime.*

33. *Appleton Crescent,* November 21, 1863.

34. "Milwaukee County Soldiers' Family Relief Committee Payroll," 1864; and "Descriptive Roll of the Milwaukee County Volunteers & Drafted Soldiers," both in Soldiers Relief Commission Collection, Milwaukee County Historical Society, Milwaukee, Wisconsin.

35. *North Western Times,* February 8, 1865.

36. *Revised United States Army Regulations of 1861,* 244; Young, *Labor in America,* 68.

37. Edith Abbott, "Wages of Unskilled Labor," 364; US Census Office and Edmunds, *Statistics of the United States,* 512.

38. Married Soldiers Database, DSR.

39. Married Soldiers Database, DSR.

40. Married Soldiers Database, DSR.

41. John Ticknor pension record, Co. K, WC no. 12108; Frederick Bunzell pension record, Co. A, WC no. 56040; John Scott pension record, Co. K, WC no. 146566; and Arnoldus Zweerink pension record, Co. I, WC no. 80324, all in Fold3.

42. Asbury Bates pension record, Co. A, WC no. 73043; Dennis N. Johnson pension record, Co. A, WC no. 108734; and Sylvester Russell pension record, Co. C, WC no. 88478, all in Fold3.

43. N. K. Miller to Cornelia Bragg, September 21, 1862; and Jos Conklin to [illegible] Patch, September 21, 1862, both in Bragg Papers, WHS.

44. *Wisconsin State Journal,* September 22, 1862; Bragg to Cornelia Bragg, September 28, 1862, Bragg Papers, WHS. The *State Journal* had earlier reported Bragg wounded and Lysander Cutler killed at Brawner's Farm. *Wisconsin State Journal,* September 1, 1862.

45. Bragg to Cornelia Bragg, October 8, 1862; and Gen. John Gibbon to Cornelia Bragg, October 1, 1862, both in Bragg Papers, WHS.

CHAPTER 6

1. Dawes, *Full-Blown Yankee of the Iron Brigade: Service with the Sixth Wisconsin Volunteers,* 231–32 (hereafter cited as Dawes, *Service with the Sixth Wisconsin*).

2. Herdegen, *Iron Brigade,* 450–55. Gerald Lindermann argues more or less the same thing in *Embattled Courage,* 262–63.

3. Dawes, *Service with the Sixth Wisconsin,* 235.

4. James H. Shultz pension record, no. 35303, NARA.

5. Fry, *Republic in the Ranks,* 198; Herdegen, *Iron Brigade,* 465.

6. McPherson, *For Cause and Comrades,* 173; Marvel, *Lincoln's Mercenaries,* 204–5; *North Western Times,* July 6, 1864.

7. Cyrus Spooner pension record, no. 171265, NARA; Absent and Detached Database, DSR; *Milwaukee Sunday Telegraph,* April 19, 1881.

8. Master Sixth Wisconsin Database, DSR; *Roster of Wisconsin Volunteers in the War of the Rebellion.*

9. Master Sixth Wisconsin Database, DSR.

10. Costa and Kahn, *Heroes and Cowards*, esp. 5–6.

11. Cheek and Pointon, *History of the Sauk County Riflemen*, 85.

12. Park Benjamin, "Return of the Three Month's Volunteers," *Baraboo Republic*, January 20, 1864; copied from *Prescott Journal*, January 16, 1864.

13. *Baraboo Republic*, January 20, 1864; *Prescott Journal*, January 16, 1864.

14. Quoted in Herdegen, *Iron Brigade*, 465; *Daily Milwaukee News*, January 15, 1864.

15. *Prescott Journal*, January 16, 1864; *Baraboo Republic*, January 27, 1864.

16. *North Western Times*, March 30, February 17, 1864.

17. Master Sixth Wisconsin Database, DSR; Henry McDougall record, Co. B, Sixth Wisconsin Regimental Muster and Descriptive Rolls, WHS.

18. *North Western Times*, February 3, 1864; Master Sixth Wisconsin Database, DSR.

19. Dawes, *Service with the Sixth Wisconsin*, 242–43.

20. *Baraboo Republic*, February 14, 1864.

21. Master Sixth Wisconsin Database, DSR; and Thomas A. Polleys pension record, Co. H, WC no. 34104; John L. Snyder pension record, Co. G, WC no. 53535; Caleb C. Wright pension record, Co. I, WC no. 32808; and Milo Sage pension record, Co. F, WC no. 40679, all in Fold3.

22. Washburn, *Life and Writings of Jerome A. Watrous*, 92.

23. Dawes, *Service with the Sixth Wisconsin*, 235–38.

24. *Roster of Wisconsin Volunteers in the War of the Rebellion*.

25. Herdegen, *Iron Brigade*, 474; Wert, *Sword of Lincoln*, 372.

26. Haller, *Battlefield Medicine*, 37; Hess, *Trench Warfare*, 11–12.

27. Absent and Detached Database, DSR.

28. The Absent and Detached Database provides the basis for the remaining paragraphs in this section.

29. For the summer campaigns of 1864, see Gordon C. Rhea's many books, including *Battle of the Wilderness*, *To the North Anna River*, and *On to Petersburg*.

30. Reardon, "Impact of Continuous Operations," 170–202, quote 170–71; Meier, "Fighting in 'Dante's Inferno,'" 39–56, quote 54–55.

31. Ketner to his mother, April 8, 27, 1864, Ketner Papers, WHS.

32. *North Western Times*, August 24, 1864.

33. Kellogg, *Capture and Escape*, 5–6.

34. Kellogg, *Capture and Escape*, 10–13.

35. *North Western Times*, August 24, 1864.

36. Dawes, *Service with the Sixth Wisconsin*, 257, 266–69.

37. Dawes, *Service with the Sixth Wisconsin*, 284.

38. Reports of Lt. Col. Rufus R. Dawes, Sixth Wisconsin Infantry, August 7, 1864, *OR* 36(1):618.

39. Reports of Lt. Col. Rufus R. Dawes, August 7, 1864, 618.

40. Reports of Lt. Col. Rufus R. Dawes, August 7, 1864, 619–20; Hess, *Trench Warfare*, 74.

41. Reports of Lt. Col. Rufus R. Dawes, August 7, 1864, 620. The most complete account of the nightmare of the Bloody Angle is Wert, *Heart of Hell*.

42. Reports of Lt. Col. Rufus R. Dawes, August 7, 1864, 618–21.

43. Beaudot and Herdegen, *Irishman in the Iron Brigade*, 121.

44. Marc Storch and Beth Storch, eds., "'And All I Loved in It Has Gone Hence': The 1864 Letters of Sgt. John O. Johnson, Co H, 6th Wisconsin Infantry," 11–12, unpublished manuscript, Personal Papers, Beaudot Archival Collection, KCWM.

45. Dawes, *Service with the Sixth Wisconsin*, 299–300.

46. Dawes, *Service with the Sixth Wisconsin*, 301.

47. Dawes, *Service with the Sixth Wisconsin*, 284, 286–87.

48. Dawes, *Service with the Sixth Wisconsin*, 305.

49. Dawes, *Service with the Sixth Wisconsin*, 284.

50. Storch and Storch, "'And All I Loved in It Has Gone Hence,'" 3.

51. Storch and Storch, "'And All I Loved in It Has Gone Hence,'" 5.

52. *North Western Times*, July 6, 1864.

53. Waller Civil War Diary, July 29, August 19, 1864, VCHS.

54. Stratton to his wife, July 4, 1864, box 8, folder 26, Manuscript Small Collections, WVM.

55. Storch and Storch, "'And All I Loved in It Has Gone Hence,'" 14, 16.

56. Matrau to his brother, June 26, 1864; to his mother, July 25, 1864; and to his mother and father, August 8, 27, 1864, all in Reid-Green, *Letters Home*, 81, 86, 91, 94–95.

57. Beaudot and Herdegen, *Irishman in the Iron Brigade*, 127.

58. Nathaniel Burchell pension record, no. 91356, NARA.

59. Wert, *Sword of Lincoln*, 380.

CHAPTER 7

1. Kellogg, *Capture and Escape*, 199.

2. Master Sixth Wisconsin Database, DSR. Officers suffered almost exactly the same percentage of total casualties as the regimental average, although they were killed and wounded at slightly higher rates. Establishing reliable casualty rates for Civil War regiments has been a bit of a cottage industry since the nineteenth century. Different methodologies have resulted in somewhat different statistics. William F. Fox's *Regimental Losses in the Civil War*, long the standard reference, has been challenged recently but nevertheless provides a useful comparison. Fox featured the Sixth Wisconsin as one of 300 "fighting regiments" and came up with 244 men who were killed or died of their wounds and 113 who died of disease, for a total of 357. My own research in the roster and descriptive roll finds fewer total deaths. Fox, *Regimental Losses*, 396. For more on the thorny problem of establishing the true death toll of the Civil War, see Faust, "'Numbers on Top of Numbers,'" 995–1009; and Hacker, "Census-Based Count of the Civil War Dead," 307–48.

3. Absent and Detached Database, DSR.

4. Handley-Cousins, *Bodies in Blue*, 14–15, 17; Absent and Detached Database, DSR; Master Sixth Wisconsin Database, DSR. Draftees were discharged at far higher rates (44.4 percent for illness, 75.7 percent for wounds). By the time the sick and wounded had spent any amount of time on the absent list, the war would have been winding down or, for all practical purposes, over.

5. Cashin, "Deserters, Civilians, and Draft Resistance," 262–85.

6. Master Sixth Wisconsin Database, DSR.

7. Charles Mevis record, Co. G; and Andrew Tuttle record, Co. E., both in Sixth Wisconsin Regimental Muster and Descriptive Rolls, WHS.

8. *Baraboo Republic*, June 25, 1862; Current, *Civil War Era*, 144–49, 219–20, 224–36, 260–76, 281–92, 357–58, 391, 402–5, 411.

9. *Appleton Crescent*, February 9, 1862, January 30, 16, 1864.

10. *Appleton Motor*, October 16, 1862.

11. *Appleton Motor*, June 11, 1863, April 28, 1864.

12. *Appleton Crescent*, June 11, 1864; *Daily Milwaukee News*, October 9, November 13, 1864.

13. Quote in Herdegen, *Iron Brigade*, 541–42; White, *Emancipation*.

14. Fry, *Republic in the Ranks*, 162–63; *North Western Times*, August 24, 1864; Loring Winslow to his parents and siblings, September 21, 1864, Winslow letters, WHS.

15. Waller Civil War Diary, November 5, 1864, VCHS; *Daily Milwaukee News*, November 13, December 1, 1864. Overall, Wisconsin soldiers voted 11,372 to 2,428 for the Union Party ticket. Current, *Civil War Era*, 411.

16. Current, *Civil War Era*, 408–11.

17. *Wood County Reporter*, May 19, August 18, 1864.

18. *Daily Milwaukee News*, February 14, 11, 15, 1865; *Appleton Crescent*, February 18, 1865.

19. *North Western Times*, February 8, 1865.

20. Ingalls diary and memoir, November 30, December 7, 1864, GNMP.

21. Ingalls diary and memoir, December 10, 1864.

22. Ingalls diary and memoir, December 13, 14, 1864.

23. Ingalls diary and memoir, December 15, 1864.

24. Ingalls diary and memoir, December 17 and 18, 1865.

25. Ingalls diary and memoir, January 14 and 15, 1865; J. B. Ingalls record, Co. E, Sixth Wisconsin Regimental Muster and Descriptive Rolls, WHS.

26. "Wisconsin Civil War Regiments," Wisconsin Genealogy Trails, accessed July 1, 2024, http://genealogytrails.com/wis/CivilWarIndex.html.

27. "Wisconsin Civil War Regiments."

28. Master Sixth Wisconsin Database, DSR; Geary, *We Need Men*, 168.

29. James M. Eastland pension record, no. 822383, NARA.

30. Master Sixth Wisconsin Database, DSR.

31. "Registers of Deaths of Volunteers, 1861–1865," Records of the Adjutant General's Office, 1780s–1917, Record Group 94, NARA, accessed via Ancestry on July 1, 2024, https://www.ancestry.com/discoveryui-content/view/378497:2123?tid=&pid=& queryid=7575b5b1-f37a-4582-934d-6e99ce96e732&_phsrc=RFX74&_phstart =successSource.

32. Master Sixth Wisconsin Database, DSR.

33. *Roster of Wisconsin Volunteers in the War of the Rebellion*. The descriptive roll sometimes lists both a hometown and the name of the town that received "credit" for enlistees in some cases but not often enough to provide a reliable measure.

34. Master Sixth Wisconsin Database, DSR.

35. Hans Rasmussen pension record, no. 872298, NARA.

36. Master Sixth Wisconsin Database, DSR; Absent and Detached Database, DSR.

37. Master Sixth Wisconsin Database, DSR.

38. Dennis N. Johnson pension record, Co. A, WC no. 108734; and Stanley Vander-walker pension record, Co. C, WC no. 86820, both in Fold3.

39. Warren to Meade, October 1, 1864, *OR* 42(3):20; Miles to Maj. H. H. Bingham, *OR* 42(3):160; Hancock to Meade, October 15, 1864, *OR* 42(3):238; Frederick Wion pension record, no. 43511, NARA.

40. Loring to his parents, December 1, 1864, Winslow letters, WHS.

41. Alexander Lowrie pension record, no. 81816; Andrew Gallup pension record, no. 68621; and John A. Kellogg pension record, no. 164271, all in NARA.

42. Hall to Dawes, January 5, 1865, Dawes letters, DA; Beaudot and Herdegen, *Irishman in the Iron Brigade*, 133–34.

43. Gottlieb Torke to Elizabeth Torke, December 20, 1864, January 12, 1865, Torke letters, Sheboygan County Historical Research Center, Sheboygan Falls, Wisconsin.

44. Cheek and Pointon, *History of the Sauk County Riflemen*, 155–56.

45. Frederick Brandt pension record, no. 411373; and Frederick Schoephoester pension record, no. 405007, both in NARA.

46. *Boscobel Broad-Axe*, January 11, 1865.

47. Matrau to his parents, February 13, 1865, in Reid-Green, *Letters Home*, 109; Herdegen, *Iron Brigade*, 624; Kellogg, *Capture and Escape*, 199.

48. Gibbon, *Personal Recollections*, 229–30.

49. Henry Matrau to his parents, February 13, 1865, in Reid-Green, *Letters Home*, 109.

50. Gottlieb Torke to Elizabeth Torke, February 9, 1865, Torke letters, Sheboygan County Historical Research Center, Sheboygan Falls, Wisconsin.

51. Herdegen, *Iron Brigade*, 556–57.

52. Henry Matrau to his parents, April 10, 1865, in Reid-Green, *Letters Home*, 114; Cheek and Pointon, *History of the Sauk County Riflemen*, 161.

53. Report of Col. John Kellogg, *OR* 46(1):884–86.

54. Report of Col. John Kellogg, 883; Robert C. McMinn pension record, no. 237263, NARA; Conrad Bates pension record, no. 273548, NARA.

55. Report of Col. John Kellogg, 883.

56. Herdegen, *Iron Brigade*, 584.

57. Matrau to his parents, April 10, 1865, in Reid-Green, *Letters Home*, 115.

58. *Roster of Wisconsin Volunteers in the War of the Rebellion*.

59. William H. Darrow pension record, no. 288068, NARA; Herdegen, *Iron Brigade*, 587–91; Wert, *Sword of Lincoln*, 419.

60. Madison Brower record, Co. C, Sixth Wisconsin Regimental Muster and Descriptive Rolls, WHS; Brower to Julia Brower, May 13, 1865, in "Pvt. Madison H. Brower Memorial," Find a Grave, accessed July 1, 2024, www.findagrave.com/memorial/65941189/madison-h-brower.

61. Absent and Detached Database, DSR; Table of Sixth Wisconsin Soldiers in Other Regiments, DSR.

62. Master Sixth Wisconsin Database, DSR.

63. Master Sixth Wisconsin Database.

64. Master Sixth Wisconsin Database; Matrau to his parents, June 6, 1865, in Reid-Green, *Letters Home*, 119.

65. Herdegen, *Iron Brigade*, 592–95; Master Sixth Wisconsin Database, DSR.

66. Herdegen, *Iron Brigade*, 596.

67. *Daily Milwaukee News*, June 14, 1865; Cheek and Pointon, *History of the Sauk County Riflemen*, 183–84.

68. *Appleton Motor*, June 15, 1865.

69. Allen, "Wisconsin's Reluctant Heroine," 1–13.

70. Cheek and Pointon, *History of the Sauk County Riflemen*, 182.

71. Henry M. Jones pension record, Co. K, WC no. 107265; and Frederick Fischer pension record, Co. B, WC no. 142788, both in Fold3; annual report, Wisconsin Soldiers' Home, in *Journal of the Wisconsin Senate for the year 1867 A.D.*, 297.

72. Kellogg, *Capture and Escape*, 201; Catherine Cutler pension record, no. 184226, NARA.

73. *Appleton Motor*, May 11, 1865; *North Western Times*, May 31, 1865.

CHAPTER 8

1. Peter Mohrbacher pension record, no. 956484, NARA; Master Sixth Wisconsin Database, DSR.

2. *Journal of the Assembly of Wisconsin for the Year, A.D. 1866*, 44, 36, 90; *Private and Local Laws Passed by the Legislature of Wisconsin*, 17; *Journal of Proceedings of the Twentieth Annual Session of the Wisconsin Legislature*, 92; *Journal of Proceedings of the Thirty-Seventh Annual Session of the Wisconsin Legislature*, 1241, 49; *State of Wisconsin, Senate Journal*, 704.

3. *Lancaster Teller*, April 18, 1889, copied from *Portage Register*.

4. Master Sixth Wisconsin Database, DSR.

5. Master Sixth Wisconsin Database.

6. Kutzler, *Living by Inches*, 3, 4. Tongue was one of the men captured during the Brooks Expedition discussed in chapter 9 of this book.

7. Levi L. Tongue pension record, no. 96035, NARA.

8. Kellogg, *Capture and Escape*, xv–xvi.

9. John A. Kellogg pension record, no. 164271, NARA.

10. Dean, *Shook over Hell*, 70, 91–114; Sommerville, *Aberration of Mind*, 151–78; Pizarro, Silver, and Prause, "Physical and Mental Health Costs," 193–200. Another study of Confederate veterans and psychological trauma that provides useful points of comparison is McClurken, *Take Care of the Living*.

11. *Lake Geneva Herald*, April 12, 1901; Sixth Wisconsin Demographic Database, DSR.

12. Logue and Blanck, *Heavy Laden*, 35, 214, 150.

13. Divorce, Addiction, Suicide Table, DSR; for Case, Winkleman, Clumb, and Hobbs, see Master Sixth Wisconsin Database, DSR; James Burrell census record, 1880 Census for Washington, DC, accessed via Ancestry on August 27, 2023, www.ancestry.com/imageviewer/collections/6742/images/4240113-00369?treeid=&personid=&usePUB=true&_phsrc=QMb233&_phstart=successSource&pId=49173119; Richard Corcoran record, Register of Members, National Homes for Disabled Volunteer Soldiers, accessed via Ancestry on August 27, 2023, www.ancestry.com/discoveryui-content/view/326311:1200?tid=&pid=&queryId=91083bbe4d4e0f90a516b7f30bce3ebc&_phsrc=rnM5391&_phstart=successSource; Herman J. Langhoff record, Register of

Members, National Homes for Disabled Volunteer Soldiers, accessed via Ancestry on August 27, 2023, www.ancestry.com/discoveryui-content/view/209647:1200?tid =&pid=&queryId=7cd69b84d6e07e9859e98533356f906e&_phsrc=rnM2182&_phstart =successSource; Reuben Pettit record, Register of Members, National Homes for Disabled Volunteer Soldiers, accessed via Ancestry on August 27, 2023, www.ancestry.com /imageviewer/collections/1200/images/MIUSA1866_113873-00389?usePUB=true &_phsrc=rnM100&_phstart=successSource&usePUBJs=true&pId=202683; Carroll, *Invisible Wounds*, 223–42.

14. Investigation of the National Home for Disabled Volunteer Soldiers, H.R. 2676, 48th Cong., 2nd sess. (1886), at 264.

15. Laws of Wisconsin, chap. 304, no. 9, A, published April 28, 1887, pp. 323–25, https://docs.legis.wisconsin.gov/1887/related/acts/304.pdf.

16. *Stevens Point Journal*, April 21, 1888.

17. *Waukesha Freeman*, January 5, 1888; *Journal Times*, October 23, 1896; *Wisconsin State Journal*, March 3, 1891; Cunningham, *Blue Book of the State of Wisconsin*, 583.

18. *Daily Telegram*, December 8, 1897; *Boscobel Dial*, March 10, 24, 1892.

19. *Wood County Reporter*, February 28, 1901.

20. *Lancaster Teller*, November 29, 1894, November 18, 1909; *Grant County Herald*, December 25, 1912.

21. Soldiers' Relief applications for Abraham Brill, Clara Riley, Mary Herdeg, Alexander Johnston, and Mary Halls, all in Biographical Files, Beaudot Archival Collection, KCWM.

22. Kelly, *Creating a National Home*, 93–98; Skocpol, *Protecting Soldiers and Mothers*, 140–41.

23. *History of the Wisconsin Veterans Home at King*.

24. Logue, "Union Veterans and Their Government," 423.

25. Soldiers Home Database, DSR; Sixth Wisconsin Master Database, DSR.

26. Andrew Arneson record, Register of Members, National Homes for Disabled Volunteer Soldiers, 1866–1938, accessed via Ancestry on August 26, 2023, https://search .ancestry.com/cgi-bin/sse.dll?indiv=1&dbid=1200&h=210147&tid=&pid=&queryId =e957fdf5cd58eca22e61be657ecbe438&usePUB=true&_phsrc=TkW17&_phstart =successSource.

27. Philip Schardt record, Register of Members, National Homes for Disabled Volunteer Soldiers, 1866–1938, accessed via Ancestry on August 26, 2023, www.ancestry .com/imageviewer/collections/1200/images/MIUSA1866_113883-00585?treeid =&personid=&rc=&usePUB=true&_phsrc=uOi3200&_phstart=successSource &pId=217844; James Blue record, Register of Members, National Homes for Disabled Volunteer Soldiers, 1866–1938, accessed via Ancestry on August 26, 2023, https://search .ancestry.com/cgi-bin/sse.dll?indiv=1&dbid=1200&h=220210&tid=&pid=&queryId=4d2 c73df80090a333f482871367d48ec&usePUB=true&_phsrc=TkW480&_phstart=success Source. The Soldiers Home Database provided the statistical information for this section.

28. Valentine Brehl pension record, no. 270526, NARA; Linares, "Civil War Pension Law," 8–13, 16, 26–30; Skocpol, "America's First Social Security System," 102. Blanck and Song provide an excellent brief summary of pension ratings and processes in "'Never Forget What They Did Here,'" 1111–116.

29. Logue, *To Appomattox and Beyond*, 124; Costa, *Evolution of Retirement*, 162; Morton, "Federal and Confederate Pensions Contrasted," 73–74; Master Sixth Wisconsin Database, DSR.

30. By the late 1870s, the success rate for pension applications had fallen from 67 percent to 47 percent. Bentley, *Annual Report*, 15.

31. For excellent descriptions of the pension process, see Prechtel-Kluskens, "'Reasonable Degree of Promptitude,'" 26–35; and Prechtel-Kluskens, "Anatomy of a Union Civil War Pension File."

32. Hare pension file, Personal Papers, Beaudot Archival Collection, KCWM.

33. Mathias Steinmetz pension record, no. 440366, NARA; Douglass pension file, Personal Papers, Beaudot Archival Collection, KCWM.

34. Isaac Fort pension record, no. 391403; Silas W. Morrison pension record, no. 349225; Martin B. Hull pension record, no. 421225; Hiram H. Palmer pension record, no. 406211, all in NARA; Douglass pension file, Personal Papers, Beaudot Archival Collection, KCWM.

35. Owen Powderly pension record, no. 183547; Seth H. Morey pension record, no. 657042, both in NARA.

36. George Barrett pension record, Co. B, WC no. 52049, Fold3.

37. This is made abundantly clear in the chapter devoted to pensions for Black soldiers in Dale Kretz's recent book on African Americans after the closing of the Freedmen's Bureau; veterans and especially their widows encountered suspicious and often hostile pension officials. White veterans did not, of course, have to navigate the complexities caused by race and enslavement, but many veterans did face a bureaucracy that seemed unsympathetic and rigid. Kretz, *Administering Freedom*, 100–143; Blanck, "Civil War Pensions and Disability," 109–237. The oft-cited article by Megan J. McClintock suggests that the pension system for Civil War veterans was intended to "reconstruct" families separated by war or stressed by the disability of husbands and fathers. See McClintock, "Civil War Pensions," 456–80.

38. Thomas Lalor pension record, Co. E, WC no. 140129, Fold3.

39. James Rhoades pension record, no. 315340; Alexander H. Turk pension record, no. 150463, both in NARA.

40. Mathias Steinmetz pension record, no. 440366; Marcel[la] Kota pension record, no. 426503, both in NARA.

41. John A. Coughran pension record, no. 466351, NARA.

42. Revels pension file, Personal Papers, Beaudot Archival Collection, KCWM; Klinehaus pension file, Personal Papers, Beaudot Archival Collection, KCWM; Charles M. Taylor pension record, no. 424477, NARA; Charles F. Bohn pension record, no. 254321, NARA; Martin B. Hull pension record, no. 421225, NARA; William Hartman pension record, no. 688297, NARA; Silas W. Morrison pension record, no. 349225, NARA.

43. Jerome A. Hall pension record, no. 156626, NARA.

44. Skocpol, *Protecting Soldiers and Mothers*, 2, 92; Trattner, *From Poor Law to Welfare State*, 44–93.

45. Master Sixth Wisconsin Database, DSR.

46. Hans Rasmussen pension record, no. 872298, NARA.

47. Ole Rosenwater pension record, no. 397397, NARA.

48. *Wisconsin State Journal*, September 15, 1887; Hardgrove, "General Edward S. Bragg's Reminiscences," 292; Marten, *Sing Not War*, 201–2.

49. *Portage Daily Register*, September 15, 1887; *Wisconsin State Journal*, August 27, 1889; *Oshkosh Northwestern*, August 29, 1889.

50. Copied in *Milwaukee Sunday Telegraph*, March 20, 1887.

51. *Milwaukee Sunday Telegraph*, February 27, 1887; *Vernon County Censor*, August 24, 1887.

52. *Milwaukee Sunday Telegraph*, March 16, 1884; "Go Ahead, Boys: I'll Take Care of the Wives and Babies. God Bless You!," *Harper's Weekly*, August 23, 1862, 544.

53. Master Sixth Wisconsin Database, DSR.

54. Jabez A. Hyatt pension record, Co. G, WC no. 225, Fold3; John P. Johnson pension record, Co. I, WC no. 116617, Fold3; Ignatz Winkler pension record, Co. A, WC no. 65333, Fold3. A half dozen children of deceased soldiers from the Sixth would live at least briefly in the Wisconsin Soldiers' Orphans' Home in Madison. "Committee on Benevolent Institutions, Report on Soldiers' Orphans' Home," in *Journal of the Wisconsin Senate for the year 1867 A.D.*, 635; financial papers, Soldiers' Orphans' Home Records, 1866–94, box 6, Certificates, WHS.

55. Caleb C. Wright pension record, Co. I, WC no. 32808; and Milo Sage pension record, Co. F, WC no. 40679, both in Fold3.

56. "1860 Methodist Wedding Vows," *Stone of Orthanc* (blog), November 4, 2011, http://stoneoforthanc.blogspot.com/2011/11/1860-methodist-wedding-vows.html.

57. George W. Atwood pension record, Co. I, WC no. 52041, Fold3.

58. Ferdinand Lauersdorf pension record, no. 52139, NARA.

59. John J. Aney pension record, no. 445837, NARA.

60. Hiram B. Merchant pension record, no. 205498, NARA.

61. James P. Sullivan pension record, no. 132539, NARA.

62. Chauncey A. Green pension record, no. 874345, NARA.

63. Darwin W. Kinney pension record, no. 93456, NARA.

CHAPTER 9

1. Tongue to Driggs, Dillan, Georgia, December 14, 15, 1901, GNMP.

2. Fahs, *Imagined Civil War*, 311. For an excellent description of the trope of "idealized suffering" that characterized many accounts, see Clarke, *War Stories*, 25.

3. Caroline E. Janney provides the most nuanced account of war memory in *Remembering the Civil War*. There are many other books about veterans and commemoration; see, for example, Harris, *Across the Bloody Chasm*. For a short but thorough summary of the recent historiography on veterans and ideas for future research, see Jordan, "Veterans in New Fields." The original essays assembled in Jordan and Rothera, *War Went On*, provide an excellent sampling of current research.

4. For the ways in which funerals of prominent figures shaped national memory in meaningful ways, see Purcell, *Spectacle of Grief*.

5. Zeitlin, "In Peace and War."

6. *Milwaukee Daily Sentinel*, July 19, 1875.

7. *Biographical History of La Crosse, Trempealeu, Buffalo Counties*, 636–37.

8. Kellogg, *Capture and Escape*, 15–16.

9. Beaudot and Herdegen, *Irishman in the Iron Brigade*, 82–83.

10. Parsell, *Eliza Scidmore*, chap. 1 (Brooks was Scidmore's half brother); Mark Gajewski, "David Atwood," Historic Madison, Inc., accessed August 31, 2024, www .historicmadison.org/davidatwood; *Milwaukee Telegraph*, May 13, 1893; Lincoln to Butler, telegram, March 18, 1864, Telegrams Sent and Received by the War Department Central Telegraph Office, 1861–82, Record Group 107: Records of the Office of the Secretary of War, 1791–1947, NARA, https://catalog.archives.gov/id/1636088.

11. Grant to Maj. Gen. George G. Meade, June 20, 1864, in *Papers of Ulysses S. Grant*, vol. 11, *June 1–August 15, 1864*, 96–97, digital ed., University Libraries, Mississippi State University, https://scholarsjunction.msstate.edu/usg-volumes/16.

12. *New York Times*, July 7, 1864.

13. *Milwaukee Sunday Telegraph*, September 19, 1886.

14. *Milwaukee Sunday Telegraph*, January 30, 1881; and Samuel Waller record, Co. I; Silas Lowery record, Co. B; and John St. Clair record, Co. K, all in Sixth Wisconsin Regimental Muster and Descriptive Rolls, WHS.

15. *Milwaukee Sunday Telegraph*, February 1, 1880, January 30, 1881, August 17, 1884.

16. Richard H. Abbott, *For Free Press and Equal Rights*, 33, 212n25; Edward P. Brooks pension record, no. 29388, NARA.

17. *Milwaukee Telegraph*, May 13, 1893. The *Milwaukee Telegraph* succeeded the *Milwaukee Sunday Telegraph* in the early 1890s.

18. Crompton B. Burton, "'Let Every Comrade Lend Us a Hand'"; Marten, *Sing Not War*, 152–56; *American Tribune*, September 22, 1904.

19. *Grand Army Sentinel*, no. 1 (April 1874), WHS; *Boscobel Dial*, May 24, 1887.

20. Washburn, *Life and Writings of Jerome A. Watrous*, 100, 120, 123; Watrous obituary, undated, untitled newspaper clipping, scrapbook, box 1, folder 5, Watrous Papers, WHS; Hosea Rood, "Grand Army Corner," *Wisconsin Democrat*, October 24, 1920.

21. *Milwaukee Sunday Telegraph*, December 3, 1882, June 10, 1883; *Weekly Herald*, December 11, 1885.

22. *Milwaukee Sunday Telegraph*, April 1, October 14, 1883.

23. *Milwaukee Sunday Telegraph*, May 4, 1884, June 17, November 11, 1883, March 5, 1882.

24. *Milwaukee Sunday Telegraph*, February 29, March 7, 1880, January 15, 1882, October 28, 1883.

25. *Vernon County Censor*, February 11, 1880.

26. *Vernon County Censor*, January 4, 1880. In fact, the descriptive roll has Malloy deserting from Satterlee General Hospital in Philadelphia. Nathan Malloy record, Co. E, Sixth Wisconsin Regimental Muster and Descriptive Rolls, WHS.

27. Berry, *Count the Dead*, 37–42.

28. *Milwaukee Sunday Telegraph*, May 18, 23, 1886.

29. *Milwaukee Sunday Telegraph*, March 16, 1884.

30. *Wisconsin Soldiers Reunion Association, Reunion Roster*.

31. "Capt. Perry Dead," *Shawano County Journal*, April 28, 1910, accessed via Ancestry, https://sites.rootsweb.com/~wishawa4/CW_Index/Soldiers/Perry%20Leslie

/Perry,%20Leslie.htm. Yael A. Sternhell shows the often conflicting uses of the *Official Records* during their compilation and after their publication in *War on Record*.

32. Blake, "'First in the Path of the Firemen,'" 64–81.

33. Marten, *Sing Not War*, 253.

34. *Biennual Report of the Adjutant General* [. . .] *Ending September 30, 1886*, 5; *Biennial Reports of the Secretary of State*, 142.

35. *Biennual Report of the Adjutant General* [. . .] *Ending September 30, 1884*, 4, 7.

36. Quoted in Lindermann, *Embattled Courage*, 280; *Wisconsin State Journal*, March 7, 1867; *Daily Milwaukee News*, September 28, 29, 1870.

37. McCrory, *Grand Army of the Republic*, 4–5.

38. McConnell, *Glorious Contentment*, 30–38, 85; McCrory, *Grand Army of the Republic*, 1–14, 128.

39. McConnell, *Glorious Contentment*, 45, 85–86; McCrory, *Grand Army of the Republic*, 298–307.

40. *Dodgeville Chronicle*, June 28, 1866; McCrory, *Grand Army of the Republic*, 103, 145, 203–4, 205–6, 212–13, 225, 237,157–58, 173, 299–304.

41. "Gettysburg Reunion," box 1, folder 18, Watrous Papers, WHS; Flagel, *War, Memory and the 1913 Gettysburg Reunion*, 5–8, 30–31; Chubachus, "Iron Brigade Tent at Gettysburg Reunion, 1913" (photograph), CivilWarTalk, April 29, 2015, https://civilwartalk.com /threads/iron-brigade-tent-at-gettysburg-reunion-1913.112934.

42. Chubachus, "Map Where Civil War Veterans and Other Attendees of the 50th Anniversary Reunion of the Battle of Gettysburg Camped, July 1913" (photograph), Imgur, November 16, 2017, https://imgur.com/8eYuFVk; Gettysburg National Military Park Commission, "Map of Gettysburg Battlefield Showing Routes That Must Be Taken by All Wheeled Conveyances During the Anniversary Celebration, from June 28 to June 30, July 1 to 5" (photograph), Library of Congress, accessed July 1, 2024, www.loc.gov /item/99439188.

43. *Milwaukee Sunday Telegraph*, July 30, 1882.

44. Marten, *Sing Not War*, 171, 221, 235, 239; McConnell, *Glorious Contentment*, 125–65.

45. *Appleton Crescent*, May 27, 1882; *Oshkosh Northwestern*, May 31, 1886; *Wood County Reporter*, May 10, 1894.

46. *Badger State Banner* article copied in *Soldiers Record*, September 18, 1869; *Daily Milwaukee News*, March 16, 1870.

47. *Vernon County Censor*, June 25, 1890; Rufus Dawes to Company K, in *Mauston Star*, ca. November 23, 1884, copied in, no. 25, pp. 2–3, 8–9, KCWM; *Juneau County Chronicle*, July 13, 1899.

48. *Grant County Herald*, September 18, 1879; *Lancaster Teller*, August 30, 1883, June 23, 1898.

49. McCrory, *Grand Army of the Republic*, 292–95; Herdegen, *Iron Brigade*, 603. On the Texas Brigade, see Ural, *Hood's Texas Brigade*.

50. *Lancaster Teller*, September 20, 1883, September 4, 1885; *Wisconsin State Journal*, September 18, 1885. The "Quickstep" was composed in 1863. Never mentioned was another composition produced at the end of the war: Mrs. A. W. Kellogg's "Sixth Wisconsin Volunteers March" (Chicago: H. M. Higgins, 1865). She seems not to have been related to the Sixth's John Kellogg.

51. *Lancaster Teller*, December 23, 1897.

52. "Program of the Iron Brigade Reunion, 1924," Miscellaneous, WVM.

53. The preceding two paragraphs are drawn from the Master Sixth Wisconsin Database, DSR. Stuart McConnell argues that 351,244 out of 1,034,073—or 34 percent—of the men found in the 1890 veterans' census belonged to the GAR. At the height of the GAR in Wisconsin, Thomas J. McCrory estimates, 44.3 percent of veterans were members. McConnell, *Glorious Contentment*, 54; McCrory, *Grand Army of the Republic*, 290–91.

54. *Roster of Lucius Fairchild Post No. 11*, n.p.

55. *Redwood Gazette*, October 19, 1893; *Rochester Post and Record*, September 6, 1907; *Reedsburg Free Press*, October 9, 1902.

56. *Stevens Point Journal*, June 16, 1908; *Kenosha News*, April 20, 1927; *Capital Journal*, December 12, 1927; *Albany (OR) Democrat*, January 14, 1926; *Door County Advocate*, January 22, 1926; *Green Bay Gazette*, March 16, 1896; *Barron County Shield*, May 3, 1901; *Union Grove Enterprise*, October 12, 1904.

57. "Washington Palmer Force," Find a Grave, accessed July 1, 2024, www.findagrave.com/memorial/122255502/washington-palmer-force; *Wiley Warbler*, October 9, 1919; *Neenah Times*, March 20, 1909.

58. *Redwood Gazette*, October 19, 1893; *Barron County Chronotype*, April 20, 1888; *Galesville Republican*, February 6, 1908; *Spirit Lake Beacon*, May 11, 1922.

59. *Cumberland Advocate*, July 11, 1907; *Appleton Crescent*, March 31, 1894; *Albany Democrat*, January 14, 1926; *Wiley Warbler*, October 9, 1919; *Daily Northwestern*, August 28, 1919.

60. *Galesville Republican*, February 6, 1908; *Englewood Chicago Times*, April 11, 1924; *Wisconsin State Journal*, June 12, 1923; *National City Star-News*, March 15, 1935; *La Crosse Tribune*, March 24, 1939.

61. *Daily Milwaukee News*, October 5, 1862. See Lindermann, *Embattled Courage*, 248–49.

62. Wisconsin, U.S., Wills and Probate Records, 1800–1987, for George Johnson, accessed via Ancestry on July 1, 2024, www.ancestry.com/imageviewer/collections/9088/images/004467533_00159?usePUB=true&_phsrc=rnM1645&_phstart=successSource&usePUBJs=true&pId=1393807.

63. Master Sixth Wisconsin Database, DSR.

64. Dawes Diary, vol. 2, June 1, 1893, WHS.

65. Dawes Diary, vol. 2, June 1, 1893.

66. Dawes, *Full-Blown Yankee of the Iron Brigade: Service with the Sixth Wisconsin*, 316–17.

EPILOGUE

1. *Lancaster Teller*, August 11, 1898.

2. "Stephen Bennett," Find a Grave, accessed August 27, 2023, www.findagrave.com/memorial/355839/stephen-bennett; Master Sixth Wisconsin Database, DSR; John C. Piron record, Burial Registers, Military Posts and National Cemeteries, 1862–1960, accessed via Ancestry on August 27, 2023, www.ancestry.com/discoveryui-content/view/393275:3135.

3. Master Sixth Wisconsin Database, DSR.

4. Public Service Database, DSR.

5. We can establish at least one postwar location for about 90 percent of Sixth Wisconsin veterans. Master Sixth Wisconsin Database, DSR; Emory Wyman census record, 1910 U.S. Federal Census, accessed via Ancestry on August 26, 2023, www.ancestry.com /discoveryui-content/view/15393646:7884?tid=&pid=&queryId=3025b1e4cb998e84a01 da88404161d32&_phsrc=QMb322&_phstart=successSource; Fawcett and Hepper, *Veterans of the Civil War*, 60. For a good, if brief, introduction to postwar migration of Civil War veterans, see Cimbala, *Veterans North and South*, 74–82. See also Hackemer, "Union Veteran Migration Patterns," 84–108; and Mack, *Bucking the Railroads*.

6. *Journal of Proceedings of the Thirty-Eighth Annual Session of the Wisconsin Legislature*, 57–60; *Wood County Reporter*, April 21, 1887; *Wisconsin State Register*, March 10, 1888; *Weekly Wisconsin*, February 18, 1888. A tiny stone marker also notes where the exhausted survivors of the Sixth and other Iron Brigade regiments dug breastworks on Culp's Hill.

7. *Journal of the Assembly of Wisconsin for the Year, A.D. 1866*, 221, 471; *Journal of Proceedings of the Twenty-Eighth Annual Session of the Wisconsin Legislature*, 408; "Wisconsin's Civil War Monuments," Recollection Wisconsin, November 10, 2015, https://recollectionwisconsin.org/civil-war-monuments; *Oshkosh Northwestern*, June 28, 1898; Thomas J. Brown, *Civil War Monuments*, 27–29, 41–55, 65; "Pierce County War Memorial," Tour of Honor, accessed June 19, 2023, www.tourofhonor.com/pages/2013wi _ellsworth.html; "Veterans Memorial," Historical Marker Project, accessed June 19, 2023, https://historicalmarkerproject.com/markers/HM1E3W_veterans-memorial_Alma-WI .html; "Prairie du Chien Veterans Memorial," Historical Marker Database, accessed June 19, 2023, www.hmdb.org/m.asp?m=53014.

8. "Sandwiches and Wraps," Blue Gray Bar and Grill, accessed June 19, 3023, www .bluegraybargrill.com/sandwiches-wraps.php; "Commemorative Highways and Bridges," Wisconsin Department of Transportation, accessed April 12, 2020, https://wisconsindot .gov/Pages/travel/road/comm-hwys/default.aspx; "The Iron Brigade," Historical Marker Database, accessed June 19, 2023, www.hmdb.org/m.asp?m=4119; "Iron Brigade Association," Civil War Round Table of Milwaukee, accessed July 14, 2023, www.milwaukeecwrt .org/iron-brigade-association.

9. Chris Lese, "Teaching Civil War Memory," *Commonplace*, accessed June 11, 2023, http://commonplace.online/article/teaching-civil-war-memory; "I Hope to Do Something Brave," clip from "Juneau County," special episode of *Wisconsin Hometown Stories*, aired April 17, 2014, on PBS, https://video.pbswisconsin.org/video/wisconsin -hometown-stories-juneau-county-i-hope-do-something-brave; "Memorial Hall's Civil War History," Beloit College website, accessed June 19, 2023, www.beloit.edu/logan /exhibits/ongoing-exhibits; William Beaudot, "1961: Forming the 6th," *Blackhat*, no. 6 (ca. 1984), 2–7, Beaudot Archival Collection, KCWM; *Juneau County Star-Times*, June 2, 1987.

BIBLIOGRAPHY

PRIMARY SOURCES

Archives

Davee Library, University of Wisconsin–River Falls
    Archives and Special Collections
        Andrews, A. D., Papers
        Saunders, Ainsworth, letter
Dawes Arboretum, Newark, Ohio
    Dawes, Rufus R., letters
Fold3 Military Records Database, www.fold3.com
Gettysburg National Military Park Library, Gettysburg, Pennsylvania
    Crawford, John A., service record and medical report
    Delaglise, F. A., service record and pension exam record
    Gunderson, Ole, service record and pension exam record
    Harris, Lloyd G., pension and service papers
    Holford, Lyman C., diary, June–September 1863 (photocopies from Lyman C.
        Holford Papers, 1861–92, Library of Congress, Washington, DC)
    Huntington, H. J., memoir of the attack on the Railroad Cut, 1887
    Ingalls, J. B., diary and memoir, 1864
    Johnson, C. J., "Personal Recollections of the Battle of Gettysburg, of a Soldier
        of the Iron Brigade" (unpublished manuscript, typescript)
    Muller, Dr. Auguste, obituary
    "Report on the Removal of the Bodies to the Cemetery. Notes on
        the Bodies Removed Near the Railroad Cut"
    Stedman, Levi, service papers
    Tongue, Levi, personnel record
Kenosha Civil War Museum, Kenosha, Wisconsin
    William J. K. Beaudot Archival Collection, 1982–98
        Biographical Files
            Brill, Abraham, Co. G

Bruce, Charles, Co. B
Burchel, Nathan, Co. I
Charlesworth, John, Co. D
Cleveland, Thomas J., Co. K
Costigan, John., Co. D
Douglass, William, Co. B
Hall, Leverett C., Co. B
Halls, George, Co. D
Hare, Frank, Co. B
Hart, Lewis, Co. I
Harter, Charles, Co. B
Herdeg, John, Co. H
Johnston, Alexander, Co. C
Korbe, William, Co. H
Leach, William, Co. K
Nelson, Lars M., Co. C
Newton, John F., Co. B
Riley, James
Sherman, Reuben, Co. D

The Blackhat [newsletter], issues 1–90, ca. 1970s–80s

Iron Brigade Files
Bachelder Gettysburg Map Correspondence: Sixth Wisconsin
Cemeteries
Iron Brigade Association
Iron Brigade at Antietam Papers
Iron Brigade photos
Miscellaneous notes, papers, and articles
Nebraska Veterans
Soldier biographies
South Dakota Veterans

Personal Papers
Brown, Edwin A., letters
Douglass, William, Co. B., pension file
Fairfield, George, diary
Hare, Frank, Co. B., pension file
Huntington, Howard, letters and records
Johnson, John O., letters
Klinehaus, Frederick, pension file
Revels, Henry, pension file
Storch, Marc, and Beth Storch, eds., "'And All I Loved in It Has Gone
    Hence': The 1864 Letters of Sgt. John O. Johnson, Co H, 6th
    Wisconsin Infantry," 11–12 (unpublished manuscript)
Sullivan, James P., papers

Milwaukee County Historical Society, Milwaukee, Wisconsin
　　Military Order of the Loyal Legion of the United States,
　　Wisconsin Commandery Memorials, 1886–1917
　　Records of Milwaukee, Wisconsin, Grand Army of the Republic Posts, 1865–1943
　　　　Robert Chivas Post: membership books, list of deceased members,
　　　　　　meeting minutes
　　　　Clippings, 1889, 1899–1962
　　　　E. B. Wolcott Post No. 1, history and rosters/misc.
　　　　1889 GAR Encampment (Milwaukee), souvenir booklets/miscellaneous clippings
　　　　GAR National Encampments, miscellaneous programs and material, 1887–1910
　　　　GAR and Auxiliary Units, General and Special Orders/Letters
　　　　GAR miscellaneous
　　　　Memorial Day Programs, 1870–1941
　　　　Veteran and Reunion pamphlets and booklets
　　　　E. B. Wolcott Post No. 1, index and catalog, 1 volume
　　　　E. B. Wolcott Post No. 1, personal war sketches
　　Soldiers' Relief Commission Collection, Mss-1372
National Archives and Records Administration, Washington, DC
　　Pension records
Rare Books and Manuscripts, New York Public Library
　　US Sanitary Commission Records, Series 7
　　　　Andrew, George, camp inspection return, Sixth Wisconsin, November 21, 1861
　　　　Camp inspection return, Sixth Wisconsin, August 19, 1861
　　　　Chamberlain, W. M., camp inspection return, Sixth Wisconsin, February 10, 1862
　　　　Collyer, A., report, August 20, 1861
Raynor Memorial Libraries, Marquette University, Milwaukee, Wisconsin
　　Digital Scholarship Repository
　　　　Absent and Detached Database
　　　　Divorce, Addiction, Suicide Table
　　　　Married Soldiers Database
　　　　Master Sixth Wisconsin Database
　　　　Officers Database
　　　　Public Service Database
　　　　Roster of the Sixth Wisconsin
　　　　Sixth Wisconsin Demographic Database
　　　　Sixth Wisconsin Geography Database
　　　　Soldiers Home Database
　　　　Table of Sixth Wisconsin Soldiers in Other Regiments
Sheboygan County Historical Research Center, Sheboygan Falls, Wisconsin
　　Torke, Gottlieb, letters, 1864–65 (translated by Leona Torke Kane)
Vernon County Historical Society, Viroqua, Wisconsin
　　Rogers, Earl M., "Autobiography" (unpublished manuscript, transcription)
　　Waller, Francis, Civil War Diary (transcription)

Wisconsin Historical Society, Madison

    Adjutant General Records, Series 1200

        Iron Brigade

    Bragg, Edwin, Papers

    Chapman, Chandler P., Papers

    Church, William Henry, Papers

    Cook, John H., Papers

    Dawes, Rufus R., Diary (2 vols.)

    Gallup, Andrew, Papers

    Grand Army Sentinel (1874–75)

    Haskell, Frank A., Papers

    Huntley, Reuben, Papers

    Iron Brigade Association, miscellaneous papers

    Ketner, William J., Papers

    Murray, Julius A., Family Papers

    Quiner, E. B., "Quiner Scrapbooks: Correspondence of the Wisconsin
            Volunteers, 1861–1865," 10 vols., https://content.wisconsinhistory
            .org/digital/collection/quiner/id/12959

    Sixth Wisconsin Regimental Muster and Descriptive Rolls, Series 1144

    Soldiers' Orphans' Home Records

        Harrsch, Patricia, "The Soldiers' Orphans Home: A Roster of
            Its Residents" (typescript)

        Vouchers, rosters, financial papers

    St. Clair, John W., Papers

    Watrous, Jerome, Papers

    Winslow, Loring B. F., letters

Wisconsin Veterans Museum, Madison

    Grand Army of the Republic, Department of Wisconsin Records, 1861–1986

        GAR Post No. 11, Lucius Fairchild Post, Madison, WI, roster, 1922

        GAR Post No. 32, J. B. Wyman Post, Clintonville, WI, descriptive book

        GAR Post No. 35, N. S. Frost Post, Prairie du Sac, WI, descriptive book

        GAR Post No. 38, Wilson-Colwell Post, La Crosse, WI, roster, 1906

        GAR Post No. 67, Samuel F. Curtis Post, Lima, WI, Information on
            Charter Members and Officers

        GAR Post No. 68, James Comerford Post, Chippewa Falls, WI
           Membership applications, 1883–1900
               Roll of Members from Organization of Post, March 15, 1883–January 1, 1890

        GAR Post No. 88, W. A. Barstow Post, Kendall, WI, descriptive book

        GAR Post No. 129, H. J. Lewis Post, Neenah, WI

        GAR Post No. 130, E. A. Brown Post, Fond du Lac, WI, descriptive book

        GAR Post No. 132, Tom Cox Post, Lancaster, WI, records, 1884–1916

        GAR Post No. 133, Geo. D. Eggleston Post, Appleton, WI, roster, 1898

        GAR Post No. 138, Joseph Bailey Post, Palmyra, WI, records, 1884–1916

        GAR Post No. 221, C. McCarthy Post, Rockbridge, WI, descriptive book

    Manuscript Small Collections

Miscellaneous

    Dedication, Sauk County Soldiers' Monument, Saturday, May 29, 1897

    "The Following Lists of Members of the G.A.R. Have Trees at Cushing Park . . ."

    Membership Ledger Book, 1866–80, Soldiers' and Sailors' National Union
        League of Wisconsin

    Miscellaneous Department [1876–1933]

    Patriotic letters from teachers, 1909

    "Program of the Iron Brigade Reunion, 1924"

    Reunion and Banquet of the Iron Brigade, 1900

    School essays, 1910

        Adams County Schools

        Madison Schools

        Marinette, Menasha

    Wisconsin Veterans Home, records and photographs, 1866–1986

        Applications (1887–1914)

Personal Papers

    Harland, John, letter, 1862

    Smith, Erastus, letter, 1863

    Stratton, Alcinous, letter, 1864

    Torke, Gottlieb, letters, 1864–65

    Tucker, Isaac, diary, 1861–62

Published Works

    Hardtack, Pork, Beans: Encampment Souvenir, Camp-Stories and Songs of the
        Veterans of 1861–1865. Eau Claire: Department of Wisconsin, GAR, 1909.

    Index to Residents of the Grand Army Home for Veterans Home,
        1887–1937. Compiled by Abbie Norderhaug and Katy Marty.
        Madison: Wisconsin Veterans Museum, 2008.

    The Knapsack. Journal. Madison: Grand Army of the Republic,
        Department of Wisconsin, Patriotic Commission, 1928–29.

    The Muffled Drum: The Muster-Out Roll of Civil War Burials, Central
        Wisconsin Veterans Memorial Cemetery, King, Wisc. Compiled by
        James G Gardner King, WI: Hannah I. Gardner Library, 2013.

    Notes Taken at the Wisconsin Veterans' Home with Reports of Officers. Edited
        by Hannah E. Patchin. Waupaca, WI: D. L. Stinchfield, 1891.

    Patriotic Instruction: Report of Patriotic Instructor, Department of Wisconsin, G.A.R.
        Madison: Grand Army of the Republic, Department of Wisconsin, 1909–11.

Registers of National and State Encampments

    National Encampment Register: Wisconsin Infantry Reg. 1–10, ca. 1908

    National Encampment Register: Wisconsin Regiments 1–12, 1905–20

        1905 Denver

        1910 Atlantic City

        1911 Rochester

        1916 Kansas City

        1917 Boston

        1918 Portland, OR

1919 Columbus, OH

1920 Indianapolis

Register of Comrades Visiting the Wisconsin Department Headquarters at the
National Encampment at Boston, MA, August 17–18, 1904

Register of Names, National Encampment, Department of Wisconsin, Infantry

1901 Cleveland

1902 Washington, DC

1903 San Francisco

[State] Encampment Register, Chippewa Falls, 1903

[State] Encampment Register, Madison, 1904

[State] Encampment Register, Inf. Regiments 1–20, La Crosse, 1905

[State] Encampment Register, Oshkosh, 1907

Newspapers

Baraboo Republic

Mauston Star

New York Times

National Tribune

Soldiers Record (Madison)

Sunday Telegraph (Milwaukee)

Newspapers.com Database

Albany (OR) Democrat

American Tribune (Indianapolis, IN)

Appleton (WI) Crescent

Appleton (WI) Motor

Badger State Banner (Black
River Falls, WI)

Baraboo (WI) Republic

Barron County Chronotype
(Rice Lake, WI)

Barron County Shield
(Barron, WI)

Boscobel (WI) Broad-Axe

Boscobel (WI) Dial

Brandon (VT) Monitor

Capital Journal (Salem, OR)

Cumberland (WI) Advocate

Daily Milwaukee (WI) News

Daily Northwestern (Oshkosh, WI)

Daily Telegram (Eau Claire, WI)

Dodgeville (WI) Chronicle

Door County Advocate
(Sturgeon Bay, WI)

Englewood Chicago Times

Galesville (WI) Republican

*General Orders: The Newsletter of the Civil
War Round Table of Milwaukee, Inc.,
and the Iron Brigade Association*

Grant County Herald (Lancaster, WI)

Green Bay (WI) Gazette

Harper's Weekly

Journal Times (Racine, WI)

Juneau County Chronicle (Mauston, WI)

Juneau County Star-Times (Mauston, WI)

Kenosha (WI) News

La Crosse (WI) Tribune

Lake Geneva (WI) Herald

Lancaster (WI) Teller

Madison (WI) State Journal

Mauston (WI) Star

Milwaukee (WI) Daily Sentinel

Milwaukee (WI) Sunday Telegraph

Milwaukee (WI) Telegraph

Manitowoc (WI) Herald

Mineral Point (WI) Weekly Tribune

National City (CA) Star-News
National Tribune (Washington, DC)
Neenah (WI) Times
New York Times
North Western Times (Viroqua, WI)
Oshkosh (WI) Northwestern
Portage (WI) Daily Register
Prescott (WI) Journal
Prescott (WI) Transcript
Redwood Gazette (Redwood Falls, MN)
Reedsburg (WI) Free Press
Rochester (MN) Post and Record
Soldiers Record (Madison, WI)

Spirit Lake (IA) Beacon
Stevens Point (WI) Journal
Union Grove (WI) Enterprise
Vernon County Censor (Viroqua, WI)
Waukesha (WI) Freeman
Weekly Herald (Chippewa Falls, WI)
Weekly Wisconsin (Milwaukee)
Wiley (KS) Warbler
Wisconsin Democrat (Madison)
Wisconsin State Journal (Madison)
Wisconsin State Register (Portage)
Wood County Reporter
    (Grand Rapids, WI)

Wisconsin State Government Documents

Annual Report of the Adjutant General of the State of Wisconsin, for the Year 1861. Madison, WI: State Printer, 1861.

Annual Report of the Adjutant General of the State of Wisconsin, with Reports from the Quartermaster General and Surgeon General for the Year Ending December 31, 1864. Madison, WI: State Printer, 1865.

Biennual Report of the Adjutant General of the State of Wisconsin for the Two Fiscal Years Ending September 30, 1884. Madison, WI: State Printer, 1885.

Biennial Report of the Adjutant General of the State of Wisconsin for the Two Fiscal Years Ending September 30, 1886. Madison, WI: State Printer, 1887.

Biennial Reports of the Secretary of State, Commissioners of Public Printing, and the Superintendent of Public Property of the State of Wisconsin for the Fiscal Term Ending September 30, 1886. Madison, WI: State Printer, 1886.

Journal of Proceedings of the Thirty-Eighth Annual Session of the Wisconsin Legislature. Madison, WI: State Printer, 1887.

Journal of Proceedings of the Thirty-Seventh Annual Session of the Wisconsin Legislature. Madison, WI: State Printer, 1885.

Journal of Proceedings of the Twentieth Annual Session of the Wisconsin Legislature, for the Year 1868. Madison, WI: State Printer, 1868.

Journal of Proceedings of the Twenty-Eighth Annual Session of the Wisconsin Legislature. Madison, WI: State Printer, 1875.

Journal of the Assembly of Wisconsin for the Year, A.D. 1866. Madison, WI: State Printer, 1866.

Journal of the Assembly of Wisconsin, Fourteenth Annual Session for the Year A.D. 1862. Madison, WI: State Printer, 1862.

Journal of the Thirty-First National Encampment of the Grand Army of the Republic. Lincoln, NE: State Journal, 1897.

Journal of the Wisconsin Senate for the year 1867 A.D. Madison, WI: State Printer, 1867.

Private and Local Laws Passed by the Legislature of Wisconsin in the Year Eighteen Hundred and Sixty-Seven. Madison, WI: State Printer, 1867.

State of Wisconsin, *Senate Journal, Fortieth Session.* Madison, WI: State Printer, 1891.

United States Government Documents

Bentley, John. *Annual Report of the Commissioner of Pensions, 1879.* Washington, DC: Government Printing Office, 1879.

Final Report Made to the Secretary of War, by the Provost Marshal General. Washington, DC: Government Printing Office, 1866.

Revised United States Army Regulations of 1861: With an Appendix Containing the Changes and Laws Affecting Army Regulations and Articles of War to June 25, 1863. Washington, DC: Government Printing Office, 1863.

U.S. Census Office and James M. Edmunds. *Statistics of the United States (including Mortality, Property, &c.) in 1860.* Washington, DC: Government Printing Office, 1866.

War of the Rebellion: A Compilation of the Official Records of the Union and Confederate Armies. 128 vols. Washington, DC: Government Printing Office, 1880–1989.

Published Primary Sources

Aroostook War: Historical Sketch and Roster of Commissioned Officers and Enlisted Men. Augusta, GA: Kennebec Journal Print, 1904.

Beaudot, William J. K., and Lance J. Herdegen. *An Irishman in the Iron Brigade: The Civil War Memoirs of James P. Sullivan, Sergt., Company K, 6th Wisconsin Volunteers.* New York: Fordham University Press, 1993.

Brinton, John H. *Personal Memoirs of John H. Brinton, Major and Surgeon, U.S.V., 1861–1865.* New York: Neale, 1914.

Buell, August. *"The Cannoneer": Recollections of Service in the Army of the Potomac.* Washington, DC: National Tribune, 1890.

Carr, Jo Ann Daly. *Such Anxious Hours: Wisconsin Women's Voices from the Civil War.* Madison: University of Wisconsin Press, 2019.

Chandler, R. *Chandler's Tactics, Compiled from Scott and Hardee, for the Use of Wisconsin Volunteers.* Milwaukee, WI: Herman and Brightman, 1861.

Cheek, Philip, and Mair Pointon. *History of the Sauk County Riflemen, Known as Company "A" Sixth Wisconsin Veteran Volunteer Infantry, 1861–1865.* N.p.: Philip Cheek, 1909.

Corbett, Elizabeth. *Out at the Soldiers' Home: A Memory Book.* New York: Appleton-Century, 1941.

Cunningham, Thomas J., ed. *The Blue Book of the State of Wisconsin.* Milwaukee, WI: Milwaukee Litho and Engraving, 1891.

Dawes, Rufus. *A Full-Blown Yankee of the Iron Brigade: Service with the Sixth Wisconsin Volunteers.* Lincoln: University of Nebraska Press, 1999.

———. "With the Sixth Wisconsin at Gettysburg." In *Sketches of War History, 1861–1865: Papers Read before the Ohio Commandery of the Military Order of the Loyal Legion of the*

United States, 1888–1890, edited by Robert Hunter, 3:364–88. Cincinnati, OH: Robert Clarke, 1890.

de Thulstrup, Thule. *Battle of Antietam*. Boston: L. Prang, ca. 1887.

Dumont, Frank. *The Half-Breed: A Western Drama in Three Acts*. Philadelphia: Penn, 1912.

Fitch, Michael H. *Echoes of the Civil War as I Hear Them*. New York: R. F. Fenno, 1905.

Fox, William F. *Regimental Losses in the American Civil War, 1861–1865*. Albany, NY: Albany Publishing, 1889.

Gibbon, John. *Personal Recollections of the Civil War*. New York: G. P. Putnam's Sons, 1928.

Grand Army of the Republic, Department of Wisconsin, *Journal of the Sixtieth Encampment, Racine, June 14–16, 1926*. Madison, WI: Democrat, 1926.

Grand Army of the Republic, Department of Wisconsin, *Journal of the Sixty-Fourth Annual Encampment, Appleton., June 11, 12, 13, 1934*. Madison, WI: Democrat, 1934.

Gross, S. D. *A Manual of Military Surgery*. Philadelphia: J. B. Lippincott, 1861.

Haight, Lt. Theron W. "Among the Pontoons at Fitzhugh Crossing." In *War Papers Read before the Commandery of the State of Wisconsin, Military Order of the Loyal Legion of the United States*, 1:416–23. Milwaukee, WI: Burdick, Armitage, and Allen, 1891.

Hardgrove, J. G. "General Edward S. Bragg's Reminiscences." *Wisconsin Magazine of History*, no. 3 (March 1950): 281–309.

Haskell, Frank. *The Battle of Gettysburg*. N.p., ca. 1881.

Henshaw, Sarah Edwards. *Our Branch and Its Tributaries: Being a History of the Work of the Northwestern Sanitary Commission and Its Auxiliaries during the War of the Rebellion*. Chicago: Alfred L. Sewell, 1868.

Journal of the Thirtieth Annual Encampment of the Grand Army of the Republic. Indianapolis: William B. Hurford, 1896.

Keen, William W. *Surgical Reminiscences of the Civil War*. Philadelphia: College of Physicians of Philadelphia, 1905.

Kellogg, John A. *Capture and Escape: A Narrative of Army and Prison Life*. Madison: Wisconsin History Commission, 1908.

King, Gen. Charles. *The Iron Brigade: A Story of the Army of the Potomac*. New York: G. W. Dillingham, 1902.

Morton, M. B. "Federal and Confederate Pensions Contrasted." *Forum*, September 1893, 68–74.

Otis, George A., ed. *Medical and Surgical History of the War of the Rebellion, 1861–1865*. 3 pts. Washington, DC: Government Printing Office, 1870–88.

Paddy's Wedding. New York: Andrews, n.d. Library of Congress. www.loc.gov/resource /amss.as110710.

Pocket Register, Commandery of Wisconsin, Military Order of the Loyal Legion of the United States. Milwaukee, WI: Burdick and Allen, 1905.

Proceedings of the Sixth Annual Encampment of the Grand Army of the Republic, Department of Kansas. Topeka, KS: C. B. Hamilton, 1887.

Quiner, E. B. *Military History of Wisconsin: A Record of the Civil and Military Patriotism of the State in the War for the Union, with a History of the Campaigns in Which Wisconsin Soldiers Have Been Conspicuous, etc.* Chicago: Clarke, 1866.

Register of the Military Order of the Loyal Legion of the United States. Boston: Edwin L. Slocomb, 1906.

Reid-Green, Marcia, ed. *Letters Home: Henry Matrau of the Iron Brigade*. Lincoln: University of Nebraska Press, 1993.

Rogers, Earl. *Memoirs of Vernon County, from the Earliest Historical Times down to the Present*. Madison, WI: Western Historical Association, 1907.

Roster of Lucius Fairchild Post No. 11, Department of Wisconsin, Grand Army of the Republic. Madison, WI: n.p., 1922.

The Roster of Wisconsin Volunteers in the War of the Rebellion, 1861–1865. Madison, WI: State Printer, 1886.

Smart, William R. E. "On Hospital Gangrene." In *The Half-Yearly Abstract of the Medical Sciences*, vol. 52:178. Philadelphia: Henry C. Lean, 1871.

Smith, William, ed. *Smaller Specimens of English Literature: Selected from the Chief English Writers and Arranged Chronologically*. London: John Murray, 1869.

Thwaites, Reuben Gold, ed. *Civil War Messages and Proclamations of Wisconsin War Governors*. Madison: Wisconsin History Commission, 1912.

Washburn, William H. *The Life and Writings of Jerome A. Watrous: Soldier-Reporter Adjutant of the Iron Brigade*. Milwaukee: William H. Washburn, 1992.

Watrous, Jerome A., ed., *Memoirs of Milwaukee County, from the Earliest Historical Times down to the Present*. Madison, WI: Western Historical Association, 1909.

Wisconsin Soldiers Reunion Association, Reunion Roster. Fond du Lac, WI: Star Steam Job and Book, 1880.

Woolsey, Jane Stuart. *Hospital Days: Reminiscence of a Civil War Nurse*. Edited by Daniel John Hoisington. Roseville, MN: Edinborough, 1996.

SECONDARY SOURCES

Abbott, Edith. "The Wages of Unskilled Labor in the United States, 1859–1900." *Journal of Political Economy* 13, no. 3 (June 1905): 321–67.

Abbott, Richard H. *For Free Press and Equal Rights: Republican Newspapers in the Reconstruction South*. Athens: University of Georgia Press, 2004.

Adams, Michael C. C. *Living Hell: The Dark Side of the Civil War*. Baltimore: Johns Hopkins University Press, 2014.

Allen, Anne Beiser. "Wisconsin's Reluctant Heroine: Cordelia Perrine Harvey." *Wisconsin Magazine of History* 95, no. 2 (Winter 2011–12): 1–13.

Berry, Stephen. *Count the Dead: Coroners, Quants, and the Birth of Death as We Know It*. Chapel Hill: University of North Carolina Press, 2022.

———. "When Metal Meets Mettle: The Hard Realities of Civil War Soldiering." *North and South* 9 (August 2006): 12–21.

Bever, Megan L. *At War with King Alcohol: Debating Drinking and Masculinity in the Civil War*. Chapel Hill: University of North Carolina Press, 2022.

Biographical History of La Crosse, Trempealeu, Buffalo Counties. Chicago: Lewis, 1892.

Blake, Kellee. "'First in the Path of the Firemen': The Fate of the 1890 Population Census." *Prologue* 28 (Spring 1996): 64–81.

Blanck, Peter. "Civil War Pensions and Disability." *Ohio State Law Journal* 62, no. 1 (2001): 109–237.

Blanck, Peter, and Chen Song. "'Never Forget What They Did Here': Civil War Pensions for Gettysburg Union Army Veterans and Disability in Nineteenth-Century America." *William and Mary Law Review*, no. 44 (2003): 1111–117.

Bledsoe, Andrew S. *Citizen-Officers: The Union and Confederate Volunteer Junior Officer Corps in the American Civil War*. Baton Rouge: Louisiana State University Press, 2015.

Bollet, Alfred Jay. "Amputations in the Civil War." In *Years of Change and Suffering: Modern Perspectives on Civil War Medicine*, edited by James M. Schmidt and Guy R. Hasegawa, 57–67. Roseville, MN: Edinborough Press, 2009.

Brown, Thomas J. *Civil War Monuments and the Militarization of America*. Chapel Hill: University of North Carolina Press, 2019.

Brown, William Fiske. *Rock County, Wisconsin, a New History of Its Cities, Villages, Towns, Citizens and Varied Interests, from the Earliest Times, Up to Date*. Vol. 1. Beloit, WI: C. F. Cooper, 1908.

Burbick, William George. "Columbus, Ohio, Theater from the Beginning of the Civil War to 1875." PhD diss., Ohio State University, 1963.

Burton, Crompton B. "'Let Every Comrade Lend Us a Hand': George E. Lemon and the *National Tribune*." In *Buying and Selling Civil War Memory in Gilded Age America*, edited by James Marten and Caroline E. Janney, 63–77. Athens: University of Georgia Press, 2021.

Carmichael, Peter S. *The War for the Common Soldier: How Men Thought, Fought, and Survived in Civil War Armies*. Chapel Hill: University of North Carolina Press, 2018.

Carroll, Dillon J. *Invisible Wounds: Mental Illness and Civil War Soldiers*. Baton Rouge: Louisiana State University Press, 2021.

Carroon, Robert G., and Dana B. Shoaf. *Union Blue: The History of the Military Order of the Loyal Legion of the United States*. Shippensburg, PA: White Mane Books, 2001.

Cashin, Joan E. "Deserters, Civilians, and Draft Resistance in the North." In *The War Was You and Me: Civilians in the American Civil War*, edited by Joan E. Cashin, 262–85. Princeton, NJ: Princeton University Press, 2002.

Catton, Bruce. *Glory Road*. New York: Doubleday, 1952.

———. *Mr. Lincoln's Army*. New York: Doubleday, 1951.

Cimbala, Paul A. *Veterans North and South: The Transition from Soldier to Civilian after the American Civil War*. Santa Barbara, CA: Praeger, 2015.

Clarke, Frances M. *War Stories: Suffering and Sacrifice in the Civil War North*. Chicago: University of Chicago Press, 2011.

Coco, Gregory A. *Killed in Action: Eyewitness Accounts of the Last Moments of 100 Union Soldiers Who Died at Gettysburg*. Gettysburg, PA: Thomas, 1992.

———. *A Strange and Blighted Land: Gettysburg; The Aftermath of a Battle*. Gettysburg, PA: Thomas, 1995.

Conner, Albert Z., Jr., and Chris Mackowski. *Seizing Destiny: The Army of the Potomac's "Valley Forge" and the Civil War Winter That Saved the Union*. El Dorado Hills, CA: Savas Beatie, 2016.

Costa, Dora L. *The Evolution of Retirement: An American Economic History, 1880–1890*. Chicago: University of Chicago Press, 1998.

Costa, Dora L., and Matthew E. Kahn. *Heroes and Cowards: The Social Face of War*. Princeton, NJ: Princeton University Press, 2008.

Current, Richard N. *The Civil War Era, 1848–1873*. Vol. 2 of *The History of Wisconsin*. Madison, WI: State Historical Society of Wisconsin, 1976.

Curtiss-Wedge, F., and George Jones. *History of Dunn County, Wisconsin*. Minneapolis: H. C. Cooper Jr., 1925.

Dean, Eric T., Jr. *Shook over Hell: Post-traumatic Stress, Vietnam, and the Civil War*. Cambridge, MA: Harvard University Press, 1997.

Devine, Shauna. *Learning from the Wounded: The Civil War and the Rise of American Medical Science*. Chapel Hill: University of North Carolina Press, 2014.

Dunn, Craig L. *Iron Men, Iron Will: The Nineteenth Indiana Regiment of the Iron Brigade*. Fort Wayne: Guild Press of Indiana, 1995.

Etcheson, Nicole. *A Generation at War: The Civil War in a Northern Community*. Lawrence: University Press of Kansas, 2011.

Ezratty, Harry A. *Baltimore in the Civil War: The Pratt Street Riot and a City Occupied*. Charleston, SC: History Press, 2010.

Fahs, Alice. *The Imagined Civil War: Popular Literature of the North and South, 1861–1865*. Chapel Hill: University of North Carolina Press, 2002.

Faust, Drew Gilpin. "'Numbers on Top of Numbers': Counting the Civil War Dead." *Journal of Military History*, no. 70 (October 2006): 995–1009.

———. *This Republic of Suffering: Death and the American Civil War*. New York: Vintage, 2008.

Fawcett, Winifred, and Thelma Hepper. *Veterans of the Civil War Who Settled in Potter County, Dakota Territory*. Gettysburg, PA: Self-published, 1993.

Figg, Laurann, and Jane Farrell-Beck. "Amputation in the Civil War: Physical and Social Dimensions." *Journal of the History of Medicine and Allied Sciences* 48, no. 4 (October 1993): 454–75.

Fish, Carl R. "The Raising of the Wisconsin Volunteers, 1861." *Military Historian and Economist*, no. 1 (July 1916): 258–73.

Flagel, Thomas R. *War, Memory and the 1913 Gettysburg Reunion*. Kent, OH: Kent State University Press, 2019.

Foote, Lorien. *The Gentlemen and the Roughs: Violence, Honor, and Manhood in the Union Army*. New York: New York University Press, 2010.

Frassanito, William A. *Antietam: The Photographic Legacy of America's Bloodiest Day*. New York: Charles Scribner's Sons, 1978.

Fry, Zachery A. *A Republic in the Ranks: Loyalty and Dissent in the Army of the Potomac*. Chapel Hill: University of North Carolina Press, 2020.

Gaff, Alan D. *Brave Men's Tears: The Iron Brigade at Brawner's Farm*. Dayton, OH: Morningside Bookshop, 1985.

Gallagher, Gary W., and Kathryn Shively Meier. "Coming to Terms with Civil War Military History." *Journal of the Civil War Era*, no. 4 (December 2014): 487–508.

Gallman, J. Matthew. *Defining Duty in the Civil War: Personal Choice, Popular Culture, and the Union Home Front*. Chapel Hill: University of North Carolina Press, 2015.

———. *Mastering Wartime: A Social History of Philadelphia during the Civil War*. Cambridge: Cambridge University Press, 1990.

Gamble, Richard M. *A Fiery Gospel: The Battle Hymn of the Republic and the Road to Righteous War*. Ithaca, NY: Cornell University Press, 2019.

Gannon, Barbara. *The Won Cause: Black and White Comradeship in the Grand Army of the Republic.* Chapel Hill: University of North Carolina Press, 2011.

Garland, Hamlin. *Main-Travelled Roads.* New York: Harper, 1899.

Geary, James W. *We Need Men: The Union Draft in the Civil War.* DeKalb: Northern Illinois University Press, 1991.

Giesberg, Judith. *Army at Home: Women and the Civil War on the Northern Home Front.* Chapel Hill: University of North Carolina Press, 2009.

———. "Orphans and Indians: Pennsylvania's Soldiers' Orphan Schools and the Landscape of Postwar Childhood." In *Children and Youth during the Civil War Era,* edited by James Marten, 188–206. New York: New York University Press, 2012.

Glasson, William H. "The National Pension System as Applied to the Civil War and the War with Spain." *Annals of the American Academy of Political and Social Science,* no. 19 (March 1902): 40–62.

Glatthaar, Joseph T. *Soldiering in the Army of Northern Virginia: A Statistical Portrait of the Troops Who Served under Robert E. Lee.* Chapel Hill: University of North Carolina Press, 2014.

———. "A Tale of Two Armies: The Confederate Army of Northern Virginia and the Union Army of the Potomac and Their Cultures." *Journal of the Civil War Era* 6, no. 3 (September 2016): 315–46.

Glazer, Walter S. "Wisconsin Goes to War: April, 1861." *Wisconsin Magazine of History* 50, no. 2 (Winter 1967): 146–64.

Gleeson, David T. "Immigrant America and the Civil War." In *Affairs of the People,* edited by Aaron Sheehan-Dean, 173–93. Vol. 3 of *The Cambridge History of the American Civil War.* Cambridge: Cambridge University Press, 2019.

Glymph, Thavolia. *The Women's Fight: The Civil War's Battles for Home, Freedom, and Nation.* Chapel Hill: University of North Carolina Press, 2020.

Gordon, Lesley J. *A Broken Regiment: The 16th Connecticut's Civil War.* Baton Rouge: Louisiana State University Press, 2014.

Greene, A. Wilson. *The Final Battles of the Petersburg Campaign: Breaking the Backbone of the Rebellion.* Knoxville: University of Tennessee Press, 2008.

Greer, Anna Lennarson. "Health Care Delivery." In *Encyclopedia of Milwaukee.* University of Wisconsin-Milwaukee, 2008–20. https://emke.uwm.edu/entry/health-care-delivery.

Groeling, Meg. *The Aftermath of Battle: The Burial of the Civil War Dead.* El Dorado Hills, CA: Savas Beatie, 2015.

Hackemer, Kurt. "Union Veteran Migration Patterns to the Frontier: The Case of Dakota Territory." *Journal of the Civil War Era* 9, no. 1 (March 2019): 84–108.

Hacker, J. David. "A Census-Based Count of the Civil War Dead." *Civil War History* 57, no. 4 (December 2011): 307–48.

Haller, John S., Jr. *Battlefield Medicine: A History of the Military Ambulance from the Napoleonic Wars through World War I.* Carbondale: Southern Illinois University Press, 1992.

Handley-Cousins, Sarah. *Bodies in Blue: Disability in the Civil War North.* Athens: University of Georgia Press, 2019.

Harris, Keith. *Across the Bloody Chasm: The Culture of Commemoration among Civil War Veterans.* Baton Rouge: Louisiana State University Press, 2014.

Harrsch, Patricia G. "'This Noble Monument': The Story of the Soldiers' Orphans' Home." *Wisconsin Magazine of History*, no. 76 (Winter 1992–93): 82–120.

Hartwig, D. Scott. *I Dread the Thought of the Place: The Battle of Antietam and the End of the Maryland Campaign*. Baltimore: Johns Hopkins University Press, 2023.

———. "'I Dread the Thought of the Place': The Iron Brigade at Antietam." In Nolan and Vipond, *Giants in Their Tall Black Hats*, 30–52.

———. *To Antietam Creek: The Maryland Campaign of September 1862*. Baltimore: Johns Hopkins University Press, 2012.

Hennessy, John J. *Return to Bull Run: The Campaign and Battle of Second Manassas*. Norman: University of Oklahoma Press, 1993.

Herdegen, Lance J. *The Iron Brigade in Civil War and Memory*. El Dorado Hills, CA: Savas Beatie, 2012.

———. *The Men Stood Like Iron: How the Iron Brigade Won Its Name*. Bloomington: Indiana University Press, 1997.

Herdegen, Lance J., and William J. K. Beaudot. *In the Bloody Railroad Cut at Gettysburg: The 6th Wisconsin of the Iron Brigade and Its Famous Charge*. 2nd ed. El Dorado Hills, CA: Savas Beatie, 2015.

Hess, Earl J. *Trench Warfare under Grant and Lee: Field Fortifications in the Overland Campaign*. Chapel Hill: University of North Carolina Press, 2007.

———. *The Union Soldier in Battle: Enduring the Ordeal of Combat*. Lawrence, KS: University Press of Kansas, 1997.

History of Fond du Lac County, Wisconsin. Chicago: Western Historical Company, 1880.

History of the Wisconsin Veterans Home at King. King: Wisconsin Department of Veterans Affairs, n.d. https://dva.wi.gov/Documents/newsMediaDocuments/WDVA%20 Toolkit/Brochures/WDVA_B3402_History_of_the_Wisconsin_Veterans_Home.pdf.

Humphreys, Margaret. *Marrow of Tragedy: The Health Crisis of the American Civil War*. Baltimore: Johns Hopkins University Press, 2013.

Hurn, Ethel Alice. *Wisconsin Women in the War between the States*. Madison: Wisconsin History Commission, 1911.

Huston, James L. *The Panic of 1857 and the Coming of the Civil War*. Baton Rouge: Louisiana State University Press, 1987.

Janney, Caroline E. *Remembering the Civil War: Reunion and the Limits of Reconciliation*. Chapel Hill: University of North Carolina Press, 2013.

Johnson, Russell L. *Warriors into Workers: The Civil War and the Formation of Urban-Industrial Society in a Northern City*. New York: Fordham University Press, 2003.

Jones, Jonathan S. "Opium Slavery: Civil War Veterans and Opiate Addiction." *Journal of the Civil War Era*, no. 10 (June 2020): 185–212.

Jordan, Brian Matthew. *Marching Home: Union Veterans and Their Unending Civil War*. New York: Liveright, 2014.

———. "Veterans in New Fields: Directions for Future Scholarship on Civil War Veterans." In Jordan and Rothera, *War Went On*, 307–19.

———. "What I Witnessed Would Only Make You Sick: Union Soldiers Confront the Dead at Antietam." In *The Civil War in Maryland Reconsidered*, edited by Charles Mitchell and Jean H. Baker, 195–208. Baton Rouge: Louisiana State University Press, 2022.

Jordan, Brian Matthew, and Evan C. Rothera. *The War Went On: Reconsidering the Lives of Civil War Veterans*. Baton Rouge: Louisiana State University Press, 2020.

Keating, Ryan W. *Shades of Green: Irish Regiments, American Soldiers, and Local Communities in the Civil War Era*. New York: Fordham University Press, 2017.

Kehoe, Karen. "The Wisconsin Soldiers' Aid Society and the Civil War." PhD diss., Marquette University, 2003.

Kelly, Patrick J. *Creating a National Home: Building the Veterans' Welfare State, 1860–1900*. Cambridge, MA: Harvard University Press, 1997.

Klement, Frank L. *Wisconsin in the Civil War: The Home Front and the Battle Front, 1861–1865*. Madison: Wisconsin Historical Society Press, 2013.

Kreiser, Lawrence A., Jr. *Marketing the Blue and Gray: Newspaper Advertising and the American Civil War*. Baton Rouge: Louisiana State University Press, 2019.

Kretz, Dale. *Administering Freedom: The State of Emancipation after the Freedmen's Bureau*. Chapel Hill: University of North Carolina Press, 2022.

Kutzler, Evan A. *Living by Inches: The Smells, Sounds, Tastes, and Feeling of Captivity in Civil War Prisons*. Chapel Hill: University of North Carolina Press, 2019.

Lang, Andrew F. *In the Wake of War: Military Occupation, Emancipation, and Civil War America*. Baton Rouge: Louisiana State University Press, 2017.

Lavery, Dennis S., and Mark H. Jordan. *Iron Brigade General: John Gibbon, a Rebel in Blue*. Westport, CT: Greenwood, 1993.

Lee, Chulhee. "Health, Information, and Migration: Geographic Mobility of Union Army Veterans, 1860–1880." *Journal of Economic History*, no. 68 (September 2008): 862–99.

Levine, Peter. "Draft Evasion in the North during the Civil War, 1863–1865." *Journal of American History*, no. 67 (March 1981): 816–34.

Linares, Claudia. "The Civil War Pension Law." CPE Working Paper Series, University of Chicago, Center for Population Economics, 2001.

Lindermann, Gerald. *Embattled Courage: The Experience of Combat in the American Civil War*. New York: Free Press, 1987.

Logue, Larry M. *To Appomattox and Beyond: The Civil War Soldier in War and Peace*. Chicago: Ivan R. Dee, 1995.

———. "Union Veterans and Their Government: The Effects of Public Policies on Private Lives." *Journal of Interdisciplinary History* 22, no. 3 (Winter 1992): 411–34.

Logue, Larry M., and Peter Blanck. *Heavy Laden: Union Veterans, Psychological Illness, and Suicide*. Cambridge: Cambridge University Press, 2018.

Luskey, Brian P. *Men Is Cheap: Exposing the Frauds of Free Labor in Civil War America*. Chapel Hill: University of North Carolina Press, 2020.

Mack, John N. *Bucking the Railroads on the Kansas Frontier: The Struggle over Land Claims by Homesteading Civil War Veterans, 1867–1876*. Jefferson, NC: McFarland, 2013.

Manning, Chandra. *What This Cruel War Was Over: Soldiers, Slavery, and the Civil War*. New York: Knopf, 2007.

Marsh, John L. "Drama and Spectacle by the Yard: The Panorama in America." *Journal of Popular Culture* 10, no. 3 (Winter 1976): 581–92.

Marten, James. *The Children's Civil War*. Chapel Hill: University of North Carolina Press, 1998.

———. *Sing Not War: The Lives of Union and Confederate Veterans in Gilded Age America*. Chapel Hill: University of North Carolina Press, 2011.

Marvel, William. *Lincoln's Mercenaries: Economic Motivation among Union Soldiers during the Civil War*. Baton Rouge: Louisiana State University Press, 2018.

Mattern, Carolyn J. *Soldiers When They Go: The Story of Camp Randall, 1861–1865*. Madison: State Historical Society of Wisconsin, 1981.

McClintock, Megan J. "Civil War Pensions and the Reconstruction of Union Families." *Journal of American History* 83, no. 2 (September 1996): 456–80.

McClurken, Jeffrey W. *Take Care of the Living: Reconstructing Confederate Veteran Families in Virginia*. Charlottesville: University of Virginia Press, 2009.

McConnell, Stuart. *Glorious Contentment: The Grand Army of the Republic, 1865–1900*. Chapel Hill: University of North Carolina Press, 1992.

McCrory, Thomas J. *Grand Army of the Republic: Department of Wisconsin*. Black Earth, WI: Trail Books, 2005.

McPherson, James M. *For Cause and Comrades: Why Men Fought in the Civil War*. New York: Oxford University Press, 1997.

Meier, Kathryn S. "Fighting in 'Dante's Inferno': Changing Perceptions of Civil War Combat in the Spotsylvania Wilderness from 1863 to 1864." In *Militarized Landscapes: From Gettysburg to Salisbury Plains*, edited by Chris Pearson, Peter Coates, and Tim Cole, 39–56. London: Continuum, 2010.

Merk, Frederick. *Economic History of Wisconsin during the Civil War Decade*. Madison: State Historical Society of Wisconsin, 1916.

Mitchell, Reid. *The Vacant Chair: The Northern Soldier Leaves Home*. New York: Oxford University Press, 1993.

Murdock, Eugene C. *Patriotism Limited 1862–1865: The Civil War Draft and the Bounty System*. Kent, OH: Kent State University Press, 1967.

Neugent, Robert J. "The National Soldiers' Home." *Historical Messenger*, no. 31 (Autumn 1975): 88–96.

Nolan, Alan T. *The Iron Brigade: A Military History*. Bloomington: Indiana University Press, 1961.

———. "John Brawner's Damage Claim." In Nolan and Vipond, *Giants in Their Tall Black Hats*, 1–12.

Nolan, Alan T., and Sharon Eggleston Vipond, eds. *Giants in Their Tall Black Hats: Essays on the Iron Brigade*. Bloomington: Indiana University Press, 1998.

Parsell, Diana P. *Eliza Scidmore: The Trailblazing Journalist Behind Washington's Cherry Trees*. New York: Oxford University Press, 2023.

Pfanz, Harry W. *Gettysburg—the First Day*. Chapel Hill: University of North Carolina Press, 2001.

Pinheiro, Holly A. *The Families' Civil War: Black Soldiers and the Fight for Racial Justice*. Athens: University of Georgia Press, 2022.

Pizarro, Judith, Roxane Cohen Silver, and JoAnn Prause. "Physical and Mental Health Costs of Traumatic War Experiences among Civil War Veterans." *Archives of General Psychiatry* 63, no. 2 (February 2006): 193–200.

Prechtel-Kluskens, Claire. "Anatomy of a Union Civil War Pension File." *NGS Newsmagazine* 34, no. 3 (July–September 2008): 42–47.

———. "'A Reasonable Degree of Promptitude': Civil War Pension Application Processing, 1861–1885." *Prologue* 42 (Spring 2020): 26–35.

Preston, Samuel H., and John McDonald. "The Incidence of Divorce within Cohorts of American Marriages Contracted since the Civil War." *Demography*, no. 16 (February 1979): 1–25.

Purcell, Sarah J. *Spectacle of Grief: Public Funerals and Memory in the Civil War Era*. Chapel Hill: University of North Carolina Press, 2022.

Quaife, M. M. "The Panic of 1862 in Wisconsin." *Wisconsin Magazine of History* 4, no. 2 (December 1920): 166–95.

Reardon, Carol. "The Impact of Continuous Operations on the Army of the Potomac and the Army of Northern Virginia in May 1864." In *The Spotsylvania Campaign*, edited by Gary W. Gallagher, 170–202. Chapel Hill: University of North Carolina Press, 1998.

———. "Writing Battle History: The Challenge of Memory." *Civil War History*, no. 53 (September 2007): 252–63.

Reimer, Terry. *One Vast Hospital: The Civil War Hospital Sites in Frederick, Maryland after Antietam*. Frederick, MD: National Museum of Civil War Medicine, 2001.

Rhea, Gordon C. *The Battle of the Wilderness, May 5–6, 1864*. Baton Rouge: Louisiana State University Press, 1994.

———. *On to Petersburg: Grant and Lee, June 4–15, 1864*. Baton Rouge: Louisiana State University Press, 2017.

———. *To the North Anna River: Grant and Lee, May 13–28, 1864*. Baton Rouge: Louisiana State University Press, 2000.

Royster, Charles. *A Revolutionary People at War: The Continental Army and American Character, 1775–1783*. Chapel Hill: University of North Carolina Press, 1979.

Rutkow, Ira M. *Bleeding Blue and Gray: Civil War Surgery and the Evolution of American Medicine*. New York: Random House, 2005.

Sacher, John M. *Confederate Conscription and the Struggle for Southern Soldiers*. Baton Rouge: Louisiana State University Press, 2021.

Shively, Kathryn. *Nature's Civil War: Common Soldiers and the Environment in 1862 Virginia*. Chapel Hill: University of North Carolina Press, 2013.

Silber, Nina. *Daughters of the Union: Northern Women Fight the Civil War*. Cambridge, MA: Harvard University Press, 2005.

Skocpol, Theda. "America's First Social Security System: The Expansion of Benefits for Civil War Veterans." *Political Science Quarterly* 108, no. 1 (Spring 1993): 85–116.

———. *Protecting Soldiers and Mothers: The Political Origins of Social Policy in the United States*. Cambridge, MA: Harvard University Press, 1994.

Smith, Adam I. P. "Beyond Politics: Patriotism and Partisanship on the Northern Home Front." In *An Uncommon Time: The Civil War and the Northern Home Front*, edited by Paul A. Cimbala and Randall M. Miller, 145–69. New York: Fordham University Press, 2002.

Smith, Donald L. *The Twenty-Fourth Michigan of the Iron Brigade*. Harrisburg, PA: Stackpole, 1962.

Smith, John David, and Raymond Arsenault, eds. *The Long Civil War: New Explorations of America's Enduring Conflict*. Lexington: University Press of Kentucky, 2021.

Smith, Mark M. *The Smell of Battle, the Taste of Siege: A Sensory History of the Civil War*. Oxford: Oxford University Press, 2015.

Sommerville, Diane Miller. *Aberration of Mind: Suicide and Suffering in the Civil War–Era South*. Chapel Hill: University of North Carolina Press, 2018.

Steplyk, Jonathan M. *Fighting Means Killing: Civil War Soldiers and the Nature of Combat*. Lawrence: University Press of Kansas, 2018.

Sternhell, Yael A. *War on Record: The Archive and the Afterlife of the Civil War*. New Haven, CT: Yale University Press, 2024.

Taylor, Amy Murrell. *Embattled Freedom: Journeys through the Civil War's Slave Refugee Camps*. Chapel Hill: University of North Carolina Press, 2018.

Trattner, Walter I. *From Poor Law to Welfare State: A History of Social Welfare in America*. 6th ed. New York: Simon and Schuster, 1999.

Ural, Susannah J. *Hood's Texas Brigade: The Soldiers and Families of the Confederacy's Most Celebrated Unit*. Baton Rouge: Louisiana State University Press, 2017.

Weeks, Jim. *Gettysburg: Memory, Market and an American Shrine*. Princeton, NJ: Princeton University Press, 2003.

Wert, Jeffrey D. *A Brotherhood of Valor: The Common Soldiers of the Stonewall Brigade, C.S.A., and the Iron Brigade, U.S.A.* New York: Simon and Schuster, 1999.

———. *The Heart of Hell: The Soldiers' Struggle for Spotsylvania's Bloody Angle*. Chapel Hill: University of North Carolina Press, 2022.

———. *The Sword of Lincoln: The Army of the Potomac*. New York: Simon and Schuster, 2005.

White, Jonathan W. *Emancipation, the Union Army, and the Re-election of Abraham Lincoln*. Baton Rouge: Louisiana State University Press, 2014.

Wiley, Bell I. *The Life of Billy Yank: The Common Soldier of the Union*. Indianapolis: Bobbs-Merrill, 1952.

———. *The Life of Johnny Reb: The Common Soldier of the Confederacy*. Baton Rouge: Louisiana State University Press, 1943.

Young, Edward. *Labor in America: Showing the Rates of Wages and Cost of Subsistence in the United States and British America, in the Year 1874, as Compared with Previous Years*. Washington, DC: Government Printing Office, 1875.

Zeitlin, Richard H. "In Peace and War: Union Veterans and Cultural Symbols—The Flags of the Iron Brigade." In Nolan and Vipond, *Giants in Their Tall Black Hats*, 160–78.

Zimm, John. "'On Wisconsin!': Celebrating Camp Randall." *Wisconsin Magazine of History*, no. 102 (Autumn 2018): 28–37.

INDEX